BESTSELLING
BOOK SERIES

The Vietnam War For Dummies®

D1072911

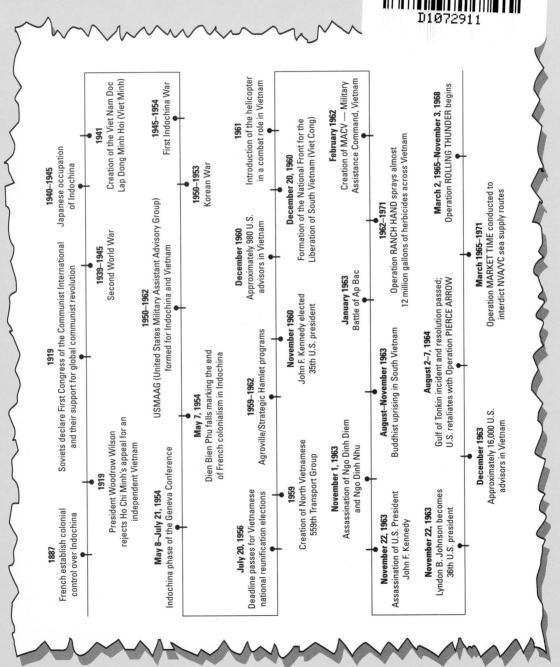

1887
French establish colonial control over Indochina

1919
Soviets declare First Congress of the Communist International and their support for global communist revolution

1919
President Woodrow Wilson rejects Ho Chi Minh's appeal for an independent Vietnam

1940–1945
Japanese occupation of Indochina

1939–1945
Second World War

1941
Creation of the Viet Nam Doc Lap Dong Minh Hoi (Viet Minh)

1950–1962
USMAAG (United States Military Assistant Advisory Group) formed for Indochina and Vietnam

1945–1954
First Indochina War

1950–1953
Korean War

May 8–July 21, 1954
Indochina phase of the Geneva Conference

May 7, 1954
Dien Bien Phu falls marking the end of French colonialism in Indochina

1961
Introduction of the helicopter in a combat role in Vietnam

July 20, 1956
Deadline passes for Vietnamese national reunification elections

1959–1962
Agroville/Strategic Hamlet programs

December 1960
Approximately 980 U.S. advisors in Vietnam

December 20, 1960
Formation of the National Front for the Liberation of South Vietnam (Viet Cong)

February 1962
Creation of MACV — Military Assistance Command, Vietnam

November 1960
John F. Kennedy elected 35th U.S. president

1959
Creation of North Vietnamese 559th Transport Group

January 1963
Battle of Ap Bac

1962–1971
Operation RANCH HAND sprays almost 12 million gallons of herbicides across Vietnam

March 2, 1965–November 3, 1968
Operation ROLLING THUNDER begins

November 1, 1963
Assassination of Ngo Dinh Diem and Ngo Dinh Nhu

August–November 1963
Buddhist uprising in South Vietnam

August 2–7, 1964
Gulf of Tonkin incident and resolution passed; U.S. retaliates with Operation PIERCE ARROW

March 1965–1971
Operation MARKET TIME conducted to interdict NVA/VC sea supply routes

November 22, 1963
Assassination of U.S. President John F. Kennedy

November 22, 1963
Lyndon B. Johnson becomes 36th U.S. president

December 1963
Approximately 16,000 U.S. advisors in Vietnam

For Dummies: Bestselling Book Series for Beginners

The Vietnam War For Dummies®

Cheat Sheet

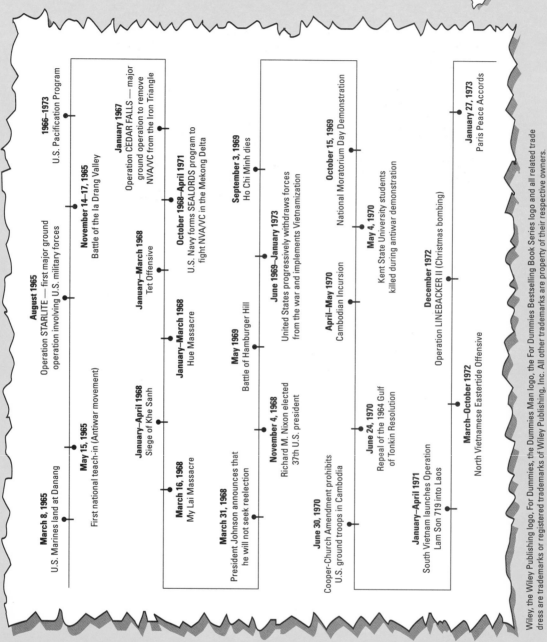

March 8, 1965
U.S. Marines land at Danang

May 15, 1965
First national teach-in (Antiwar movement)

August 1965
Operation STARLITE — first major ground operation involving U.S. military forces

November 14–17, 1965
Battle of the Ia Drang Valley

1966–1973
U.S. Pacification Program

January 1967
Operation CEDAR FALLS — major ground operation to remove NVA/VC from the Iron Triangle

January–March 1968
Tet Offensive

January–April 1968
Siege of Khe Sanh

January–March 1968
Hue Massacre

March 16, 1968
My Lai Massacre

March 31, 1968
President Johnson announces that he will not seek reelection

October 1968–April 1971
U.S. Navy forms SEALORDS program to fight NVA/VC in the Mekong Delta

November 4, 1968
Richard M. Nixon elected 37th U.S. president

May 1969
Battle of Hamburger Hill

June 1969–January 1973
United States progressively withdraws forces from the war and implements Vietnamization

September 3, 1969
Ho Chi Minh dies

October 15, 1969
National Moratorium Day Demonstration

April–May 1970
Cambodian Incursion

May 4, 1970
Kent State University students killed during antiwar demonstration

June 24, 1970
Repeal of the 1964 Gulf of Tonkin Resolution

June 30, 1970
Cooper-Church Amendment prohibits U.S. ground troops in Cambodia

January–April 1971
South Vietnam launches Operation Lam Son 719 into Laos

March–October 1972
North Vietnamese Eastertide Offensive

December 1972
Operation LINEBACKER II (Christmas bombing)

January 27, 1973
Paris Peace Accords

For Dummies: Bestselling Book Series for Beginners

The Vietnam War

FOR

DUMMIES®

by Ronald B. Frankum, Jr. and
Stephen F. Maxner

Wiley Publishing, Inc.

The Vietnam War For Dummies®

Published by
Wiley Publishing, Inc.
909 Third Avenue
New York, NY 10022
www.wiley.com

Copyright © 2003 by Wiley Publishing, Inc., Indianapolis, Indiana

Published simultaneously in Canada

For general information on our other products and services or to obtain technical support, please contact our Customer Care Department within the U.S. at 800-762-2974, outside the U.S. at 317-572-3993, or fax 317-572-4002.

Wiley also publishes its books in a variety of electronic formats. Some content that appears in print may not be available in electronic books.

Library of Congress Control Number: 2002110310

ISBN: 0-7645-5480-8

Manufactured in the United States of America

10 9 8 7 6 5 4 3 2 1

1B/ST/RQ/QS/IN

About the Authors

Ronald B. Frankum, Jr.: Ron is archivist for the Vietnam Archive at Texas Tech University and has an adjunct appointment in the Department of History. He teaches Vietnam War seminars in the Honors College. He recently published a book on United States-Australian relations during the Vietnam War, *Silent Partners: The United States and Australia in Vietnam, 1954-1968,* and is working on books examining the air war during the Vietnam War and Operation Passage to Freedom, the 1954 evacuation of Vietnamese from North Vietnam to South Vietnam.

Stephen Farris Maxner: Stephen is assistant archivist and oral historian for the Vietnam Archive at Texas Tech University. He has served nearly six years in the U.S. Army as an enlisted legal specialist and as a commissioned officer and mechanized infantry platoon leader. He is currently working on his Ph.D. dissertation, which examines American attitudes toward death in war and how such attitudes have affected national security policy formulation and decision-making.

About the Sculptor of the Three Soldiers

See cover image

The Legacy of Frederick Hart: 1943–1999

Frederick Hart is America's greatest figurative sculptor since Daniel Chester French. Hart not only created works of great beauty and gravitas, he was singularly responsible for restoring to American public monuments and memorials an iconology worthy of a great nation.

Hart's works address those transcendental themes a civilization must retain if the arts are to remain relevant and vigorous: creation, beauty, virtue, spirituality and God. His desire to create a living myth from stone, marble, acrylic and bronze was both profoundly artistic and deeply personal.

He pioneered the use of cast acrylic resin, thereby creating a new medium of expression for generations of artists to come. Hart's genius was recognized by many including Pope John Paul II who on the occasion of receiving the clear acrylic resin sculpture entitled, *Cross of the Millennium* in his papal study, proclaimed, "This work represents a profound theological statement for our day."

Upon the dedication of the *Three Soldiers* statue Frederick Hart said, "I see the wall as a kind of ocean, a sea of sacrifice that is overwhelming and nearly incomprehensible in its sweep of names. I place these figures upon the shore of that sea, gazing upon it, standing vigil before it, reflecting the human face of it, the human heart."

The Creation Sculptures at Washington National Cathedral: *Ex Nihilo, Creation of Day*, *Creation of Night*, *Adam*, *St. Peter* and *St. Paul*, took Hart almost thirteen years to complete, and are among the most important religious commissions of the century.

"I believe that art has a moral responsibility, that it must pursue something higher than itself. Art must be a part of life. It must exist in the domain of the common man. It must be an enriching, ennobling, and vital partner in the public pursuit of civilization. It should be a majestic presence in everyday life just as it was in the past." — Frederick Hart

Authors' Acknowledgments

This book would not be possible without the resources of the Vietnam Archive at Texas Tech University. The authors also wish to thank Tara Lennon and Sherri Lynn Brouillette for their constant support and assistance in editing the chapters in this book. The authors also wish to thank the hard-working and dedicated staff at Wiley Publishing, Incorporated. Special thanks go to Greg Tubach, Tonya Cupp, Jennifer Ehrlich, and Neil Johnson for their patience and encouragement. Additional thanks go to John Ernst and Jim Willbanks the technical editors, for their poignant remarks and attention to detail.

Publisher's Acknowledgments

We're proud of this book; please send us your comments through our Dummies online registration form located at www.dummies.com/register/.

Some of the people who helped bring this book to market include the following:

Acquisitions, Editorial, and Media Development

Project Editors: Tonya Maddox Cupp and Tere Drenth

Acquisitions Editors: Greg Tubach and Kathy Cox

Copy Editor: E. Neil Johnson

Acquisitions Coordinator: Joyce Pepple

Technical Editors: Dr. John Ernst and Dr. James H. Willbanks

Senior Permissions Editor: Carmen Krikorian

Editorial Manager: Jennifer Ehrlich

Editorial Assistant: Carol Strickland

Cover Photos: PHX-Hagerstown

Cartoons: Rich Tennant, www.the5thwave.com

Production

Project Coordinator: Bill Ramsey

Layout and Graphics: Jackie Nicholas, Heather Pope, Jacque Schneider, Jeremey Unger, Erin Zeltner

Special Art: Photos and maps inside book courtesy the Vietnam Archive, Texas Tech University

Proofreaders: John Greenough, Dwight Ramsey, TECHBOOKS Production Services

Indexer: TECHBOOKS Production Services

Publishing and Editorial for Consumer Dummies

Diane Graves Steele, Vice President and Publisher, Consumer Dummies

Joyce Pepple, Acquisitions Director, Consumer Dummies

Kristin A. Cocks, Product Development Director, Consumer Dummies

Michael Spring, Vice President and Publisher, Travel

Brice Gosnell, Publishing Director, Travel

Suzanne Jannetta, Editorial Director, Travel

Publishing for Technology Dummies

Andy Cummings, Vice President and Publisher, Dummies Technology/General User

Composition Services

Gerry Fahey, Vice President of Production Services

Debbie Stailey, Director of Composition Services

Contents at a Glance

Table of Contents

Part III: Taking to Air and Sea 151

Chapter 7: Learning to Fly: 1950–1964 153

Introduction

• •

*T*he Vietnam War was unlike any war the United States ever fought in during the course of its history. Unlike the First and Second World Wars and the Korean War, U.S. involvement has no definitive beginning in the Vietnam War nor has any single day received consensus from scholars as being that war's end. The Vietnam War also was unique in that each country involved in the conflict committed different levels of its nation's resources toward winning the war.

The Vietnam War is best understood once you accept that competing and conflicting perspectives were involved during the duration of the war. Some questions that plagued the United States during the 1960s and 1970s are easier to understand once the North Vietnamese Army (NVA) and Viet Cong (VC) perspectives are understood. For instance, it was difficult for those conducting the war from Washington, D.C., to understand how the NVA/VC could absorb the tremendous losses from engagements with the United States and the various air campaigns. Understanding the 2,000-year tradition of the Vietnamese people in resisting foreign invaders regardless of the cost helps to put the steadfastness of the NVA/VC into perspective. Conversely, Democratic of Vietnam (DRV or North Vietnam) leaders couldn't understand why the United States placed the Vietnamese independence movement within the Cold War struggle against the Soviet Union. They didn't see the conflict of interest as they garnered Soviet assistance whenever and wherever they could gain an advantage.

The legacies left by the Vietnam War are an important part of its aftermath that have changed the way many view conflict and the extent to which the United States ever becomes involved in other foreign policy entanglements. Unlike the First or Second World Wars, the Vietnam War left the United States divided, and it continues to influence U.S. domestic and foreign policy. Without question, the Vietnam Syndrome that emerged after the war's end altered the policies of Presidents Jimmy Carter and Ronald Reagan. The lessons of the Vietnam War were applied to President George Bush's military campaign in the Persian Gulf.

The Vietnam War story is one that never has been fully understood and probably never will be explained to the satisfaction of those who experienced it directly or indirectly. Few debate that Japan overtly attacked the United States at Pearl Harbor in 1941 and started the U.S. involvement in the Second World War. Neither do historians debate with much fervor the U.S. military and political strategy leading to the defeat of German and Japan in 1945. The same, however, can't be said for the Vietnam War, which is what makes it such an interesting event to study. The Vietnam War will continue to spark debate and controversy for each new generation of scholars. Anyone interested in learning more about this most interesting time in history needs to be commended. We don't guarantee that all of your questions will be answered in the pages that follow, nor that the history provided here is devoid of controversy, but we hope you will use this book as a guide as you begin exploring the Vietnam War.

About This Book

If you haven't read much about the Vietnam War, but you're interested in gaining a quick and accurate overview of the significant events that occurred and people who made history during the war, then *The Vietnam War For Dummies* is the right book for you.

This book doesn't claim to provide a description of every event or incident. In a recent study for The Vietnam Archive at Texas Tech University, a staff member identified more than 1,100 named military operations that occurred during the war. Listing them all here is as impractical as naming every important person who took part in conducting the war. Historians and veterans agree on certain turning points and significant events during the war. This book describes them.

This book is designed to meet the needs of the following types of readers:

- ✔ Individuals who want a general history of the Vietnam War that answers questions that begin with How, Why, What, Where, and When.
- ✔ Those who want a compact reference guide to the major subjects about the Vietnam War.
- ✔ Those who have an interest in one of the most remarkable times in U.S. modern history and want to understand how the Vietnam War helped shape their politics, society, and personal views of the world.

Remember that having an understanding of the Vietnam War means knowing that its history is based upon perspectives. For any one book that argues a point in a specific way, at least two other books will interpret that point in another way. Knowing all of this, you can use *The Vietnam War For Dummies* as a guide for beginning your examination of this most important historical event in American history.

How to Use This Book

A dangerous trend has been set in the history profession to create works that are not accessible to the public. Many historians of these new schools of thought use jargon-laden text that is confusing even to professional historians. The study and writing of history need not be confusing, boring, or inaccessible. Even a history of the Vietnam War, as complex as the war was to those who experienced it, can provide basic facts in an easy-to-read format that provides a beginning, middle, and end to every subject that is discussed. This book is designed that way. This is not a book that you must read from front cover to back cover to understand it. You can read each part, chapter, or section independently. You can use this book as a good beginning point to studying the war or as a reference tool during your continuing exploration. It is designed to satisfy both requirements and should be used both ways.

Conventions Used in This Book

Where chapters include specialized terms, we have identified and explained them as early in the text as possible. We have included a number of maps on the major ground operations to help guide you through the text; tables also help you identify the most common aircraft used in the air war. All named U.S. and Allied military operations are capitalized. This is the standard convention for the military and also helps you identify the operation being discussed. Although we retained the Vietnamese order in names, we weren't able to include the tonal or diacritical marks associated with the Vietnamese language. For that we do apologize.

Additionally, we chose to use the name North Vietnamese Army (NVA) for all of the DRV regular forces though they could have also been called the People's Army of Vietnam (PAVN) just as we used the term Viet Cong instead of the National Liberation Front for the irregular forces fighting against the South Vietnam. What is in a name...we recognize that there is much when it comes to the Vietnam War but we needed to chose something and remain consistent throughout the book.

How This Book Is Organized

We have organized this book into six parts, each examining a major subject in the war. Within each part, the subject is dealt with chronologically to make it easier to understand.

Part 1: Returning to the Start of the Vietnam War

This part provides an overview of America's longest war and a background to the conflict. Understanding that the Vietnam War began before the first U.S. soldiers set foot in Vietnam is just as important as realizing that the American commitment in Southeast Asia was a part of the larger Cold War struggle against the new enemy of the post–Second World War — communism. This part also examines major figures and the perspective of the Vietnamese people — North and South — as war intensified in the 1950s and 1960s. To truly understand the Vietnam War, knowing its origins and the motives of all of its participants is important. This part will provide all of the background information you need to know to begin studying the war.

Part 11: Fighting the Ground War in Southeast Asia

This part examines the political and military policies of Presidents Eisenhower, Kennedy, Johnson, and Nixon, and how they dealt with the situation in Vietnam and American involvement there. It examines the escalation of hostility within South Vietnam and the many issues involved with deciding to send American military personnel to do what some people thought the South Vietnamese should do for themselves — defend their nation against communism. This part looks at the various strategies and tactics employed and many of the major battles and turning points.

Part 111: Taking to Air and Sea

The intensity of the air and sea war paralleled the progression of the war as the U.S. Armed Forces faced challenges and obstacles in the environment of Southeast Asia that tested it from the beginning. This part examines these challenges and obstacles and outlines the progression of air and sea campaigns between the United States and South Vietnam and the NVA/VC.

Part 1V: The "Other Wars"

This part looks at the various activities of the United States and Republic of Vietnam (RVN or South Vietnam) and their attempts to pacify and maintain the support of South Vietnamese people. It also looks at American activities in the other countries in Southeast Asia that had a direct bearing on the war in South Vietnam.

Part V: A War at Home and a Home at War

This part examines the origins, development, and eventual demise of the antiwar movement and the effort to support the American troops in Vietnam. In it, you'll discover some of the factors that caused the antiwar movement to grow, the reasons why it faded away in the early 1970s, and how those who supported the U.S. involvement in Vietnam worked to assist the U.S. Armed Forces and government in their attempt to keep South Vietnam free from communism.

Part VI: The Part of Tens

For those of you familiar with the *For Dummies* books (or if this is your first *For Dummies* book), this part can be one of the most interesting. The Part of Tens gives the authors an opportunity to provide important information about the subject that doesn't fit in to the general flow of the book. The lists are designed to create some discussion and debate and to provide resources for continued examination of the Vietnam War.

Icons Used in This Book

Although the information provided in this book has been selected for its significance, you may need to quickly find something that's important within a chapter. The icons designate passages about four general subjects. These little pictures next to the text are easy to spot and identify, once you know what each one represents:

This icon identifies general military strategy used by the United States, DRV, South Vietnamese, or Viet Cong during the course of the war.

This icon gives you a piece of historic information that can add to your understanding or appreciation of a particular event in the Vietnam War.

This icon draws your attention to detailed information about different kinds of military equipment, units, and the language used during the Vietnam War.

This icon points out especially important information that you need to keep in mind as subsequent events unfold.

Where to Go from Here

Once you read *The Vietnam War For Dummies,* its solid overview of the major aspects of the war provides you with many opportunities for future study of the Vietnam War. We provide, in Chapter 17, different resources that are found on the Internet and at your local library. These resources are only the tip of the iceberg. More and more books, articles, documentaries, and oral history interviews are released on a daily basis. In fact, it can easily become overwhelming once the full range of material on the Vietnam War is revealed. You need to use this to your advantage, because regardless of what your area of interest may be, you're likely to find a book or an article that deals with the topic. The Internet is a powerful tool for studying the Vietnam War, but we caution about using it as the final word on any subject. Instead, you need to use the Internet to find additional resources about your topic and as a supplement to the documents, books, and articles that are available at most research libraries.

You don't have to start with Chapter 1 and read through to the end. If you're interested only in the ground war during the Nixon presidency, start with that chapter. We have provided several cross-references to guide you to other areas in the book. For example, in the Nixon ground war chapter, we have cross-referenced other events that occurred in the same time frame such as the air war in Laos and Cambodia (Chapter 9) and the antiwar movement (Chapter 14). However, if you want to learn it all, start with the first chapter and work your way through.

Part I

Returning to the Start of the Vietnam War

The 5th Wave

By Rich Tennant

"Our committee has determined that going into Vietnam, neutralizing the spread of Communism, and getting out again should be as easy as putting one foot in front of the other."

In this part . . .

When the first U.S. combat troops landed on the beach in Danang in 1965 starting what many considered the Vietnam War for the U.S., the most current conflict in Vietnam had been raging for nearly twenty years. In this part, you will have an opportunity to examine an overview of the Vietnam War from the Second World War though the French struggle with the Viet Minh and finally the U.S. experience in Vietnam. You will get a list of the important individuals and organizations that helped to shape the war on the Vietnamese side as well as explore in greater detail the critical turning point in 1954 – the Geneva Conference – when the U.S. took over assisting the South Vietnamese from the French. The result was the beginning of more active U.S. involvement in Southeast Asia, which would lead to the troops landing on the Danang beach in 1965.

Chapter 1

Looking at America's Longest War

*T*he Vietnam War can be seen as a time of lost opportunities. The United States engaged in a struggle that lasted almost 25 years and cost more than 58,000 lives and billions of dollars spent in Southeast Asia. The Vietnam War lasted through the tenures of five presidents (some would argue seven presidents) and played a role in the downfalls of two of these men.

For South Vietnam, the conflict that had emerged from the 1954 division of Vietnam along the 17th parallel forced that newborn country to alter its focus and resources toward fighting a war when it needed all of its people and industry for the development of a country hampered by a French colonial past.

The same is true for North Vietnam, which suffered greater perils than South Vietnam, because it didn't have U.S. dollars or technical advisors to improve the day-to-day lives of its people. Vietnam, both North and South, was virtually destroyed by the war's end. Twenty-five years after the final collapse of South Vietnam, parts of the countryside still have no electricity or proper sanitary facilities.

Despite many attempts to determine the human cost of the war for Vietnam, no definitive numbers have been posted. Estimates, however, indicate that the North Vietnamese lost between 1 million and 2 million soldiers and civilians and the South Vietnamese suffered at least 1 million casualties. Similarly, no numbers are available for Laos or Cambodia, but each of those countries underwent periods of destruction that continue to plague them today.

From a World War to a Cold War in Southeast Asia

The first soldiers from the United States to operate in Vietnam arrived during World War II, representing what many consider the start of the U.S. involvement in Vietnam. *Operatives* (those working in foreign countries) from the U.S. Office of Strategic Services (OSS) established observation stations in Indochina (Vietnam, Laos, and Cambodia) enabling them to monitor Japanese military movements and provide *intelligence,* such as troop and ship locations, to the Allied Forces fighting Japan.

The OSS was formed in August 1941 as the Office of the Coordinator of Information and was headed by William Joseph "Wild Bill" Donovan. Less than a year later, President Franklin Delano Roosevelt (FDR) renamed the organization the Office of Strategic Services until it eventually became the Central Intelligence Group in 1946 and finally the Central Intelligence Agency (CIA) in 1947.

These OSS operatives worked with the Vietnamese, rescuing downed pilots and supporting Vietnamese resistance against Japanese forces who had occupied most of Indochina. The U.S. operatives left Vietnam at the end of World War II with promises that the United States would support Vietnamese independence. The United States, however, was unable to live up to those promises because of the emergence of the Cold War.

Prelude to the Vietnam War: World War II, Southeast Asia, and the Grand Strategy

FDR hoped that the end of World War II also would bring an end to *colonialism* (the policy of one country ruling another by force). He believed the United States was obligated to work with emerging nations that had been exploited during colonial rule. "France has milked it," Roosevelt argued when speaking of Indochina, "for 100 years. The people of Indochina are entitled to something better than that."

But America's major WWII ally, the United Kingdom, and its leader, Winston Churchill, were not pleased with FDR's ideas of postwar decolonization. If the United States and other allies dismantled France's empire after the war, Churchill feared the British Empire soon would follow. Churchill refused to preside over such a chain of events in the United Kingdom and took action to prevent it by convincing FDR to wait until the war was over before discussing the postwar question (see Chapter 2 as well as *World War II For Dummies,* published by Wiley, Inc., for more information).

Playing the Soviet card: De Gaulle responds to Roosevelt

FDR presented to the U.S. wartime allies the idea of establishing trusteeships in the former colonies. In a *trusteeship,* more-developed countries would oversee and assist in the development of the former colony into independent nations. FDR proposed just such a plan for Indochina for after WWII, but Charles De Gaulle, the leader of France, argued that Roosevelt's plan would result in the collapse of France and the real possibility that France would fall under Soviet and communist influence in Europe.

Although his worldview was much larger than the fate of France and Europe and De Gaulle's warnings went largely unheeded, Roosevelt unfortunately took the idea of an Indochina trusteeship with him to the grave, and his successor, President Harry S. Truman, dealt with circumstances that Roosevelt could not have predicted.

In the aftermath of WWII, President Truman dealt with a different set of foreign policy considerations than those FDR faced. Truman's attention was focused on the Soviet influence in Europe and international communism. He believed France was an important ally in the new battle, as he saw it, of defending freedom and democracy around the world. He also saw a valuable partner in the North Atlantic Treaty Organization (NATO). NATO brought together free-market economies and democracies in Europe and North America in a defense league. If the Soviet Union attacked any member of NATO, the remaining members promised to retaliate against the Soviet Union.

Facing not only these larger political and diplomatic issues, but also the threat of Soviet and communist expansion, Truman was left with no choice but to abandon the ideal of an Indochina trusteeship for the sake of a Franco-American alliance and NATO.

Truman believed that the people of Indochina needed to be independent, but he also argued that they needed to work under a French framework and on a French timetable to gain that independence. Throughout the early part of his presidency, Truman maintained that the United States needed its attention focused on Europe, because the Soviet Union remained a real threat to world peace.

Dividing Vietnam: The British and Chinese in 1946

After World War II, Indochina was divided along the 16th parallel with Great Britain occupying the southern half and the Peoples Republic of China (PRC) occupying the northern half until Japanese troops were gathered and returned to Japan. According to agreements reached during the war, France was to retain her colonial empire in Indochina. Great Britain used its presence in Indochina to support the return of France, and the PRC assisted the Viet Minh (Vietnamese Independence League) in its forthcoming struggle against France to gain its independence.

Before Americans Fought: Learning from the French Indochina War

The French or First Indochina War lasted from 1945 through 1954 with the French fighting the Viet Minh for control of Indochina. During the course of the nine-year war, the United States increasingly supported France militarily and politically. President Truman believed that global security rested in Europe through the containment of the Soviet Union. The French government used this posture to gain U.S. assistance in Indochina by arguing consistently that if the French lost Indochina, their government would fall to the Communist Party, which then would result in greater Soviet influence in Europe. To maintain strength in France, the United States had to support French claims in Indochina.

Helping in the war: The U.S. Military Assistance Advisory Group

The United States established the Military Assistance Advisory Group, Indochina (MAAG-I) after President Truman signed National Security Council Memorandum 64 in September 1950, declaring Indochina a strategic area in the struggle against communism.

MAAG-I officers were instructed to serve as liaisons between the French and the Vietnamese, determining what type of training and equipment was necessary to ensure a French victory in the region. The presence of MAAG-I represented the first organized U.S. military force in Vietnam and, for many observers, the start of the American war there.

Faltering: The French empire

Even though they received U.S. assistance during the First Indochina War, the French had a tough time containing the Viet Minh and the independence movement. Although French Union Forces had better weapons and advantages in air power and mobility, the Viet Minh chose when and where they fought the French. This allowed them to choose battles that took advantage of French weaknesses while maximizing Viet Minh strengths and allowed the Viet Minh to sustain fewer casualties while inflicting higher casualties on the French. In 1953, the United States increased its commitment to France as the war progressed to the point where the United States was providing 70 percent (or more) of the war budget. In Indochina, the French never were able to fight in a European-style battle in which they used air power and artillery to defeat the Viet Minh.

So, the French formulated a strategy in 1953 to lure the Viet Minh into a decisive battle at the village of Dien Bien Phu in the northwest part of Vietnam near the Laotian border. Dien Bien Phu was situated on the only major northern road between Vietnam and Laos. Gaining control over the village meant cutting off the Viet Minh from Laos and isolating the Pathet Lao (see Chapter 13), who had also been fighting the French. However, the French underestimated Viet Minh forces around the Dien Bien Phu and misjudged their own ability to reinforce, resupply, and defend such an isolated fortress, or grouping of fortified outposts. Poor weather and U.S. reluctance to join in a failing effort brought on by France's refusal to acknowledge the future independence of Vietnam, Laos, and Cambodia led to the fall of the fortress and marked the beginning of the end of French rule in Indochina.

Searching for peace: The 1954 Geneva Conference

The fall of Dien Bien Phu occurred the day before the Indochina phase of the 1954 Geneva Conference convened in Switzerland. Losing the fortress and suffering more than 15,000 casualties, the French were forced to negotiate from a weak position. Conference participants had a tough time agreeing on an end to the fighting in the region, and although the United States wasn't satisfied with the final declaration signed July 20, 1954 by the Viet Minh and France, it had little choice but to accept the fate of the French in Indochina.

The United States moved into Indochina with the sole purpose of providing Vietnamese in the south with an opportunity to develop a form of government akin to American democracy. As the United States became more involved in the struggle in Vietnam, its original purpose expanded into building a nation in South Vietnam that could stand in Southeast Asia as a barrier against the communist threat emanating from North Vietnam. Throughout nearly 20 years of this new phase, the efforts of more than 2.7 million Americans eventually were committed to the war in Indochina.

Second Indochina War: The American Vietnam War

The Vietnam War, also known as the Second Indochina War in Europe, Asia, and elsewhere, began in 1954 and lasted until the last American combat troops left Vietnam early in 1973. The early phase of the war was fought at a low intensity, because the United States was more concerned with supporting the South Vietnamese government than with fighting against the North Vietnamese Army and Viet Cong (NVA/VC).

However, the American response to North Vietnam's eventual escalation of the war in the south caused the NVA/VC to increase its commitment toward overthrowing the South Vietnamese and ousting the United States. As the two forces responded to one another, the total number of troops involved in the conflict continued to rise.

Finding a leader: The Ngo Dinh Diem experiment and Nation Building

During the presidency of Dwight D. Eisenhower, the United States supported Ngo Dinh Diem as the man who would lead South Vietnam against Ho Chi Minh, leader of North Vietnam. Ngo Dinh Diem proved his worth in the mid-1950s by eliminating rebellious factions in the south and rallying the Vietnamese people to his side. Diem had the potential to work well with the U.S. strategy of Nation Building during the mid-1950s, though by the late 1950s and early 1960s it became clear that Diem was more of an obstacle than a benefit to U.S. Nation Building efforts, which is discussed in more detail in Chapters 3, 4, and 12. The United States sent military and civilian advisors to South Vietnam to work with the South Vietnamese Armed Forces and civilian servants.

Nation Building was partially effective in training the army and providing the necessary advice to form the basis of a democratic government. As the NVA/VC exerted more pressure in the south, the Nation Building strategy began to falter. Diem blamed the United States for encouraging an attempt on his life in November 1960. He began mistrusting advice provided by the United States. Conversely, U.S. officials in South Vietnam grew discouraged with Diem, frustrated by his failure to enact recommended reforms. At the same time, the United States and NVA/VC were matching military escalation with military escalation, American officials and Diem moved farther apart, and U.S. and South Vietnamese strategies and tactics took separate paths.

Kennedy's Vietnam and the fall of Ngo Dinh Diem

The day before John F. Kennedy entered the White House in 1961, he met with Eisenhower to discuss foreign policy concerns. The discussion centered on the situation in Laos, which Eisenhower saw as the key to Southeast Asian security. Although they didn't discuss the situation in Vietnam in detail, it and the fate of Ngo Dinh Diem nevertheless became a significant part of Kennedy's legacy. Kennedy opted for increasing U.S. military presence in Vietnam to combat the NVA/VC threat.

During the course of Kennedy's presidency, U.S. strength in Vietnam increased from approximately 980 to more than 16,000 personnel. Kennedy introduced the Special Forces, helicopters, and increased military activity during his first year. He spoke eloquently during his three years in office in defense of South Vietnam, warning the Soviet Union about aiding the NVA/VC.

The fracture that began with a November 1960 attempted coup d'état against Diem's regime grew in the early 1960s. By 1963, few in the United States believed Diem could lead South Vietnam against the NVA/VC. In the summer of 1963, Diem moved against the Buddhists, whom he believed were supporting the communist insurgency in the south. The international community viewed Diem's move against the Buddhists as religious intolerance. In the United States, Diem's actions were seen as another example of how he had lost touch with the Vietnamese people.

The United States was reluctant to support the replacement of Diem until another leader emerged who could lead the war-torn country. Diem used American indecision to further his control of the opposition to his rule, becoming more reliant on his brother, Ngo Dinh Nhu. Although the United States refused, in the summer of 1963, to support opposition to Diem until that opposition proved capable of ruling the country, by the middle of October 1963, Diem's actions pushed the United States toward making a decision supporting the best possible non-Diem solution.

When South Vietnamese generals made known their intentions to oust Diem, the United States neither officially supported the coup nor argued against it. The planners took the U.S. refusal to stop them as a sign that they had U.S. support. So, Diem and his brother Nhu were captured November 1, 1963, and executed. Diem's death was a major turning point in the American Vietnam War, enabling the NVA/VC to take advantage of weakened leadership by increasing pressure on the resulting turmoil in the South Vietnamese countryside and thereby toppling its unstable government.

At the same time in the United States, the assassination of John F. Kennedy and the new presidency of Lyndon Baines Johnson signaled a new phase of U.S. involvement — one in which the next logical step was the deployment of American combat troops in Vietnam.

Americanizing the war in Vietnam

Post-Diem governments were unable to maintain military pressure against NVA/VC forces in South Vietnam. In 1964, the United States cited two attacks against the U.S. Navy (the second never was confirmed) in the Gulf of Tonkin as reasons for beginning its slow military escalation in South Vietnam.

President Johnson began an air campaign against North Vietnam, hoping that overwhelming American firepower might force North Vietnam into rethinking its strategy and negotiating a peaceful resolution to the conflict. Instead the bombing made most of the North Vietnamese people angry and prompted them to support their government and the war in South Vietnam. The intro-duction of U.S. warplanes into Vietnam required additional U.S. personnel to maintain and protect them, so, by the end of 1964, approximately 23,000 Americans were in Vietnam. (We cover the early air war in Chapter 7 and the air war against Vietnam, Laos, and Cambodia in Chapters 8 and 9.)

Seizing the initiative: The American military buildup

In the first months of 1965, the NVA/VC launched an offensive aimed at cut-ting South Vietnam in two. U.S. and Army of the Republic of Vietnam (ARVN) forces stalled the offensive, but it was enough to convince the United States that further involvement was necessary if South Vietnam was to be saved.

President Johnson ordered a prolonged air offensive against the Democratic Republic of (North) Vietnam (DRV) and ordered U.S. Marines in Danang to protect aircraft stationed there. The United States continued sending troops to South Vietnam and established *enclaves,* or defensive bases, used to defend strategic military facilities. This enclave strategy pulled the United States further into the war. By the end of 1965, almost 200,000 U.S. personnel were in Vietnam. That number increased to nearly 365,000 by the end of 1966 and approximately 475,000 through 1967.

Being secretive in Laos and Cambodia

The war in Vietnam was not the only conflict in Southeast Asia. The NVA/VC also threatened Laos and Cambodia, and at one time or another, the United States supported the governments in each of those countries against commu-nist insurgencies that were attempting to overthrow them. However, the United States had a more difficult time dealing with Laos and Cambodia, because each had proclaimed neutrality. U.S. military forces weren't officially allowed within the borders of either country and, therefore, had to act secretly.

The U.S. Central Intelligence Agency covertly worked within those countries supporting forces arrayed against the communists. CIA case officers worked with Laotian forces on the ground, and Air America and other pilots provided air support. Laos and Cambodia held the key to controlling the land supply route from North Vietnam to South Vietnam and the safe havens from the U.S. military and its allies operating within South Vietnam. The United States never reconciled the advantage that the NVA/VC had in operating freely in Laos and Cambodia with the political realities of fighting in a neutral country. (We discuss the details of U.S. operations and activities in Laos and Cambodia in more detail in Chapter 13.)

Military successes and political failures

The United States engaged in a *strategy of attrition* against the NVA/VC that relied on killing more NVA/VC soldiers than the losses it and its allies incurred. The *body count,* the number of NVA/VC reported killed in a battle, became the mark by which U.S. military officials determined how successful the war was going. U.S. military operations during the period between 1965 and 1968 were engaged in the tactic of *search-and-destroy,* or finding the NVA/VC and using superior firepower to destroy them.

Although the United States achieved a certain amount of success using this strategy, it nevertheless allowed the NVA/VC to maintain the initiative whereby they determined when and where to engage U.S. forces. General William C. Westmoreland (shown in Figure 5-3), commander of U.S. forces in Vietnam, never gained the initiative from the NVA/VC by using search-and-destroy tactics, and yet the United States never lost a major military engagement with them during the course of the war. As a consequence, military success didn't result in political victory, and in the end, victory in Vietnam wasn't measured by military means alone. The United States never achieved the success it desired because North Vietnam ultimately defeated South Vietnam and communism spread throughout Southeast Asia.

The turning point: The 1968 Tet Offensive

The 1968 Tet Offensive was a significant event in the Vietnam War and it is discussed in greater detail in Chapter 5. During the *Tet holiday,* an event described as Christmas, New Year's Eve, Easter, and your birthday rolled into one, NVA/VC forces launched a nationwide attack against the Republic of (South) Vietnam, attempting to overthrow the South Vietnamese government and oust the United States from Southeast Asia. The United States, however, repelled all but a few of the attacks in the first day of the offensive and scored a military victory that devastated the Viet Cong and set back the NVA for years.

Understanding where in the world Southeast Asia and Vietnam are

Knowing the geography — political and physical — of Southeast Asia is important to understanding the Vietnam War. The war extended beyond the borders of Vietnam into Laos and Cambodia and indirectly affected surrounding countries in the Asian and Pacific regions.

Using countries that surrounded South Vietnam as sanctuaries was advantageous to the NVA/VC, because the United States, for the most part, limited its own military operations to areas within the borders of South Vietnam. The map at the beginning of Chapter 2 provides a good visual of Southeast Asia for beginning your examination of the Vietnam War.

The country of Vietnam — North and South — is bordered on the east by the China Sea. To the north, the Peoples Republic of China (PRC) lingers as a constant reminder of a threat to its independence, and the countries of Laos and Cambodia border Vietnam to the west. Vietnam's shape is similar to an elongated *S*, measuring approximately 1,200 miles from its northern to southern tips. Renowned scholar Bernard Fall described Vietnam as a long pole with two rice baskets on either end. Fall's imagery is fitting when you consider that the two deltas formed at the mouths of the Red River in the north and the Mekong River in the south are Vietnam's principle areas of agricultural production. The Annamite Mountains run along nearly the entire western border of Vietnam forming the pole in Fall's description.

Vietnam is a country of contrasts, from rugged mountains to the central plains and from expansive rice paddies to the dense canopy jungles and mangroves. It also is a rugged yet beautiful country in which to live and a difficult one in which to fight a war. Its geography and tropical climate challenged the United States in its war against the NVA/VC. In the southern part of Vietnam, there are two seasons: the wet and the dry. It is not uncommon to have continuous rain for several days during the wet season and have unbearably hot temperatures in the dry season. The northern part of Vietnam has an additional season of winter, though the average temperature seldom falls below 70 degrees during the day.

The U.S. military victory shriveled in comparison to the political defeat that the United States suffered because of the offensive. Johnson, Westmoreland, and others conducting the war all but promised an end to fighting, arguing prior to the Tet Offensive that the NVA/VC forces had all but been eliminated. No one could explain the NVA/VC resurgence, leading many in the United States to believe that the leaders running the war had lied to the American people. In keeping with one of the ongoing ironies of Vietnam, the United States won on the battlefield but lost the battle politically. Johnson suspended the U.S. bombing campaign against North Vietnam and announced that he would not accept the Democratic Party's nomination for president in the November 1968 elections.

Nixon inherits the war

Richard Nixon entered the White House on the heels of one of the largest electoral victories the United States has ever seen. He offered the American people the hope of ending the war in Vietnam (see Chapter 6) and a chance to regain some of the prestige lost during the Johnson years. Nixon's first move was determining how to disengage the United States from Vietnam and, at the same time, maintain American credibility.

Nixon's planners devised a strategy of *Vietnamization* — turning the war over to the Vietnamese and withdrawing U.S. troops in the process. For Vietnamization to work, the United States had to continue training and equipping the Army of the Republic of Vietnam (ARVN) and supporting the South Vietnamese government. Nixon exercised greater military control over decisions made in Vietnam and authorized the invasion into Cambodia. To learn more about Nixon, Vietnamization, and the Cambodian Incursion, you should definitely read Chapter 6.

The price of Vietnamization, however, was a backlash within American society against the presidency that was led by people who opposed the war. (For more on such opposition, see Chapter 14.) Many thought Nixon was expanding the Vietnam War rather than withdrawing U.S. troops. That perception aside, Nixon's strategy furthered Vietnamization and the withdrawal of U.S. troops from Southeast Asia. Vietnamization failed in 1971 with a botched invasion into Laos but later achieved notable success with a victory against the NVA in the 1972 Eastertide Offensive, which is discussed in Chapter 6.

The fall of South Vietnam

After the failure of the NVA/VC Eastertide Offensive of 1972, Nixon and the United States pushed harder to negotiate an end to American military involvement in Vietnam. After convincing North Vietnam of the serious intentions of the United States to end the war with the Christmas bombing raids (see Chapter 8), representatives from the United States, South Vietnam, North Vietnam, and the Viet Cong signed the "Agreement on Ending the War and Restoring the Peace in Vietnam," commonly referred to as the *Paris Peace Accords,* on January 27, 1973. At the same time, the United States privately assured a reluctant South Vietnamese government that it would come to its aid if the North Vietnamese violated the agreements.

The agreements, however, signaled the end of U.S. military involvement in South Vietnam. The United States was a country tired of war, and Congress ensured the United States wouldn't become reinvolved in South Vietnam by passing legislation limiting military spending and the president's ability to wage war. Nixon resigned the White House in August 1974 amid the Watergate scandal, and Gerald Ford assumed the presidency only to watch as the DRV violated the agreements by invading South Vietnam. Bound by law and unable to garner enough domestic support, Ford watched as Saigon fell to the DRV on April 30, 1975, and the Republic of Vietnam ceased to exist. The Vietnam War ended for the United States with the signing of the Paris Peace Accords in 1973, sealing the fate for South Vietnam.

Its legacy lives on even today in ways that people born after the Vietnam War hardly recognize. But for a generation that grew up during the Vietnam War, the lessons learned, and the memories, remain a part of U.S. history and heritage.

Assessing the Effect of the War

When the United States exited South Vietnam in 1973 and stood by as the country fell to the North Vietnamese in 1975, the perception was that the United States had lost in war for the first time in the country's history. Whether that is a true observation continues to elicit debate among the scholarly, military, political, and other interested parties.

Without question, the Vietnam War left a series of legacies that remain in U.S. society at the beginning of the 21st century. Debate about the causes, course, and outcome of the war also continue to interest not only people who lived through the period but also newer generations who study this divisive period in history. The Vietnam War changed the society, culture, military, and political structure of the United States, and remains the single most important event that has occurred in the past half century.

A failure of political or military will?

One strain of debate during the postwar period has been assessing and assigning blame for the fall of South Vietnam. Several conflicting opinions have emerged:

> ✔ Some people believe the United States lost in Vietnam because of the political restrictions placed upon the U.S. Armed Forces. Supporters of this theory point to the limited air war against North Vietnam, which was guided by Johnson's White House rather than the military, and the failure to attack the NVA/VC units that used neutral Cambodia and Laos as bases of operations against South Vietnam. (See Chapters 5, 6, and 13.) When restrictions were lifted — the argument surmises — the

United States was able to force the DRV to concede to its will (see Chapter 9), although the U.S./ARVN still did not win decisively.

✔ Another group of people who think the war could have been won have been very critical of the emphasis the United States placed on conventional strategies and tactics that focused on bombing and killing as many NVA/VC as possible. These people argue that the United States should have focused more attention on pacification and other activities, which are discussed in Chapters 5 and 12. This group emphasizes that the United States could have won if it had focused on winning over the people of South Vietnam.

✔ Some people maintain that Vietnam was not a winnable war at all and argue that little could have been done by U.S. military or political leaders that would have resulted in a more positive outcome. U.S. authorities running the war, they say, failed to understand Vietnamese society, history, and culture. The American experience in Vietnam was only a small part of Vietnam's 2,000-year struggle for independence, and the North Vietnamese understood that in spite of the damage sustained, they could outlast U.S. activities in the region.

Readers who venture forward into the rest of this book will see that all of these arguments have their strengths and weaknesses.

Hitting a crossroads in American foreign policy: The Carter Administration

When the Republic of Vietnam fell in April 1975, the United States found itself in a unique position — one not yet experienced in the brief history of the United States. It had lost a war in spite of proclaiming it had won peace with honor. James E. Carter replaced Gerald Ford as President of the United States, inheriting remnants of a 25-year conflict. Carter was unable to immediately heal the country after Vietnam and, in many respects, allowed U.S. foreign policy to react to the *Vietnam syndrome* that emerged: the fear that the U.S. foreign policy would lead the country into another Vietnam War.

When the U.S. embassy in Iran was taken over by militant Muslims after the overthrow of the Shah, the shadow of Vietnam lingered over Carter even more. The United States was seen as weak because it was unable to forcibly rescue the hostages. Carter spent his last 444 days as president with the reminder in Iran of the depths to which the United States had fallen in international opinion. He never was able to conquer the Vietnam syndrome (see Chapter 18).

Forgetting the veterans: America turns its back on those who fought

The worst casualties of the Vietnam War were caused by the failure of the U.S. government and citizens, for the most part, to recognize and support the Vietnam veterans when they returned from Southeast Asia. They were greeted with few parades down Main Street in small towns across the country and no larger shows of support in the cities (see Chapters 14 and 15 for more on the antiwar movement and supporting the veterans during the war). Tired of war, the United States wanted to forget the long and costly struggle.

As a constant reminder of the American experience in Vietnam, veterans turned inward, relying on family and friends rather than a nationwide support group. Among Vietnam veterans, the perception grew that the U.S. government had failed to provide the resources and support that it had promised the veterans' community. Animosity between the veterans and the government grew during the Ford and Carter administrations. The Vietnam syndrome was well entrenched through the 1970s and into the early 1980s.

Return of the imperial president: The Reagan Doctrine

When Ronald Reagan entered the White House in 1981, he promised the United States a return to the days when Americans held their heads high. Well versed in Cold War terms, Reagan was quick to confront people who were opposed to his patriotic views and who actively opposed the Vietnam War. He brought back a sense of pride to many in the United States.

Under his presidency, Reagan involved the United States in a series of small winnable conflicts aimed at restoring U.S. prestige and confidence. During his administration, the Vietnam syndrome began to fade slightly, even though the syndrome and other legacies of the war remain a part of American society and culture.

Remembering the veterans: The return of honor

Not until the final construction of the Vietnam Veterans Memorial (dedicated in 1982) on the mall in Washington, D.C., did the healing process begin for many veterans. The stark monument of black marble, nearly 500-feet long and inscribed with the names of soldiers killed in action, was the first national recognition of the sacrifice this generation made for its country. The 1980s saw the rise of the Vietnam veterans' associations. Veterans, previously denied entry — or uncomfortably accepted — into the American Legion and Veterans of Foreign War posts, organized themselves by the units in which they served during the war. For more on postwar concerns, see Chapter 18.

The fall of the Soviet Union and communism in Eastern Europe, combined with the successful military campaign against Iraq in 1990–1991, brought the Vietnam War and Vietnam veterans into perspective for many people in the United States. Prior to that, many Vietnam veterans hid and lied about their service in Southeast Asia and few Americans showed any appreciation for their service. Following the successes against communism and in the Gulf War, the U.S. military enjoyed a lot of recognition and appreciation from the American people. This prompted many Vietnam veterans to "come out of the closet" and reveal to their communities that they too served their nation many years ago in Southeast Asia, and the reception most received was equally positive. By the early 1990s, Vietnam veterans began actively recounting their experiences to current generations of Americans, sharing the lessons of the past, and offering their knowledge for the future.

Chapter 2

Warring Ideologies: The Two Vietnams

*W*ar in Vietnam did not begin with the entry of U.S. combat soldiers in the 1960s. Since the founding of the country over 2,000 years ago, Vietnam's history has been one of conflict. The Vietnamese people periodically fought against the Chinese for 2,000 years, the French for 100 years, and the Japanese during World War II. In order to really understand the Vietnam War, you first have to have some sense of the history leading up to the war. Vietnam struggled for 2,000 years to gain its independence of which the fight against the United States lasted for approximately 20 years. In this chapter, we give you all the information you need (and none of what you don't) to understand the Vietnam War.

In the Beginning: The Early Days of Conflict in Vietnam

Vietnam was identified as a country as early as 208 B.C. and was founded by Trieu Da, a renegade Chinese *warlord* (someone who rules the people with military might) from the northern part of the country. For nearly 100 years, Nam Viet, as the Chinese referred to it, remained free of Chinese control and governed itself.

Enter China, stage right

Self-rule changed for Vietnam in 111 B.C., with the rise of the Han Dynasty in China, which tried to return Vietnam to China's control. The people of Vietnam resisted the Chinese for 300 years. The most notable protestors, the Trung Sisters, took their own lives in A.D. 40 rather than submit to Chinese rule. Since that time, the Vietnamese people have developed a strong history of resistance to foreign invaders — a trait that has remained with them for 2,000 years.

From A.D. 220 to 542, because of weak leadership, China went through a period of decay. Vietnam reexerted control of its destiny and began building an *autonomous* (independent) culture and society, taking what it believed were the best characteristics from the Chinese. But with the rise of the T'ang Dynasty in China in 618, the Chinese returned to Vietnam for another 300 years of struggle.

In 939, the Ngo Dynasty emerged in Vietnam, fighting back the Chinese and leading to nearly 900 years of semi-independence for Vietnam. During that period, Vietnam grew from a small nation bordering China and concentrated in the Red River Delta to its currently recognized boundaries.

Enter France, stage left

The French entered Indochina (shown in Figure 2-1) in the mid-nineteenth century. Why? They were

- ✓ Hoping to secure a series of land and sea bases from Europe to Asia.
- ✓ Competing with the British for colonial possessions.
- ✓ Trying to convert that area of the world to Catholicism.

As part of an 1862 treaty, the French secured control of the southern section of Vietnam, a reasonably secure base area from which they expanded their control over *Indochina* (a name derived from the combination of India and China, which at the time were part of the British Empire — France's competition). The expansion of the French into Indochina led to an 1887 treaty that combined present-day Cambodia, Laos, and Vietnam with Indochina. Although a growing number of Vietnamese started a resistance movement to oust the French colonial power, the French remained in power until World War II.

Figure 2-1:
The Indochina of the 1950s, comprised of North Vietnam, South Vietnam, Laos, and Cambodia, kept similar geographical features for much of the last 200 years leading to the reunification of Vietnam in 1975.

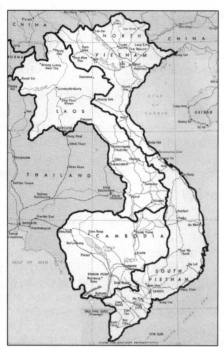

Figure 2-1:
The Indochina of the 1950s, comprised of North Vietnam, South Vietnam, Laos, and Cambodia, kept similar geographical features for much of the last 200 years leading to the reunification of Vietnam in 1975.

Demoting France

The French suffered a serious setback during World War II when Germany defeated the French Armed Forces after a short campaign in June 1940. France was out of the war in Europe and soon found itself defeated at the hands of the Japanese in Indochina. In Europe, France's declaration of neutrality enabled Germany to control its countryside. Similarly, France worked out an arrangement with Japan that enabled the French to remain in symbolic control of Indochina, while allowing the Japanese to exploit the area for war materials and other resources.

The Japanese defeat of the French provided hope for the Vietnamese people that they would be able to finally achieve independence. With the French weakened, Vietnamese leaders created organizations to fight the Japanese, believing that the French were finished in Vietnam. If the Vietnamese helped to defeat the Japanese in Indochina during World War II, they hoped it would lead to their independence.

The groups formed during this period to fight the Japanese were the same ones that emerged after World War II as the leading oppositional organization fighting the French from 1945 to 1954 and the United States during the 1960s and 1970s.

Fighting with the French

At the end of World War II, Indochina was divided in two at the 16th parallel to disarm the Japanese, who had taken control of the area from the French during the war.

The British controlled the southern section of Indochina, and the Chinese controlled the northern section. Both the British and the Chinese received the same postwar instructions from the victors of World War II:

- Concentrate, disarm, and return to Japan the defeated Japanese armies.
- Remain outside of the internal disputes.

But neither the British nor the Chinese stayed out of the internal disputes. The Chinese helped the Viet Minh forces (a group formed in 1941, opposed to French rule), which had fought the Japanese. The Chinese and the Viet Minh were united in the effort to oust the French from Indochina. The British also disarmed Japanese soldiers but moved toward the return of the French by working against the Viet Minh. In reasserting French command over Indochina, the British and French used Japanese soldiers to fight Viet Minh soldiers. Ultimately, the country was in turmoil after four years of Japanese occupation and France's desire to reclaim its empire. In 1946, France regained control of Vietnam, Laos, and Cambodia though it had begun to reassert itself in Southeast Asia in 1945.

The return of French rule to Indochina after World War II resulted in a nine-year struggle for the Vietnamese people in what often is called the First Indochina War (1945–1954). During this time, the French, with some Vietnamese assistance, desperately fought to hold onto their Indochina empire. A growing group of nationalists among the Vietnamese people, under the political leadership of Ho Chi Minh and the military leadership of Vo Nguyen Giap, fought for Vietnamese independence and an end to the foreign presence in Vietnam.

The Hatfields and the McCoys, Vietnamese style

The first division of Vietnam did not occur in 1946. In the seventeenth century, fighting between the Nguyen family in the South and the Trinh family in the North resulted in an armed stalemate. A wall was built near the 18th parallel, close to the town of Dong Hoi, dividing the country in two. Three hundred years later, in 1954, Vietnam was divided for the last time, along the 17th parallel, with the signing of the Geneva Agreements.

OSS for the USA

The OSS was created as an intelligence branch for the U.S. government. The elite group of operators provided much of the early intelligence for the United States and played an important role in World War II. OSS officers had strong working relationships with the Viet Minh and were strong supporters of Vietnamese independence at the end of World War II.

Declaring independence: Ho Chi Minh

The Viet Minh forces were active during World War II and opposed the return of the French after the war. Ho Chi Minh (for more information on Ho Chi Minh, see the "Understanding Ho Chi Minh and Ngo Dinh Diem" section later in the chapter) and the Viet Minh supported members of the Office of Strategic Services (OSS), the predecessor to the U.S. Central Intelligence Agency (CIA), in Indochina. The OSS had set up *listening posts* (stations to listen to Japanese radio broadcasts) throughout Indochina to spy on the Japanese and rescue downed American pilots before the Japanese captured them.

In August 1945, the Viet Minh met in a congress at Cao Bang near the Chinese border, forming a provisional government as an alternative to French rule. Viet Minh forces fought against remaining Japanese occupation troops in the Tonkin Delta and took control from them on August 19 in Hanoi. The Vietnamese people, sensing an opportunity to gain their independence, staged massive demonstrations around the country. Nearly 100,000 people participated in a display of nationalism on August 25 in Saigon.

The Vietnamese people had cause for celebration. Japanese invaders were defeated, and France, their former colonial ruler, suffered a significant defeat in the war, abandoning its right to govern when it failed to protect the colony. On September 2, Ho Chi Minh issued a Declaration of Independence, modeled after the U.S. Declaration of Independence (1776) as a sign of respect to the United States and its fight against the British during the American Revolution. In doing so, he hoped the Americans would recognize and support Vietnam as it began a similar struggle against France.

The red, white, and blue stick together: U.S. support of France

Ho Chi Minh's declaration didn't have the effect on the United States and France that he had hoped. In fact, neither country recognized his declaration.

France proceeded with reclaiming its lost colony, and the United States faced a choice in 1945 of either supporting the new regime of Ho Chi Minh or supporting France. President Harry S. Truman's foreign policy was focused on Europe and the danger that the Soviet Union posed to the world. Because the United States thought France played a greater role in the future of peace in the world, Truman gave it a higher priority than Vietnam. When the British and Chinese withdrew from Indochina, the French returned, confident that they'd receive international support.

During the late 1940s and early 1950s, a Cold War mentality was developing in the United States. This philosophy argued that the Soviet Union was crusading to communize the world and that containing Soviet advances whenever and wherever possible was a U.S. responsibility. The United States developed a containment policy in 1947: Any country that didn't join the United States and the Western world was a gain for the Soviets and communism. This Cold War mentality maintained that only one communist philosophy existed, and it emerged from Moscow. The United States maintained that communists were responsible for many revolts erupting in former colonial countries around the world.

Nationalist revolutions were seen as communist insurgencies (or revolts), and the following American policies became American objectives:

- Containing communism
- Aiding embattled countries
- Exporting democracy

The United States met those objectives, in part, by giving aid to France (and Indochina) in the form of money, weapons, and advice.

France used the Cold War mentality to obtain aid for Indochina from the United States, arguing that if it lost Indochina, France would become so weak that the government would fall and the French Communist Party, supported by the Soviets, would rise to power. If that happened, the United States couldn't rely on France to fight the Soviets in Europe. By playing the Indochina trump card, France was able to get American aid during the First Indochina War. By 1952, the United States provided one-third of the French military budget in Indochina. And by 1954, the amount of American aid had increased to nearly 70 percent.

The French Union Forces in Indochina found that fighting the Viet Minh was more difficult than expected. General de Lattre had some successes in 1950 and 1951, but his forces never were able to destroy the Viet Minh.

The United States military and political leaders were divided about how to fight the war. Some members of the U.S. military didn't believe the United States had enough resources to become involved in less significant areas of interest, such as Indochina. The reasons for their opposition included the following:

- Europe was the main battlefield, and participating in a conflict in Indochina only drained resources away from the main fight. So if the United States committed its limited resources to Indochina, the Soviets and Communist Chinese ultimately would benefit.

- The American military didn't trust the French to remain in Indochina if it looked like the Democratic Republic of Vietnam (DRV, or North Vietnam) would defeat the South Vietnamese. Before the United States committed itself to the region, the military wanted another ally, preferably the United Kingdom. The United States acting alone was deemed unwise, especially when the French lacked effective leadership and control in Indochina.

- The military stationed in Vietnam recognized that the Vietnamese were fighting for their independence. Even if communism was their ideology, the overriding philosophy driving the movement was nationalism. The fact that Ho Chi Minh and Vo Nguyen Giap were popular leaders throughout Vietnam didn't help, either.

- The nature of the war being fought by the French was different than the training received by U.S. troops. A guerilla war fought in Indochina would, at best, result in a stalemate and, at worst, a defeat.

In 1953, French General Henri Navarre assumed command of the French Union Forces in Indochina. Navarre's plan was to negotiate a greater independence for the Vietnamese in exchange for Vietnamese support against the Viet Minh. The Navarre Plan also called for additional French and indigenous troops and combining forces that were scattered throughout the Red River Delta (see Figure 2-2) in preparation for a major offensive. The United States supported the Navarre Plan with financial assistance and equipment, believing that it finally would end the threat of communism in Indochina.

And yet, before Navarre even started, he abandoned his plan. The Viet Minh launched an attack that scattered French forces and placed them on the defensive. Navarre improvised an alternative strategy known as Operation CASTOR, establishing a fortress (a grouping of fortified outposts) in the remote village of Dien Bien Phu. The principal mission of Operation CASTOR was stopping the flow of Viet Minh personnel and material between Laos and Vietnam. Navarre also hoped to lure the Viet Minh into a Western-styled battle and destroy them with superior firepower and air power. The battle at Dien Bien Phu eventually turned out differently for the French. Rather than an opportunity to destroy the Viet Minh, the battle turned into a desperate fight for the survival of the French fortress and an end of French rule in Indochina.

Figure 2-2:
Red River
Delta was
the scene of
the majority
of French–
Viet Minh
battles
during the
First
Indochina
War. Dien
Bien Phu is
on the
western
border with
Laos.

Map courtesy of the Vietnam Archive, Texas Tech University

The loss of an empire: Dien Bien Phu: 1954

The village of Dien Bien Phu is situated in North Vietnam in a valley on the border with Laos. Under the command of Colonel Christian Marie Ferdinand de la Croix de Castries, the French believed that, with only a small force, they would be able to hold off anything the Viet Minh threw at them. Dien Bien Phu was surrounded by a series of hills on which the French created *strongholds* (small forts), each of which was named for one of de Castries's mistresses.

Early in the operation, the French abandoned patrols they'd been conducting from the strongholds after the Viet Minh bloodied the small groups of men. Disabling the patrols enabled the Viet Minh to place more soldiers around the fortress at Dien Bien Phu and to attack the strongholds one-by-one. Because of harsh weather in the valley, de Castries was unable to reinforce his garrison the way he wanted and Viet Minh General Giap was able to significantly increase the number of Viet Minh troops in the area after calling off his Northern offensive. By March 1954, the Viet Minh had positioned approximately 40,000 troops around Dien Bien Phu.

With the aid of the Communist Chinese, the Viet Minh gathered their artillery around the surrounding hills of Dien Bien Phu by carrying each gun piece-by-piece up the mountains, assembling them, and then firing on the French Union troops stationed in the French fortress. The French tried to destroy the artillery and surrounding Viet Minh troops but discovered that doing so was difficult because of the weather and the perfect cover afforded by the dense surrounding jungle. Firepower was a key to victory and the French underestimated the Viet Minh's ability to match its artillery.

The Viet Minh bombardment and siege of Dien Bien Phu began March 13, 1954. One of the French strongholds was overrun and another was captured a few days later. The French had no strategy for countering the Viet Minh, who, after heavy bombardments, launched massive attacks against the French. When another stronghold fell nine days later, the ability of the French to hold onto Dien Bien Phu became questionable. The French were unable to provide relief for de Castries over land, and attempts to resupply the fortress by air were insufficient. Monsoons settled over the valley and kept aircraft on the ground. Plus, the Viet Minh placed a number of antiaircraft guns along the fly routes of French airplanes, inflicting moderate damage when those planes were able to fly.

The French had several plans for relieving the garrison, each more desperate than the last. The plans show how the French position in Indochina was slipping away and how the United States became an unwilling replacement:

- Operation CONDOR would link the fortress with troops from Laos, and Operation ALBATROSS was designed for the garrison to break out, linking with troops from the east. Neither plan was executed because of poor weather conditions and the danger of Viet Minh ambush along the single road into Dien Bien Phu.

- Operation VULTURE was a plan the French developed for using U.S. air power to rescue the forces at Dien Bien Phu. It called for American B-29 bombers to raid Viet Minh positions around Dien Bien Phu and destroy the concentrated forces. If this attack proved inadequate, the B-29s also were to strike the Viet Minh supply routes leading into the valley. Neither plan was implemented, but American officials seriously considered the proposal.

Another strategy discussed in the United States was a plan of United Action — an international force led by the United States that would come to the aid of the French. The Americans wouldn't move without allied support, especially from the British, and the British refused to become involved in the fight. When United Action failed to materialize, the fate of the French fortress was sealed.

Australia, New Zealand, and United Action

Although the United Kingdom was the primary ally for any U.S. involvement in Indochina during the battle for Dien Bien Phu, Australia and New Zealand received their fair share of pressure from the United States to actively plan and participate in joint operations and to encourage the United Kingdom to join United Action. But after United Action failed, the United States turned to its Pacific allies for support in Vietnam. Australia was the first ally to provide advisors to Vietnam in 1962. Australia and the United States proved to be valuable allies after 1965, and so were the South Koreans, because all three committed troops to the war effort.

Although the French had suffered at Dien Bien Phu, the Viet Minh also were bloodied. General Giap changed strategies by the end of March, moving away from massive human-wave attacks toward a *strategy of attrition* (a strategy to kill more French than the Viet Minh lost) and pointed attacks aimed at defeating the French. With time on his side, Giap recognized that the French couldn't maintain the fortress indefinitely. The Viet Minh weakened the remaining strongholds around Dien Bien Phu earlier in April and then launched the final phase of the battle at the end of the month. The Viet Minh dug trenches to the edge of the strategic areas, enabling them to attack at close range and overwhelm the defenders. By May 6, the Viet Minh overran all but a small area around Dien Bien Phu, and the final French Union Forces surrendered May 7.

The Viet Minh suffered greater casualties than the French, by a margin of almost two-to-one, but won the battlefield. Coming on the eve of Indochina's portion of the Geneva Conference (see the "Searching for Peace: The 1954 Geneva Conference" section that follows), the victory at Dien Bien Phu placed the Viet Minh in a stronger negotiating position. The French people were tired of the war, and the French government had promised peace at any cost. The defeat at Dien Bien Phu effectively ended the French colonial empire in Indochina. Vietnam had suffered from nine additional years of war, but its victory wouldn't be an end to the conflict. One more chance for peace came in 1954.

Searching for Peace: The 1954 Geneva Conference

The Indochina phase of the Geneva Conference began May 8, 1954, the day after Dien Bien Phu fell to the Viet Minh. The objectives of this phase of the conference were

- ✔ Negotiating an end to hostilities
- ✔ Achieving the independence of Vietnam from French rule

U.S. representatives, under the leadership of Secretary of State John Foster Dulles and Undersecretary of State Walter Bedell Smith, tried to negotiate the best possible treaty for themselves and the State of Vietnam. However, the Viet Minh had the upper hand and, with Soviet and Communist Chinese assistance, signed a treaty that would get the French out of Indochina on July 21, 1954.

The 1954 Geneva Agreements, which featured several significant points, included separate peace plans for Vietnam, Laos, and Cambodia. The final agreements created the International Commission for Supervision and Control (ICSC) to oversee the treaty. The commission was responsible for overseeing the treaty and addressing any violations by either side. It was not as effective as the United States would have liked, because the commission required all three of its representative members (India, Canada, and Poland) to agree before it would act. Canada represented the United States, while Poland took care of DRV (North Vietnam) interests. As you can guess, the two country's representatives rarely agreed.

So what was the treaty that the ICSC was supposed to oversee? The treaty did the following:

- ✔ Temporarily divided Vietnam into two countries near the 17th parallel.

- ✔ Ordered an election in July 1956, under the supervision of the ICSC, at which time the country would be reunited.

- ✔ Prohibited entry of foreign troops, military personnel, weapons, and munitions into North and South Vietnam.

- ✔ Prohibited new military bases under foreign control.

- ✔ Permitted the Vietnamese to move freely between North and South Vietnam until May 1955.

- ✔ Prohibited violence against persons (or members of their families) who had collaborated in any way with the French or Viet Minh during the war.

- ✔ Called for the withdrawal of French Union Forces from Vietnam, Laos, and Cambodia. (By 1956, the French presence in Vietnam, Laos, and Cambodia had diminished.)

The United States wasn't pleased with the outcome of the Geneva Conference and didn't sign the document. The United States, however, realized that the treaty was the best it could hope for given the consequences at Dien Bien Phu. In fact, only representatives from France and the Viet Minh signed the final agreement. Yet, the United States had little choice in accepting conclusions reached at Geneva. The United States wasn't prepared to become directly involved in the conflict but, instead, believed its best opportunity to make a difference in Vietnam was supporting the Republic of Vietnam (South Vietnam) in the two years prior to the general elections.

After the signing of the agreements, a statement by Undersecretary of State Bedell Smith, the U.S. representative in Geneva after Dulles left, indicated that the United States would work toward strengthening the agreements and would "refrain from the threat or the use of force to disturb them." Bedell Smith argued that the United States would seek to achieve the unity of Vietnam through the 1956 general elections, but despite these public statements, the American position mirrored Diem's contention that a free election in Vietnam was a contradiction.

Dividing Vietnam again: The 17th parallel

The division of Vietnam along the 17th parallel created the Republic of Vietnam in the south and the Democratic Republic of Vietnam in the north. Ngo Dinh Diem led South Vietnam, and Ho Chi Minh governed North Vietnam. The separation of the Vietnams would remain temporary as long as the Geneva Agreement was in effect. The 1956 general elections were expected to reunify the country after the people had an opportunity to resume their normal lives.

Although South Vietnam received more land in the settlement, North Vietnam had a greater population. This disparity in population didn't give Diem much confidence in 1954, because he believed the Viet Minh would fix the elections in favor of the North's Ho. Because more of the population was in the North, Ho would not have had to "fix" the election, but it did give Ngo Dinh Diem, with U.S. agreement, cause to cancel the mandated elections.

Identifying the Vietnam War Players

Knowing who is fighting whom during the Vietnam War is sometimes difficult. Many individuals and organizations involved on both sides of the 17th parallel fought for control of the beleaguered country. The following sections provide a good background of the various factions.

Democratic Republic of Vietnam (North Vietnam)

The Democratic Republic of Vietnam (DRV), or North Vietnam (NV), consisted of the land in Southeast Asia located north of the 17th parallel, as defined by the 1954 Geneva Agreements. The Soviet Union, the People's Republic of China, and their allies supported the DRV in its fight against the United States and its attempts to overthrow the Republic of Vietnam (South Vietnam). In 1975, the DRV defeated South Vietnam, and the two countries combined to make the Socialist Republic of Vietnam (SRV).

The DRV leadership consisted of:

- **Ho Chi Minh:** Leader and founder of anticolonial groups that opposed the French and the United States, and president of the DRV from 1945 until his death in 1969.

- **Vo Nguyen Giap:** Commander of all military forces in North Vietnam from 1945 through 1973. His power diminished when his military advice was ignored by Ho Chi Minh during the American Vietnam War. Giap was the mastermind behind the Vietnamese victory over the French at Dien Bien Phu, but he lost power after the failed 1972 Eastertide Offensive.

- ✔ **Le Duan:** An early leader in the anticolonial movement and follower of Ho Chi Minh. Le Duan believed in an offensive military campaign in South Vietnam and was involved in an internal struggle for power and direction of the military with Vo Nguyen Giap during the 1960s. Following the death of Ho Chi Minh, Le Duan took over leadership of the Lao Dong Party (described later in this section) and led the country through the end of the war.

- ✔ **Pham Van Dong:** After Ho Chi Minh and Vo Nguyen Giap, Pham Van Dong was one of the most powerful individuals in North Vietnam. He also was an active anticolonialist, an early member of the Communist Viet Minh, and a skillful diplomat, serving at the 1954 Geneva Conference and later at the Paris Peace Negotiations between 1970 and 1973. After Ho Chi Minh's death, Pham Van Dong played a crucial and more public role in the war.

The DRV's struggle against the French began well before World War II and the introduction in the 1950s of American personnel. The foundation and mainte-nance of the DRV can be traced to the following organizations:

- ✔ **Viet Nam Doc Lap Dong Minh Hoi (also known as the Viet Minh or the Vietnamese Independence League):** The Viet Minh was established in May 1941 as a loose-knit organization of committed communists, social-ists, labor unions, nationalists, and others opposed to French rule. The group began as a force to oust France from Vietnam, but as the war con-tinued, and France's role diminished, its ideology became more radical.

- ✔ **Dong Lao Dong Viet Nam (also known as the Lao Dong Party, or the Vietnamese Workers' Party, it was renamed in 1976 as the Dang Cong San Viet Nam, or Vietnamese Communist Party [VCP]):** This political party ruled the Democratic Republic of Vietnam from 1951 to 1986 and was responsible for all domestic legislation. Ho Chi Minh used the Lao Dong to rule over North Vietnam until his death in 1969.

- ✔ **National Front for the Liberation of South Vietnam (also known as the National Liberation Front [NLF] or the Viet Cong [VC]):** This group was formed December 20, 1960, in Tay Ninh Province to fight in South Vietnam. The NLF organized other groups in opposition to the govern-ment of the Republic of Vietnam with the ultimate goal of overthrowing Ngo Dinh Diem, who is described in the following section.

- ✔ **People's Liberation Armed Forces (PLAF):** PLAF was the military branch of the National Liberation Front and was responsible for organiz-ing military resistance in South Vietnam.

- ✔ **Provisional Revolutionary Government of South Vietnam (PRG):** The PRG was formed in 1969 as a parallel government in the Republic of Vietnam, combining organizations that had been working in the South to overthrow the existing government. The primary role of the PRG was legitimizing and representing the Southern insurgency in international affairs and negotiations.

The Republic of Vietnam (South Vietnam)

Also known as the RVN or South Vietnam (SV), the Republic of Vietnam consists of land south of the 17th parallel as defined by the 1954 Geneva Agreements, described earlier in this chapter. The United States and its allies supported the RVN (which was seen as a counterforce to communism in North Vietnam) in its war against North Vietnam. The RVN was ruled by a number of men during its existence from 1954 to 1975:

- **Ngo Dinh Diem:** Diem served as prime minister and then as the first president of the RVN from 1954 to 1963. He was an anticolonialist who worked with the United States to secure the future of South Vietnam.

- **Duong Van Minh:** General Duong Van "Big" Minh served in the Army of the Republic of Vietnam and as a member of the group of military officers that overthrew Ngo Dinh Diem in 1963. He served in the military until April 1975 and as RVN president for the last two days before the country ceased to exist.

- **Nguyen Khanh:** General Khanh served in the Army of the Republic of Vietnam until 1964 when he took over as RVN prime minister and president for a short period in 1965. He served with the Viet Minh and French in his efforts to gain independence for Vietnam.

- **Nguyen Cao Ky:** Air Marshall Ky joined Nguyen Khanh when he took over from General Minh in 1964. He served as RVN prime minister in 1965 after ousting the U.S.-backed President Phan Huy Quat. He remained in that position until 1967 and then served as vice president until 1971.

- **Nguyen Van Thieu:** General Thieu was involved in the overthrow of Ngo Dinh Diem and served on the Military Revolution Council during the post-coup period. Thieu became President of the Republic of Vietnam in 1967, a position he retained until late April 1975 when he fled the country before Saigon's fall.

Understanding Ho Chi Minh and Ngo Dinh Diem

You can get a better understanding of the Vietnam War by taking a look at the leaders of North Vietnam (Ho Chi Minh) and South Vietnam (Ngo Dinh Diem). Learning more about the two leaders in Vietnam will help you better understand their reactions to the United States as it became more involved in Vietnam and answer those nagging questions about the Vietnam War.

Understanding Ho Chi Minh

In many respects, Ho Chi Minh (shown in Figure 2-3) remained a mystery throughout his life and until his death in September 1969. Little is known about his birth date, his early childhood, or his family, leaving considerable speculation about how these events shaped his worldview. His father was a strong Vietnamese nationalist who passed along to Ho a belief that Vietnam belonged to the Vietnamese. Ho Chi Minh was not a good student and, because of his anticolonial views, left the Lycee Huoc-Hoc before graduation. He left for Europe in 1911 on a French ship departing from Saigon, learning about different cultures and gaining alliances for Vietnam. His journeys took him to the United States, Europe, and Asia, and during that time, Ho Chi Minh began formulating his philosophy for Vietnamese independence.

Figure 2-3:
In the first session of the second legislature, the National Assembly (1960) unanimously maintained Ho Chi Minh in his function as President of the Democratic Republic of Vietnam and elected Ton Duc Thang as vice president.

Photograph courtesy of the Vietnam Archive, Texas Tech Universityß

Ho Chi Minh used the mystery of his early life to his advantage during the Vietnam War, projecting his image as a man of the people. He was often photographed in peasant clothes and sandals and among the North Vietnamese people and was viewed as a simple man who required little and wanted only to see his country through to independence. He claimed that his birthday coincided with his introduction to communist ideology. Often referred to as Uncle Ho, Ho Chi Minh stood in stark contrast to his South Vietnamese adversary, Ngo Dinh Diem.

Looking to the West: A political education abroad

Ho Chi Minh's first contact with the West was with sailors visiting Indochina. His recollections suggest that he was less than impressed with their abilities, and these encounters did much to undermine the notion of Western superiority.

Working as a pastry chef and retouching photographs for part of the time that he spent in Europe during World War I, the effects of the war helped shape Ho's vision of the West and the role it would play in Vietnam. The same was true of his trip to the United States. At the end of World War I, Ho found himself in Europe and traveled to Versailles to represent Vietnam at the Peace Talks even though his country was still controlled by the French and not recognized as an official member of the Treaty of Versailles peace talks. Although President Woodrow Wilson's Fourteen Points promised hope for Ho's quest for Vietnamese independence, he failed to gain a meeting with the president and was not treated seriously by the participants.

See *World War II For Dummies* by Keith D. Dickson (published by Wiley) for additional background information on the First World War and the Treaty of Versailles.

Communist or nationalist?

Ho stayed in France after the war and was a founding member of the French Communist Party. His expectations were that he could work from within to end France's control over Vietnam. Ho became the colonial expert within the French Communist Party because of his knowledge of French colonial control in Indochina but didn't have the influence that he needed to change party doctrine. When the French Communist Party failed to meet his expectations, Ho traveled to the Soviet Union, condemning Western communism for its wait-and-see attitude and revealing his preference for the more active philosophies in Russia.

During the 1920s and 1930s, Ho also traveled to China where he became familiar with Mao Tse-tung's anticolonial revolutions based on peasantry. In 1925, Ho founded the Vietnam Revolutionary Youth Group and helped organize the Indochina Communist Party in 1929. During World War II, Ho was imprisoned in China, accused of being a spy for the communists and the French. Upon his release from prison, Ho returned to Vietnam and worked with offices of the American Office of Strategic Services (OSS), rescuing Allied pilots who were shot down over Indochina.

Ho Chi Minh supported the U.S. effort during World War II, because he wanted to develop a relationship with the only country capable of aiding in Vietnam's independence movement and influencing France. In trying to gain an understanding of Ho Chi Minh, the question of whether he was communist or nationalist isn't most important.

Ho actively resisted France, Japan, China, and the United States when doing so meant advancing Vietnamese independence, and by the same token, he actively supported them whenever doing so meant advancing Vietnamese independence. Ho Chi Minh wanted Vietnam's independence first, free of colonial or foreign interference, and he would use any country — regardless of philosophy — to achieve his goal.

Understanding Ngo Dinh Diem

Unlike his counterpart to the North, no mystique surrounded Ngo Dinh Diem (shown in Figure 2-4). Born in 1901 in Quang Binh Province (part of North Vietnam), Diem was the son of a well-educated *mandarin* (Vietnamese civil servant who took part in running the country) who served as the Minister of Rites and Grand Chamberlain to Emperor Thanh-Thai (1889–1907). Diem's family was one of the earliest to convert to Catholicism, a religion he took with him to the south early in his career. Similar to Ho Chi Minh's father, Diem's father was an ardent nationalist, resigning his government post in protest against French rule in Indochina. Although Diem and Ho went to the same school, Diem was a good student and skillful debater, who graduated at the top of his class. Unlike Ho Chi Minh, Diem's rise to power took a different path.

Figure 2-4:
President of the Republic of Vietnam Ngo Dinh Diem.

Photograph courtesy of the Vietnam Archive, Texas Tech University

Creating South Vietnam: Diem re-creates the mandarin

Similar to Ho, Diem followed the path established by his father and was a strong nationalist who demanded an end to French rule in Indochina. He compared himself with Emperor Gia Long, who reunified Vietnam at the end of the eighteenth century after pushing out foreign invaders. In the same way that Gia Long created a series of codes and laws for the people, Diem believed that only he could bring order back to his worn-torn country. In Vietnamese history, the rule of the Emperor always was secondary to the rule of the village. Diem, however, maintained that in a time of crisis, Vietnam needed a strong leader making tough decisions for the Vietnamese people. During the early years of the Republic of Vietnam, this philosophy worked, but it backfired when Diem strengthened his hold in the South Vietnamese countryside as the struggle against communism intensified in the late 1950s.

Opportunist or nationalist?

When the Japanese occupied Indochina, Diem refused to collaborate with them. He, however, supported the Vietnamese emperor Bao Dai, who had been yielding his waning power on Vietnam from France. Bao Dai, the last of the Vietnamese emperors, was a weak leader who worked with the French to retain his power and then with the Japanese during World War II. Because of this collaboration and his unwillingness to return to Vietnam to rule the country, many Vietnamese did not trust or support him. Diem's association with Bao Dai resulted in many Vietnamese people also labeling him a collaborator by association. Diem believed in the power of the Vietnamese monarchy when it complemented his theories of a strong central government, and yet he abandoned the emperor when he concluded that it had become incapable of providing Vietnam with the kind of king it needed to achieve independence. Diem knew that he could provide that leadership.

Diem also recognized that France never would give Vietnam its independence, and based on how the Catholics were treated by the Viet Minh after the 1954 Geneva Conference, he didn't believe that Catholics could live peacefully in a Viet Minh–led country. To counter both powers, Diem created Phong Trao Quoc-Gia Qua Kich, a political party known as the Nationalist Extremist Movement. Diem's mission during his nine-year rule of South Vietnam was to create a stable country, but his rise to power all but ensured that he never would achieve that goal.

The return of the empire: Diem's rise to power

On June 19, 1954, Bao Dai gave Diem dictatorial powers over South Vietnam. Bao Dai still believed he could control Diem from France. Diem, however, was an all-or-nothing person with a strong stubborn streak. He refused the offer of becoming chief of state until Bao Dai gave him what he wanted, settling for no less than the next highest position in order for the emperor to prove that he was capable of ruling the country. Diem wanted Bao Dai to take responsibility for the country and when Diem realized that Bao Dai was incapable, he began assuming responsibility for South Vietnam. Before Diem could effectively rule

South Vietnam and make it a viable anticommunist state, he needed to successfully consolidate his power.

Three major political-religious sects — the Binh Xuyen, Cao Dai, and Hoa Hao — stood in the way of Diem's ultimate goal in South Vietnam. Each sect believed it was strong enough to rule Vietnam without Diem. Buying influence into the Cao Dai and Hoa Hao sects in 1955, Diem focused them against one another and used his forces to defeat the Binh Xuyen. In April, the Binh Xuyen and Hoa Hao merged, forming the United Front of Nationalist Forces in an attempt to overthrow Diem; however, Diem's forces were swift and efficient in their response, overpowering the Binh Xuyen. By early May, Diem had decimated the Binh Xuyen and diffused the effectiveness of the Hoa Hao and Cao Dai by using a combination of force and persuasion. His consolidation of the three factions was completed May 15, 1955, when he abolished Bao Dai's Imperial Guard.

In October 1955, Diem officially replaced Bao Dai as chief of state in an election in which Diem received 98.4 percent of the vote. Although many political and military leaders within the United States would rather Diem had provided freer elections and a more reasonable result, few were concerned that he wouldn't win the election fairly. Nevertheless, Diem consolidated his power and began his focus on the *insurgency* (communist) movement in South Vietnam. True to the principles of many Vietnamese, the family played an extremely important role. Diem never considered negotiating with the Viet Minh after the Geneva Conference, primarily because the Viet Minh assassinated his brother as a French collaborator.

Regardless of the Geneva Agreements, Diem knew that creating a viable anticommunist state in the South was his first mission. He established unchallenged control through a centralized government and prepared South Vietnam for an inevitable invasion from the North. Knowing that general elections scheduled in 1956 could never be free because of the Viet Minh, Diem announced in 1955 that South Vietnam would not participate.

South Vietnam remained under Ngo Dinh Diem's control until November 1963, when he was assassinated by young military officers who believed that he no longer possessed the confidence of the Vietnamese people or the United States.

Personalism countering communism

Ngo Dinh Diem adopted the philosophy of personalism (called Nhan-Vi in Vietnamese) in an effort to create a viable democratic state. The philosophy was developed in the 1930s based on the European personalism of France's Emmanuel Mounier. Diem combined this philosophy with Vietnamese Catholicism and anticommunism to create Nhan-Vi. Personalism emphasizes human dignity or individualism instead of being part of the masses — the perfect counterforce to communism. Diem's personalism, however, proved weak compared with the communist ideology and failed to rally the South Vietnamese to his cause.

Pitting North against South

The two Vietnams were divided geographically, politically, and ideologically:

- ✔ The Republic of (South) Vietnam based itself, in part, on a democratically elected government modeled after the United States, but problems emerged with the rule of Ngo Dinh Diem. (See "Understanding Ngo Dinh Diem" earlier in this chapter for more about this topic.)

- ✔ The Democratic Republic of (North) Vietnam based itself on a Vietnamese-style communist model under the leadership of Ho Chi Minh.

The two Vietnams offered conflicting ideologies between which (for the most part) the Vietnamese people had to decide. This choice formed the basis for the conflict that lasted for more than 20 years.

Practicing poor politics: Diem's policies in South Vietnam

Diem knew that the Communist Party was his greatest nemesis, so he organized anticommunist denunciation campaigns to search for the Viet Minh who stayed in South Vietnam after the Geneva Conference as well as their supporters. The campaign turned into a manhunt where those seeking the communists used their power to settle old debts and damage potential adversaries. Diem's tactics actually forced as many Vietnamese to the communist side as it exposed when eliminating the communists.

Diem organized the campaign at the village level in order to root out the communist supporters. In forming the anticommunist campaign, Diem:

- ✔ Decreed that three- to five-man committees appointed by the province chief were to replace elected village councils.

- ✔ Proclaimed four months later that province chiefs were to be appointed directly by the president and were responsible for all administration within their respective provinces. This took power away from the village leaders who knew the committee members and placed it in the hands of the provinces, allowing for more potential corruption.

- ✔ Declared in 1957 that province chiefs were commanders in control of all military forces within the province. This further strengthened the role of the province chief who often did not know the needs of the people in his province.

If you wanted to keep your job in Diem's Vietnam, you had to be completely loyal to him, which frustrated many of his followers. As a countermeasure to Viet Minh and their propaganda, Diem organized small civic-action teams that went from village to village denouncing communism and taking care of the people's complaints about corruption, poor living conditions, and a number of other day-to-day problems. Unfortunately, the villagers viewed these teams as highly paid outsiders compared to the Vietnamese commoner, who was barely staying alive. Many members of the teams were chosen because of political or family ties and not based on merit. As a result, many of the civic-action teams were corrupt and did more damage than good in the villages.

Throwing fuel on the south's instability

Fueling the seeds of unrest in the South was to the benefit of the Democratic Republic of Vietnam. Although the Viet Minh conducted political assassinations (known as *Tru Gian*) on a small but effective scale between 1957 and 1959, the Communist Party of the Democratic Republic of Vietnam adhered to the policy of political rather than violent resistance, preferring to allow Diem policies to work for them. The Viet Minh also targeted Diem's secret police (Cong An), honest or effective government employees, influential anticommunist teachers, and serious civic-action personnel. At the same time, the Viet Minh ignored the corrupt and inefficient officials.

After Diem launched his most active campaign against the southern communist in 1959 and enforced a decree providing for harsh punishment of antigovernment activity, the Communist Party Central Committee in Hanoi responded by supplementing its political onslaught with armed aggression from the North. The North Vietnamese military created the 559th Transport Group to organize the logistics for returning Vietnamese people who left South Vietnam and regrouped in North Vietnam after the Geneva Conference to help train the southern insurgency. The Viet Minh also dramatically increased the Tru Gian campaign at the end of 1959, assassinating almost 1,000 people within a 12-month period.

Reforming North Vietnam: Ho Chi Minh's vision of a "free" Vietnam

The DRV had a difficult start in 1954 and 1955 as it worked to organize the people and land to create a viable country to counter the Republic of Vietnam (South Vietnam). The immediate results created dangerous conditions in the north as the DRV was cut off from the rich food supplies in the south and instituted a policy of retribution against those who had supported the French and had not taken advantage of Operation Passage to Freedom (see Chapter 10).

This policy, along with a failed economic strategy, resulted in a difficult start for the DRV:

- ✔ **They were wrongly imprisoned.** The Vietnamese who had supported the French and stayed in North Vietnam after the Geneva Conference or possessed large areas of land were placed in labor camps (they were considered a threat to the Communist way of life). In late 1955, Ho ordered the release of the majority of these individuals.

- ✔ **A poorly executed plan nearly resulted in famine.** Land reform was important in the new Communist State, but the DRV did not have the expertise or equipment to make this experiment work. Less food was produced, and had it not been for the aid of the Soviet Union, hundreds of thousands would have starved.

- ✔ **The five-year plan failed.** A five-year plan was created to improve all industries in North Vietnam but the DRV's allies did not have the resources of the United States. The DRV's economic revolution never took place and its economy advanced at a slower pace than South Vietnam, which had the advantage of U.S. economic and technical assistance. With the introduction of the United States and its bombings of North Vietnam, the DRV industry suffered.

Counting Diem's final days

In November 1960, an attempted coup d'état against Ngo Dinh Diem in South Vietnam nearly succeeded (see Figure 2-5). Diem believed that those who had organized the coup had received the assistance and approval of the United States. As a result, Diem turned away from his American advisors, and began relying more on the advice of his younger brother Ngo Dinh Nhu.

The failure to consult the U.S. military and political advisors stationed in South Vietnam further alienated American leaders in Washington. Diem had always been very loyal to his family and inserted his family in important political positions throughout Vietnam. His reliance on family advice, especially Nhu's, caused many within the U.S. military involved in Vietnam to question Ngo Dinh Diem's value as leader of South Vietnam. The failed Strategic Hamlet Program in 1962, which is described in Chapter 4, and the increasing authoritarian nature of Diem's rule caused discontent to swell within the Vietnamese military and the American political and military community.

Diem proved unwilling to initiate reforms the United States believed were necessary for South Vietnam to gain acceptance as a member of the international community. He lost the confidence of the people in his failed effort to rid the South of the insurgency. As a result, only one significant incident during the summer of 1963 was necessary to serve as a catalyst for the removal of Diem from power.

Figure 2-5:
Scenes of devastation resulting from the November 1963 coup d'état of Ngo Dinh Diem show one of the turning points of the American war in Vietnam.

Photograph courtesy of the Vietnam Archive, Texas Tech University

May 8, 1963, was the 2,527th birthday of Buddha. Buddhists planning their annual celebration of the event gathered in Hue, the old imperial capital of Vietnam, thinking they'd recognize the occasion with Buddhist flags and a show of religious faith. The Diem regime, however, issued orders for the national flag to be flown with any other flags that were flying in public. The deputy province chief in Hue, a Catholic, took that order to mean the Buddhists were prohibited from flying their flags.

The protest that ensued turned violent when a grenade was thrown at Buddhist protestors, killing and wounding several of them. This event triggered a series of protests throughout South Vietnam, inspired by Buddhists whom Diem believed were the communists who had rallied behind the North Vietnamese cause. Diem suppressed the crowds, but in the process, caused additional and larger protests. The crisis came to a crossroads on July 11, 1963, when a Vietnamese Buddhist, Thich Quang Duc, sat down on a busy Saigon street and set himself on fire in protest of Diem's religious persecution. The international reaction was immediate and strongly against Diem, causing him to retreat further from American advice and rely more on his brother Ngo Dinh Nhu and sister-in-law Madame Nhu, who gained notoriety in the early 1960s as the "dragon lady" after she delivered some insensitive remarks regarding the Buddhist crisis.

The U.S. reaction was critical of Diem, causing many within the Kennedy Administration to believe that Diem must be replaced. Several factions in South Vietnam secretly inquired whether the United States would support them in a coup; however, they were rebuffed until Generals Duong Van Minh and Tran Van Don approached American officials in late October 1963. Although the United States didn't officially sponsor the coup, it also did nothing to stop it. Diem and Nhu surrendered on November 1, 1963, to the coup planners (Generals Minh and Don) with the understanding that they'd be exiled from Vietnam. Taking no chances, the Ngo brothers were assassinated by the coup followers, ending the Ngo Dinh Diem experiment and setting in motion a downward spiral for the South Vietnamese. Madame Nhu survived the coup because she was out of the country; today, she lives in Rome.

Seeing America's Entry from the Vietnamese Perspective

The assassination of Diem was followed three weeks later by the assassination of U.S. President John F. Kennedy. The new administration, under President Lyndon Baines Johnson, continued Kennedy's Vietnam policy, leading to the eventual introduction of U.S. ground forces in Vietnam (see Chapter 5). For North Vietnam and South Vietnam, the American presence permanently altered the war that had been raging for nearly 20 years.

The southern revolving door

Less than three months after the overthrow of Diem, General Nguyen Khanh staged another coup d'état against the military leadership in South Vietnam. General Khanh urged a more active war against North Vietnam but was forced to concern himself more with internal struggles within the South Vietnamese Government and increased U.S. pressure for more positive military results against the Viet Cong.

During the struggle of various factions for leadership in South Vietnam — seven changes occurred in 1964 alone — the Viet Cong were able to fill the void of leadership in the South Vietnamese countryside. The South Vietnamese Government was faced with expending so much of its resources fighting for political power that it was unable to fight the Viet Cong, who were using this period of South Vietnamese insurrection to consolidate their military and political gains.

This revolt forced the United States to either increase its commitment or risk the loss of South Vietnam to the communists. One of President Johnson's first statements after being sworn in as president was that he was "not going to be the president who saw Southeast Asia go the way China went." A military *triumvirate* (government by three groups or individuals) consisting of Khanh, Minh, and General Tran Thien Khiem, ruled in South Vietnam during the last half of 1964. In December, a group of officers known as the "Young Turks" overthrew the older generals. Generals Nguyen Cao Ky and Nguyen Van Thieu led the Young Turks.

Bringing change via stability: Ky and Thieu

Another series of bloodless coups occurred during the first few months of 1965 and resulted in the return of Khanh, but he had earned many enemies within the United States, among his Vietnamese colleagues, and among fellow officers, and was forced out of power in February 1965. An uneasy peace followed until June 1965 when Air Marshall Nguyen Cao Ky forced the United States–backed Phan Huy Quat away from the presidency.

Ky served as prime minister of South Vietnam until 1967 when national elections brought Nguyen Van Thieu to power. Thieu served as president, with Ky as his vice president. Although these two men remained in power during the critical years of the war, they constantly struggled against one another to gain power. Thieu finally rid himself of Ky in 1971 by having him disqualified as a presidential candidate. By that time, however, South Vietnam was divided between Thieu and Ky and the schism reached too deep into the military and politics for the country ever to heal. The revolving door of leadership in the South Vietnamese government required the expenditure of too many resources at a time when none could be spared. The internal struggle for power enabled the Viet Cong to consolidate its power in the South thus matching the U.S. military buildup after 1965.

A view from Hanoi

The DRV had two primary goals to accomplish during the war:

- ✔ Defeat the United States and expel foreign troops.
- ✔ Continue the social and economic revolution in the North and expand it to the South through the reunification of North and South Vietnam.

The fight in the South was more than a military crusade. It sought a complete transformation of South Vietnamese society and economy based on the communist model in the North. The Viet Cong were linked to the liberation of the peasants, and the national revolution would end only with the complete domination of the Communist Party.

Because it was controlled by a communist ideology, North Vietnam was going through the period of ideological transition from French colonialism to socialism. Key components to North Vietnam's struggle in the South were freedom and independence for other repressed peoples and for world peace. DRV leaders saw the war as a testing ground for the world struggle against American imperialism. If the DRV defeated the United States, then all former colonies had a chance to gain their own independence. The struggle required — and justified — violence. Revolutionary violence was needed to destroy the South's military resistance and see the United States defeated, but it also was necessary to destroy South Vietnam's social and economic resistance to the new ideology.

Changing of the guard: Ending an era in North Vietnam

South Vietnam's scrapes with instability in South Vietnam in the 1960s did not go unnoticed in the DRV, nor was North Vietnam immune from internal struggle. Differing political and military factions were evident as early as the late 1950s. However, the conflicting political parties in the DRV were able to work together under Ho Chi Minh to achieve the objectives of eliminating the United States and allied forces in the South and finishing the social and economic revolution in the North. As long as Ho Chi Minh retained his power, dissention within the party was secondary to these primary concerns.

Ron & Steve: Regarding highlighted, Veteran/ TE asks . . . "or were they just factions of the Lao Dong Party? No. These were outside of the Lao Dong Party and nationalist (non-communist) in ideology. Ron

Ho Chi Minh held the position of president of the Democratic Republic of Vietnam until his death in September 1969, but some speculate that as he drew nearer his death, his role became only ceremonial and a younger generation of Vietnamese was actually running the country. Upon Ho's death, North Vietnam politics underwent a change as the young guard eased its way into power. Without question, a split developed between the first and second generations of revolutionaries in North Vietnam in dealing with military strategy.

During the early 1960s, Vo Nguyen Giap vied for power over the North's military and its strategy against Le Duan and Nguyen Chi Thanh. Giap advocated a political settlement in the South at the same time the North was developing its social and economic revolution. Le Duan and Thanh favored a more aggressive war in the South, and after the United States escalated its military commitment, they convinced Ho Chi Minh they were right. Giap regained power, however, after Thanh's death and the failure of the 1968 Tet Offensive (see Chapter 5). Giap then was eased out of power after the failure of the 1972 Easter Offensive (see Chapter 6). He left the top military position in the North's armed forces and, in 1980, resigned as minister of defense. In 1982, his direct influence on political events ended when he lost his governmental positions.

Assessing Vietnam

Understanding that the Vietnam War was more than a conflict between the United States and North Vietnam is important because of the many threads of conflict between the Vietnamese that were unrelated to American involvement but nevertheless intensified the conflict. Vietnam had fought for its independence for more than 2,000 years before the United States ever became a participant. The desire for independence and the nationalist zeal were strong on both sides of the 17th parallel. Perhaps one of the greatest failures of the American experience in Vietnam was the inability of the United States to understand the history, culture, and society of Vietnam. The task of building and maintaining South Vietnam was difficult enough without those handicaps. With them, the task was impossible.

Part II
Fighting the Ground War in Southeast Asia

The 5th Wave   By Rich Tennant

"Remember men, when you're out there, be ready for the unexpected – booby traps, snipers, CBS camera crews..."

In this part . . .

The American military ground presence in Vietnam started with a handful of military advisors in the 1950s. After the Gulf of Tonkin Incidents in 1964, it exploded to more than 500,000 men and women at its peak in 1968. Most of these Americans provided support to a much smaller but significant core of soldiers, marines, sailors, and airmen actually engaged in combat operations. This part examines the political and military policies of Presidents Dwight Eisenhower, John Kennedy, Lyndon Johnson, and Richard Nixon and how they dealt with the situation in Vietnam and American involvement there. It focuses on the principal leaders and commanders and their decisions, as well as various strategies and tactics employed and many of the major battles and turning points.

Chapter 3

Eisenhower, Korea, and Southeast Asia: Hot Flashes in a Cold War

In This Chapter

▶ Ending the Korean War

▶ Identifying American interests in Southeast Asia

▶ Advising the French and the South Vietnamese

▶ Staying out of the fight

▶ Passing the torch to JFK

Dwight "Ike" Eisenhower ran for president in 1952 on a platform that he would go to Korea to help end that war. Americans carried banners claiming, "I Like Ike," and they must have meant it, because Eisenhower won by a landslide. This wasn't surprising because Eisenhower, formerly General Eisenhower, was the person who led American military forces to victory in Europe during World War II. See *World War II For Dummies* (Wiley, Inc.) for more information.

Americans hoped Eisenhower would work that same WWII-era magic on the Korean Peninsula, where Americans and South Koreans had been fighting against the Communist North Koreans and Chinese for two years. Ending the Korean War became President Eisenhower's principal focus upon entering office in 1953. His experience in Korea, although brief, had a powerful effect on his policies toward Southeast Asia.

Fighting During a Cold War: Korea

Like Vietnam after the Geneva Accords of 1954 (discussed later in this chapter), the Korean Peninsula was divided after World War II along the 38th parallel, the line of latitude that splits the nation in halves: North and South. Like in Vietnam, the Soviet Union and China supported North Korea, while the United States supported South Korea. And like in Vietnam, both sides developed competing systems of government and economy, hoping one day to reunite the nations under their rule.

In the Korean War, North Korea made the first move to reunite the two Koreas in June 1950 when it attacked South Korea and pushed the South Korean Army to the southernmost tip of the Korean Peninsula. The U.S. responded quickly as they already had a small military force pre-positioned in the region and in July 1950, additional U.S. troops entered the war on the side of South Korea. Eventually, U.S., South Korean, and United Nations (U.N.) forces pushed the North Korean Army back north of the 38th parallel and continued to push them all the way north to the border with China. Threatened by this approach of U.S. forces into the strategic and heavily industrialized Yalu River region, Communist China entered the war on the side of North Korea and helped the North Korean Army push the U.S., South Korean, and U.N. forces back down to the 38th parallel. There, the war remained in bloody stalemate until Eisenhower took office

Ike to the rescue

By 1951, neither side was gaining ground in Korea, and the peace talks between North and South Korea were going nowhere fast. A fresh approach was needed if the war was to end quickly. Eisenhower promised to provide that new approach as commander in chief to bring the war to "an early and honorable end." Eisenhower traveled to Korea in late November 1952, immediately after he won the election earlier that month.

Eisenhower soon realized that North Korea had little incentive to negotiate an end to the war, because it continued to receive significant support from China. He further realized that the key to ending the war in Korea lay not with the North Koreans but with ending this Chinese support. The question was, "How do you convince China to end the War in Korea?" The answer involved the one weapon they lacked and feared most.

Ending the war in Korea: Ike likes nukes

Early during the Korean War, some Americans thought the United States should employ atomic bombs against targets in communist China. President Truman resisted such calls because he and other military commanders thought the Korean War was only a diversion and that the Soviet Union actually planned to attack Europe after American forces were committed to Korea. The U.S. atomic arsenal had to be reserved in the event of war with the Soviets, who also possessed the bomb.

But important differences existed between 1951 and 1953:

- **The United States had lost more than 30,000 men:** This meant the United States couldn't simply quit the war but had to bring about a peace that would justify the level of sacrifice endured.

- **Josef Stalin died:** The Soviets never did attack Europe and with the death of this totalitarian ruler, the Union of Soviet Socialist Republics (Soviet Union) was in a state of political disarray. This meant that a prompt military response by them into Europe became even less likely.

- **The United States had more — and better — bombs:** The American arsenal of atomic bombs now exceeded 1,600 and included a significant number of smaller-yield, artillery-fired, tactical atomic bombs. And the United States detonated a hydrogen (or nuclear) bomb in 1952, a bomb thousands of times more powerful than the atomic bombs dropped on Japan during WWII.

- **Eisenhower became president of the United States:** In the eyes of many Americans, Eisenhower won WWII. If he thought nukes were the way to go in Korea, most Americans would back him.

Eisenhower threatened communist China, indicating that he would approve the use of tactical nuclear weapons against targets in China and against Chinese forces in Korea if they didn't pressure North Korea to end the war. China realized the Soviet Union was in no position to respond in this event and pressured North Korea to sign an armistice in July 1953. Eisenhower had done it and the Korean War ended.

Taking away lessons from Korea

Eisenhower took away a very important lesson from his experience in Korea: Never get bogged down in a land war in Asia. This became especially important as such wars became part of the larger global competition called the Cold War, which this chapter explains in more detail.

Although the United States could feel secure in being the dominant nuclear and atomic power for years, Eisenhower had these concerns to consider:

- The Soviet Union would challenge the dominance of the United States as soon as the Soviets recovered from Stalin's death.

- It was unreasonable to think the United States and the Soviet Union would remain the only nuclear or atomic powers for very much longer. In particular, communist China remained a potential atomic and nuclear rival to the United States.

As a result, future wars with Asian nations might not be so easily resolved through nuclear threats. At the same time, Asian nations with China as an ally had that nation's huge population as a possible support base. Despite American advances in weapons and technology, the potential costs of a future war in Asia would likely prove too high for the United States to sustain.

The French-Indochina War

While the United States helped South Korea fight against North Korea and China, another war raged on in Southeast Asia (see Figure 2-1) in a place called French Indochina, or Vietnam. The French returned to their colony in Indochina after WWII and tried to end a revolution bent on overthrowing French colonial rule there, as described in Chapter 2.

France couldn't fight this war alone. Having been devastated by WWII, France depended heavily on American military and financial assistance to wage their war against the *Viet Minh*, a revolutionary group discussed in Chapter 2. President Truman and President Eisenhower both felt compelled to provide some form of assistance to the French, who threatened to pull out of the European Defense Community (the bulwark in Western Europe against Soviet Communist expansion) if the United States failed to provide the support it needed in Indochina.

Soon after taking office in 1953, Eisenhower agreed to continue supplying the French as they fought against the Viet Minh. U.S. support for the French included American planes, technical advisors, and maintenance personnel, all of which were sent to Vietnam in 1953. Eventually, fighting between the French and Viet Minh centered on Dien Bien Phu, a French fortification situated in a valley that was surrounded by the Viet Minh on high ground on three sides.

The battle at Dien Bien Phu lasted for several months and resulted in the total defeat and capture of the French forces. Shortly after, peace negotiations began in Geneva, and both sides signed the Geneva Accords in 1954. (For the lowdown on the battle for Dien Bien Phu, the Geneva negotiations, and the resulting peace accords, see Chapter 2.) Two significant conditions in the accords stipulated that

- Vietnam was to be split in half along the 17th parallel.
- Both North and South Vietnam were to participate in the reunification of Vietnam through national elections in 1956.

Deciding What to Do: America, the Cold War, and Southeast Asia

Having learned valuable lessons from both the Korean and French Indochina Wars, President Eisenhower approached Vietnam and the rest of Southeast Asia with deliberate caution. He and the members of his cabinet were all firm believers in the domino theory: They reasoned that if South Vietnam fell to communism, so, too, would the remainder of Southeast Asia like a row of dominos. In deciding what the United States should do, Eisenhower had to consider a complex web of international and domestic political issues.

Maintaining alliances against communism

First, in order to thwart the spread of communism in Europe, Asia, and elsewhere, the United States had to maintain various alliances with different groups of nations. This included the North Atlantic Treaty Organization (NATO), which served as a defensive alliance against Soviet communist expansion into Western Europe. But unlike the European members of NATO who faced the threat of direct war with the Soviet Union on a constant basis, the United States was surrounded by a buffer zone of security that included oceans to the east and west and friendly countries to the north and south. Although fear of war existed between the United States and Soviet Union, most people agreed that the bulk of the fighting, and by extension, most of the destruction and killing, would occur in Europe. So, as a show of commitment to European and other allies, the United States had to help thwart communist expansion by sending military forces to places like Korea and Vietnam.

Sharing responsibility: The creation of SEATO

Building on the Australia/New Zealand/United States (ANZUS) Pact signed after WWII between those three nations, U.S. Secretary of State John Dulles conceived of a broader regional treaty organization similar to NATO but for Southeast Asia. The purpose behind this treaty organization, called SEATO (Southeast Asia Treaty Organization), was to create a regional defense league that would provide military and other assistance in the event that member nations (or those considered under their protection) came under attack.

The member nations included Australia, New Zealand, Pakistan, the Philippines, Thailand, the United States, Great Britain, and France. Of course, South Vietnam, Laos, and Cambodia were included under SEATO protection. It was hoped by Dulles and others that the existence of SEATO would deter communist expansion into Southeast Asia. However, SEATO wasn't able to succeed because most of the Vietnam War involved fighting between internal parties, not just foreign or external aggression.

Trying to stay out of a land war in Asia

After he ended the war in Korea, Eisenhower realized that the United States couldn't afford to get bogged down in another land war in Asia. Although the United States possessed significant industrial and military capabilities, Americans were weary from fighting four years during WWII and then another three years in Korea. After all, Americans were just beginning to enjoy the freedom and security they helped create after the defeat of Germany and Japan when the conflict in Korea arose. Many Americans wondered when the United States would finally enjoy the fruits of its collective sacrifices and labors.

With the end of the Korean War, many Americans enjoyed a prosperity and level of comfort not enjoyed since before the Great Depression. Going to war in Southeast Asia had the potential to damage this American domestic economy and prosperity and spell political defeat for the Republican Party in the election in 1956.

At the same time, the Republican Party, Eisenhower's political party, couldn't afford to lose Southeast Asia to communism. Many political analysts thought that Americans held the Democratic Party responsible for losing China to communism in 1949 and voted Republican in 1952 as a result. Of course, American politicians were not really responsible for countries like China and South Vietnam deciding to adopt communism as their form of government and economy. But Americans have rarely been driven by such rational considerations at the voting booth. The Republican Party and President Eisenhower realized this.

As a result of all of these considerations, Eisenhower chose to show commitment against communism in Southeast Asia by providing American advice and support to South Vietnam and Laos. This included political, economic, and military aid and initially involved very few Americans serving on the ground in Southeast Asia.

Eisenhower's decision to send American advisors to Vietnam after the end of the French Indochina War was simply a continuation of American policy dating back to the Second World War. During that war, the United States sent men from the Office of Strategic Services (OSS), what later became the CIA, to assist the Viet Minh as they fought against the Japanese in Vietnam. In 1954, the enemy had changed, but the American goals had not: prevent the total collapse of Southeast Asia, this time, to communists. Americans serving in South Vietnam under Eisenhower engaged in an additional mission called *nation building,* improving South Vietnam's political, social, and economic condition.

Expanding U.S. Assistance under MAAG and Creating Other Acronyms

One of the first steps Eisenhower took was to rename the American military advisory effort in Vietnam. Established in 1950 by the Truman administration, the first Military Assistance Advisory Group–Indochina (MAAG-I) was created to provide assistance to the French while they reestablished their colonial empire in Southeast Asia. With the removal of the French, the United States needed to change the form and appearance of this organization.

In mid-1955, the United States officially disbanded MAAG-I and created Military Assistance Advisory Group–Vietnam (MAAG-V) in its place. MAAG-V directed all American military assistance in Vietnam, including the shipment of military supplies and the training of the Army of Vietnam (ARVN) until 1962, when it was replaced by yet another acronym (MACV) and an increased focus on a joint advisory effort discussed in Chapter 4.

The training done by MAAG-V emphasized a conventional military approach to war under the assumption that communist North Vietnamese would attack South Vietnam, much the same way communist North Korea had attacked South Korea. Eisenhower himself thought that a potential invasion from North Vietnam might occur, and he theorized that it would not happen through the narrow passage of the Demilitarized Zone (DMZ), the small strip of land from the coast to Laos along the 17th parallel connecting North and South Vietnam. The DMZ was an area where neither side was supposed to have forces or fortifications but where both nations stood poised for an attack. Instead, Eisenhower thought North Vietnam would attack along the lengthy border area that connects South Vietnam with Laos and Cambodia. Eisenhower was right about the North Vietnamese approach — but he and the MAAG-V personnel failed initially to consider the importance of the guerilla war brewing in South Vietnam that was initiated and fought by the Viet Cong (VC).

Choosing the Right People: The Strong Personalities Involved

Because so few U.S. personnel were deployed during the early years of American involvement in Southeast Asia, success and failure hinged on which Americans were chosen to serve there. Fortunately, Ike could choose from a pool of talented men who had firsthand experience in Asia. But the small number of personnel involved meant Ike had to choose people with strong personalities. As these personalities clashed, they sometimes fought against one another and slowly undercut American policy in the region.

Enter the ugly Americans

At the recommendation of Secretary of State John Foster Dulles, President Eisenhower handpicked General "Lightning Joe" Collins to go to Vietnam to take charge of the situation. As a testament to his trust, Eisenhower gave Collins sweeping authority to act and speak on behalf of the president and the United States about U.S. policies in Vietnam. But Lightning Joe's success depended much less on Eisenhower and this authority and much more on the people who lived and worked in Vietnam.

The government of South Vietnam, under the leadership of President Ngo Dinh Diem, remained unstable in the months following the Geneva Accords (see Chapter 2). American prestige was on the line, because the United States couldn't afford to lose South Vietnam to communism. In other words, the United States had a vested interest in stabilizing the government under Ngo Dinh Diem (shown in Figure 2-4). As a surprise to Collins, this factor eventually became a stumbling block to his efforts in Vietnam.

A juggling act by an artful dodger: President Ngo Dinh Diem of South Vietnam

Major obstacles stood in the way of U.S. attempts to stabilize South Vietnam. South Vietnam was not a nationalistic and homogenous whole but consisted of various groups all vying for power. And they all disagreed on who should be leader of South Vietnam.

Major religious differences between prominent groups in Vietnamese society created some of the complexity of the situation in South Vietnam. The vast majority of South Vietnamese practiced Buddhism, whereas the new President, Diem, and many of his political appointees, were Catholic. This became a serious issue when Diem enacted policies that supported Catholics and discriminated against Buddhists, including

- ✔ Giving preference to Catholics for positions in the military and government agencies

- ✔ Giving land to Catholics

- ✔ Appointing Catholics to be province, district, hamlet, and village chiefs

- ✔ Banning the display of Buddhist flags

When this happened, matters were made worse by the fact that many of South Vietnam's Catholics were originally from North Vietnam, and they spoke a different dialect of Vietnamese. Because Vietnamese is a tonal language, regional identity is based, in part, on how one speaks Vietnamese.

Diem also had to deal with opposition from his own Army. General Nguyen Van Hinh, who commanded the ARVN, openly opposed Diem and challenged the legitimacy of the Diem government. Hinh even publicly threatened to stage a coup to overthrow Diem. When Diem issued an order expelling Hinh from Vietnam, Hinh rode around Saigon defiantly on his motorcycle. Ultimately, Hinh did go to France at the behest of the exiled Emperor of Vietnam, Bao Dai, who under pressure from both the United States and France, asked Hinh to join him there. Diem was rid of one major obstacle to his rule, but others remained.

Although the French had lost against the Viet Minh, as part of the Geneva Convention, they remained in the region to provide support for South Vietnam until national elections could be held in 1956. The French were supposed to limit their involvement in Vietnamese affairs to training the Vietnamese military but, being a former colonial power, the temptation to meddle was too great. The French refused to support Diem because they knew they had no influence over him. Instead, they hoped to turn South Vietnam back over to Bao Dai, the Vietnamese Emperor in exile, who was at that time living in a villa on the French Riviera and who was easily influenced and controlled by the French. Eventually, French opposition to Diem included support for one of his major rivals, the organized crime ring called the Binh Xuyen. (See the "Destroying the Sects for Good: The Battle for Saigon" section, later in this chapter.)

HISTORIC TRIVIA

J. Lawton Collins: Soldier and statesman

General J. Lawton Collins, also known as Lightning Joe, served with Eisenhower during WWII and commanded some American forces during the Invasion of Normandy. A graduate of the United States Military Academy at West Point in 1917, Collins served in WWI and then commanded American forces in the Pacific against the Japanese during WWII.

It was during WWII that Collins earned the nickname, "Lightning Joe," and it was either for his hot temper or his aggressive pursuit of the Japanese during the Battle for Guadalcanal while commanding the American 25th Infantry, which was also called the Tropic Lightning Division — or perhaps it was for both reasons.

As the Army's highest-ranking officer during the Korean War, Collins served as the Army Chief of Staff from 1949 to 1953. Then, in 1954, Eisenhower asked Lightning Joe to serve as a U.S. special representative to Vietnam with the rank (but not title) of ambassador, a role he filled until 1955. Although only in Vietnam a short time, Collins quickly concluded that President Ngo Dinh Diem had little chance for success in stabilizing that country and thwarting communist expansion.

So Diem had his hands full! By extension, so did Collins. When Collins arrived in Vietnam in 1954, he found himself in a morass of power struggles between various groups of Vietnamese, with the French in the middle playing all sides off each other.

Riding the lightning: Collins in Vietnam

Upon his arrival, Collins took immediate action to reorganize the American mission in South Vietnam. The U.S. mission had been under the leadership of Ambassador Donald Heath, appointed in June 1952 by President Truman. Heath remained at the post until 1954 but Collins held much authority and influence as Eisenhower's special representative. Contrary to Heath's more relaxed approach to diplomacy, Collins applied a military mentality to the U.S. diplomatic mission, and based on his initial observations, concluded that Diem needed the support of the French if he was going to succeed. But the French didn't trust Diem to maintain their interests in Vietnam, saw Diem as a potential American puppet, and wanted to install their own puppet, the playboy emperor in exile, Bao Dai.

Dealing with the French

Although the French played a diminishing role in South Vietnam, they maintained a mission there under the command of General Paul Ely. Ely didn't look forward to the arrival of Collins, a new American player, and even refused to be in Saigon when Collins arrived. Instead, in order for the two to meet, Collins had to track Ely down at his villa in Da Lat, a mountain resort city in central South Vietnam. When Collins arrived there, the two men hit it off immediately; no doubt this was assisted by Collins' reputation and experience in Europe during WWII as well as his command of the French language. By the end of their first meeting, Ely promised Collins that he would not support the sects in opposition to Diem.

Several days later, Ely and Collins drafted a proposal to support the Diem government, and it contained several major components:

- **Military reorganization and training:** Collins had already recommended reducing the size of the Vietnamese army from 170,000 to 77,000 personnel. He and Ely called for more intensive training and support for the army and a deployment of the ARVN that would optimize its effectiveness for internal security and prepare it in the event of a communist attack. Ely also agreed to turn over training of the Vietnamese Army to the United States.

- **Government and political reform:** This component of Ely's and Collins's agreement included the creation of a National Assembly and reforms in the civil service.

> ✔ **Refugee relocation and settlement:** After Vietnam split in half under the Geneva Accords and the Viet Minh took over North Vietnam, many North Vietnamese Catholics fled South, following Diem and "the Virgin Mary." Operation Passage to Freedom resulted in the resettlement of nearly 710,000 North Vietnamese into South Vietnam. This included approximately 500,000 Catholics.
>
> ✔ **Economic and land reform:** This portion of the agreement included lots of money from the United States and the redistribution of land to the large number of refugees who migrated south from North Vietnam. This caused problems for the Diem government, because the land had to come from somewhere, and typically it was taken away from South Vietnamese Buddhists and Montagnards (mountain people).
>
> ✔ **Psychological operations:** The CIA and other American operatives needed funding and support to thwart communist attempts to propagandize the South Vietnamese. Colonel Ed Lansdale, discussed in more detail later in this chapter, handled much of the American propaganda during this early period. (See the "Seeing Diem through rose-colored glasses: Ed Lansdale in South Vietnam" section, later in this chapter.)

Although the program indicated a growing trust between Collins and Ely, neither man seriously considered the problems that lay ahead, due to their failure to include President Ngo Dinh Diem in their discussions and deliberations.

Dealing with Diem: Ignoring America's man in Vietnam

Collins didn't discuss his initial plans with Diem for a number of reasons, including the impression he had that Diem wasn't a strong leader and didn't have the support of Vietnamese military, let alone most of the people of South Vietnam. But Collins also realized that he couldn't just dictate policies to the President of South Vietnam, so he hoped to convince Diem that the program was best for his embattled country.

Collins also thought he had leverage over Diem, given the amount of money and military aid the United States was providing South Vietnam. The Collins-Ely proposal emphasized the role of American aid in stabilizing South Vietnam and, if implemented, Collins thought it would show progress quickly. This was important to Collins because he thought American aid for South Vietnam, both economic and military, should be predicated on clear indications of progress toward stabilizing Vietnam and defending the country against communist attack. Unfortunately, neither Diem nor Diem's major supporters in Washington shared this particular view.

Resisting the Americans: Diem consolidates his power at home and abroad

Collins had serious doubts about Diem's abilities to both remain as President of South Vietnam and reform and stabilize South Vietnam along the American model of democracy and free market economy, which was necessary in order to fend off communist aggression. Diem quickly proved he could survive as president, but ultimately, his reforms left much to be desired.

Still, Diem's self assessment that he was the right man for Vietnam wasn't without supporters. A group of supporters from the United States, dubbed the "Vietnam Lobby," included Cardinal Francis Spellman, a prominent Catholic religious figure, and U.S. Senators Mike Mansfield and John F. Kennedy. In addition to government officials, Diem received support from many U.S. universities, including Wesley Fishel at Michigan State University, and from many other Catholic Americans throughout the nation.

Reigning in the Lightning: Dulles on Collins

By the end of 1954, Collins reported back that he lacked confidence in Diem and thought the United States should increase pressure on Diem by threatening to withdraw U.S. support. Collins went so far as to air his opinion that, unless the situation changed dramatically, the United States should consider a complete withdrawal from Vietnam, turning everything back over to the French. Dulles immediately attacked these ideas.

As far as Dulles was concerned, the United States had no choice but to support Diem because Americans had too much at stake in Vietnam. If the United States didn't support Diem and South Vietnam fell to communism, the entirety of Southeast Asia would fall: Laos, Cambodia, Thailand, Malaysia, and so on would follow Vietnam. Dulles convinced President Eisenhower that America couldn't let that happen. Eisenhower agreed.

In a strongly worded memo, Dulles informed Collins that he had no choice but to work with Diem. Even if Diem ultimately failed, at least current American policy in Vietnam would stave off communist expansion for a time, allowing the other nations in Southeast Asia to stabilize and develop so as to prevent further expansion of communism. No matter what Collins thought personally, Eisenhower and the United States stood firmly behind Diem, and Diem knew it.

The fact that the United States had such a powerful vested interest in propping up South Vietnam seriously eroded the amount of influence Americans wielded while advising Diem and subsequent South Vietnamese leaders. As a result, American recommendations usually fell on deaf ears. The South Vietnamese knew the United States was not going to just pull out and leave them high and dry to fall to communism . . . at least not yet.

Who were these "ugly" Americans?

The phrase "ugly American" is probably one of the most controversial expressions to come out of Vietnam War–era literature. Used broadly to refer to the American sense of superiority and arrogance while traveling and serving abroad, the term "ugly American" comes from a book called *The Ugly American* by William Lederer and Eugene Burdick. First published in 1958, the book is composed of a series of short stories focusing on fictional characters set in fictional landscapes that, at times, closely resemble actual people and events in Southeast Asia.

The stories involve arrogant and corrupt American and foreign officials as well as kind-hearted and humble Americans serving with people of Southeast Asia. One of the greatest ironies of the book is that the title's literal namesake, the character, named Colonel Hillendale, who is referred to as the "ugly American," is called this because his facial features are not considered attractive. In actuality, he is the most kind-hearted and generous character in the book and represents Americans in the best possible way. Traveling the countryside, learning Asian languages, and getting to know the people of Southeast Asia, Hillendale was always ready to pull out his harmonica so that he could learn and play the local folksongs. In fact, the character of Colonel Hillendale was based on none other than Colonel Edward Lansdale . . . who carried around a guitar, not a harmonica.

Seeing Diem through rose-colored glasses: Ed Lansdale in South Vietnam

As his most ardent supporter, Ed Lansdale helped cement U.S. policy behind Diem. But where did Lansdale come from and why did he so powerfully support Diem?

Lansdale (shown in Figure 3-1) worked in advertising before WWII, joined the OSS during the war, and eventually received a commission in the U.S. Army in 1943. He worked in military intelligence during most of WWII and was transferred to the Philippines in 1945, where he became Chief of the Intelligence Division for the Headquarters of Air Forces Western Pacific. Commissioned in the newly created United States Air Force in 1947, he simultaneously went to work for the newly created Central Intelligence Agency.

The National Security Act of 1947, the same piece of legislation that created the United States Air Force, also created the Central Intelligence Agency to replace the wartime Office of Strategic Services.

Figure 3-1:
Ed Lansdale.

Photograph courtesy of the Vietnam Archive,
Texas Tech University

Lansdale worked in the Philippines for several years after WWII and returned in 1950 to assist the American mission that was helping the Philippine government fight off a communist led insurgency called the *Huk Rebellion*. Lansdale quickly immersed himself into the nuances of the Philippine conflict and became a strong supporter of Ramon Magsaysay, the man who ultimately led the Philippines out of the rebellion. Based in part on propaganda and psychological warfare employed by Lansdale, Magsaysay gained significant popular support and defeated most of the guerillas through an aggressive combination of political, economic, and land-reform programs that left only a small group of hard-core communist guerillas remaining. This small group was eventually defeated by the Philippine military forces, and the leader of the Huks, Luis Taruc, surrendered in 1954.

Building on the lessons he learned fighting communist Huk guerillas in the Philippines, Lansdale went to Vietnam in 1954 hoping to repeat the magic of Magsaysay in Vietnam. In fact, President Ngo Dinh Diem was even referred to as the Magsaysay of Vietnam. But Lansdale quickly ran into various problems because the model of the Philippines did not match completely the events occurring in Vietnam.

Much of Lansdale's success in Vietnam hinged on his creation of an intelligence network that could keep him informed of various activities concerning President Diem. This network helped him prevent the coup of 1954. But in addition, Lansdale relied on the old fashioned method of getting people to do what he wanted: bribery. Using a secret fund set up by the CIA, Lansdale bought off Diem's opposition left and right using millions of American dollars until almost no more opposition existed. One of the toughest groups to deal with was the Binh Xuyen, the criminal ring. But even for them, Lansdale devised an offer they couldn't refuse.

Lansdale devised a plan involving the Binh Xuyen whereby they would build a road connecting Saigon with the rest of the Mekong Delta. Of necessity, the road would go through lands owned and operated by the Binh Xuyen so they would directly profit from the road, given that people would have to make stops along the way in their territory. In addition, the Binh Xuyen would make legal profits through a hefty road building contract with the government of South Vietnam. Although Lansdale and the Binh Xuyen thought this was a grand scheme, Diem had other ideas.

At a meeting set up by Lansdale, Diem insulted Bai Vien, the leader of the Binh Xuyen, and refused to go along with the road building scheme. Bai Vien stormed out of the meeting and called a meeting of the remaining sect leaders and crime bosses. Diem took further action against the Binh Xuyen and replaced the Chief of National Police with one of his own men. As a result, the sect leaders all agreed to issue Diem an ultimatum: share governmental power by appointing sect members to government cabinet posts or suffer the consequences. Diem chose the consequences.

Destroying the Sects for Good: The Battle for Saigon

The Binh Xuyen formed an Army of 40,000 men in Saigon and surrounded the Presidential Palace and grounds with *mortars,* a small, portable, crew-served weapon. At midnight on March 29, 1955, the Binh Xuyen opened fire, turning Saigon into a war zone. The Army of South Vietnam stood their ground and repulsed attacks made by Binh Xuyen; eventually, fighting erupted street to street.

The French moved their forces into the streets as well and, as Lansdale later discovered, acted to thwart the movement of Diem's forces. The French did this because they still supported the idea of Emperor Bao Dai returning, and the Binh Xuyen wanted to facilitate this change in government as well, because the group had profited under Bao Dai in the past. The French instituted a cease fire in early April and an uneasy peace lasted for several weeks.

During the pause in the fighting, General Collins vehemently restated his opposition to Diem and argued that Diem would fall from power very soon. Diem's American opponents argued that he had precipitated a civil war in South Vietnam by picking a fight with the Binh Xuyen and other sects. In order to discuss the issues in more detail, Collins was called back to Washington to convince Eisenhower and Dulles that he was right and they were wrong about Diem.

Over several days, Collins argued and eventually succeeded in convincing John Dulles and President Eisenhower that the United States needed to back another horse in Vietnam. Dulles went so far as to send telegrams to the Embassy staff in Saigon, ordering them to prepare for a change in leadership because Diem wouldn't last. But Diem and his American supporters back in Saigon had other plans.

Diem realized that Collins didn't truly support him and that his trip back to Washington was designed to remove Diem from power. If Diem was to survive, he had to act fast. Here's what he did:

- **Holding elections:** Diem made a radio address that many thought would be his resignation but was instead an announcement that he would hold elections for the National Assembly within the following few months. This announcement was designed to undercut criticisms that he was not enacting political reforms designed to strengthen democracy and thwart communism in South Vietnam.

- **Forming an alliance with the sect:** With the assistance of Lansdale, Diem secretly approached various members of the loose alliance of sect leaders. Lansdale and Diem both realized that the coalition between the sects was weak at best and that many of the leaders could be bribed, especially those of the smaller religious sects like the Hoa Hao. Lansdale used up nearly 10 million dollars from his CIA fund to bribe and court away members of the sect alliance.

With that done, Diem let the Army loose on the remaining Binh Xuyen. As promised, the other sect leaders and members took no action when the Army of South Vietnam attacked the Binh Xuyen positions. The French had no choice but to back down and let the fighting resume as the Army slowly but progressively destroyed the Binh Xuyen forces and positions. Contrary to what everyone feared, widespread civil war didn't erupt in South Vietnam, and Diem emerged victorious in defeating the Binh Xuyen. When word of Diem's success reached Washington, Dulles informed Eisenhower, and they issued a complete reversal of policy to the Saigon Embassy Staff: The United States would continue supporting Diem.

The last of these events occurred while General Collins was in transit back to Vietnam from Washington. He fully anticipated arriving back in Saigon and leading a new mission to replace Diem. When he arrived in Vietnam, however, he learned of the defeat of the sects and the reversal of American policy. Although angry that various members of the mission, including Colonel Lansdale, had acted outside of their proscribed authority, Collins had no choice but to heed the new order from Washington to support Diem with any and all American resources. Collins didn't remain long in Vietnam — he was recalled to Washington in May 1955.

HISTORIC TRIVIA

The power behind the throne: Brother Nhu and the Dragon Lady

Many people criticized President Diem for his obvious nepotism, especially as it related to his Brother, Ngo Dinh Nhu, and Nhu's wife, Madame Nhu, also known as the "Dragon Lady." Diem appointed his brother head of the Vietnamese Secret Police and Intelligence. With a trusted relative in this position of power, Diem felt more secure, and this security helped Diem during the more tumultuous periods of his tenure.

After helping Diem get rid of the remnants of the Binh Xuyen and other Sects, Nhu used his position to help Diem consolidate power further by tracking down and killing former members of the Viet Minh who were born in and continued to live in South Vietnam. The campaign to eradicate former Viet Minh succeeded so well that, in 1958, Diem boasted that no Viet Minh existed in South Vietnam, a claim believed by members of the Eisenhower administration and used as further promotion that Diem was effectively countering communists in South Vietnam. What Eisenhower and others didn't admit publicly was that Nhu had resorted to terror and murder to accomplish this feat and that many innocent Vietnamese had suffered during this campaign.

While her husband worked behind the scenes helping President Diem consolidate power, Madam Nhu was a more public and controversial figure. Asked her thoughts on the *self-immolation* of Buddhist Monks in 1963, when several monks doused themselves with gasoline and burned themselves to death, Madame Nhu responded that she would applaud another "monk barbeque." Although they eventually became political liabilities, Diem remained loyal to his brother and sister-in-law.

Making Diem's victory complete, the French, which had backed the Binh Xuyen during the Sect crisis, lost the remainder of its influence in South Vietnam. France's deliberate actions to thwart the U.S.-backed Diem government increased tension between the United States and France. French forces withdrew completely from South Vietnam in April 1956. Diem had won on all fronts.

Where Diem Went from There

After consolidating his power in Saigon, Diem undertook a massive campaign to rid himself of all potential enemies throughout the rest of South Vietnam. In this campaign, he received the support of his brother Nhu and his national police force, as well as the backing of the U.S. mission in South Vietnam.

Chief among Diem's concerns were the former Viet Minh who remained in their homes and villages in South Vietnam after the war ended with the French. In order to deal with this potential threat, Diem allowed his brother

Nhu to engage in a campaign of terror against suspected former Viet Minh. In addition, and at the urging of his closest American advisor, Ed Lansdale, Diem devised a population relocation and control program called the *Agroville Program,* which was later renamed the *Strategic Hamlet Program.*

In essence, Diem used American assistance and built cement and cinder block villages that were surrounded by barbed wire. He then ordered villagers to be placed in these controlled areas, supposedly to protect them from communists. Circumstances led these Strategic Hamlets to become breeding grounds for hostility against Diem and foster support for the Viet Cong. The details of this program and the reasons it failed are discussed in Chapter 12 of the book. But Diem and his brother engaged in various activities during the remainder of the 1950s, all of which were designed to consolidate their power and control of the country, often times ignoring the actual and perceived needs of the Vietnamese people.

With the decision to back Diem without question and increase American economic and military aid to South Vietnam, the United States had to accept increased responsibility for Diem's continued success or failure. For his part, Diem held national elections in South Vietnam in 1955 and with the assistance of his closest American advisors, Diem won a whopping 98.6 percent of the popular vote. Needless to say, such a lopsided outcome could result only from massive amounts of voter corruption and election fraud. However, with the newly elected National Assembly, Diem established the Republic of Vietnam, the formal political entity of South Vietnam, and further consolidated his power by doing away with the exiled Emperor, Bao Dai, once and for all having him deposed through a national referendum.

For the United States, all of this meant broadening and increasing the amount of support provided Diem. From 1955 until 1961, when President Eisenhower left office, the United States provided more than $2 billion in aid to Vietnam.

Assessing the Situation: The Soldiers and the Statesmen

Assessments of the situation in Vietnam and the progress of the United States there usually depended on who was asked. The military approached the subject from the standpoint of how well prepared the ARVN forces were in the event of an attack. Many members of the diplomatic mission looked at it from the standpoint of US/RVN relations and the political stability of the nation. The two perspectives were not without conflicts regarding goals and missions, as well as assessments.

Planning for war: The MAAG-V perspective

American military commanders resisted escalating the U.S. military presence in Vietnam. But having received their orders from the Commander in Chief, the U.S. MAAG-V pushed on with training and preparing the ARVN for an eventual war with the Viet Minh and North Vietnam. Early assessments of ARVN by American military advisors were not very positive. Perhaps one of the most important observations was that the Vietnamese military lacked an adequate officer corps to lead them in the event of a war.

Another major problem that plagued the MAAG-V was that it lacked adequate personnel to carry out the mission of training the ARVN. The French played a key role in training ARVN from 1954 to 1956, but the United States took over all ARVN training responsibilities in 1956. The French had employed more than 5,000 soldiers in their endeavor to train the ARVN, but according to the Geneva Accords, the United States could not set up more than 342 military personnel in Vietnam. Many American advisors thought that the French had done a poor job of training ARVN and many felt part of that poor job was an inadequate number of training personnel. If the United States was to do a better job of it, they would need more than 5,000 personnel in Vietnam. Although MAAG-V requested an increase in personnel, the group met resistance from the most unlikely of places, the U.S. Department of State and the Embassy in Saigon.

Planning for peace: The embassy perspective

The Embassy and State Department had long been calling for an American commitment to Vietnam that included a U.S. military presence. Although the two groups pushed hard for this American presence in Vietnam, they argued against reneging on the Geneva Accords–mandated limits of 342 American military personnel in Vietnam. If the United States was to maintain the diplomatic high ground in the contest for freedom in Southeast Asia, it would have to behave in accordance with the agreements signed.

Rather than break with the 342 man ceiling, the U.S. State Department thought the United States should employ more civilians or employ military men in civilian clothes. Ultimately, Eisenhower compromised, and the U.S. military advisory presence had increased to about 700 when he left office in 1961. Eisenhower also sent more CIA personnel to include intelligence analysts, paramilitary specialists, and case officers to train and collect intelligence in South Vietnam and Laos. In this way, the United States got around restrictions on the number of military personnel allowed in South Vietnam by bringing in civilians instead.

The uneasy alliance: American soldiers and civilians in Vietnam

It is difficult to say with certainty why a difference in perspective existed between the American soldiers and statesmen who served under Eisenhower. But this difference in perspective highlights an issue that plagued American efforts in Southeast Asia for the next two decades. Bureaucratic turf battles, control over American policy, competition for the ear of the President, and competition for slices of the American budget all contributed to an adversarial atmosphere. Sometimes, it was impossible to detect such competition, while at other times it literally crippled American efforts in Southeast Asia.

Passing the Torch from Eisenhower to Kennedy: The Meeting That Never Was

Through his actions and policies, President Eisenhower committed the United States to preventing the spread of communism in Southeast Asia. The problems facing the United States at that time included growing dissent among the Vietnamese population in opposition to Diem, as well as a growing revolt in other Southeast Asian nations, including Laos. It was Laos that concerned Eisenhower most because the Soviet Union had increased its presence in that neighboring country in the hopes of turning the tide in favor of the Pathet Lao, the Laotian communists.

After Kennedy won the election of 1960, Eisenhower held a series of meetings with the president-elect, and there has been a lot of speculation as to the content of those meetings. Although Eisenhower apparently talked at length about Laos, he said nothing to Kennedy about Vietnam. When Kennedy took office in 1961, he and his newly appointed cabinet concluded that Laos was too inhospitable for the United States to do any good, so they instead focused most of their attention on Vietnam.

But whether it was Laos or Vietnam, it didn't really matter much. In an attempt to make up for the losses suffered by the Democratic Party almost a decade previously when his party "lost China," Kennedy vowed during the election of 1960 that he and the Democrats were going to make a stand against the spread of communism in Asia. How Kennedy went about this is the subject of Chapter 4.

Chapter 4
Kennedy's Green Berets

• •

In This Chapter

▶ Facing Cold War challenges

▶ Supporting South Vietnam

▶ Expanding American activity in Southeast Asia

▶ Developing new strategies

• •

*W*hen President John F. Kennedy (JFK) took office in 1961, he faced enormous challenges in the international arena. President Dwight D. Eisenhower left office having accomplished much, but with the Cold War in progress, which is discussed at length in Chapter 3, new threats constantly and quickly emerged to challenge the new president. President Kennedy, a Democrat, ran on an election platform criticizing his predecessor, claiming that the Republican Eisenhower hadn't done enough in the international arena to prevent the spread of communism. Publicly criticizing Eisenhower for such transgressions made Kennedy's life as president more difficult, because he couldn't afford the appearance of being "soft on commies" (in the words of his critics), lest his Republican opponent attack that stance in the 1964 national elections. In addition, several events that occurred much closer to home had a powerful effect on Kennedy's decisions and policies concerning Southeast Asia.

Kennedy and the Cold War

When Kennedy took office, the most pressing matters he faced centered on the Cold War and the spread of communism globally. Of immediate importance was the 1961 planned invasion of Cuba by United States–supported Cuban expatriates. Although thousands of miles from Vietnam, Kennedy's dealings with Cuba set the stage for his policies later in Vietnam as both tried to rollback or prevent the expansion of communism.

Fighting with Cuba: Failure in the Bay of Pigs

Fidel Castro, leader of the revolutionary forces in Cuba, had removed Cuban dictator Fulgencio Batista from power. Batista was friendly to U.S. business interests but didn't always look out for the interests of his people. Castro's revolution and rise to power occurred as a "people's revolution." Although Castro was a self-proclaimed communist, he also was a nationalist. Yet the fear of the spread of communism blinded Americans to anything but Castro's commitment to communism.

To most Americans, the Cold War meant communism, which, in turn, constituted a monolith, a single-minded monster controlled by the Soviet Union that was determined to destroy everything good and decent that Americans believed in — in particular free market capitalism and democracy. Someone, anyone, who admitted to being a communist was judged to be under the control of the Soviet Union and had to be stopped. This mind-set required action on the part of the U.S. government, and the Bay of Pigs invasion plan was hatched to turn back the communist revolution in Cuba. Although planned and organized by Eisenhower, implementation was left to Kennedy.

The invasion proved to be a massive failure that resulted in the death or capture of almost all of the Cuban invasion forces. Some observers blamed the failure of the Bay of Pigs on Kennedy's lack of resolve to fully utilize American military resources to support the Cuban invasion, principally American air forces that were supposed to provide close air support during the invasion.

The Bay of Pigs was the first major American foreign policy action under Kennedy, and it became his first major failure and a serious embarrassment that hurt American interests in Latin America and globally. Kennedy took away plenty of experience from the mission, and in future dealings with Cuba and other communists, Kennedy became determined to show more resolve. The next major test of his resolve came just a year later, also in Cuba (see the following section).

Protecting America's backyard: The Cuban missile crisis

Because the United States set up an embargo against Cuba and Cuba could get little support from anyone, Castro turned to the Soviet Union and its Premier Nikita Khrushchev for support. This cozying up to the communist superpower increased American mistrust of Castro, so the United States began gathering intelligence from overflights of the island by U2 spy planes (see Chapter 7), which provided high-quality photographs from high altitudes.

In September of 1962, U2 photos revealed that Castro was allowing the Soviets to set up nuclear-tipped missiles in Cuba. The crisis that followed this discovery lasted for several weeks and literally took the United States and Soviet Union to the brink of nuclear war.

For the United States, the only one acceptable solution was the complete removal of all nuclear missiles from Cuba. No compromise was possible, because JFK wouldn't survive politically if he allowed the Soviets to plant nuclear missiles 90 miles off the coast of the United States.

JFK mobilized American naval, air, and ground forces to prepare for an all-out assault on Cuba in the event that Khrushchev and Castro refused to back down. American warships cordoned off the entire island, preventing the passage of Soviet ships into the ports of Havana and elsewhere. The United States and Soviet Union stood poised for war, and with no apparent alternative in sight, Kennedy was hours from giving the order to launch the American assault on Cuba. Fortunately, Khrushchev backed down on October 28 and war was averted.

To the public, Kennedy had shown resolve and won a major psychological and diplomatic Cold War victory. In reality, back channel negotiations had led to an unofficial agreement between the United States and the Soviet Union that the Soviets would remove their missiles from Cuba if the United States removed its nuclear missiles from Turkey and the area around the Black Sea, which happened to be approximately 90 miles from targets inside of Russia.

Understanding the relevance to Vietnam

All of this Cold War activity off the coast of Florida coincided with Kennedy's policies and activities in Vietnam and Southeast Asia. The highly visible and frightening activities in Cuba bolstered American resolve to take action elsewhere, before it arrived again so close to American shores. JFK believed fighting the spread of communism was far better and safer as near to the source as possible — including Southeast Asia — than was fighting it only 90 miles off the coast of the United States. Most Americans agreed with this policy well into the war. See Chapter 15 for more information on American public's support for the war.

A New Strategy: JFK in Vietnam

With the heightened tensions that existed between the United States and the Soviet Union, Kennedy and his advisors looked at the situation in Vietnam from a different perspective than Eisenhower (whose policies are discussed in Chapter 3). Although American advisors had worked in Southeast Asia all the way back to the Second World War, Kennedy brought a new emphasis and strategy to the advisory program. Although President Eisenhower expanded American economic and military assistance, the number of actual American military personnel on the ground in Vietnam remained at rather constant levels of between 700 and 1,000 people. This personnel policy changed dramatically under Kennedy, but the shift represented more than just a change in executive leadership.

Capturing the spirit of a nation: JFK and American idealism

When President Kennedy took the oath of office and delivered his inaugural address in 1961, he captured the spirit of America when he uttered those oft repeated words, "Ask not what your country can do for you, ask what you can do for your country." JFK tapped into the idealism of many Americans to export democracy and capitalism, the twin ideologies that had made the United States the most prosperous nation in the world. To this end, JFK created the Peace Corps, which funneled American civilian volunteers abroad to help improve other nations and peoples.

Kennedy's idealism also affected his choice of members for his cabinet. Kennedy chose men who represented "the best and the brightest" from American business and government service. Two of Kennedy's closest foreign-policy advisors were Secretary of State Dean Rusk and Secretary of Defense Robert McNamara, seen with Kennedy in Figure 4-1. In addition, JFK fostered the expansion of a military organization that shared this idealistic mission of exporting American prosperity to places like Vietnam to help prevent the spread of communism. And, according to President Ngo Dinh Diem of South Vietnam, that was exactly what was happening in his nation in 1961.

Getting worse before it got even worse: Diem needed help . . . and fast

When JFK became president, the situation in Vietnam appeared fairly stable. In reality, however, Vietnam teetered on the brink of civil war and total collapse.

President Ngo Dinh Diem, shown in Figure 3-2, proved to be a capable leader (see Chapter 3), but he maintained power in South Vietnam through fear, intimidation, repression, and terror, usually at the hands of his brother, Chief of the Secret Police Ngo Dinh Nhu. The Diem government became particularly repressive just before Kennedy took office, so that by the time JFK arrived at the White House, Vietnam was in a state of open revolt.

Photo courtesy of the Vietnam Archive, Texas Tech University

The repressive policies of President Diem and his brother Nhu alienated many Vietnamese, and increasing numbers of South Vietnamese people voluntarily and openly rebelled against them.

But Diem understood American fears concerning the spread of communism and the widely held belief in the domino theory (see Chapter 3). To get additional help quickly from the United States, Diem screamed, "Communists!" The effect was little different than yelling, "Shark!" at the beach, and Americans were panicked into action.

Diem's request in 1961 differed significantly from his previous requests for American assistance. Before 1961, Diem preferred and accepted the very limited American physical presence and as much economic and military assistance as the United States was willing to provide. Prior to 1961, the number of American military advisors serving in Vietnam never really exceeded the cap of 700 imposed by the Geneva Accords (although the number of American "civilian advisors" was in the thousands). However, the deteriorating situation in Vietnam in 1961 changed Diem's priorities and concerns.

In early 1961, the Kennedy administration planned to send Vietnam additional money and military equipment that would enable Diem to expand his military forces to about 170,000 personnel (up from 150,000). Then, in mid-1961, Diem requested an increase in economic and military assistance that would boost his forces to 270,000. Unsure of how to address the request, JFK turned to his special military representative, General Maxwell Taylor.

Despite this shift in strategic thinking in the United States, Diem faced the reality of insurgency in South Vietnam. The *Viet Cong (VC)* insurgents, South Vietnamese people who became disgruntled with the government of South Vietnam, took up arms against the government, trying to bring about change by openly defying the Diem government and attacking targets at will. In the fall of 1961, Viet Cong attacks included various Army of the Republic of Vietnam (ARVN) military outposts. Desperate for American assistance, Diem requested that the United States send American combat soldiers, more as a symbol of American support than anything else. He also requested that the United States enter a defense pact with South Vietnam to deter communist expansion and military aggression from North Vietnam. This shift was a major one in Diem's position because he had always resisted Americans who recommended he allow the United States to send its ground forces to help fight the communists in South Vietnam. This reluctance was in part because of his desire to maintain complete control of events in his country. If American combat forces arrived, he knew he wouldn't have total control of those forces.

Deciding what to do: Rostow joins Taylor in Vietnam

By September of 1961, President Kennedy already had decided to send a special mission to South Vietnam to evaluate the situation. General Taylor and Walt Whitman Rostow (Kennedy's special assistant for national security affairs) left in October, conducting a two-week tour of South Vietnam. Their study concluded the following:

- ✔ The domino theory was still applicable. If South Vietnam fell to communism, the rest of Southeast Asia would fall, and as a result, the United States would lose prestige globally and the containment of communism in other places would be in jeopardy.

- ✔ The United States needed to increase the number of American advisors working in South Vietnam.

- ✔ The United States needed to send American military support units, including several helicopter squadrons with American pilots and support personnel that could be used to rapidly transport ARVN soldiers to areas under VC attack.

- ✔ The United States needed to send 8,000 American troops. At first, they would be deployed for humanitarian relief in dealing with a massive flood plaguing the Mekong River Delta, but once there, they could serve as an advanced party in preparation for sending a larger American ground force.

The lonely voice of dissent: George Ball

A number of prominent Americans spoke out against certain aspects of American policy in Vietnam. Some thought the United States should support Diem no matter what; others thought the United States shouldn't. But almost no one thought the United States needed to stay out of Vietnam completely. That distinction is reserved for one man, Undersecretary of State for Economic Affairs George Ball. In 1961, when most advisors to JFK agreed with increasing the American military presence in Vietnam, Ball viewed such a move as "a tragic error." He told the president on November 7 of that year that

after military support started, there would be no turning back, and within five years, the United States would have more than 300,000 men fighting in the rice paddies and jungles of Vietnam. Kennedy apparently responded to Ball, "George, you're just crazier than hell. That just isn't going to happen."

Both men were correct. In 1969, at the height of American presence in Vietnam, the United States had more than 500,000 men fighting in Southeast Asia. Ball merely was off by three years and 200,000 fewer men.

Nowhere in the report submitted to President Kennedy was any warning that the introduction of American ground forces might precipitate a similar response by North Vietnam. In fact, Taylor argued the opposite: He said that North Vietnam was vulnerable to American air power, so much so that if North Vietnam attempted to build up conventional forces to invade South Vietnam, Laos, or Cambodia, the U.S. Air Force could decimate the North Vietnamese forces. According to Taylor, no legitimate fear of a North Vietnamese response existed with regard to the introduction of American ground forces.

Dissenting voices to the Taylor-Rostow mission and recommendations

Other people who accompanied Taylor and Rostow walked away with slightly different observations. Chief among those viewpoints was that many South Vietnamese officials had lost confidence in President Diem. In addition, someone on the mission team observed that the war in South Vietnam was being fought in the villages and rural areas and that such a war would be a difficult one for American (or any foreign) forces to win. By contrast, Taylor suggested to President Kennedy that South Vietnam was not an unpleasant or difficult place in which to operate military forces.

Kennedy also received a conflicting recommendation from Secretary of Defense McNamara and the American Joint Chiefs of Staff (JCS). They thought Taylor's recommendation didn't go far enough. So McNamara and the JCS recommended that the president send six U.S. divisions (200,000 troops) to Vietnam. Doing so, they said, would be proof of American resolve and would show the communists that the United States meant business in South Vietnam.

JFK chooses a policy

JFK was left with two proposals to choose from. Both advocated the introduction of American ground forces, but at opposite ends of the spectrum — 8,000 versus 200,000. Kennedy rejected both. Instead, he ordered an increase in the amount of American aid for Vietnam but held off on sending more American advisors or ground troops. However, because so many Americans placed stock in the domino theory (see the preceding section), they argued persuasively that the United States had to prevent the fall of South Vietnam to communism. The question was not "if" the United States needed to intervene, but rather, "how?"

Minting a new COIN: Kennedy and counterinsurgency

In 1961, after evaluating the situation for himself, Kennedy adopted a new policy toward South Vietnam that focused on making life better for the South Vietnamese people. An extensive study commissioned by the White House revealed persuasively that the revolt in South Vietnam resulted more from internal political disaffection than from external communist subversion. In other words, the South Vietnamese people who were revolting against the Diem government weren't just communist infiltrators; instead, they were revolting because they hated Diem's policies. South Vietnam was in a state of insurgency — and the cure for insurgency was counterinsurgency, also known as COIN.

For the United States, counterinsurgency in Vietnam took on many different names. In rural Vietnam, it included nation building with Civil Operations Revolutionary (Rural) Development Support (CORDS) and using terms like "the other war" and "winning the hearts and minds," all of which are discussed in more detail in Part IV. Addressing the concerns of the South Vietnamese people and making their lives better according to how *they* defined "better" was all it boiled down to.

In most cases, *counterinsurgency* meant:

- ✔ Building schools
- ✔ Providing medical assistance
- ✔ Improving irrigation and roads
- ✔ Protecting Vietnamese peasants from the Viet Cong

These methods were intended to counteract the effects of the Viet Cong's mistreatment of the Vietnamese, which included:

- ✔ Taxing them
- ✔ Drafting their young men into service
- ✔ Terrorizing them

Counterinsurgency also meant not having government officials doing the same deeds as the Viet Cong. More than anything else, the peasants of South Vietnam wanted to be left alone to live their lives, but neither the government of South Vietnam nor the Viet Cong was willing to let that happen.

Making matters even more difficult, the Diem government was unwilling to share power with the urban Vietnamese who were growing tired of Diem's discrimination and autocratic administration, especially the favoritism of and reliance on fellow Catholics (see Chapters 3 and 12). Diem consistently rebuffed the idea of expanding his government to include the professional and middle classes of South Vietnam. The importance of this factor was not lost on many American military advisors and civilian observers who didn't think South Vietnam could survive unless Diem revamped his administration to include the disenfranchised and disenchanted South Vietnamese professional and middle classes. In addition, many Americans and South Vietnamese professionals didn't think Diem was engaging in an effective counterinsurgency policy.

The Blind Leading the Blind: Americans in Vietnam

One of the first shifts in American leadership occurring under President Kennedy was the appointment of Frederick Nolting as American Ambassador to South Vietnam in 1961. A career diplomat, as a rule, Nolting avoided controversy, but he nevertheless soon placed himself squarely in the middle of it in Vietnam.

Perhaps one of the better examples of Nolting's foibles occurred in February 1962 when he spoke to the Saigon Rotary Club. As a sign that he understood very little of what was happening in Vietnamese politics at the time, Nolting chastised the elite of Saigon society for criticizing the Diem government rather than rallying behind him in support of his policies.

Apparently, Nolting didn't think it appropriate for these Saigon professionals to criticize Diem's leadership just because Diem refused to include them in the South Vietnamese government. With that single speech, Nolting sent the message to these members of South Vietnam's middle and upper classes that the United States was squarely behind Diem, whether they liked it or not. They didn't and proved it the next day when two disgruntled ARVN Air Force pilots bombed the presidential palace. Diem survived, but the incident marked a continuation of challenges to Diem's leadership, not at the hands of sinister communist infiltrators but rather by disgruntled South Vietnamese professionals.

Ambassador Nolting was not alone in his calls for blind obedience to what many South Vietnamese thought was an unfair and illegitimate government under President Ngo Dinh Diem. General Paul Harkins, the American commander of the newly created Military Assistance Command–Vietnam (MACV), also shared this view.

American advice and support in South Vietnam was organized and coordinated by the Military Assistance Advisory Group–Vietnam (MAAG-V), which initially was created in 1950 and continued into the Kennedy administration (see Chapter 3). Under Kennedy, American commitment expanded beyond the scope of the MAAG-V organization, so it was changed to MACV (Military Assistance Command–Vietnam) in 1962. General Paul Harkins took over as commander of MACV in February of that year and remained until 1964, when he handed over command to his young, dashing, deputy commander, General William Westmoreland.

For his part, General Harkins provided highly optimistic appraisals of the situation in South Vietnam in spite of reports coming in from his American subordinates in the field in South Vietnam. One of the worst examples of this ordeal occurred with regard to the Strategic Hamlet program, which is discussed in much more detail in Part IV. In late 1962, after Diem announced that the program was a remarkable success, Harkins' subordinates reported the opposite, citing examples where hamlets (see Chapter 3) provided fertile recruiting grounds for Viet Cong. According to these more negative assessments, a vast majority of the peasants didn't appreciate being forced from their ancestral lands only to be placed behind barbed wire and forced to work for the government for no wages. Making matters worse, many government officials funneled supplies away from the hamlets, selling the materials on the black market, lining their own pockets, and depriving the hamlets of basic necessities, including weapons to fight off the Viet Cong.

Harkins reported back to Washington that he agreed with Diem's assessment, stating his optimism regarding the situation in Vietnam and promising not to allow pessimistic attitudes to form within his MACV command.

Special Forces, Kennedy-Style

As the commander in chief of U.S. military forces, Kennedy also tried to make sure that MACV included more than just advisors of the conventional stripe: Under Kennedy, U.S. Special Forces took on increasing responsibilities to train and fight in South Vietnam.

American Special Forces (SF) date back to the American colonial experience in the eighteenth century, when they modeled themselves after the guerrilla style of fighting employed by many Native Americans. But the mission of U.S. Special Forces working in Vietnam (see Figure 4-2) was significantly different. Comprising 10- to 12-man teams, U.S. Green Berets (named for the special headgear authorized by President Kennedy) trained Vietnamese forces to fight for and defend themselves.

Figure 4-2: U.S. Special Forces camp in Vietnam.

Photo courtesy of the Vietnam Archive, Texas Tech University

In Vietnam, a SF team was staffed with various light- and heavy-weapons specialists, a medic, a communications specialist, and other personnel. Before they were sent to Vietnam, SF team members underwent training designed to help them communicate and work with the people of Vietnam. The SF teams in Vietnam set up base camps in some of the more remote areas of Vietnam and trained the mountain people of Vietnam, who also were known as the *montagnards,* to defend against VC and North Vietnamese attacks.

Adopting a policy of living with the villagers, SF team members proved highly effective in training the people of Vietnam and serving as a model for later American attempts to win the war in Vietnam. Although important during the Kennedy administration, the SF model of living and working in the villages didn't receive as much support or attention later in 1964, after the United States began committing large numbers of conventional forces. You can read more about the Special Forces in Chapter 12.

Understanding the Limits of American Tactics and Equipment

Although U.S. Special Forces enjoyed a certain degree of success in training montagnard forces to defend their villages, the conventional training of ARVN did not meet with nearly as much success.

Being air-mobile: The helicopter in Vietnam

The helicopter introduced some significant changes to war-fighting strategies during the Vietnam War. One of the first contingents of American soldiers to arrive in Vietnam included the 54th Transportation Company, flying H-21 (Flying Banana) helicopters.

Although manufactured and used in limited numbers during the Second World War, helicopters tended to be poorly powered and proved to be of little use until after the war. Designed mainly for search and rescue, Americans used larger numbers of helicopters during the Korean War for transporting the sick and wounded to Mobile Army Surgical Hospitals (MASH units). Still, helicopters remained relatively small and poorly powered until later in the 1950s.

In 1955, Arthur Young of Bell Helicopters designed a helicopter around a new turbine engine that provided significantly more power to newer model helicopters. Prior to 1955, helicopters relied on standard reciprocating (internal combustion) engines. The new models used engines based on jet-turbine technology and significantly increased the power of these aircraft.

Bell started manufacturing the Model 204 UH-1 (Utility Helicopter-1) helicopter in 1956. Derivations of this model, also known as the *Huey,* soon became the symbol of American helicopter use and mobility in Vietnam. The primary mission of the Huey in Vietnam was as a transport vehicle, in essence, making it a flying truck for transporting troops and materiels anywhere they were needed. Later, weapons (machine guns, rockets, and grenade launchers) were added, resulting in the gunship concept.

As a much more flexible transport vehicle (one not requiring roads), the helicopter first surprised the Viet Cong, forcing them to adjust their tactics and activities in significant ways to effectively deal with this new technology. Even so, helicopters were particularly vulnerable when they were taking off and landing, and the VC soon were able to take advantage of the aircraft's various weaknesses, some of which are discussed in Chapter 11.

Pointing out problems: The battle of Ap Bac

The battle of Ap Bac, which served as the test case for using helicopters, armored vehicles, and various tactics in Vietnam, occurred in January 1963 when ARVN units in the Mekong Delta received orders to seize a VC radio transmitter near the village of Ap Bac. American intelligence had collected radio intercepts from this VC radio transmitter and knew its exact location. Lieutenant Colonel John Paul Vann served as the U.S. advisor to the ARVN, and he thought this operation would provide a good opportunity for the ARVN to test their combined mobility, armor, and firepower alongside the helicopter and armored personnel carriers (APCs).

Vann and his Vietnamese counterparts thought the VC transmitter was being protected by about 100 VC troops. They planned to assault the transmitter site using a two-pronged attack, bringing in elements of the 7th Division (ARVN) by helicopter and supporting them from the south with APCs with 50-caliber machine guns on revolving mounts, enabling the weapons to be fired in all directions regardless of the direction in which the vehicle was headed. The plan ran afoul from the beginning, because the VC transmitter was actually being protected by more than 350 VC soldiers.

Because of the bad intelligence and underestimation of VC strength, the ARVN assault also ran into problems because of a failure to realize that the VC force was dug in, well supplied, and ready for a fight. The VC also knew of the ARVN assault from intercepted radio messages.

When the first U.S. helicopters arrived on the morning of January 3, 1963, they encountered heavy VC gunfire and, within minutes, four U.S. helicopters carrying ARVN soldiers were shot down. The remaining aircraft also were hit by VC gunfire, and when the ARVN soldiers dismounted the aircraft, they refused to move lest they be killed. Making matters worse, the ARVN armored force became bogged down when the VC killed gunners manning the .50-caliber machine guns, because they were exposed and vulnerable.

Not even the ARVN Airborne could effectively assist in the fight, because they were deliberately dropped to the west of the initial position. This half-hearted and ineffective deployment of ARVN reserve forces occurred on the orders of General Huyen Van Cao because he was under orders from President Ngo Dinh Diem to minimize ARVN casualties.

In fact, minimizing causalities and seeking a victory was so important that during a lull in the fighting, when the VC units left the area, the ARVN staged a mock assault on empty VC positions, claiming victory.

The results of the battle, however, were hardly mixed. Although determining VC losses is impossible, because they carried off their dead and wounded, the ARVN lost more than 80 soldiers killed and more than 100 wounded. According to Vann, the American advisor, the ARVN forces failed in their objectives to use air mobility, armor, and firepower to easily destroy VC defenses and seize the VC radio transmitter. In addition, the battle proved that the VC had successfully developed new tactics and effective strategies for dealing with the increased mobility and firepower provided by helicopters and APCs. Although the VC fled their positions, the ARVN failed in all of its objectives.

General Cao, Vann's Vietnamese counterpart, didn't share his assessment. Cao called the battle an ARVN victory. The commander of MACV, General Paul Harkin, chose to accept the inflated post-battle assessment of General Cao and thus ignored Vann's critical assessment. When Harkin went public with his assessment to the press and in his reports back to Washington, Vann lodged a protest by informing the press of what really happened.

From this early conflict between official reports to Washington and a ground commander's assessment emerged the beginning of the *credibility gap*. When the United States became increasingly involved with the fighting in Vietnam in later years, Washington reports said one thing and ground commanders and other eyewitness reports frequently said something else; reporters and the American public were left to decide who was telling the truth. Because reporters eventually uncovered lying by Washington officials, the American people started believing the press more than their elected officials.

Although the Battle at Ap Bac wasn't initially recognized as a battle of significance, it since has received increased attention as an important battle that foreshadowed the future problems and failures for ARVN and the United States, despite advantages they had in air mobility. That the American decision makers in Vietnam and the United States ignored these problems and failures also was extremely important in revealing problems with the American involvement in and mentality concerning Vietnam.

Overthrowing an Oppressive Dictator: Getting Rid of an American Ally in Vietnam

By the fall of 1963, the situation in South Vietnam could not have been much worse. The country was plagued by internal turmoil and strife, much of it caused by the repressive policies of President Ngo Dinh Diem and his brother, Nhu:

- ✔ The Agroville and Strategic Hamlet Programs (discussed in Chapters 3 and 12) fostered anger and resentment among most of the peasants who were forced to reside in them, behind barbed wire and away from their ancestral lands.

- ✔ The cancellation of village elections and imposition of direct (usually Catholic) appointees by President Diem fostered even more resentment among the vastly Buddhist majority of South Vietnam.

- ✔ Buddhist monks engaged in the highest form of protest against Diem's policies through the act of *self-immolation* — lighting themselves on fire and burning themselves to death. As if that weren't bad enough, this situation worsened when Madam Nhu, the Dragon Lady (see Chapter 3), announced publicly that she would applaud another "monk barbeque show" and hinted she'd gladly provide the necessary gasoline.

In addition to internal strife, the battle at Ap Bac had shown that ARVN forces were unwilling to engage the VC effectively. The United States couldn't win the war for Vietnam but could provide only money, materiel, and advice that effective South Vietnamese leaders could use to defeat communism within their borders. This scenario did not appear possible given the apparent void in Vietnamese leadership. Something had to change.

Questions about whether the United States should support Diem stemmed from President Eisenhower and the very beginning of U.S. involvement in Vietnam (see Chapter 3). Under President Eisenhower, the United States protected Diem, even from internal Vietnamese attempts to overthrow him. The men advising President Kennedy, however, were at odds about what to do.

On one side you had General Harkin, Ambassador Nolting, General Taylor, and others in Washington advising that the United States needed to continue its support of Diem. On the other side, Far East specialists like Roger Hilsman, Averill Harriman, and new U.S. Ambassador to South Vietnam Henry Cabot Lodge advocated the removal of Diem. After much deliberation, President Kennedy decided to reverse nearly a decade of U.S. policy in South Vietnam by ending U.S. support for President Ngo Dinh Diem.

Rather than protect Diem, in early November 1963, Kennedy gave final authorization for the U.S. mission in Saigon to step aside if a coup plot emerged to overthrow him. The difficulty of making this decision was surpassed only by the bitter consequences of allowing a coup.

Although the United States didn't actively participate in the coup, the overthrow attempt couldn't and wouldn't have happened without U.S. acquiescence. That the United States supported the coup (as opposed to all previous times when it acted to stop coups from occurring) is enough to seal U.S. responsibility for this ultimate debacle. Although the United States expected ARVN military leaders to form a *junta*, or group of military commanders acting in concert to take over the country, and rally against Diem and his brother Nhu, they nevertheless expected Diem and Nhu to survive the ordeal at least with their lives. That didn't happen.

Apparently no one in the Kennedy administration was concerned that if Diem survived, he might form a government in exile and wreak international havoc in the United Nations and elsewhere, constantly challenging and making life difficult for whomever emerged as the new ruler of South Vietnam. That is what had happened in China when the communist Chinese failed to kill off the nationalist Chinese before they made it to Formosa (Taiwan). Since then, Taiwan has been a constant thorn in the side of Communist China, creating problems and challenges whenever and wherever possible. Apparently, the Vietnamese plotting the coup against Diem were not going to let that happen to them, so they decided to kill Diem and his brother Nhu, removing any possibility of the brothers returning to power.

The assassination of Diem and Nhu surprised many Americans in Vietnam and in the United States. Rather than removing an unstable leader and replacing him with someone or something better, the coup resulted in a series of *revolving door governments* in Vietnam in which one member of the military junta emerged victorious one month only to be plotted against and removed by another member of the junta the following month. The murder of Diem only made South Vietnam even more unstable, and it took three years for a strong leader to emerge and reunite the country. In the interim, the United States suffered its own abrupt change in national leadership when President John Kennedy was assassinated that same month.

The Assassination of President Kennedy and Its Meanings for Vietnam

When bullets rang out in Dealey Plaza in Dallas on the morning of November 22, 1963, few drew any links to American policy in Vietnam. As the investigation into the assassination of President Kennedy concluded, it appeared that one man had killed the president and his motivations had nothing to do with American policy in Asia. But that conclusion didn't prevent the creation of many conspiracy theories concerning the death of JFK, including some that draw a link between the president's death and his last decisions concerning Vietnam.

A number of people speculate that President Kennedy wanted to withdraw the United States from Vietnam, and his assassination occurred at the hands of people opposed to that policy. Although it is true that Kennedy ordered the withdrawal of 1,000 U.S. advisors from Vietnam in National Security Action

Memorandum (NSAM) 263, it is not apparent or obvious that he would have been able to follow through with a complete withdrawal of all American advisors during his administration for the following reasons:

- Kennedy ran for election in 1960 on the platform that he'd take a hard stand against communist expansion. Staying true to his word, JFK was responsible for increasing the American presence in Vietnam more than 20-fold during his first two years as president. When Kennedy arrived in office, the U.S. military presence in Vietnam numbered approximately 700 advisors. Upon his death, that number was more than 16,000 and consisted of conventional U.S. military forces that included helicopter and other support units.

- With the instability caused by the Diem coup and the revolving door governments that followed, the situation in South Vietnam worsened considerably and the fall of South Vietnam to communism would have been all but certain except for the massive amounts of U.S. assistance propping up the government and ARVN military forces.

- Kennedy faced an election the following year (in 1964). Although Kennedy ordered the withdrawal of 1,000 U.S. advisors by the end of 1963, he based that order on the questionable assessments that the situation in Vietnam would get better with Diem gone, when in fact, it got much worse. Kennedy couldn't expect to win reelection in 1964 while at the same time reversing his position on the U.S. support for Vietnam and the prevention of communist expansion there. Little doubt exists that Kennedy's successor, Lyndon Johnson, did exactly what Kennedy himself would have done — continue supporting South Vietnam to stop the spread of communism.

Chapter 5

Johnson's Regulars

. . . .

In This Chapter

▶ Carrying Kennedy's torch

▶ Sending American ground troops to Vietnam

▶ Fighting, American-style

▶ Winning battles but losing the war

. . . .

On November 22, 1963, Lyndon Baines Johnson (also known as LBJ) woke up vice president of the U.S. When he went to bed that evening, he was president. After the assassination of President John F. Kennedy in Dallas, Texas, Johnson took the oath of office and returned to Washington, D.C. That evening, he nervously talked with his *cabinet* (the group of people who make up the president's closest advisors) about what he would try to accomplish as president. According to those present, Johnson didn't even mention Vietnam. He focused, instead, on his domestic agenda and his hopes to expand government support for education and business, civil rights reforms, and other domestic issues. The absence of Vietnam in that discussion didn't mean Johnson was unaware of that small nation, half a world away. It merely reflected his conviction and trust that the U.S. and South Vietnam would prevail against communism there, so that Johnson would be able to focus his attention and talents on a meaningful domestic policy legacy.

Johnson's domestic-policy dreams emerged from his experiences as a junior congressman serving with one of his heroes, President Franklin D. Roosevelt, who revolutionized the role of the U.S. government in the 1930s with his Depression era "New Deal" legislation. Ultimately, however, Johnson's domestic dreams became overshadowed by the nightmare of war in Vietnam.

Picking Up Where JFK Left Off

As commander in chief, Johnson inherited a policy in Vietnam that emphasized expanding the U.S. presence and role in South Vietnam and Southeast Asia, which is discussed in more detail in Chapter 4. When President Kennedy took office in 1960, the U.S. military presence in Vietnam numbered fewer than 1,000 military advisors. At the time of his death in late 1963, the U.S. presence had been increased to more than 16,000. This included an increased U.S. Air Force presence that involved both pilots and ground crews. As a result, during his brief time as President, Kennedy further linked U.S. interests and prestige to the success of a free South Vietnam against the communist-supported North Vietnam.

In addition to expanding the U.S. military influence in Vietnam, Kennedy also expanded U.S. meddling in South Vietnamese politics. Just weeks before his assassination, Kennedy gave a nod to coup plotters in South Vietnam, who overthrew and assassinated President Ngo Dinh Diem (see Chapter 4). In Vietnam, the murder of Diem led to political anarchy and a series of revolving-door governments.

Meanwhile, as the U.S. was struggling with the Kennedy assassination, Johnson (shown in Figure 5-1) took over where Kennedy left off. This peaceful transition of power between Kennedy and Johnson served as a testament to the strength of American political institutions. Few realized in late 1963, however, that this transition would ultimately lead to the introduction of U.S. regular ground combat forces in Southeast Asia. Fewer still could predict that American political strength would ultimately dwindle in the face of a protracted guerilla war in Southeast Asia.

Figure 5-1: President Johnson sitting in the Oval Office of the White House.

Photograph courtesy of the Vietnam Archive, Texas Tech University

Inheriting and keeping a cabinet

When he took over as president, Johnson made few changes to Kennedy's cabinet. The key members of Johnson's national security team remained Secretary of State Dean Rusk, Secretary of Defense Robert McNamara,

National Security Advisor McGeorge Bundy, and Director of Central Intelligence John McCone. Because the players remained the same, so, too did the momentum behind U.S. involvement in Vietnam.

Johnson found himself dealing with the same issues as his predecessor. The U.S. was still involved in a massive Cold War contest with communists around the world, including the Soviet Union, China (PRC), North Korea, North Vietnam, and many other nations. Like Kennedy, Johnson believed strongly that American security ultimately depended on the ability of the U.S. to show force and help other nations resist communism. He also believed in the *domino theory,* which stipulated that if South Vietnam fell to communism, the surrounding countries would subsequently fall to communism like a row of dominoes. In Southeast Asia, this meant defending free South Vietnam from communist North Vietnam. The problem that persisted for both Kennedy and Johnson was that the enemy wasn't entirely from outside South Vietnam.

Kennedy and the South Vietnamese government dealt not just with the threat of communism from North Vietnam but also with communist-led insurgency from within South Vietnam (see Chapter 4). In other words, some people who were born and raised in South Vietnam were angry with their own government and actively sought to overthrow it. Some of this internal discontent in South Vietnam was based on religion, because the Catholic President Diem had appointed mostly Northern Vietnamese Catholics to positions of authority in a 90 percent Southern Vietnamese Buddhist nation. With the murder of President Diem, few of the intervening governments provided very much political stability or social order, and by the time they addressed these issues, it was too late. All of this ultimately made Johnson's job difficult at best and impossible at worst.

Americanizing the war in Vietnam

Because Johnson continued to expand U.S. support to South Vietnam, the U.S. military presence continued and took a more aggressive posture in 1964. The American advisory effort remained the same, as did the shipments of American military and economic assistance to the government and armed forces of South Vietnam. Changes in American envoys to South Vietnam (see Figure 5-2) occurred when vacancies opened at the American Embassy in Saigon and MACV headquarters. This section discusses the changes that occurred soon after Johnson took office.

Militarizing the American embassy: A Taylored response

In June 1964, Johnson selected General Maxwell Taylor to take over as U.S. Ambassador to South Vietnam. Taylor had been serving as Chairman of the Joint Chiefs of Staff and, prior to that, served as a special advisor to President Kennedy (see Chapter 4). Taylor had made several trips to Vietnam, including one in 1961 and another in 1963. After the first trip,

Taylor recommended an increase in the American troop presence in South Vietnam and asserted that a protracted ground war in Vietnam was highly unlikely. Within a year, the U.S. troop presence in Vietnam swelled from almost 700 to more than 15,000. After the second trip, Taylor reported "great progress" in the war against the communists but cautioned against continued U.S. backing of President Diem who lacked the popular support of the South Vietnamese people. Within weeks, Diem was dead. Although Taylor didn't order the troop increase or coup, himself, they stand as a testament to his influence in the Kennedy administration and, subsequently, in Johnson's.

Getting a facelift: Westy takes over MACV

Military Assistance Command–Vietnam (MACV), discussed in Chapter 4, received a boost in June 1964 in the form of a young and vibrant new commander, General William C. Westmoreland. Referred to as Westy, General Westmoreland served as deputy commander of MACV for six months under General Paul Harkin before taking over as commander in June.

The appointment of Westmoreland (see Figure 5-3) meant that South Vietnam gained a strong ally who had experience as an artillery commander in WWII. Westmoreland came away from his WWII experience as a firm believer in conventional warfare; he ultimately concluded that such strategies and tactics could win in Vietnam. Westmoreland endorsed and implemented a strategy that reflected his military training and WWII experiences and that focused on using firepower and conventional military tactics.

Figure 5-2:
Map of
South
Vietnam.

How to start a war: The U.S. Navy in the Gulf of Tonkin

The U.S. also implemented a strategy of sending American naval vessels to the South China (PRC) Sea and to the Gulf of Tonkin, where they gathered electronic and signals intelligence on North Vietnamese Army (NVA) radar sites and communications systems. U.S. naval forces also supported South Vietnamese military attacks along the coast of North Vietnam as part of OPLAN 34A and The Desoto Missions, which are discussed in much more detail in Chapter 11. These joint U.S. and South Vietnamese navy operations brought North Vietnamese and American boats and ships into close proximity, making a confrontation likely.

And that is exactly what happened on August 2, 1964. The USS *Maddox*, an American destroyer, came under fire from three North Vietnamese PT (patrol torpedo) Boats, four miles off the coast of North Vietnam. The *Maddox* returned fire and received support from U.S. Navy fighters, forcing the PT boats to flee. Two days later, it was alleged that the North Vietnamese again attacked U.S. ships, which are alleged to have counterattacked.

Figure 5-3:
General William Westmoreland in Vietnam.

Photograph courtesy of the Vietnam Archive, Texas Tech University

Since then, U.S. personnel who served on those ships have refuted whether this second attack ever took place. Nevertheless, Johnson took this "evidence" to Congress and the American people and requested their authorization and support for taking all necessary means to protect U.S. forces in the area. Although information was readily available at the time, only years after the U.S. started fighting in Vietnam did anyone question the validity of Johnson's claims concerning the second attacks. On August 7, 1964, Congress passed the *Southeast Asia Resolution*, better known as the *Gulf of Tonkin Resolution*, and

Johnson received a blank check to take whatever action he deemed necessary to secure and safeguard U.S. forces in and around Southeast Asia. Ultimately, this meant introducing U.S. ground forces into South Vietnam, and that led to the American escalation of the Vietnam War.

At first, taking all necessary action meant bombing targets in North Vietnam to punish them for allegedly attacking the USS *Maddox* and USS *Turner Joy*. The American retaliatory air strikes over North Vietnam involved military and industrial targets; they're covered in more detail in Chapter 8. From the perspective of the ground war in Vietnam, the increase of American air operations ultimately meant that the U.S. had to expand existing American airfields and create new airfields, and this meant sending American ground forces to provide security for those air bases. But first, Johnson became very preoccupied by a domestic event: the election of 1964.

Campaigning against war: Promises made only to be broken

In the months following the Gulf of Tonkin incidents and the U.S. bombing of North Vietnam, Johnson turned away from events in Vietnam and focused on getting reelected, a major concern for all U.S. presidents. The Democratic Party nominated Johnson, while the Republican Party nominated Barry Goldwater. In an ironic twist, Goldwater ran as a *hawk*, on a conservative and pro-military platform, calling for the bombing of North Vietnam.

Although Johnson sent American ships to the Tonkin Gulf to counter Goldwater's appeal as a hawk, Johnson ran for president as a *dove*, focusing on a domestic agenda that emphasized civil rights and Kennedy's *New Frontier* platform (a domestic legislative agenda focusing on economic and social reform to include Medicare and raising the minimum wage), and he called for a limited American response in Vietnam. According to Johnson at the time, the U.S. shouldn't send Americans to fight and do what the Vietnamese ought to be doing for themselves.

The dove wins in 1964

By all accounts, Johnson won by a landslide, receiving more than 43 million in the popular vote to Goldwater's 27 million. Apparently, most Americans in 1964 either feared Goldwater's more hawkish position or simply agreed with Johnson that the U.S. shouldn't send Americans to die in the rice patties, jungles, and mountains of South Vietnam. But this was a campaign pledge that Johnson couldn't keep, even if he wanted to. Johnson had few options, given the momentum behind supporting South Vietnam, the commitment of the U.S. to prevent the spread of communism there, and the American prestige that was on the line when Johnson started bombing North Vietnam in 1964.

Although he won on a peace platform, Johnson couldn't abandon Vietnam to communism. If he did, he and his fellow members of the Democratic Party would likely suffer serious political defeat during the off-year elections of 1966, because Republicans would accuse them of losing Vietnam to communism, just as Truman and the Democratic Party lost in 1950 for losing China (PRC) to communism. More important, losing in Vietnam could jeopardize the presidential election of 1968. So, more was at stake than freedom and democracy in a small Southeast Asian nation.

The dove becomes a reluctant hawk

Despite the emphasis he placed on domestic issues during the campaign of 1964, Johnson quickly became preoccupied with Vietnam in early 1965. The Viet Cong (VC) had already stepped up their attacks in South Vietnam and, as early as November 1964, had killed four American servicemen. Johnson did nothing at the time, and the VC continued to attack in South Vietnam. Making things worse, increasing numbers of North Vietnamese Army (NVA) units entered the South in late 1964 and early 1965. And complicating matters even more, various religious and political groups in South Vietnam threatened political and social stability in the capital of Saigon. Events turned ugly in February during the Vietnamese Tet holiday in 1965 (a Lunar New Year Celebration) when the Viet Cong attacked U.S. military units near Pleiku and killed nine Americans. Something had to be done to stop this killing and stabilize the situation. General Westmoreland requested sending in the U.S. Marines. Although he had grave doubts concerning the ability of U.S. forces to succeed in South Vietnam, Johnson approved Westmoreland's request.

Promise broken: Sending in the Marines

March 1965 was a busy month for U.S. forces in Vietnam. First, the U.S. 9th Marine Expeditionary Force (MEF) arrived in Danang, South Vietnam, where they initially provided security for the air base there. Within a month, Johnson authorized their use for offensive military operations, including patrolling in the area around Danang. Shortly thereafter — based on the recommendations of Defense Secretary McNamara, General Westmoreland, Ambassador Taylor, and the Joint Chiefs of Staff — Johnson authorized sending an additional 40,000 American troops to Vietnam. This introduction of American conventional ground forces represented the beginning of an ever-expanding American ground combat presence in Vietnam. In terms of fighting the war, it meant American troops took increasing amounts of responsibility for engaging the enemy. But would these American soldiers with conventional military training be able to win a war in Vietnam? The following section attempts to answer that question.

Emerging Perspectives on the War

As the U.S. and North Vietnam became increasingly involved in fighting in South Vietnam, the two sides developed different perspectives on the war.

For North Vietnam, this became an old and familiar kind of war, and for the U.S., a new and different kind of war.

Perceptions in North Vietnam

Until 1965, most of the fighting in South Vietnam occurred between indigenous South Vietnamese forces on both sides of the conflict. Most Army of the Republic of Vietnam (ARVN) soldiers came from South Vietnam, as did their principal enemy, the Viet Cong (VC). The composition of communist forces started to change in late 1964 and early 1965. Following the American bombing of 1964, North Vietnam started to send more troops to South Vietnam. They hoped that these additional North Vietnamese Army (NVA) units could quickly defeat the ARVN. The NVA/VC could then overthrow the American-supported government of South Vietnam, reuniting North and South under communism, before the U.S. could mobilize and send large numbers of American troops across the Pacific. North Vietnam failed in these goals in 1965, but, to them, this was only the beginning of the war. North Vietnam had time and a willingness to suffer almost total annihilation in the pursuit of their cause: the reunification of Vietnam under their governmental control. For the North Vietnamese, this was an old way of war. The war with the U.S. was no different than the war with the French, the Chinese, or any other colonial threat. To North Vietnam, the Vietnam War was a contest of wills more than a contest of armies. Whichever country and people could politically and socially stomach the war longer would win.

Perceptions in the United States

From the U.S. perspective, and as Johnson said in July 1965, Vietnam was a different kind of war. The U.S. was fighting a limited war in support of the Cold War policy of containing communism. The Vietnam War was somewhat different from previous American experiences because the government of South Vietnam faced a threat from within, in the form of communist insurgency, as well as a threat from without, in the form of communist North Vietnam. The U.S. also had to be careful in fighting the war since imprudent military action could lead to the introduction of communist forces from China (PRC) or the Soviet Union, and Johnson didn't want to start World War III.

Although many American analysts agreed that the war in South Vietnam started as an internal civil war, by 1965, increasing amounts of communist supplies and troops entered South Vietnam to help the Viet Cong overthrow the government of South Vietnam. American officials repeatedly stated — and Johnson and most Americans believed — that if South Vietnam fell to communism, so, too, would the rest of Southeast Asia and many neighboring nations (including, quite possibly, India and Australia). Such a chain of events would threaten freedom and democracy around the world, and Americans couldn't stand by idly and watch that happen.

How perceptions affected North Vietnamese strategies and expectations

The views and early perceptions of the war as they emerged in Hanoi, North Vietnam, and Washington, D.C., ultimately affected the strategies each side employed in fighting in South Vietnam.

For North Vietnam, its biggest assets were time, a strong will to fight, and an ability to mobilize the entire country to engage in a total war for national survival. The North Vietnamese perception that they were fighting a total war for national survival received consistent reinforcement every time an American aircraft bombed targets in North Vietnam. With a preponderance of time and national will on their side, North Vietnam strategically sought to engage in a protracted and lengthy war designed to slowly erode American will to continue fighting. Tactically, this meant NVA/VC forces had to limit their fighting in order to continue on, year after year, until the U.S. finally gave up and left, mirroring their success against the French during the French–Indochina War (see Chapter 2). To this end, NVA/VC forces had to avoid large American and ARVN forces in the field unless they could hit them and run, inflicting casualties on U.S. and ARVN forces while sustaining few in return if possible. At times, the NVA/VC would have to accept losses, which was fine, as long as they could replenish their numbers and fight again.

How perceptions affected American strategies and expectations

The U.S. had superior military assets, including a large military-industrial base, superior war-fighting technology, and superior firepower. Because Johnson and most of his advisors agreed that a lengthy war in Asia would be difficult to sustain politically and socially within the U.S., American war planners tried to devise strategies and tactics that capitalized on these perceived American strengths in order to bring the war to a rapid conclusion. At the same time, the U.S. wasn't physically threatened by North Vietnam and couldn't justify a total-war mentality. This meant the U.S. couldn't use nuclear missiles. In addition, Johnson refused to mobilize the reserves in order to maintain the appearance that the U.S. regular forces, bolstered by the draft, could handle the situation in Vietnam. The ever-present fear that the Soviet Union or PRC could become militarily involved in the war if the U.S. wasn't careful further complicated American strategic and tactical planning: The U.S. had to fight a limited war to prevent a world war.

As a result, Americans developed a strategy of attrition and erosion, mirroring their success in WWII.

- ✔ *Attrition* meant that U.S. ground force operations focused on finding and killing NVA/VC forces in the field. U.S. planners expected that if they could engage and kill enough NVA/VC, the communists would eventually run out of troops and have no choice but to stop fighting.

- ✔ *Erosion* meant bombing military and industrial targets in North Vietnam, bombing the road network leading from North Vietnam to South Vietnam through Laos and Cambodia (also known as the *Ho Chi Minh Trail* or *HCM Trail*, and searching for and destroying NVA/VC facilities and caches in South Vietnam, eroding their material capability to wage war.

By combining these two strategies, the U.S. expected to win quickly because the NVA/VC couldn't even come close to competing with American technology, industrial capacity, manpower, or firepower. It would take time for the U.S. to move enough ground forces to Vietnam to engage in attrition, but it already had naval and air force fighters and bombers in Thailand, South Vietnam, and off the coast of Vietnam. So the U.S. embarked quickly upon missions to erode the traffic of people and material from North Vietnam into South Vietnam. They are discussed in the two following short sections.

Was attrition the only viable strategy available?

President Johnson, Defense Secretary McNamara, and General Westmoreland all agreed that attrition was the best strategy for U.S. forces in Vietnam. It maximized the American strengths of mobility and firepower and it made it easy to quantify American progress through the *body count,* or the number of men killed and wounded on each side in an operation or battle. But was attrition actually relevant to the war in Vietnam and was it the only viable ground war strategy available? This question became one of the most contested issues during the war and continues to the present because historians, military personnel, politicians, veterans, and others continue to argue all sides of the issue.

During the Vietnam War, the debate was between attrition and the "other war," which focused on winning over the people of Vietnam (see Chapter 12). With regard to the ground war,

the Marine Corps introduced a different strategy in 1966 called *Combined Action.* Eventually, this evolved into the CAP or Combined Action Platoon program (also discussed in Chapter 12) in which the Marines placed specially selected platoons right next to Vietnamese villages. These Marines shied away from the war of attrition and focused instead on training and helping Vietnamese villagers to defend themselves against the NVA/VC. Instead of the body count, the CAPs measured their success on their ability to train friendly Vietnamese civilians, to help prevent the VC from coming into villages for food and other supplies, and to stop the forced conscription of the young Vietnamese men into the ranks of the VC. The CAP program ended prematurely but it remains an interesting potential alternative to the conventional American strategy of attrition.

First by sea: Interdicting the communist supply routes

Operation MARKET TIME was one of the first and longest of the American-led operations in Vietnam, and it combined American and Vietnamese air and naval forces in an attempt to cut off coastal supply routes used by the Viet Cong (see Chapter 10). Until 1965, the Viet Cong received an estimated 70 percent of their supplies through infiltration of the 1,200-mile coast of South Vietnam. If U.S. and ARVN forces could cut off these sea lanes of supply, they could strike a devastating blow to the capabilities of North Vietnam to supply materiel to NVA/VC units in the field.

Operation MARKET TIME lasted from 1965 until 1971, and in many instances succeeded in accomplishing the goal of cutting off the coastal supply missions. This meant that the North Vietnamese had to rely more heavily on land routes to access South Vietnam.

Second by air: More interdiction of the communist supply routes

As the U.S. undertook the bombing of North Vietnam, it included attacks on the growing network of roads and trails (the HCM Trail) leading from North to South Vietnam through Laos and Cambodia. By 1965, the HCM trail started to blossom into a series of road networks that carried many thousands of people and tons of supplies per day to the South. The U.S. engaged in two campaigns in an attempt to slow or halt NVA/VC traffic along the HCM Trail.

- ✔ **Secret War in Laos (see Chapter 13):** The U.S. Central Intelligence Agency (CIA) worked with Laotian people near the trail network in an attempt to gather intelligence and interdict movement along the trail. To this end, the CIA ran the largest civilian airline in Southeast Asia called *Civil Air Transport and Air America,* discussed in more detail in Chapter 13. Although the CIA and Laotian forces couldn't close down the trail on their own, they did a remarkable job of providing intelligence and closing *choke-points* (very narrow points in areas where no alternative routes could be easily found) along the Ho Chi Minh Trail in Laos as the trails and roads wound through treacherous and mountainous terrain.

- ✔ **The conventional air campaign over Laos and the HCM (see Chapter 9):** There is little doubt that the combined American and ARVN Air Force bombing campaign slowed the movement of people and supplies down the trail, given the many tons of bombs dropped.

Despite the air campaign and the CIA work in Laos, the trail remained open because no significant U.S. or South Vietnamese ground force presence prevented using the trail network. Instead the U.S. and South Vietnam focused on using their ground forces on fighting in South Vietnam — and there was plenty of that to go around.

The Ground War Begins

After March 1965, the U.S. Marine Corps continued to send units to Vietnam in order to secure coastal facilities, ports, and airfields and provide safe staging areas for the anticipated influx of U.S. forces. In order to succeed, the Marines couldn't just sit back and let the VC attack these U.S. bases, but had to engage in offensive operations as opportunities presented themselves. This is how the American ground war in Vietnam started — it's the subject of this section.

Off to a good start: Operation STARLITE

Operation STARLITE was the first major ground combat operation for U.S. forces in Vietnam. The operation involved elements of the U.S. 3rd Marine Amphibious Force stationed at Chu Lai against elements of the 1st Viet Cong Regiment. General Lewis Walt, commander of the Marines at Chu Lai learned of an impending attack on his base from a VC deserter and devised Operation STARLITE to preempt that attack. On August 18, 1965, the assault began as American artillery and bombers prepared the battlefield, attacking the known concentrations of enemy units and preparing the landing zones. Marine ground forces quickly moved in and met little resistance from the VC until they reached Hill 43. For an explanation of Hill numbers, see Chapter 6.

On Hill 43, the VC fought from bunkers and other defensive works and staunchly defended their positions, to the death. The Marines called in heavy artillery and air strikes and after several days of fighting, destroyed the VC. Operation STARLITE ended on August 24. For Americans, the battle couldn't have had better results. The 1st VC Regiment lost 614 soldiers and saw 9 captured; for a time, the regiment ceased to exist. The Marines lost 45 soldiers killed with 120 wounded. The low number of American dead resulted, in part, from the use of Marine helicopters that came in and evacuated the wounded. The high number of VC deaths resulted from their decision to stay and fight, ill-prepared for the massive amounts of firepower the U.S. forces could bring to bear on their positions.

STARLITE was an important initial tactical victory for the U.S. because it boosted morale just as much as a defeat would have seriously dampened it. It also proved the effectiveness of U.S. firepower capabilities. To the Americans who believed in the strategy of attrition, the *kill ratio* of 13 to 1 (13 VC killed to each American) showed that the U.S. could win and win quickly if similar body counts and kill ratios could be generated in future battles. But the question remained whether the strategy could work over the long term.

U.S. forces move into Vietnam

As the Marines secured coastal bases and facilities in South Vietnam and fought in Chu Lai and elsewhere, the U.S. Army mobilized and started sending in ground combat units to fight inland in such places as Central Highlands, the Mekong Delta, and the Hobo Woods. The number of U.S. forces in Vietnam expanded rapidly, and during 1965 alone, increased from 23,000 to more than 184,000. At their peak in 1969, the U.S. forces in Vietnam numbered more than 540,000.

As larger numbers of U.S. troops arrived in Vietnam, different strategies emerged concerning their deployment and employment. Ambassador Taylor and General Harold Johnson, U.S. Army Chief of Staff, both recommended an *Enclave Strategy,* where U.S. forces would occupy static defense bases along the coast and would limit operations to within 50 miles of such bases. This would limit the number of American casualties and let ARVN do most of the fighting. Although Johnson initially agreed with this cautious approach, senior advisors, members of the Joint Chiefs of Staff (JCS), and General Westmoreland all convinced Johnson that the U.S. forces had to take a more active role in the fighting in order to defeat communism in South Vietnam.

As increasing numbers of American soldiers occupied and patrolled parts of South Vietnam, they sought contact with NVA/VC units in order to continue the strategy of attrition. In order to maximize American force capabilities and to make them less vulnerable to the NVA/VC attacks, the U.S. forces developed a system of *firebase.* Firebases constituted semipermanent, heavily fortified defensive bases that military units used for security and for launching offensive patrolling operations.

In addition, U.S. forces integrated new tactics involving helicopters, the workhorses of the Vietnam War, which rapidly moved U.S. and ARVN forces to distant battlefields in order to find and destroy the NVA/VC. American cavalry units used helicopters during one of the earliest and most significant battles against well-trained and well-equipped NVA units in the Vietnam War in October and November of 1965.

The valley of death: Battle for the Ia Drang

Before deploying to Vietnam, the 1st Cavalry Division trained in the U.S. using helicopters as their primary means of transportation. When they arrived in Vietnam, the 1st Cav was deployed inland to Pleiku, an area in the Central Highlands, in order to relieve pressure on American Special Forces units in the area who had been under attack since early 1965 as increasing numbers of NVA/VC moved into the area. The battle for the Ia Drang Valley started when the NVA 33rd and 66th Regiments attacked the American Special Forces Camp at Plei Me, just south of Pleiku. On November 14, the 7th Cavalry deployed to *LZ X-Ray* (Landing Zone X) using helicopters, and inadvertently landed in the middle of the 66th NVA Regiment base camp. *Landing zones* were usually predetermined cleared areas where helicopters could land and drop off or pick up troops and supplies.

Strike: Killing NVA at LZ X-Ray

During the next two days, elements of the U.S. 7th Cavalry fought against the 66th NVA Regiment, bringing in massive amounts of artillery fire and close air support (aircraft that fly slow and close to the ground and bomb or fire their weapons in close proximity to ground forces). The battle for LZ X-Ray ended when the NVA left the battlefield, having suffered more than 2,000 casualties compared to the American body count of 200. The battle at LZ X-Ray proved yet again the devastating capabilities of superior U.S. mobility and firepower. But the battle for the Ia Drang Valley didn't end there.

Counterstrike: Killing Americans at LZ Albany

The day after the battle at LZ X-Ray ended, the 2nd Battalion of the 7th Cavalry Regiment (2/7th) moved to a new landing zone, LZ Albany, approximately two miles north of LZ X-Ray. Unfortunately, the American commanders didn't realize that the 33rd NVA Regiment and the remaining elements of the embattled 66th NVA Regiment waited in ambush for just such a movement of U.S. forces. As the 2/7th arrived to the edge of the clearing of LZ Albany, the NVA opened fire and used machine gun and sniper fire to pin down the American force, killing or wounding nearly 280 Americans.

Talking in an alphabet soup: Acronyms in Vietnam

The language of war can be rather confusing. In Vietnam, the U.S. military developed strange acronyms and words that they used as a sort of shorthand to facilitate more rapid or accurate communication. At times, these were simple acronyms, where the first letter (or letters) in a string of words was used to more quickly communicate. Sometimes they stood for groups of people like VC (Viet Cong) or for individuals like COMU.S.MACV (Commander of United States Military Assistance Command in Vietnam — General William Westmoreland). Other times

they indicated locations, such as LZ, which stood for landing zone.

In addition to the acronyms, the military also used a phonetic alphabet system designed to increase accuracy in communication, especially over the radio. Soldiers would not say something like "LZ X" because over a radio it might sound like "LZ S" or even "LZ F", depending on the quality of radio transmission. Because the lives of men depended on the accuracy of the information provided, soldiers would say, "LZ X-Ray."

HISTORIC TRIVIA

Allies against communism: The Republic of Korea

Perhaps no U.S. or ARVN ally had as powerful and fearful a reputation as did the Republic of Korea or ROK forces (pronounced rock). Trained in the martial arts, especially tai kwon do, the ROK forces had a reputation for ruthlessness like no other army fighting in Vietnam. ROK forces remained highly active throughout the war, arriving in 1965, and primarily engaged in search-and-destroy operations, including Operations WHITEHORSE, BOONE, CRAZY HORSE, and RIO GRANDE, to name a few. They operated along the coast in I and II CTZ, and their TAOR (Tactical Area of Responsibility) was one of the few very secure areas in South Vietnam.

To achieve this high level of security, ROK forces followed a strict code of taking no prisoners, and rumors abounded during the Vietnam War that if a ROK unit received gunfire from a village, it would kill everyone and destroy the village. The ROK's apparent mercilessness even extended to their own. For example, if a ROK soldier fell asleep on guard duty, he would be severely beaten, if not summarily executed. It is difficult to say with certainty how much of this information concerning ROK cruelty and ruthlessness was truth and how much was propaganda. But according to some Americans who worked closely with ROK forces or entered areas after ROK forces left, the death and destruction left in their wake was nothing short of terrifying. The ROK left the same impression on surviving Vietnamese peasants who did all they could to avoid ROK soldiers and reported this to Americans. And even VC commanders cautioned their units to avoid the ROK forces unless absolutely certain of victory. The ROK sent both ground infantry and Marines to Vietnam, and at their peak, numbered 50,000. Over the course of the war, the Koreans lost 4,400 soldiers and the last of the ROK forces didn't leave until March 1973.

Lessons from the valley

The U.S. walked away from the battle of the Ia Drang Valley the clear victor in terms of the body count and the number of NVA/VC personnel killed and wounded. The 7th Cavalry proved that American air mobility and firepower, when properly employed, overwhelmed the NVA/VC advantages of sheer numbers. After the Ia Drang, the U.S. became convinced that the strategy of attrition would work and committed as many forces as possible to large unit operations that patrolled through areas in the hopes of finding and killing the NVA/VC as quickly as possible.

TECHNICAL STUFF

Although NVA suffered much heavier casualties, it left with a better appreciation of how to overcome the American strengths of mobility and firepower. The NVA realized that when they tried to stand toe-to-toe with American units, they risked being pummeled by artillery and close air fire support. The lesson it learned from Ia Drang resulted from the different outcomes at LZ X-Ray and LZ Albany. At X-Ray, U.S. forces could call in artillery and close air support because the NVA remained far enough away for the American units to safely utilize those firepower resources. The NVA learned from LZ Albany that if its troops stayed close enough to U.S. forces and surprised them, they could strike quickly, inflict heavy casualties, and close off American options for artillery and close air support (for fear of hitting the American units along with the NVA).

Major Operations in South Vietnam

With the decisions made to focus on attrition on one side and protracted warfare on the other, the ground war progressed, and each side tried to maximize the resultant combat engagements to their advantage. The next major American engagement occurred in January of 1966 and lasted until March. It started out as Operation MASHER and involved U.S., ARVN, and ROK (Republic of Korea) forces. Operation MASHER was a search-and-destroy operation designed to seek out and kill the NVA/VC units in and around the Bong Son Plain in Binh Dinh Province, South Vietnam.

Operation MASHER/WHITE WING

Shortly after it commenced, Operation MASHER was renamed Operation WHITE WING at the insistence of Washington officials because Operation MASHER didn't sound nice and wasn't consistent with the official rhetoric that the U.S. used in South Vietnam to help protect and build up that nation.

Regardless of the name, the operation lasted more than 40 days, and U.S. and ROK forces got their body count. The operation killed more than 2,100 NVA/VC, while the U.S. lost almost 230 killed and had nearly 800 wounded. While the operation proved yet again that U.S. firepower and mobility would allow U.S. and allied forces to kill more of the NVA/VC than they killed Americans or its allies, the battle was inconclusive in terms of the broader attrition strategy. The NVA/VC units showed a greater capacity to fight than they showed previously, and after the battle turned too heavily against them, they showed increased flexibility in withdrawing from the battle in an orderly fashion. This allowed the NVA/VC to save more of their forces to fight again on another day. More troublesome for the American strategy of attrition, the NVA and VC both showed an increased capacity to sustain heavy losses and replenish their numbers quickly enough in order to return their units to battle.

Operation ATTLEBORO

Similar search-and-destroy operations occurred as battalion-sized U.S. ground units (numbering from several hundred to almost a thousand personnel) throughout South Vietnam engaged in sweeps of areas, trying to find and destroy the NVA/VC. One such operation occurred in the fall of 1966 as U.S. ground forces searched for and eventually fought against a combined NVA/VC force in Tay Ninh, just northwest of Saigon. Although little fighting occurred during the first month of the operation, both sides more than made up for that lack of fighting during the first two weeks of November. Elements of the 196th Light Infantry Brigade made contact with staunch NVA/VC resistance near the Cambodian border. The fighting that ensued surprised the Americans, because the NVA/VC seemed determined to stand and fight rather then break contact and flee to sanctuaries across the border to Cambodia.

The NVA/VC had good reasons to stay and fight: After two weeks of fighting, the remaining NVA/VC forces finally withdrew on November 15 to Cambodia and left behind more than 1,100 men killed. When they secured the area, U.S. forces discovered one of the largest weapons caches captured up to that time, and it contained thousands of grenades, explosives, and Bangalore torpedoes. A *Bangalore torpedo* is a long cylindrical explosive mine that's used to get through barbed wire and other defensive barriers.

The U.S. losses totaled more than 150 killed, with nearly 500 wounded. As before, the kill ratio significantly favored the U.S. forces. Operation ATTLE-BORO, shown in Figure 5-4, showed that opportunities might still exist for American units to force NVA/VC units to stand and fight if U.S. forces could find NVA/VC in their base areas.

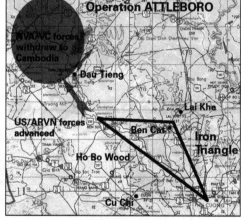

Figure 5-4:
South
Vietnam's
major battle
sites for
Operation
ATTLEBORO.

Map courtesy of the Vietnam Archive, Texas Tech University

Breaking the Iron Triangle: Operation CEDAR FALLS

The next opportunity to find and destroy NVA or VC units in an area they might have wanted to hold occurred two months after the completion of

Operation ATTLEBORO in an area north of Saigon called the *Iron Triangle*. A known VC stronghold and suspected headquarters for the VC operating in that part of South Vietnam, three Vietnamese villages — Phu Loi, Ben Suc, and Lai Khe — marked the corners of the triangle, which was just north of Cu Chi village, as shown in Figure 5-4.

Operation CEDAR FALLS, shown in Figure 5-5, involved both U.S. and ARVN ground forces as well as elements of the Vietnamese Navy Riverine forces and the collectively fought against two VC Regiments. General Westmoreland hoped that the VC units would stay and fight as they had during Operation ATTLEBORO, and that their staying to fight would enable U.S. and ARVN forces to pin them down and destroy them with superior firepower.

In terms of actual fighting, CEDAR FALLS turned out to be a disappointment, because the VC forces engaged only in small unit fighting; no major battles occurred. The operation lasted for 19 days and resulted in another tactical military victory for the U.S. and South Vietnam. The VC suffered nearly 1,000 soldiers killed or captured while the U.S. and ARVN losses numbered just over 400 killed or wounded. The VC units abandoned the area and went to Cambodia, while American and ARVN units swept through the area, where they found another cache of VC supplies that included rifles, machine guns, mortars, and more than 60,000 rounds of ammunition.

Perhaps more impressive than the cache of supplies was the massive complex of tunnels found and destroyed in the area. The VC constructed an impressive array of tunnels around Cu Chi that included storerooms, field hospitals, kitchens, sleeping areas, wells for drinking water, and everything the units needed to survive underground. During Operation CEDAR FALLS, U.S. and ARVN forces destroyed more than 500 tunnels but actually only made a dent in this immense underground system.

The U.S./ARVN victory in CEDAR FALLS also rang hollow because of political fallout that resulted from the operation. In order to effectively go through the Iron Triangle and destroy supply caches and tunnels, U.S. and ARVN troops forced the evacuation of almost 6,000 South Vietnamese villagers from Ben Suc to a refugee camp near Phu Loi. The U.S. and ARVN forces then destroyed the original village, including homes and farmland. The forced relocation of people and the destruction of peasant homes and farms created turmoil among the people of Vietnam as well as with the American public. Few people in Vietnam or in the U.S. could understand the logic of destroying a village in order to save it. More problematic for the ground war, most Vietnamese peasants enjoyed strong ancestral ties to their lands and homes, and many could trace their family lineage in these homes going back hundreds of years. The destruction of Vietnamese ancestral homes and lands created tremendous discontent among the refugees, and this ultimately added to the ranks of the Viet Cong. For more information about the refugee situation in South Vietnam, check out Chapter 12.

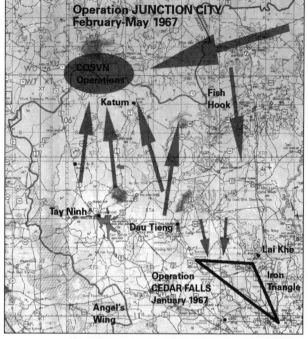

Figure 5-5:
Map of the
Iron Triangle
showing
Operations
CEDAR
FALLS and
JUNCTION
CITY.

Map courtesy of the Vietnam Archive, Texas Tech University

Giving sanctuary

One of the most difficult decisions made by the U.S. government during the Vietnam War was to limit how and where U.S. forces fought. This led to limits on the use of air power in North Vietnam, where bombers stayed away from dikes, other targets too close to or located within civilian population centers, and even some military or industrial targets (over concern of killing Soviets or Chinese and, thus, widening the war to include their nations and armies).

Another limitation more troublesome to the ground war involved the neutrality of Laos and Cambodia. Although the NVA/VC ignored such issues, the U.S. couldn't attack into either country

because of various treaties and promises. Rather than ignore American treaty obligations, the U.S. had to let the NVA/VC engage in battles near the border and then retreat across the border, where they were safe and could resupply and replenish their numbers. Although the situation angered both soldiers in Vietnam and policy makers in Washington, there was little they could do if the U.S. wanted to maintain the twin illusions that the U.S. didn't want to widen the war in Southeast Asia and that the U.S. was fighting for the right of a nation to self determine its government and alliances

Priming the JUNCTION CITY pump: Operation GADSDEN

As the NVA/VC continued to operate north of Saigon, this area remained a focus of military operations during the opening months of 1967. Immediately following Operation CEDAR FALLS, elements of the U.S. 4th and 25th Infantry Divisions, along with the 196th Light Infantry Brigade, engaged in a search-and-destroy operation in an attempt to try to track down the 9th VC Division. As an important prelude to the larger Operation JUNCTION CITY (discussed later in this chapter), Operation GADSDEN lasted for three weeks and netted an impressive cache of supplies that included not only typical ammunition and explosives but also nearly 400 tons of rice and a 100-gallon still (along with 2,000 gallons of mash). Apparently, the NVA/VC, much like their U.S./ARVN counterparts, needed to kick back and have an occasional drink.

U.S. forces also captured training facilities, including obstacle and land-navigation courses, as well as medical and weapons-producing facilities. The VC losses included 160 killed and 2 captured, and American losses included 29 killed and more than 107 wounded. Although not an impressive body count, the commander of U.S. forces for the operation reported in his after-action reports that the VC had been forced to abandon an important base area in order to reorganize. Unfortunately for the Americans preparing for Operation JUNCTION CITY, that VC reorganization didn't take long.

Operation JUNCTION CITY

Immediately following Operation GADSDEN, elements of the American 1st, 4th, 9th, and 25th Infantry Divisions, along with the 196th Light Infantry Brigade, 173rd Airborne Brigade, and 11th Armored Cavalry Regiment, joined forces with ARVN Rangers, Marines, and Cavalry to go back into the area near Tay Ninh to accomplish the following objectives:

✔ Search for and destroy the 9th Viet Cong Division

✔ Search for and destroy the 101st NVA Regiment

✔ Search for and destroy COSVN (the Central Office of South Vietnam)

✔ Establish an American Special Forces CIDG (Civilian Irregular Defense Group) camp

Operation JUNCTION CITY, shown in Figure 5-5, placed a heavy emphasis on search-and-destroy that reflected the level of American commitment to continuing the strategy of attrition. (See the "How perceptions affected American strategies and expectations" section, earlier in this chapter, for more information on attrition.)

HISTORIC TRIVIA

Operation JUNCTION CITY received a lot of public and media attention, not only because of its bold objectives but also because it featured the only American parachute assault during the entire Vietnam War.

The operation started on February 22, 1967 and continued until May. During the initial phases of the operation, the U.S. forces uncovered several large caches of supplies. And while American and ARVN met little resistance at first, by the end of February and early March, Americans started to come up against units of the 101st NVA and 272nd VC Regiments.

By mid-March, American commanders thought the area secure enough to begin construction of the U.S. Special Forces CIDG camp. While constructing and securing this camp, U.S. forces came under repeated attack by the NVA/VC forces in the area, including the 9th VC Division. All of the battles occurred at the instigation of the NVA/VC, usually at night while Americans were in temporary camps. Although the NVA/VC initiated these battles, they suffered heavily for it, usually because they didn't realize that most of the American units contained tank, armored, and artillery support. Using the artillery, American units could fire beehive rounds into the ranks of attacking NVA/VC. Each of these rounds contained 8,000 steel *fleshettes,* which were fin-stabilized darts that fanned out with a massive killing radius.

By the end of Operation JUNCTION CITY, the NVA/VC suffered tremendous losses, including more than 2,700 killed. But the U.S. forces also suffered high casualties: nearly 300 killed and almost 1,600 wounded. The Special Forces CIDG camp had been built, but the remnants of the 9th VC and 101st NVA made it out of the area and across the border into Cambodia where the sanctuary allowed them time to resupply and replenish their numbers. COSVN also escaped intact and continued to organize and direct some of the fighting in South Vietnam. Despite American superiority in firepower, mobility, and weapons technology, Operation JUNCTION CITY didn't accomplish the goals set by American military planners.

Operation THAYER II

Operations similar to CEDAR FALLS and JUNCTION CITY also occurred at the same time in other parts of South Vietnam. Further north in II CTZ, the American 1st Cavalry Division returned to Binh Dinh Province (see the "Operation MASHER/WHITE WING" section, earlier in this chapter) in February 1967 as part of Operation THAYER II, with a mission to *pacify* or subdue what was characterized as a densely populated area. This operation ultimately involved American and ARVN ground combat units who engaged in large search-and-destroy sweeps throughout the province, calling in rather large amounts of artillery and naval gunfire support, B-52 and fighter-bomber *sorties* (one plane flying one mission), and an abundance of *Napalm* (bombs containing jellied gasoline that spread out into a wave of flame on impact). The body count results were impressive for the American side: U.S. forces killed more than 1,700 VC. U.S. forces also dislocated more than 17,000 Vietnamese peasants, who relocated to refugee camps and whose homes and farms were destroyed. The question remained as to whether such tactics served the American policy goals in Vietnam of creating a political and social climate conducive to fending off communism.

Fighting in the hills of Khe Sanh

More fighting occurred even farther north in Khe Sanh, a remote base near the DMZ (the buffer zone between North and South Vietnam where neither country was supposed to have military forces). U.S. Marines had been in and out of Khe Sanh since 1964 but always with reluctance because it was remote and difficult to defend or support. A strategically significant piece of terrain, Khe Sanh sat on one of the highest points in the northern part of South Vietnam, and whomever owned Khe Sanh could easily watch the HCM trail and road network coming from North Vietnam, through Laos, and into South Vietnam. In addition, General Westmoreland hoped that President Johnson and Secretary McNamara would ultimately approve his plan to launch offensive ground operations from Khe Sanh into Laos and North Vietnam, cutting off the HCM Trail. Approval for that plan never came.

The U.S. Marines went to Khe Sanh only when ordered to by General Westmoreland and usually didn't stay long. Because of its strategic significance, Westmoreland ordered the creation of a Special Forces camp near Khe Sanh in order to collect intelligence and monitor traffic down the HCM Trail. If the U.S. couldn't launch offensive ground combat operations from there, at least they could use Khe Sanh to collect intelligence, including *passive patrolling* (patrols designed to avoid fighting) and *radio interception* (the use of radio equipment to listen in on NVA/VC personnel talking over two-way radios).

At one point in July 1964, the Marines came under heavy attack and left Khe Sanh, only to return in 1966. At that time, the Marines repeatedly patrolled the area but made no contact with either VC or NVA units and left again. But in the fall of 1966, General Westmoreland ordered the Marines back to establish a base at Khe Sanh and engage in *active patrolling* (patrols designed to engage in fighting) near the DMZ and Laos to gather intelligence on NVA/VC movements. The Special Forces camp moved south to Lang Vei and, after creating a base, patrolling for five months, and making no contact, the Marines left a small force and removed the bulk of their forces from Khe Sanh again.

Two months later, the remaining Maine Company made contact with the 325th NVA Division, which triggered fighting in the hills around Khe Sanh that initially lasted from April to May of 1967. The fighting centered on Hills 861 and 881(for additional information on hill numbers, see Chapter 6) and focused on the NVA strongholds. The Marines sent reinforcements, and requested close air support and B52 bombers, all of which forced the NVA to withdraw first from Hill 861 and then from Hill 881.

Allies against communism: The Australians

Of the nations that also participated in Vietnam in the war against communism, Australia and New Zealand also provided significant assistance during the war, including Navy destroyers and aircraft carriers, Special Operations personnel, Air Force personnel, and regular ground combat units. Australian and New Zealand forces participated in a variety of missions and operations, including naval interdiction and riverine operations, search-and-destroy missions (Operations ABILENE, DARLINGHURST, and DARWIN), pacification and refugee relocation (Operations AINSLEE and MAILED FIST), and operations that attempted to deny the NVA/VC access to certain resources, especially rice and other food (Operation FORREST).

Troops from Australia and New Zealand served in Vietnam from 1962 until December 1972 and although they participated in many of the more conventional operations, they focused more attention on counterinsurgency and pacifying the civilian population (see Chapter 4 for information on counterinsurgency). During the course of that decade, more than 50,000 troops came from "down under" to help their allies in South Vietnam. By April 1966, the Australian and New Zealand forces in Vietnam established a Task Force and became responsible for security in Phuoc Tuy Province to the northeast of Saigon. While Australians and New Zealanders concentrated on Phuoc Tuy, advisors from those two countries served throughout South Vietnam.

The Marines won and prevented the NVA from overrunning the U.S. base at Khe Sanh. The battles also resulted in a heavy body count, including 940 NVA killed. The U.S. Marines lost 155 killed, and 425 were wounded. The battle also proved that the North Vietnamese shared General Westmoreland's assessment of the strategic importance of the area. The question remained: Did the initial defeat of NVA in April and May of 1967 mean they had given up hope of controlling Khe Sanh? The U.S. Marines based there didn't have long to wait for a response (see the "Laying siege to marines: The Khe Sanh hill fights, part II" section, later in this chapter).

Progressing toward victory: More operations in 1967

Throughout the remainder of 1967, the U.S. and its allies continued to engage and try to kill off the NVA/VC units throughout South Vietnam. To name a select few, these operations included the following:

- **May 1967, Operation AHINA:** U.S. 4th and 9th Infantry Divisions conducted more offensive operations to destroy NVA/VC forces and installations in War Zone C near Tay Ninh, north of Saigon.

- **June 1967, Operation ADAIR:** U.S. 5th Marine operation was designed to destroy VC forces in Quang Tin Province.

✔ **July 1967, Operation HICKORY II:** U.S. 9th Marine operations in Quang Tri province attempted to destroy NVA forces and fortifications near the DMZ.

✔ **August 1967, Operation AKRON II:** U.S. 9th Infantry Division operation was designed to disrupt enemy activity in the area just east of Saigon in Long Khanh Province.

✔ **September 1967, Operation ARKANSAS CITY:** U.S. 11th Armored Cavalry Regiment operation set out to destroy VC units in Phuoc Tuy Province, just east of Saigon.

✔ **October 1967, Operation CORONADO VI:** U.S. 9th Infantry Division operation attempted to destroy VC forces operating in the Rung Sat Special Zone near Saigon.

✔ **November 1967, Operation LANCASTER I:** U.S. 1st, 3rd, and 9th Marines operation set out to destroy NVA/VC units operating in Quang Tri Province of I CTZ.

✔ **December 1967, Operation SARATOGA:** U.S. 25th Infantry Division operations in the provinces north of Saigon along the Cambodian Border were supposed to destroy NVA/VC units and the COSVN.

The primary emphasis for these operations remained the same throughout most of 1967. The strategic and tactical focus, although at times dressed up as pacification, usually involved search-and-destroy operations, large unit sweeps, civilian population relocation, and very heavy doses of firepower. At times, these operations netted significant body counts, as with Operation SARATOGA, which resulted in nearly 4,000 NVA/VC killed. But events outside of Vietnam near the end of 1967 and events in Vietnam in early 1968 proved much more powerful in affecting the outcome of the war than any of these various operations. As an indication, the NVA/VC launched a major offensive in September and October 1967, which is discussed in the following section.

Predicting the future: The siege of Con Thien

The DMZ remained a hotly contested area throughout the war, because the NVA/VC wanted to control and use it for the movement of troops and supplies south and the U.S. wanted to control and use it to monitor NVA/VC activity and interdict every movement. Reminding the U.S. of the strategic importance of the area, the NVA/VC attacked the Marine base at Con Thien, just miles from the DMZ in September 1967. The NVA used heavy artillery and well-constructed fortifications from which to launch several attacks, none of which succeeded. The U.S. Marines repelled all of them with the assistance of U.S. artillery, close air, bomber, and naval gunfire support.

The siege lasted until October and resulted in heavy NVA casualties. It proved once again that a smaller U.S. force could withstand a larger NVA/VC ground assault through the judicious use of supporting artillery, air, and naval gunfire support. But it also proved that the NVA could continue to maintain its forces in the field and held the *tactical initiative,* that is, they could decide when and where to engage U.S. and ARVN forces. And despite the heavy losses, the NVA/VC consistently showed it could replenish its numbers and fight again. As 1967 drew to a close, the U.S. strategy of attrition didn't appear to be working.

The Politics of War: The Difficulty of Creating and Maintaining Consensus

The events in the fall of 1967 proved more significant than anyone at the time could realize. The U.S. forces patrolling and sweeping Vietnam proved time and again that when the NVA/VC stood and fought against American units, the NVA/VC troops left the battlefield beaten, usually having sustained many more casualties than they inflicted on the American units. To General Westmoreland in Vietnam and Johnson and others back in Washington, these casualties meant the strategy of attrition was working. And in November of 1967, it was time to reinforce this message of U.S. success to the American people.

They served, too: Women at war

Women participated in the Vietnam War in a number of ways. Vietnamese women served in all capacities in North and South Vietnam, to include some women in the NVA/VC serving as active combatants. Women from Australia and New Zealand served in non-combat capacities, serving as nurses and working in orphanages. American women served in the U.S. military branches but were not allowed to serve in combat roles. They worked in communications, transportation, logistics (supply system), hospitals, military intelligence, engineering, administration, entertainment, and many other areas.

Of the almost 7,500 American women who served in Southeast Asia, it is estimated that more 80 percent served as nurses in hospitals in Thailand and Vietnam. American women also served as civilians working for various U.S. government agencies to include the Department of Defense, Department of State, Central Intelligence Agency, and others. They served as administrators, supervisors, clerks, and in many other capacities as well. American women worked as civilians for the U.S. military creating and running various clubs and they helped establish and administer a library system used by American personnel throughout South Vietnam. American women also volunteered to work with the American Red Cross and they served as "Donut Dollies" throughout Southeast Asia, engaging in recreational activities and visiting with soldiers, building up the morale of U.S. personnel.

Robert S. McNamara:
A "strange" secretary of defense

Robert Strange McNamara was one of the most controversial people involved with the Vietnam War. He served in WWII as part of the American strategic bomber planning command, defining targets for American bomber runs in Europe.

After World War II, McNamara left the service and eventually entered business, where he rose to one of the most prestigious positions in industry: chief executive officer of Ford Motor Company. McNamara was the first man to hold that position who didn't have "Ford" as a last name. He built up Ford by utilizing quantification theory and statistical analysis, identifying problems in production and supply, and further streamlining the processes of manufacturing. Without a doubt, his business acumen made him one of the most effective CEOs in the U.S.

When President Kennedy entered office in 1961, he sought out the best and the brightest of American society, including Robert McNamara. Kennedy asked McNamara to take over the Defense Department in the hopes that McNamara would bring his considerable business skills to the defense procurement system to make it as cost effective and efficient as possible. In large part, McNamara succeeded in accomplishing these peacetime goals, but it remained to be seen whether these same business skills that served so well in defense procurement would also work in running a war. McNamara continues to remain controversial: He has written two books about his service during the Vietnam War, both of which have continued to stir emotions and debates regarding the Vietnam War. To give you an example, McNamara makes some startling admissions in his book, *In Retrospect,* where he states early in the war he had serious doubts whether the U.S. could actually win.

But convincing the American people was difficult when certain members of Johnson's cabinet didn't believe in the U.S. strategy in South Vietnam. President Johnson and other officials in Washington realized that one of the chief problems they faced was maintaining popular American support for the war in Vietnam. (The sensitivity of this subject and Johnson's rejection of a public debate on Vietnam is discussed in Chapter 2.) But Johnson and most of his advisors thought that as long as they could provide proof that the U.S. made consistent progress in the war, Americans would find it easier to continue supporting it. But by late 1967, two principal camps emerged in the White House: the optimists and the naysayers.

The optimists: America is winning, really!

General Westmoreland was one of the more guarded of the optimists, but he felt confident that the U.S. was winning and would ultimately achieve its goals in Vietnam. He still held out hope that the various restrictions on U.S.

operations in Southeast Asia would be lifted and that he would get additional U.S. troops into Vietnam, but even without them, Westmoreland estimated that the U.S. could win in Vietnam within two years and could then begin removing its forces, letting the ARVN take care of any small skirmishes that might occur thereafter. This was the light at the end of the tunnel.

At the same time, Westmoreland cautioned against any pauses in bombing North Vietnam, stating that the U.S. must maintain the pressure created by bombing to meet the two-year deadline. President Johnson and National Security Advisor Walt Rostow felt buoyed by Westmoreland's uplifting and positive appraisal of the situation.

Losing the faith: Strange naysayers emerge

Perhaps the strangest of the naysayers to emerge was Defense Secretary Robert McNamara. Although he was an early supporter of bombing North Vietnam and introducing American ground forces, by November 1967, McNamara had joined a group of presidential advisors calling for the stabilization of U.S. forces in Vietnam with no expansion of the forces. In addition, McNamara advocated a halt to the bombing campaign in North Vietnam and pushed for a negotiated settlement with North Vietnam to end the war and reduce the American military presence.

McGeorge Bundy, Special Advisor to Johnson, joined McNamara in calling for the stabilization of American troop deployments to Vietnam. But the men disagreed over the bombing issue, and Bundy thought that the U.S. should keep up the pressure in order to negotiate with Vietnam from a position of strength. If nothing else, Bundy believed that bombing would continue to erode the North Vietnamese military and industrial base. Bundy also criticized the preoccupation and heavy emphasis placed on using statistics to demonstrate progress to the American people. In his words, "We have tried too hard to convert public opinion by statistics . . . I have to say also that I think public discontent with the war is now wide and deep."

McNamara and Bundy were joined by the only consistent voice of criticism regarding American military involvement in South Vietnam, that of George Ball. As mentioned in Chapter 4, Ball tried to convince President Kennedy not to increase the American military presence in Vietnam, and he continued to counsel against such action when Johnson became president. As with Kennedy, Ball's cautions that the American people couldn't long sustain the war in Vietnam fell on Johnson's deaf ears. In the end — and of little consolation — Ball's position proved correct, and an important event that brought about the decline of American support occurred in November 1967.

Counting bodies

With his appetite for quantification and analyzing statistics, numbers, and the bottom line, Defense Secretary Robert S. McNamara tackled the Vietnam War much as he would have any corporate business problem. McNamara worked with General William Westmoreland, Commander of U.S. forces in Vietnam, and they both closely monitored the NVA/VC body count in Vietnam. Both men pushed to keep these numbers rolling in and rolling in high. They agreed with the strategy of attrition, believing that the NVA/VC could fight only for so long and sustain only so many casualties until they would have to give up.

Unfortunately, the body count became a highly unreliable indicator of progress in the war. Many counts included duplicate counts and estimates, and some field commanders were pushed into either providing high body counts or receiving a low performance evaluation. In Vietnam, if a U.S. commander had any hopes of a military career, he had to produce high NVA/VC body counts in his reports. As a result,

many commanders inflated the numbers of enemy killed during their operations, sometimes counting any dead Vietnamese person regardless of age, sex, uniform, or equipment, which made the body count a meaningless statistic. Regardless, Westmoreland and McNamara both used the body count to prove that the U.S. was winning in Vietnam.

In fact, body counts and kill ratios became two of the primary tools of the daily military press briefings, dubbed the *five o'clock follies,* sending the message to the American people that the U.S. killed many more of the NVA/VC than the NVA/VC killed Americans. That constantly reinforced message came back to haunt Westmoreland, McNamara, and Johnson when it became clear that, despite the happy numbers, the NVA/VC could still launch major offensive operations throughout South Vietnam. The body count wasn't the only attempt of the U.S. to quantify victory in Vietnam. See Chapter 12 for a discussion of how they distorted numbers using the Hamlet Evaluation System (HES).

The glowing assessment that lights the fuse: Westmoreland briefs Congress

General Westmoreland returned to the U.S. on occasion to brief Johnson, Johnson's staff, and the Joint Chiefs on progress in the war in Vietnam. Westmoreland made just such a trip in November 1967 and in addition to his typical briefs, was asked to present a report to a Joint Session of Congress, a first for a serving battlefield commander. In his message to Congress and the American people, Westmoreland spoke cautiously of American success, telling Americans that while progress had been made in the fight against communism, the continued support of the public was the lynchpin of American success.

When combined with his various press briefings and other reports in November, Americans came away with the impression that the U.S. forces were winning and would win, probably sooner rather than later.

Westmoreland's visit to and briefings in the U.S. have been likened to his saying that there is a light at the end of the tunnel, meaning the end of the war was in sight. Or perhaps it was an oncoming train!

The Train in the Tunnel: The Tet Offensives of 1968

The *Tet holiday* is revered in Vietnamese society as a series of days to visit with and enjoy family and friends. It has also been a time of great victories over previous foreign invaders in Vietnam. Almost every year during the war, a Tet cease-fire was called and broken. So what made Tet of 1968 so different? First was the extent of the attack. Most people in South Vietnam expected something to happen, but few expected the massive and coordinated NVA/VC assaults that took place.

On January 31, 1968, more then 80,000 NVA/VC soldiers launched the Tet Offensives and simultaneously attacked more than 150 hamlets, district capitals, provincial capitals, and autonomous cities. They attacked Saigon and the old Imperial capital at Hue. While they attacked throughout the country, the NVA/VC hoped and expected that the people of South Vietnam would rise up and join them in overthrowing the government of South Vietnam along with (in their words) their puppet-masters, the Americans. The uprising never happened, leaving the NVA/VC at the mercy of superior American and ARVN firepower and mobility.

Fighting in the streets: The battle for Saigon

The fighting in Saigon was intense because the NVA/VC concentrated a significant force there in the hope of capturing the city and ending the war. The American Embassy even came under serious threat when a group of VC soldiers attacked into the compound. VC *Sappers* (personnel who infiltrated the defensive perimeter and threw explosives into bunkers or buildings) killed U.S. Marines and MPs guarding the embassy, but the VC couldn't hold up against the American reinforcements sent in to secure the facility and were eventually all killed. Although the NVA/VC enjoyed some initial successes in Saigon and elsewhere, U.S. and ARVN forces quickly rallied and began turning them back until the hoped-for general uprising turned into a devastating defeat. As more American and ARVN forces entered Saigon and counterattacked, they had to engage the remnants of the NVA/VC in house-to-house street fighting. By the first week of February, the ARVN assumed responsibility for the remaining operations to clean up Saigon.

Searching for a moral victory: The battle for Hue

The city of Hue is the former Imperial capital of Vietnam, and the fighting there reached an intensity and ferocity not closely matched anywhere else during the Tet fighting. The battle for Hue lasted 25 days and, unlike most of the other city battles, resulted in NVA control over much of the city. The city had been previously off limits to U.S. soldiers, which meant that soldiers were not already in the area, so Americans had to be brought in to help defend the city and help push the NVA out.

The fighting for Hue lasted until March when elements of the U.S. 1st Cavalry and 101st Airborne Division, 1st and 5th Marine Regiments, and numerous ARVN units finally forced the NVA/VC out of the city. All sides suffered heavy losses. The NVA lost 5,000 soldiers and had nearly 100 captured. The ARVN suffered more then 380 dead with nearly 2,000 wounded. 210 Americans died and 1,360 were wounded. Hue itself suffered heavy damage as the battles destroyed and damaged nearly half the city.

The most surprising losses, however, didn't occur among the fighting soldiers or in the razed buildings. Americans and South Vietnamese later discovered that, upon entering the city, NVA/VC leaders rounded up South Vietnamese teachers and government officials and killed them. In what became known as the *Hue Massacre,* the NVA/VC murdered nearly 3,000 residents of Hue and buried them in a mass grave in the jungle outside the city.

Unfortunately, such horrific atrocities were not limited to Hue. Two weeks after the battle for Hue ended, U.S. forces committed what has become the most publicized, talked about, and politicized atrocity of the Vietnam War, the My Lai Massacre which is discussed briefly in Chapter 16.

Laying siege to marines: The Khe Sanh hill fights, part II

While the fighting in Saigon started and ended rather quickly, the longest battle of the Tet Offensive occurred in the mountains overlooking the HCM Trail near Khe Sanh (see Figure 5-6). Although the initial hill fights had ended in May of 1967 (see the "Things to come: Fighting in the hills of Khe Sanh" section, earlier in this chapter), the NVA/VC hadn't given up hope that they could deliver a devastating blow to the American effort by overrunning and capturing the U.S. base at Khe Sanh. During the intervening months, from May 1967 until January 1968, the NVA/VC built up their forces and supplies and prepared for a massive siege to capture this mountain outpost.

The fighting and subsequent siege began on January 21, a little more than a week before the Tet Offensive began. General Vo Nguyen Giap, the North Vietnamese strategist who planned the attack on Khe Sanh and much of the Tet Offensive, hoped, along with the rest of North Vietnam, to accomplish several goals:

- ✔ The NVA wanted to draw American and ARVN forces from the cities in preparation for the Tet Offensive.

- ✔ If a general uprising did occur during Tet, those U.S. and ARVN forces would be forced to redeploy back to the cities in order to repel the many attacks throughout South Vietnam.

- ✔ At Khe Sanh, either the U.S. would have to start withdrawing or the remaining NVA/VC forces would be better able to overrun the base camp absent the American and ARVN reinforcements who would have left to protect the cities during Tet.

In this way, Giap and other North Vietnamese strategists hoped to repeat at Khe Sanh what they had accomplished Dien Bien Phu in 1954, the decisive battle that defeated the French and effectively ended the French Indochina War (see Chapters 2 and 3). The analogy between the two battles was apparent to Americans and at the outset of the battle for Khe Sanh, Johnson himself is quoted as saying, "I don't want any damn 'Dien Bien Phu!'"

Fortunately for Johnson, Giap and the North Vietnamese overestimated the likelihood of a general uprising among the South Vietnamese people and underestimated the ability of the U.S. and ARVN forces to deploy and redeploy as necessary to deal with all of the threats of Tet and still maintain a strong enough presence at Khe Sanh to protect and outlast the siege.

The NVA/VC massed 40,000 troops in the hills of Khe Sanh in preparation for the siege and attacks. For their part, the U.S. Marines reinforced the Khe Sanh garrison with more than 5,000 Marines of the 26th Marine Regiment. As the battle and siege continued during January, February, and March, the U.S. and ARVN tried to reinforce the U.S. Marine garrison and brought in massive amounts of artillery, close air, and naval gunfire support. The U.S. Marines also received enough ammunition, food, and other essential materials through aerial resupply to help them outlast the siege.

During the siege, the NVA bombarded the Marine base with artillery, mortars, and rocket fire and early in the process detonated much of the fuel depot and ammunition dump. They dug trenches and tried at one point to launch a ground assault, but the U.S. Marines repulsed the attacks. In addition to attacks on Khe Sanh, NVA forces also attacked and overran the Special Forces camp at Lang Vei, just south of Khe Sanh.

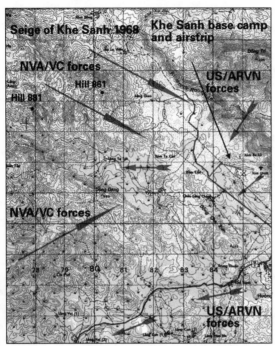

Figure 5-6:
Khe Sanh.

The siege of Khe Sanh ended on April 8 after the 1st Cavalry Division reopened Route 9 and made contact with the Marines at Khe Sanh. Both sides suffered significant casualties: U.S. forces lost nearly 300 soldiers, more than 1,400 wounded; estimates show that the NVA lost somewhere between 10,000 and 15,000 soldiers. By April, the siege of Khe Sanh and the Tet Offensive officially ended but the aftershocks resonated for months, even years.

Fighting a Mini-Tet: Dai Do and Kham Duc

Although the NVA/VC suffered heavy losses during Tet and the Khe Sanh fighting, they pressed on with several other battle plans in the spring of 1968 in what was called *Mini-Tet*. During the months of April and May, remaining NVA/VC units attacked again into more than 100 cities and military installations. The fighting eventually centered on the U.S. Marine base at Dong Ha near the DMZ (also near Dai Do) and the U.S. Special Forces camp at Kham Duc, which was farther south in I CTZ. Figure 5-6 shows this.

At Dai Do, U.S. Marine, Navy Riverine, and Army forces spoiled the NVA attack to take over Dai Do and Dong Ha. The situation at Kham Duc, however, became desperate when the base was cut off with no roads or other means of reinforcement except by air. To cut the losses there, Kham Duc had to be evacuated, which occurred successfully in May. Although the NVA suffered heavy losses again, they had successfully gained control over an important surveillance camp near the Laotian border.

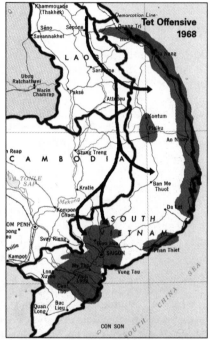

Figure 5-7:
Tet
Offensive.

Map courtesy of the Vietnam Archive, Texas Tech University

The Tet Offensives of 1968: And the winners are . . .

Without a doubt, the U.S. and, shown in Figure 5-7, ARVN forces won the various battles involved with the 1968 Tet Offensives and repelled every attack except those on Lang Vei and Kham Duc. The NVA/VC lost more than 45,000 men and had nearly 1,000 captured. But the real surprise of Tet 1968 had nothing to do with the attacks throughout the cities, the siege of Khe Sanh, Mini-Tet, or even the horrific casualties suffered by soldiers and civilians on all sides.

What no one foresaw was what became two of the most significant casualties of the Vietnam War:

✔ The trust and faith of the American people in their government, also known as the *credibility gap,* as certain public officials lost their credibility with the American people because it appeared they had been lying about progress in the war.

✔ The political and moral will of President Lyndon Johnson to continue fighting in Vietnam. On March 31, Johnson announced a halt to the bombing of North Vietnam north of the 19th parallel, and he told the world that he would not accept the nomination to run for reelection. Johnson no longer wanted to be president of the U.S.

This was so important because until 1968, the majority of Americans supported the war and believed what the U.S. government told them regarding the war. Today, Americans looking back on the events, remark about how they lost faith in the government when Tet 1968 occurred and it appeared the government had been lying to them about progress in the war.

Johnson's decision not to seek reelection was so important because the will of the American people flowed from and through the president, making him the symbolic embodiment of U.S. national will. When Johnson lost faith and gave up, it became difficult for many Americans to continue supporting a war the president no longer supported. Tet 1968 ultimately proved that the communist strategy of a protracted war designed to drain the will of the American people was a much better approach than was the U.S. strategy of attrition.

Perhaps the greatest irony of the situation was that the U.S. and ARVN forces succeeded in destroying most of the remaining Viet Cong during Tet. (What remained of the VC came under direct attack with the Phoenix Program, which is discussed in Chapter 12.) This meant that after Tet, the NVA had to take over nearly all of the fighting in South Vietnam. As a result, the U.S. and ARVN forces could put a more concerted effort behind fighting NVA units and building up South Vietnamese political, military, and social institutions. But American attitudes toward the war shifted remarkably after Tet, so the gains that the military netted during Tet 1968 were lost on their long trip across the Pacific to the U.S.

After that presidential announcement of March, the American people continued for a time to support their men and women in Vietnam, to continue the draft, and to continue sending U.S. military replacements into Vietnam. But now the U.S. looked for a leader who could help them get out of Vietnam, but with victory, not defeat — or at least the appearance of victory. The person for that job is the subject of Chapter 6.

Chapter 6

Nixon's Victory in Vietnam: A Peace with Honor?

*W*hen he arrived at the White House in January of 1969, President Richard Nixon faced serious difficulties at home and abroad. Following the 1968 Tet Offensive, which is discussed in detail in Chapter 5, the American press and American people grew increasingly impatient with the war. Student protests intensified, and major leaders throughout the United States questioned American efforts in Southeast Asia. The Viet Cong had been largely destroyed in the many city battles that occurred throughout South Vietnam during the Tet Offensive, but the North Vietnamese had shown strength in the aftermath of the offensive, laying siege to Khe Sanh for six months and attacking other American and South Vietnamese bases along borders with Laos and Cambodia.

Further complicating matters for President Nixon was the lack of progress in peace talks that began under President Lyndon B. Johnson. Problems emerged because the South Vietnamese government refused to grant the Viet Cong (VC) equal representation at the peace negotiations. This dilemma was partly Nixon's own doing because his representatives convinced the South Vietnamese to stall the peace talks until he became president, hinting that they would get a better deal under his administration. Although President Nixon continued the peace talks in Paris when he took office in early 1969, no easy diplomatic or military solutions appeared likely to bring about an acceptable peace.

Giving It the Old College Try: Nixon's Plans to End the War — 1969

Despite enduring myths to the contrary, President Nixon didn't run for president in 1968 on a platform that he had a "secret plan" to end the war. True, his election platform emphasized, _ending the war and winning the peace in Vietnam,_ but his initial plans centered on international diplomacy — and a mind-game or two.

Dick Nixon: Sailor, Congressman, Statesman

Born in California in 1913, Richard Milhous Nixon became the 37th President of the United States in 1969. After graduating from Duke University Law School, he served in World War II in the Pacific Theater as a lieutenant commander in the U.S. Navy. After WWII, Nixon entered Republican Party politics and was elected to California's 12th district seat in the U.S. House of Representatives.

In 1950, Nixon won one of his state's seats in the U.S. Senate. During this period of his political career, Nixon made a name for himself as a _red hunter,_ an anticommunist, and he became visible during investigations of Alger Hiss and other alleged communists accused of espionage while working within the U.S. government. (They were alleged to have been spying for the Soviets.) Nixon served as vice president for President Dwight Eisenhower from 1953 through 1960, but lost the presidential election of 1960 to the youthful and charismatic John F. Kennedy. Remaining active in politics during the intervening years, Nixon won the Republican nomination and was elected president in 1968. Although he was considered brilliant and successful in many respects, Nixon's legacy consistently has been tainted by the Watergate scandal and other questionable activities during his two terms as president.

Undermining support for North Vietnam

Nixon intended to bring pressure on the North Vietnamese by convincing their two main supporters, the Soviet Union and the Peoples Republic of China (PRC), to stop sending weapons and supplies to North Vietnam. Nixon figured that, without the support of the superpowers, the North Vietnamese would be more likely to make compromises at the peace negotiations.

Using a tactic know as *triangular diplomacy* (playing one country against the other) to accomplish his goal, Nixon met and talked separately with the leaders of the Soviet Union and the PRC, thinking his diplomatic activities would work because a competitive atmosphere existed (and even border disputes had occurred) between the two nations.

Eventually, Nixon made great strides in restoring relations between the United States and the Soviet Union and the United States and PRC, at the expense of a separate harmony between the other two. However, his triangular diplomacy failed to end the support provided by the Soviet Union and PRC for North Vietnam. So, Nixon moved on to plan number two, which he called "the Madman Theory."

Driving MADman

Before becoming president, Nixon made a name for himself as one of the most resolute and extreme anticommunists in the United States. He figured that his reputation as a fanatical anticommunist would convince the North Vietnamese that, if they did not agree to an acceptable peace agreement quickly, he might use nuclear weapons against them. President Eisenhower used a similar threat in 1953 to stop the Korean War. The idea may have worked for Ike, but it didn't do anything for Dick.

The problem with Nixon's concept was that ideas about using nuclear weapons had changed a great deal between 1953 and 1969. Sure, everyone knew they were horrible and every (rational) person was scared to death of them, but Americans stopped viewing their use as a real military option. Why? Because the United States wasn't the only country with nuclear weapons anymore. The Soviet Union had them, too.

And the twin theories of Massive Retaliation and Mutually Assured Destruction were born:

- **Massive Retaliation:** Use of a nuclear weapon by one country would trigger massive retaliatory strikes from other countries with nuclear capabilities.

- **Mutually Assured Destruction (MAD):** With nuclear weapons going off like firecrackers, everyone and everything would be destroyed.

With no realistic diplomatic solution to leverage his desired peace with honor, Nixon reluctantly turned to conventional military options. The first step was convincing the North Vietnamese that he meant business, and that meant escalating the war.

Expanding the war to end the war

Earlier attempts by President Johnson and General William C. Westmoreland to escalate the war didn't erode North Vietnam's materiel-support base and the attrition strategy had not killed enough NVA/VC to have much of an effect on North Vietnam's ability to continue the fight. See Chapter 5 for more information on these attempts. Nixon wanted to find out why, so he consulted his policy team. They all agreed that a major part of the problem had been Laotian and Cambodian neutrality.

Laos and Cambodia claimed to be neutral and didn't want to fight. Likewise, they didn't want others fighting within their borders. This policy effectively kept the U.S. military out of those countries (officially, at least, because the CIA fought a secret war in Laos that is discussed in Chapter 13), but it didn't hinder the North Vietnamese or the Viet Cong from using border areas for their own purposes to include supply routes and as safe havens or base camps that would not come under attack.

As a result, Nixon decided to expand the American overt conventional war already underway in North and South Vietnam into Cambodia and Laos, hoping to stop the North Vietnamese and Viet Cong (NVA/VC) from launching their assaults on South Vietnam from bases in those countries.

Fighting in Laos and Cambodia: A Belated Welcome to the Party

Because Laos and Cambodia officially declared their neutrality, the official American policy was to respect that neutrality. As a result, from 1965 to 1969, overt American military operations in Laos and Cambodia were heavily restricted. The United States couldn't openly send troops into either country. Unofficially (and even during the 1965 to 1969 timeframe), however, the U.S. Central Intelligence Agency (CIA) had been waging a secret or *covert war* in Laos since 1952, the details of which are discussed in Chapter 13.

But the same restrictions didn't apply to the NVA/VC. They traveled freely and extensively through Laos and Cambodia, and used bases there for supplying troops, launching operations into South Vietnam, and as sanctuary (see Figure 2-1). NVA/VC forces attacked American and South Vietnamese forces and then ran across the border into Laos or Cambodia where they knew they wouldn't be followed.

In March 1969, President Nixon, seeing no other options available to him and not wanting to be the first American president to lose a war, expanded the war into Cambodia and Laos.

Figure 6-1:
The principal areas used by the NVA/VC for supply routes, base camps, and sanctuary in Laos and Cambodia.

Map courtesy of the Vietnam Archive, Texas Tech University

Expanding the air war in Cambodia: Operation MENU

In early 1969, Nixon received reports that the NVA/VC were building up forces in Cambodia that were preparing to launch attacks into South Vietnam. In order to counter those attacks, he authorized Operation MENU, in which the United States launched airstrikes against communist bases in Cambodia. These raids had to be kept a secret because:

✔ The official position of the United States was to respect Cambodian neutrality.

✔ Nixon didn't want to add fuel to antiwar sentiment at home. He feared that Americans would perceive bombing raids as an escalation of the war when they were expecting more movement toward peace.

With no ground forces entering Cambodia, bombing raids didn't have much lasting effect on the North Vietnamese operations there. See Chapter 9 for more information about Operation MENU.

Supporting the ground war in Laos: Operation APACHE SNOW

Although Operation MENU was intended to hinder communist use of Cambodia, the North Vietnamese continued moving men and supplies through Laos and into South Vietnam.

The NVA/VC continued attacking South Vietnam and the A Shau Valley. They had also expanded the Ho Chi Minh Trail, the major road network that allowed rapid movement of troops and materials into the region.

These NVA forces threatened U.S./ARVN forces in the area. They also threatened the major South Vietnamese city of Hue (which the NVA temporarily had occupied during Tet in early 1968; see Chapter 5 for more information on that offensive). To push the North Vietnamese out of the A Shau Valley, the United States launched Operation APACHE SNOW in May 1969.

The purpose of Operation APACHE SNOW was twofold:

- To keep pressure on the North Vietnamese units and base camps in the A Shau Valley
- To disrupt and destroy enemy units, thus preventing attacks on the coastal provinces

A hill by any other name . . .

American forces deployed throughout Southeast Asia used a specific kind of map called a *topo* or topographical map. Unlike most road maps, topo maps have terrain features on them, meaning you can identify such things as hills and valleys.

Going up hills or down into valleys is indicated by a series of swirling lines called contour lines (see Figure 6-2). Hilltops are indicated by the smallest circle within many rings of contour lines or *circles*. The highest point of elevation on any hilltop is indicated in meters by a number on the map, such as 937, meaning the highest point on the hill is 937 meters above sea level.

Because most Americans in Vietnam didn't speak or read Vietnamese, they referred to these hills by these numbers instead of the names they could not read or speak. So, although Operation APACHE SNOW occurred on Ap Bia Mountain, Americans referred to it as Hill 937. Americans only called it Hamburger Hill after the battle.

The U.S./ARVN (Army of the Republic of Vietnam) strategy was to sweep and clear the area using overwhelming firepower in the air and on the ground.

The operation begins

Operation APACHE SNOW started on May 10, 1969. As American and ARVN (pronounced "Arvin") forces entered the area, they encountered only light resistance. What the American commanders didn't know was that most of the North Vietnamese regiment was waiting for them in the A Shau Valley around Ap Bia Mountain, also known as Hill 937.

The 3rd Battalion of the U.S. 187th Infantry was assigned the task of taking Hill 937. The North Vietnamese made a major stand there, and the name of Hill 937 eventually became known as Hamburger Hill.

Battling for Hamburger Hill: A victory of sorts

The assault on Hamburger Hill started May 11, 1969, and continued until May 20. The forces assigned to take the hill (see Figure 6-2) couldn't handle the fight alone, so the United States and the ARVN sent additional forces to help. After ten days of intense fighting, the U.S./ARVN forces finally won — but the toll had been heavy:

- More than 50 U.S./ARVN soldiers were killed.

- More than 400 U.S./ARVN soldiers were wounded.

- More than an estimated 630 NVA were killed. The exact number of NVA soldiers killed and wounded is unknown because no one is sure how many died in underground tunnels and bunkers or how many NVA bodies were carried across the border into Laos.

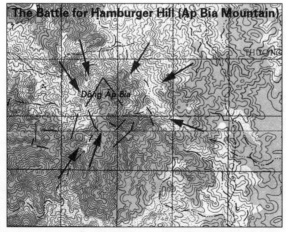

Figure 6-2:
Hamburger
Hill.

Map courtesy of the Vietnam Archive, Texas Tech University

Nevertheless, the casualties were fewer and the length of the campaign shorter when compared with many previous American operations in Vietnam. Certain factors about Hamburger Hill, however, served to create a powerful reaction on the home front. Americans found especially bothersome the fact that U.S./ARVN forces simply abandoned Hamburger Hill after having won it. NVA forces returned later unchallenged. War-weary Americans questioned the logic of sacrificing so many lives to take a hill only to abandon that same hill and allow enemy reoccupation without a fight. This was especially the case because it was all too likely that U.S./ARVN forces would eventually have to fight and sacrifice more lives for that same piece of strategic terrain some time in the future. If not, then how could it have been deemed so important as to fight for it in the first instance. Either way, Hamburger Hill became a public relations nightmare.

Feeling the sting of the American public's reaction and acting with the authority granted to him as commander in chief by the Gulf of Tonkin Resolutions (discussed in Chapter 5), Nixon

✔ Gave General Creighton Abrams, commander of U.S. Military Assistance Command, Vietnam, explicit new orders: "Conduct the war with a minimum of American casualties."

✔ Ordered the *Vietnamization* of the war (a plan already underway) to commence immediately, meaning that American forces would begin withdrawing from Vietnam while training and preparing a larger South Vietnamese army with new modern equipment to take over the bulk of fighting the war. Putting this policy into motion, Nixon announced in June 1969 that he had ordered the redeployment of approximately 25,000 men away from Vietnam. The American withdrawal had begun. At the same time, American forces returned to providing advice and support as occurred under Eisenhower and Kennedy and discussed in Chapters 3 and 4.

✔ Outlined his new policy (called the Nixon Doctrine) concerning American involvement in Asia after the Vietnam War ended: The United States would continue to honor its treaty obligations as set forth in the SEATO Treaty, and discussed in Chapter 3, but would *not* commit U.S. ground forces in a fight against direct or indirect communist aggression. The United States would provide only financial and material support in future wars like the one in Vietnam. You can read more at www.nixonfoundation.org/ Research_Center/1969_pdf_files/1969_0425.pdf.

Nixon's actions had the following effects on the U.S. and South Vietnamese fighting forces, who were still embroiled in the conflict:

✔ With news of American withdrawal from Vietnam, the attitude of American commanders and their forces changed. Before, the objective had been to win; now it was to keep casualties to a minimum.

> ✔ The Nixon Doctrine signaled to America's allies that the United States would continue to fund and supply them as they fought against the communists.

The United States Invades Cambodia; 1970

Not much changed during the remainder of 1969 as the United States pressed forward with Vietnamization (see the preceding section for details). The United States, South Vietnamese, North Vietnamese, and Viet Cong made little headway, either on the battlefield or at the peace table. But even as he announced the continued withdrawal of 150,000 American forces from South Vietnam and claimed that a just peace was in sight, Nixon called for a bold move in Cambodia, despite the potential for fallout from the American people. Cambodia continued to be a problem: The North Vietnamese and the Viet Cong continued to amass troops and conduct operations into South Vietnam from their bases in Cambodia. In addition, the country itself was a mess as rival factions and gangs vied for power and massacred one another. Slowly, Cambodia fell into anarchy. Because of its strategic importance, both the U.S./ARVN and the NVA/VC became embroiled in the power struggle within its borders:

> ✔ The United States backed a military commander, General Lon Nol, in opposition to the titular head of state, Prince Norodom Sihanouk, who is discussed in more detail in Chapter 13.

> ✔ The NVA/VC backed the Khmer Rouge under Pol Pot, also discussed in Chapter 13, whose bloody excesses surpassed any in the region and further destabilized Southeast Asia.

Nixon thought that he had to do something to stem the tide of communist attacks in South Vietnam and Cambodia and to get the NVA/VC back to the peace table. He also wanted to show North Vietnam, the Viet Cong, and the rest of the communist world that he was serious in his support for South Vietnam. The answer, he thought, was to go after the NVA and the Viet Cong inside Cambodia.

The Cambodian Incursion

Cambodia had long played a significant role in the Vietnam War and was no stranger to conflict. It was a Viet Cong sanctuary and a significant logistical center at the end of the Ho Chi Minh trail. It had even been bombed by the U.S. Air Force in Operation MENU since March 1969. So Nixon decided to send U.S. troops into Cambodia. See the earlier section "Expanding the air war in Cambodia: Operation MENU" for more about this operation.

Convincing the American people

On April 30, 1970, Nixon told the American people, "This is not an invasion of Cambodia. We take this action not for the purpose of expanding the war into Cambodia but for the purpose of ending the war in Vietnam and winning the just peace we all desire."

Regardless of whether you call it an invasion or an incursion, in May 1970, the United States attacked NVA and VC bases inside Cambodia. The goals were to:

- ✔ Disrupt the plans of the NVA/VC
- ✔ Buy time for Vietnamization

Strategy and Execution

On May 1, combined U.S./ARVN forces launched attacks on the *Parrot's Beak* and the *Fishhook* areas in Cambodia, geographical locations named for the objects they resemble on the map (see Figure 6-3). Their goal was to destroy NVA/VC bases that had been supplying those forces inside South Vietnam so U.S./ARVN troops conducted raids on the Ho Chi Minh Trail and NVA/VC bases inside of Cambodia.

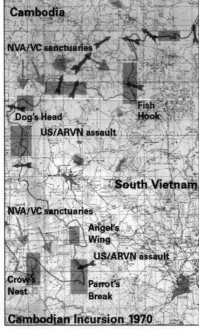

Figure 6-3: Cambodian Incursion: Parrot's Beak and Fish Hook operational prongs show which units were deployed in Cambodia.

Map courtesy of the Vietnam Archive, Texas Tech University

For the most part, the NVA/VC fled, preferring to yield ground and sacrifice bases rather than risk a direct fight with the U.S./ARVN forces. By the middle of May, U.S. forces withdrew from this area of Cambodia, turning the operation over to the ARVN, but U.S./ARVN forces continued to operate farther south in the area around the Parrot's Beak. Here U.S./ARVN forces fought the NVA/VC for two days before forcing them to flee. On June 30, the U.S. forces withdrew from this area as well, turning the entire operation over to the ARVN forces.

Victory in Cambodia

During the incursion, U.S./ARVN forces captured thousands of weapons and millions of rounds of ammunition. They also completely disrupted the supply network that fed enemy forces in South Vietnam.

During the battles, 383 American soldiers and 693 South Vietnamese soldiers died. Of the combined U.S./ARVN troops, 5,534 were wounded (1,525 of the wounded were Americans). Approximately 11,000 NVA/VC troops were killed and 2,500 were captured. Militarily, the Cambodian Incursion was a success.

When victory turns into disaster: Cambodia on the American home front

Given the military success in Cambodia, the American people initially supported the invasion, but that support didn't last. Although a military success, the invasion didn't help either the war effort or the president.

Here's why:

- ✔ The media and several prominent Americans protested the invasion of Cambodia as reckless and as a needless escalation of the war when the United States was supposed to be winding down its involvement. In this way, invasion served as a catalyst for the antiwar movement and demonstrations that led to the May 4, 1970, killings at Kent State University described in Chapter 18.

- ✔ Americans recognized the disparity between what Nixon said and what he did. The "credibility gap" grew as a problem and haunted Nixon for the remainder of his time as president. The American press and American people watched more intently and scrutinized more closely his words and deeds.

In the aftermath of the invasion of Cambodia, Congressional support for the war also decreased significantly:

- ✔ The Senate repealed the Gulf of Tonkin Resolutions, which had served as the basis for intervention in 1965.

> ✔ On December 22, 1970, Congress passed the Cooper-Church Amendment to the Defense Appropriations Bill, which further restricted the use of American military forces in Southeast Asia. This amendment forbade the deployment of any U.S. military forces, including U.S. advisors, on the ground in Cambodia, but left open the use of American air support.

Testing Vietnamization in Laos — LAM SON 719: 1971

The United States continued to withdraw forces from South Vietnam for the remainder of 1970 and into 1971. Vietnamization also continued with American advisors helping train and equip ARVN forces, preparing them to fight against the NVA/VC. The first test of their capabilities came in January 1971 in Operation LAM SON 719, when U.S. and South Vietnamese forces tried to repeat in Laos what they had accomplished in Cambodia.

From 1965 to 1971, military operations in South Vietnam almost always included significant amounts of American military forces. However, when the United States withdrew its forces from South Vietnam in 1969 and 1970, ARVN had to take over increasing shares of that burden. LAM SON 719 was the first major battle pitting ARVN alone on the ground against the NVA/VC in Laos.

LAM SON 719 was supposed to disrupt North Vietnamese movement along the Ho Chi Minh Trail by capturing the strategic city of Tchepone in Laos. ARVN forces were supposed to move in from the area near Khe Sanh in South Vietnam pushing the NVA back into Laos, advancing into A Luoi and Tchepone, and destroying any supplies they found in NVA/VC Base Areas 604 and 611. Once complete, ARVN forces would deal the NVA a staggering defeat by severing their access into South Vietnam via the Ho Chi Minh Trail (see Figure 6-4). What actually happened was a little different.

Phase 1 — American involvement on the ground

The operation contained four major components. Phase I started in January 1971 with Operation DEWEY CANYON in which elements of the American 101st Airborne Division and approximately 20,000 ARVN troops reactivated the former American base at Khe Sanh. Then they pushed up to the Laotian border, engaging NVA units along the way and forcing them back into Laos. Khe Sanh then served as a support base and launching point for the remainder of the operation.

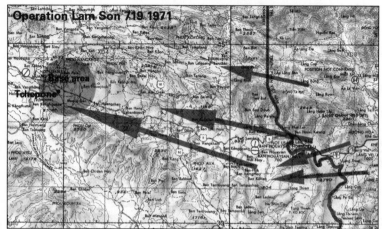

Figure 6-4:
Operation
LAM
SON 719.

Map courtesy of the Vietnam Archive, Texas Tech University

Phase II — The Vietnamese go it alone, almost

The second phase started in early February when approximately 17,000 ARVN soldiers, supported by American helicopters and other air assets launched an attack to seize A Luoi. As ARVN forces pushed into Laos accompanied by U.S. helicopter, close air, and B-52 bomber support, they met staunch enemy resistance. This was not surprising because the NVA had to stop the ARVN advance into Laos if they wanted to maintain their operations in South Vietnam. Approximately 22,000 NVA soldiers fought against the 17,000-strong ARVN. On February 10, 1971, despite being seriously outnumbered, ARVN captured A Luoi. ARVN forces then were supposed to immediately launch an attack to capture Tchepone. Instead, they halted their operations.

Unknown to Americans who helped plan and support the attack, South Vietnamese President Nguyen Van Thieu ordered his forces to stop and await reinforcements if they sustained too many casualties. Thieu set the limit at approximately 3,000 killed and wounded. By the time ARVN reinforcements arrived at A Luoi and continued on to Tchepone, 18,000 NVA armor, artillery, and antiaircraft reinforcements also arrived and dealt severe blows to ARVN forces.

Events could not have been worse for ARVN when the weather changed and heavy cloud cover prevented U.S. close air support from flying in the area. Although higher-flying B-52s can attack in spite of the weather, the blast and damage radius of such attacks prevented the United States from dropping bombs within three miles of ARVN units unless it was absolutely necessary. NVA commanders aware of that limitation stayed as close to ARVN as possible. When the weather cleared, NVA antiaircraft artillery (AAA) and machine guns kept U.S. close air support on the defensive and surface-to-air missiles (SAMs) threatened the higher-flying B-52s. Because of the U.S. domestic fallout from Hamburger Hill and orders from Nixon to minimize U.S. casualties, American commanders hesitated in risking the lives of American pilots in LAM SON 719.

President Thieu still wanted to take Tchepone, even though it had been abandoned and had little strategic value. So, U.S. helicopters transported ARVN troops into Tchepone where they searched in vain for caches of NVA supplies. In March, ARVN units began withdrawing from Laos. The NVA intensified its attacks and, in part, because of a lack of training, the ARVN retreat turned into a rout. U.S. air power was again unable to provide even a little support to the retreating ARVN because it was hindered by more weather but also by AAA fire.

Half of the ARVN force survived largely because of the bravery of U.S. helicopter pilots who flew into NVA/VC controlled landing zones in bad weather to retrieve the fleeing ARVN troops. By the conclusion of the operation, the NVA had destroyed 108 U.S. helicopters and seriously damaged an additional 618. The U.S. sustained 1,149 killed and wounded while ARVN suffered more than 1,700 killed and nearly 6,000 wounded or missing. Although determining the exact number of NVA casualties is impossible, estimates run as high as 20,000 killed, wounded, and missing.

Winners and losers, all

North Vietnam and South Vietnam each claimed victory. But South Vietnam's primary goal of cutting off NVA access to the Ho Chi Minh Trail around Tchepone failed. Like Hamburger Hill two years earlier, the NVA reoccupied Tchepone unopposed after the ARVN withdrawal. Hanoi called the operation the "heaviest defeat ever" for the allies.

Meanwhile, President Nixon also used this opportunity to claim victory for U.S. and ARVN forces, moreover to declare the U.S. Vietnamization program a success. He overlooked the facts that LAM SON 719 revealed ARVN's continued dependence on U.S. air support and firepower and proved NVA resolve and reinforcement capabilities. Regardless, America continued to withdraw its military forces from Vietnam and didn't have long to wait for a justification for that policy.

The Eastertide Offensive, 1972

Learning from the failures of LAM SON 719 proved difficult but not impossible for the South Vietnamese government and military to overcome. With massive amounts of American advisory, materiel, and financial support still sustaining them, the South Vietnamese spent the next year training and preparing for inevitable battles with their northern rival. This kind of preparation resulted in a better-prepared South Vietnam. At the same time, however, North Vietnam was preparing for Operation NGUYEN HUE, more popularly known as the Eastertide Offensive.

Confidence and calculation — The North plans the "Final Battle"

General Vo Nguyen Giap, commander of the North Vietnamese military forces, spent much of 1971 and early 1972 preparing for what he hoped would be the final battle against South Vietnam, what became called the Eastertide Offensive. Giap amassed more than 20 divisions (that's more than 200,000 men) for a three-pronged attack aimed at the total conquest of South Vietnam, as shown in Figure 6-5.

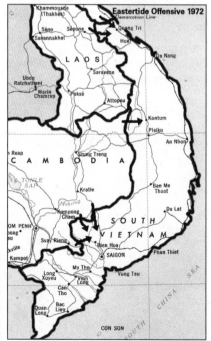

Figure 6-5:
The Eastertide Offensive.

Map courtesy of the Vietnam Archive, Texas Tech University

The North Vietnamese carefully timed the offensive and were confident that the South Vietnamese forces would fall easily, given their poor performance in Laos during LAM SON 719. General Giap didn't think the intervening year had provided enough time for South Vietnam to become better prepared for battle. Not only did General Giap want to launch the offensive once the majority of American ground forces had withdrawn from South Vietnam, but he also wanted to do battle with a token American force, easily defeating them and humiliating Nixon. 1972 was an election year and such a defeat would destroy Nixon's chances for re-election and destroy American policy in Southeast Asia for years to come.

And on a lovely spring morning . . . offensive launched

North Vietnam launched the Eastertide Offensive Thursday, March 30, 1972. The attack was supposed to occurr along three prongs or fronts:

- First, NVA forces were to enter through the DMZ and from Laos and attack Quang Tri Province in northern South Vietnam in order to capture Quang Tri city and then the royal capital of Hue.

- The second prong was to strike from Cambodia into Kontum Province in central South Vietnam, aiming for Kontum city and continuing to the sea with the goal of splitting South Vietnam in half.

- The final prong was to thrust from Cambodia into Binh Long Province in southern South Vietnam to capture the city of An Loc. Although unsuccessful during this 1972 operation, the Viet Cong did eventually capture An Loc, where they established their official seat of government and launched attacks on Saigon, the national capital of South Vietnam.

Fighting in the North

In Quang Tri, the NVA opened up with a barrage of 130mm artillery fire in preparation for a ground assault. Their better guns outranged ARVN artillery by almost 10,000 meters (2 miles), providing them with an early advantage. After a massive bombardment against the ARVN positions, the 304th and 308th NVA Divisions attacked Quang Tri Province with significant infantry, armor, and artillery regimental support. They had four NVA divisions in reserve to the north, east, and south.

The battle for Quang Tri city raged for more than a month; however, ARVN units panicked under the heavy bombardment and deserted the city, leaving it to the NVA. With Hue threatened, President Thieu fired the Vietnamese commander of I CTZ in May and replaced him with the capable General Ngo Quang Truong.

Considered the best general in the South Vietnamese Army, General Truong rallied his forces around Hue and defended the city against the NVA assault. Receiving reinforcements in June and support from American B-52 bombers and naval gunfire (which countered the advantage of the better NVA artillery), General Truong launched a counteroffensive pushing the NVA back. By September, ARVN recaptured Quang Tri city and most of the other bases along the demilitarized zone (DMZ) (see Chapter 2 for information about the DMZ).

Fighting in the center

In Kontum, the North Vietnamese launched their offensive Wednesday, April 12, 1972, with three divisions supported by tank and artillery regiments (see Figure 6-5) and an additional division that attacked along the coast. Around Kontum and to the coast, ARVN deployed four regiments from various divisions, an airborne division, two armored cavalry squadrons, and held the 23rd Division in reserve near Ban Me Thuot. The NVA overran ARVN positions to the west of Kontum city and destroyed the base for the ARVN 22nd Division, capturing the commander and his staff. Disaster continued for ARVN as units abandoned their positions around Kontum, leaving artillery pieces and other equipment that the NVA captured.

In early May, the airborne division withdrew from Kontum to reinforce Hue, and this left Kontum virtually defenseless. South Vietnam stood on the verge of being split in half. Seeing the threat, President Thieu again acted swiftly, firing the II CTZ commander and replacing him with two able combat leaders.

Reorganizing its defenses around Kontum just in time, ARVN successfully repulsed the NVA assault on May 14 and continued doing so for two more weeks with the help of American airstrikes and helicopter gunships. By the end of May, the tide turned in ARVN's favor and its forces engaged in house-to-house fighting to rid the city of remaining NVA forces. ARVN continued its reinforcement of units in the area and recaptured the remaining towns along the coast.

Fighting in the South

The NVA launched the third prong of the Eastertide Offensive on Sunday, April 2, 1972, when the 5th, 7th, and 9th Viet Cong Divisions supported by tanks, artillery, and the 24th NVA Regiment attacked Binh Long Province, which was being defended by elements of several ARVN Divisions (see Figure 6-5). As the NVA force moved toward the city of Loc Ninh, they overwhelmed the ARVN forces thereon April 7. The NVA also captured the airfield at Quan Loi, cutting off resupply to the city of An Loc. And yet, having moved so quickly, the NVA/VC units had depleted their resources and had to wait for resupply. President Thieu took advantage of this lull in the fighting to resupply and reinforce his forces at An Loc by air, a distinct advantage he had over the NVA/VC who had to rely on ground-based resupply. In addition, U.S. aircraft launched heavy attacks against the NVA/VC, who were preparing for a final assault on An Loc. By the time the NVA were able to resume their assault on April 13, ARVN was ready. South Vietnamese forces repulsed several NVA attacks, withstanding heavy artillery bombardments into May as the North Vietnamese continued fighting for the city.

At the same time, the United States continued its support of ARVN with enormous amounts of air power, decimating NVA formations while they tried to amass for their assaults on An Loc. The NVA unsuccessfully continued its attack through May, and an ARVN counteroffensive pushed the NVA out of the city and ended the siege of An Loc in July 1972, although fighting continued for months thereafter.

Overconfidence and miscalculation lead to defeat

Unlike LAM SON 719, there was no question as to the winner and loser in the Eastertide Offensive of 1972. Although he was a highly skilled and experienced strategist and tactician, General Giap fell prey to overconfidence, underestimating the combat effectiveness of ARVN and the continued American support. Giap spread his forces too thin, so that no one assault was powerful enough to accomplish the goal of defeating South Vietnam. Although the NVA continued its occupation of strategic areas in South Vietnam, for the most part they left the battlefields empty-handed and badly defeated.

North Vietnam seriously misjudged the American response to the Eastertide Offensive. General Giap and others thought Nixon would do little because the American people didn't support a continuation of the war. In other words, Giap expected token American resistance but encountered just the opposite.

Seeking to punish North Vietnam for its Eastertide Offensive and impede the flow of men and materiel south, Nixon resumed the air war over the North, launching Operation LINEBACKER I and opening the entire country to U.S. air attack with the exception of a small buffer zone along its border with China. The bombing included Hanoi and the rail lines bringing supplies in from China (see Chapter 9). The United States also mined Hai Phong and other harbors cutting off Chinese and Soviet sea-based supply routes and approximately 85 percent of the supplies coming into North Vietnam. Combined with the massive air and naval gunfire support that the United States provided ARVN, North Vietnam found that it was impossible to adequately support its own forces during the Eastertide Offensive.

The costs to North Vietnam were staggering, particularly to its 200,000-man force, which reportedly lost 100,000 *casualties* (soldiers either killed, wounded, captured, or missing in action). In addition, the North Vietnamese lost nearly half of their tanks and heavy artillery, and their government eased the revered General Giap out of power and set to the task of preparing for the next offensive. It took them almost two years to recover from the defeat.

Vietnamization Successful — Pushing for Peace in Paris

Through the brave and tenacious defense of their country, the South Vietnamese proved that they could defend themselves against the North Vietnamese. U.S. air power, naval gunfire, and ground advisory support had been important to their overall success, but an important factor remained ARVN units, on the ground, in the hands of capable ARVN commanders. With continued American support, they might hold out indefinitely.

This proof of ARVN's ability to defend South Vietnam provided Nixon with an opportunity to pursue the peace he and the American people so desperately wanted. Unfortunately, this desire for peace wasn't shared by the North Vietnamese.

Talking in Paris while fighting in South Vietnam

Vietnamese and American delegates continued to meet and negotiate for peace while the Eastertide Offensive raged on. Henry Kissinger represented the United States and, sensing compromise was near, announced just that in October 1972. As a gesture of American goodwill, he recommended a halt to the bombing of North Vietnam that same month. But the North Vietnamese stalled the peace process in December seeking to embarrass and frustrate Kissinger, Nixon, and the United States.

Talking in Paris while bombing Hanoi

Enraged by the stalling tactics of the North Vietnamese, President Nixon authorized Operation LINEBACKER II, a resumption of the bombing campaign in North Vietnam (see Chapter 8). Despite domestic and international condemnation of the so-called "Christmas Bombing," Nixon continued the campaign until

December 29, three days after Hanoi agreed to resume peace negotiations. Nixon hoped an increase in the damage suffered by NVA forces and North Vietnam might also enhance the chances of South Vietnam remaining free from communism for a longer period.

The Paris Peace Accords — A Peace with "Honor," 1973

The Paris peace talks resulted in the signing of an "Agreement on Ending the War and Restoring the Peace in Vietnam" on January 27, 1973, which also is referred to as the Paris Peace Accords. As is true of all negotiated settlements, each side made concessions.

North Vietnam agreed to:

- A cease-fire in South Vietnam

- Drop their demands for a coalition government between the Republic of Vietnam and the Viet Cong (The Provisional Government of Vietnam)

- Release all prisoners and cooperate in gathering information on those still listed as missing

The United States agreed to:

- A cease fire, a halt to all military operations against the North Vietnam and withdrawal of all American forces and advisors from South Vietnam

- Dismantle all American bases in South Vietnam and cease all military activity there

- Not interfere in the internal affairs of South Vietnam

- Commit to a reconstruction plan for North Vietnam to help "heal the wounds of the war"

South Vietnam agreed to:

- Self determination for the South Vietnamese people

- Reunification of North and South Vietnam by "peaceful means"

- Continued military occupation of various areas of South Vietnam by the NVA (In January 1973, the NVA forces numbered 13 Divisions and 75 regiments for a total of almost 160,000 soldiers in South Vietnam)

President Thieu reportedly wept when he read the Paris Peace Accords, because he realized they all but amounted to a complete, albeit looming, surrender to North Vietnam. Adding to his discouragement, he realized the emptiness of American promises for continued support in the event of another enemy offensive, despite his hopes to the contrary.

Thieu's worst fears and suspicions came true when, in June 1973, the U.S. Congress passed the Case-Church Amendment, which demanded an end to American military involvement in Southeast Asia and stipulated that no funds would be available after August 15, 1973, to support U.S. forces in North or South Vietnam, Laos, or Cambodia. Despite disagreeing with the amendment, Nixon signed it into law because he lacked support in Congress to prevent his veto from being overridden. The fall of South Vietnam seemed all but a matter of time.

Nixon and Disgrace — Thieu and Defeat, 1974

1974 turned out to be a bad year for President Nixon and his South Vietnamese counterpart, President Thieu. Nixon faced accusations of illegal activities and possible impeachment while Thieu faced a new North Vietnamese attempt to conquer his country.

Nixon's scandals and resignation

A number of scandals involving President Nixon increased the likelihood that he would be impeached. Watergate, of course, received the most attention in the press at the time and, for that matter, has ever since his resignation. The war in Southeast Asia, however, also provided a basis for investigation and charges against the president.

The expansion of the air war into Cambodia in 1969 and the contradictory public statements made by President Nixon brought about the first calls for investigations into his presidency. Unpopular decisions to subsequently invade Cambodia and later to bomb North Vietnam in late 1972 further eroded Nixon's support in Congress and with the American people. When Watergate became public knowledge, the president had no choice, resign or face impeachment. Nixon resigned August 9, 1974.

The final offensive: North Vietnam strikes, America does nothing

On the same day that Nixon resigned, Gerald Ford took the oath of office to become the 38th President of the United States. Despite the power of his position, he could do little when North Vietnam broke with the Paris Peace Accords and attacked South Vietnam in the fall of that year. Hamstrung by the Case-Church Amendment, members of the Ford administration petitioned Congress and the American people to continue supporting South Vietnam against communist aggression. Their requests, however, fell on the deaf ears of war-weary Americans and their congressional representatives.

Congress provided token assistance and, after two decades, South Vietnam stood alone with a severely constricted American aid package.

The Fall of South Vietnam, 1975

The South Vietnamese did everything that they could with dwindling military supplies and diminished forces as North Vietnam attacked first into northern South Vietnam and then progressively throughout the rest of the country. By the end of 1974, the NVA and Viet Cong controlled nearly half of South Vietnam. In December, they launched their offensive to take control of the rest of the country.

A more focused assault

Unlike the Eastertide Offensive of 1972, North Vietnam focused its final offensive on strategic areas of South Vietnam, progressively overtaking certain areas leading up to a final assault on the capitol city of Saigon.

The first major assault of 1975 occurred in Phuoc Long Province in III CTZ, which fell to the NVA/VC in January 1975. The interior cities of Ban Me Thuot, Kontum, and Pleiku along with the coastal cities of Hue, Da Nang, and Tuy Hoa all fell by the end of March. In early April, the North Vietnamese coastal advance continued as they captured Nha Trang and Cam Ranh Bay.

The fall of the first domino

By mid-April, North Vietnam controlled nearly three quarters of the country and began surrounding Saigon. Despite a heroic stand by ARVN forces, Xuan

Loc, a strategic city east of Saigon, fell April 22, 1975, to the NVA/VC. The NVA/VC then surrounded the South Vietnamese capital and Saigon fell April 30, 1975.

Toppling the remaining Asian dominos

While South Vietnam fought against communist forces from within and without, Cambodia and Laos lay under similar siege.

First Cambodia

In April 1975, the Cambodian Khmer Rouge successfully engaged the remaining nationalist forces and captured Phnom Penh, that nation's capital, April 17. (More details of what happened in Cambodia during the war are discussed in Chapter 13.) After taking control of the country, the Khmer Rouge engaged in unbelievable atrocities, massacring more than 1 million men, women, and children. When the murderous campaign crossed into Vietnam in 1978, a then recently reunified Vietnam (known as the Socialist Republic of Vietnam, or SRV) launched a full-scale invasion of Cambodia in December. By early January, SRV forces occupied Phnom Penh and remained there for the next decade.

Then Laos

The details of what happened in Laos during the war are also discussed in Chapter 13. In 1975, while heavy fighting occurred in Vietnam and Cambodia, the communist Pathet Lao of Laos met little resistance as they consolidated their forces and moved toward the Laotian capital of Vientiane in May. With government forces ordered not to resist, the city fell August 23, 1975, to the communists. The fighting continued as Pathet Lao forces engaged their former enemies, including the Hmong tribal people (see Chapter 15). More than 350,000 refugees tried to leave the country and more than 150,000 Laotian and Hmong were resettled in the United States.

The United States loses?

Despite a massive U.S. military involvement, South Vietnam fell to communism. Losses on all sides were staggering. More than 58,000 U.S. men and women were killed, more than 300,000 were wounded, and more than 3,000 were captured or missing. Furthermore, the United States spent an estimated $15 billion dollars trying to prevent the fall of South Vietnam. The defeat of the American policy to keep Vietnam free from communism also dealt a serious blow to American morale and American self-perceptions. For the first time, the United States failed in its war objectives and the effects of this defeat were long lasting.

American losses pale when compared with those of North Vietnam and South Vietnam. Although impossible to accurately state, South Vietnam's losses were estimated at more than 400,000 people killed, while North Vietnam and the Viet Cong lost more than 1 million killed, including civilians. Making matters worse for the reunited Vietnam, its entire nation had been ravaged by decades of war. The attack on South Vietnam by North Vietnam in 1974 essentially nullified the Paris Peace Accords, so the United States felt no obligation to provide any of the postwar reconstruction assistance it had initially promised. As a result, Vietnam's recovery has been a slow and painful one.

Part III
Taking to Air and Sea

The 5th Wave   By Rich Tennant

"I don't mind him doing that, just not on the smart bombs."

In this part . . .

The Vietnam War was not only fought on the ground though the majority of action did occur there. The battle in the air and on the water was equally critical to the success of U.S. and South Vietnamese strategy. In this part, you will find out how U.S. and South Vietnamese fought the Vietnam War in the air and on the water. You will discover that the air war, like the ground war, was not limited to Vietnam. The air campaigns in Laos and Cambodia were critical to the success of U.S. strategy and played a significant role in wartime planning. The air and sea wars will also demonstrate how the war in Vietnam was not just a military conflict. The politics of decision-making as the U.S. and South Vietnam directed the air and sea wars played a predominant role. In the air campaigns over North Vietnam, political decisions often outweighed military strategy as the U.S. wrestled fighting a public war where international opinion was not always on its side. In this part, you will also learn how the North Vietnamese countered U.S. air and sea power to maintain some control over its destiny. The stubborn and creativeness of the North Vietnamese provided more of a challenge than the quantity and quality of U.S. technology than anticipated.

Chapter 7

Learning to Fly: 1950–1964

- -

In This Chapter

▶ Advising the South Vietnamese Air Force

▶ Taking over the air war

▶ Taking flight with Kennedy's Special Forces

▶ Defoliating the countryside with Agent Orange

▶ Evaluating the early air war

- -

*T*he air war in Vietnam started in a fashion similar to the ground and sea campaigns. During the first 10 years (1950–1960) of United States Air Force (USAF) involvement in Vietnam, the primary focus was on training and equipping the South Vietnamese Air Force (VNAF) so that it was able to support the war against communist insurgency.

The USAF was also involved in *reconnaissance missions* (taking photographs from aircraft of strategic areas or bomb damage for future military operations). As the war progressed and the United States became more involved in the defense of South Vietnam, the commitment to air power as a means of winning the war increased. By the end of the Kennedy Administration, the United States was committed to South Vietnam, and USAF and U.S. Navy (USN) aircraft and personnel were focused on the struggle for victory. For more on the origins of air power during wartime, see *World War II For Dummies* (Wiley, Inc.).

Advising the Vietnamese: 1950–1961

The United States made a commitment to help defend South Vietnam from North Vietnam and the Viet Cong (VC) by establishing the Military Assistance and Advisory Group (MAAG) shortly after the outbreak of war in Korea. As a result, the American military organization was given the task of coordinating French, Vietnamese, and U.S. planning to fight the Viet Minh. After the defeat of the French Union Forces at Dien Bien Phu, which is discussed in Chapter 2, and the subsequent withdrawal of the French from Indochina, MAAG took over the responsibility of training the South Vietnamese.

The United States established the MAAG Air Force Section in November 1950. This section served as the primary Air Force group working with the VNAF and the French in the struggle against the Viet Minh.

Speaking the plane truth

Planes and helicopters used by the United States, VNAF, and France during the early stages of the war represent a broad range of aircraft. Table 7-1 presents descriptions of these aircraft as a cheat sheet that will help you with the sections of this chapter that follow, as well as Chapters 8 and 9. Your newfound knowledge will impress your friends:

Table 7-1	Early Warplanes and Helicopters Used by the United States, VNAF, and France	
Fighters/Bombers		
Official Reference	*Also Known as*	*History*
AD-6 (A-1)	Skyraider	The AD-6 Skyraider (later renamed the A-1) was developed by the U.S. Navy during World War II as a dive bomber and torpedo plane. The USAF adopted it as a fighter and bomber in the Korean and Vietnam wars. The USAF and VNAF liked the plane because it could take an incredible amount of damage and still fly plus it carried a large ordnance load.
B-26	Invader	This twin-engine, propeller-driven bomber was developed during the Second World War. The USAF transferred a number of B-26 planes to the French for use in Indochina during the early 1950s. The B-26 was redesigned during the Vietnam War as the A-26. RB-26, a version of the B-26, was used for reconnaissance and intelligence work during the war.

Official Reference	Also Known as	History
F-6F	Hellcat	The USAF provided the single-engine, propeller-driven F-6F to the French in Indochina. The F-6F, surplus from the Second World War, formed the basis of the French Air Force in Indochina.
F-8F	Bearcat	The USAF provided the F-8F to the French in Indochina to replace the F-6F. Also a single-engine, propeller-driven plane, the F-8F had a longer range and more armament than the F-6F.
T-28	Nomad/Trojan	The T-28 was a training plane that was armed with weapons and used during the early stages of the war in a fire support and reconnaissance role (RT-28).

Helicopters

Official reference	Also Known as	History
CH 21	Shawnee	Helicopter used by the U.S. Marines to transport Army of the Republic of Vietnam (ARVN) troops as the South Vietnamese became more aggressive in their ground war.
UH-1	Iroquois	Known as the Huey, the early stages of the war saw Model A and B carrying troops and supporting slower fixed-wing planes and gunships. Later models of the UH-1 served a variety of other functions during the war.
UH-34	Sea Horse/Choctaws	The UH-34 started as a Navy submarine-hunter helicopter. The Army used the UH-34, calling it the Choctaw, as a troop transport in Vietnam.

(continued)

Table 7-1 *(continued)*

Reconnaissance/Observation

Official Reference	Also Known as	Its Use
L-19	Bird Dog	The L-19 (later redesignated the O-1 in 1964) was a single-engine, propeller-driven Cessna Plane used for observation and directing fire support.
OV-1	Mohawk	A propeller-driven aircraft used as a photograph observation and electronic reconnaissance.
O-2	Skymaster	A small Cessna aircraft used by Forward Air Controllers (FAC) to call in artillery and air strikes against NVA/VC positions.
RF-101	Voodoo	The RF-101 served in Vietnam as a reconnaissance jet. It was a high-speed alternative to older propeller-driven planes.
RT-33	T-Bird	The RT-33 was a jet aircraft used in Vietnam as a reconnaissance plane.

Transportation

Official Reference	Also Known as	Its Use
C-119	Flying Boxcar	The C-119 was used primarily as a troop and cargo transport during the early stages of the war. As the United States escalated its involvement, the AC-119 developed a distinguished career as a gunship.
C-123	Provider	The majority of C-123's served in Vietnam as transports for cargo or personnel. The C-123 was also the preferred aircraft for Operation RANCH HAND.
C-45	Expeditor	The C-45 was used in Vietnam as a staff transport. Many of the aircraft were a part of the lend-lease program during the Second World War, during which the United States gave is allies war equipment on loan until the finish of the war.

Official Reference	Also Known as	Its Use
C-47	Skytrain	The C-47 served as a transport during the early stages of the war and as a reconnaissance (RC-47) and search-and-rescue (SC-46 "Dumbo") plane. Later in the war, the plane also served as a gunship (AC-47 "Puff the Magic Dragon").
C-54	Skymaster	The C-54 was a transport plane with four propeller-driven engines. It had a longer range and greater speed than the C-47.

An ally on the run

Between the advent of MAAG's *Air Force Section* (the group of Air Force officers assigned to advise the South Vietnamese Air Force) and the French failure at Dien Bien Phu, the United States had one major objective in Indochina: building up and maintaining air assets for the French and Vietnamese as they pursued the war. The French Air Force in Indochina consisted of an odd assortment of old-model aircraft, most of which was British and United States surplus, and captured German transports from the Second World War.

Although these aircraft served their roles admirably in Vietnam, the French had difficulties maintaining them, constantly suffering from grounded planes because of a lack of spare parts. The first priority became replacing these aircraft with more modern, if not more advanced, aircraft. Even before the official formation of the Air Force Section, the United States provided Hellcat fighters to replace older British Spitfire fighters. Ninety Bearcat fighters supplemented the Hellcats in 1951. The United States provided a number of Skytrain transport planes to replace German JU-52 transports and Invader bombers for close air support. The Air Force Section also supplied vast amounts of surplus ammunition for fighters and bombers.

The U.S. commitment to air power had an immediate impact on the war, enabling the French to more than double the number of weekly *sorties* (one sortie = one plane conducting one mission) between summer 1950 and spring 1951. The Korean War kept the number of modern aircraft available for use in Indochina to a minimum; however, when the war ended with an armistice in July 1953, the Air Force turned its attention to Vietnam and the French struggle to retain its empire.

Nonetheless, the war was going badly for the French. Air power changed from being a component of the overall strategy to a last-ditch effort to save the

French in Indochina. The United States, however, refused to dance to the French tune, choosing not to become militarily involved in the French effort to retain its Indochina colony.

Planning the air war

One key element for a French victory in Indochina was air power. The French controlled the skies but stilled needed American assistance to win the day. General Henri Navarre, leader of the French Union Forces in Indochina, created a plan to consolidate his troops and lure the Viet Minh into battle. His plan required a number of transports to deploy *paratroopers,* who would jump from the transports into Dien Bien Phu. The United States offered to loan Flying Boxcars to the French, but the French rejected the deal, requesting Skytrains instead, because they were more suitable for the Navarre Plan. Twenty-five Skytrains arrived in December 1953. The French based their hope for success in Indochina on a small, isolated outpost at Dien Bien Phu, which is discussed at-length in Chapter 2. However, they underestimated the Viet Minh and, by early 1954, were in dire straits. In mid-January, 20 Flying Boxcar and 50 Skytrain sorties per day were required just to supply troops at Dien Bien Phu.

When the Viet Minh took over the airstrip at Dien Bien Phu in March 1954, the French requested U.S. air power to turn the tide. Under President Eisenhower's Mutual Assistance Program, the United States loaned France a number of B-26 bombers. These American aircraft where supplemented with 200 USAF technicians and 12 Flying Boxcars from the Civil Air Transport (CAT). CAT pilots were American civilians, most of whom were veterans of the Second World War. They were funded through the Central Intelligence Agency (CIA). See Chapter 13 for more about CAT and the CIA.

Because Dien Bien Phu received virtually all of its supplies by air, resupplying the garrison with the 170 tons of ammunition and 32 tons of food it needed each day became impossible when transport aircraft were confronted with fully operational and deadly effective Viet Minh *antiaircraft batteries* (gun placements) in the mountains overlooking the French fortress.

Taking the last breath

The Viet Minh continued its strangle hold on Dien Bien Phu throughout the spring and it appeared the fortress might fall if major relief wasn't provided. General Ely, then commander-in-chief of the French Union Forces, traveled to Washington, D.C., informing American leaders of the predicted fate of Dien Bien Phu without a massive U.S. bombing campaign to save the day. Ely and Chairman of the Joint Chiefs of Staff Admiral Arthur Radford devised a plan for committing 60 B-29 bombers to Dien Bien Phu to heavily bomb the Viet Minh hiding in the mountains.

Operation VULTURE, as it became known during the planning stage, met stiff opposition in Washington, D.C., because American officials worried such an operation wouldn't save Dien Bien Phu and might even cause the Communist China to escalate its involvement in the war. French hopes were raised March 29 when Secretary of State John Foster Dulles called for a plan of United Action to win the day in Indochina, but the promise of Operation VULTURE remained unfulfilled.

Three primary concerns on the military's side against conducting the operation were

✔ The French didn't possess the ability to operate the planes, which would require American pilots to fly them in a heavy combat zone with the distinct possibility of suffering casualties.

✔ The French didn't possess the ability to provide maintenance for the aircraft, which therefore required a large number of American personnel to service the bombers, opening up the United States to accusations that it was involved in the war and offering Communist China the chance to justify entering the conflict.

✔ The B-29 bombers required fighter escorts and a further commitment of U.S. personnel. Without fighter escorts, the bombers were vulnerable to Communist Chinese MiG fighters if they entered the conflict. For more on the MiG fighter, see Chapter 11.

The bottom line: Operation VULTURE meant a significant U.S. escalation into Indochina, and the United States was not willing to commit to such a move without British support. And, when that support was not forthcoming, the operation and United Action fell apart. For more information on United Action, see Chapter 2.

Taking over the air war: Eisenhower's vision for Vietnam

The Geneva Conference, which is outlined in Chapter 2, placed restrictions on the amount and type of assistance the United States could provide the Republic of Vietnam. The South Vietnamese Air Force (VNAF), however, was not a top priority in 1954–1956 as South Vietnamese president Ngo Dinh Diem consolidated his power in South Vietnam (see Chapters 2 and 3).

The Republic of Vietnam (South Vietnam) Air Force (RVNAF) consisted of 4,140 personnel with one squadron of Bearcat fighters, two squadrons of Skytrains, two squadrons of Bird Dog observation planes, and one H-19 helicopter unit. In other words, South Vietnam had neither an effective nor modern air force. The French continued training the VNAF until May 1957 when the USAF finally took over. USAF trainers discovered the Vietnamese could fly the planes, but they had little or no combat experience. To be effective, the VNAF needed a complete overhaul.

As the Viet Cong increased its strength in South Vietnam, the Army of the Republic of Vietnam (ARVN) found itself engaged in larger and more deadly battles. VNAF planes provided limited support for ARVN forces. The Bearcat, an air-to-air fighter, couldn't carry large bombs, and repairing a fighter that was long past retirement age also was difficult for the VNAF.

President Eisenhower agreed to provide VNAF with a Navy plane, the AD-6, as a replacement for the Bearcat AD-6, which later was renamed the Skyraider (see Figure 7-1). The Skyraider became the workhorse of the VNAF and still is admired by American pilots who flew it in Vietnam. The Skyraider also earned the respect of the ground troops who appreciated its accuracy and ability to stay above the battlefield utilizing numerous weapons to support the troops. In addition to the Skyraider, the United States provided 11 Sea Horse/Choctaw helicopters, enabling the South Vietnamese to take a more aggressive role in the war.

The Skyraider not only was a good fighter but also carried an awesome amount of firepower. The helicopters, on the other hand, meant the South Vietnamese could move large numbers of troops within short periods of time. Despite these improvements, Eisenhower was less concerned with the development of the VNAF than he was of improving ARVN.

Specializing a "Special" Force: Kennedy's 1961 Decisions

When John F. Kennedy entered the White House, the United States stood at a crossroads in Vietnam. Fewer than 1,000 American personnel were in Vietnam supporting the South Vietnamese, but 1961 proved to be an important year for Kennedy and Vietnam. Kennedy committed additional American forces in Vietnam, promising to help increase and maintain the South Vietnamese Armed Forces. The first Air Force personnel arriving during 1961 was a detachment of the 507th Tactical Control Group, which was sent in to provide radar control and warning around Saigon and to train VNAF personnel in the use of these skills. Kennedy and Secretary of Defense Robert McNamara also provided additional fighter squadrons (T-28 training planes with guns) and another squadron of L-19s. Under Project Mule Train, the United States provided C-123 Providers to replace the C-47s. Although the Providers were considered obsolete, they found a second life in Vietnam offering tactical airlift support (moving soldiers by air from one location to another) for ARVN troops and later as the preferred plane, because of their ability to fly at a low speed and altitude, in the infamous Operation RANCH HAND.

Kennedy was interested in using U.S. Special Forces (highly trained soldiers considered the elite forces of the U.S. Army) in Vietnam for combating the Viet Cong forces that defied traditional military strategy and tactics. Special Forces personnel trained South Vietnamese to fight the Viet Cong in their own territory and take the offensive in the war. In October 1961, Kennedy agreed to establish the 4400th Combat Crew Training Squadron — Jungle Jim — so it could provide similar training for the VNAF. Detachment 2A of the 4400th arrived in Vietnam between November and December 1961 under Operation FARM GATE.

Under Operation FARM GATE, the United States provided approximately 150 Air Force personnel and an assortment of planes to help improve the VNAF. In December 1961, the United States and South Vietnam participated in their first joint operation against a Viet Cong stronghold in War Zone D, northeast of Saigon. Although American participation was kept to a minimum, and precautions were taken to limit potential casualties, the United States had taken the next step in its commitment to Vietnam.

Kennedy continued using rhetoric that indicated the USAF was in Vietnam only to train, but he authorized American forces to defend themselves whenever they were fired upon. Operation FARM GATE and the new role for the USAF made clear that Kennedy would not have minded a clash between Americans and the Viet Cong. In late December 1961, the USAF was allowed to engage in combat missions if a member of the VNAF also was in the plane or if the VNAF couldn't complete its mission. Although some have argued that Kennedy advanced this position to limit the U.S. role in Vietnam and avoid a possible conflict with the PRC, the possibility also is very real that this one step beyond what Eisenhower allowed actually drew the United States deeper into the war.

Operation FARM GATE missions in 1962 increased even as the USAF was trying to restrict its offensive capabilities to adhere to the 1954 Geneva Agreements. That the presence of Operation FARM GATE personnel was a direct violation of the original intent of the agreements didn't matter. As the war intensified, the USAF stepped up its training of the VNAF and helped create support facilities to assist the South Vietnamese in their air war. One installation, the Tactical Air Control System, consisted of radar units at Tan Son Nhut Air Base in Saigon, at Danang (on the coast), and at Pleiku (Central Highlands). These facilities provided early warning capabilities against possible North Vietnamese air strikes and organized the increasing number of flights occurring over South Vietnam.

Figure 7-1:
Mechanics at the well-equipped Air Vietnam Technical Services Center at Tan Son Nhut extend the life of an A-1 fighter-bomber by rebuilding the plane's wing structure.

Photograph courtesy of the Vietnam Archive, Texas Tech University

The VNAF suffered a setback in February 1962 when two Vietnamese pilots flying Skyraiders bombed the Presidential Palace in Saigon hoping to kill Ngo Dinh Diem. These pilots were part of a growing Vietnamese opposition to Diem, and they wanted to see a change in government. The attack failed, but thereafter, Diem distrusted the loyalty of the VNAF. Already faced with training and equipment problems, the VNAF also had to contend with politics and political intrigue. In April 1962, the United States learned that ARVN was not taking advantage of its air support in ground operations against the Viet Cong. Planes accompanied less than 10 percent of the helicopter missions. The United States immediately went to work on the problem by providing additional training and equipment, increasing the number of plane-supported helicopter missions to 40 percent.

Dirty Thirty

In April 1962, 30 USAF pilots were selected to serve with the VNAF and assigned to the 1st Transportation Group. Known as the Dirty Thirty, these pilots served with Vietnamese pilots flying the C-47s. The 30 pilots were on call 24 hours a day and flew almost 25,000 hours. As a result, they were required to always be prepared and always be dressed in their flight suits. They were christened the Dirty Thirty after a reporter made a remark about the cleanliness (or lack of it) of their flight suits. The American pilots quickly learned that their training had been successful and that the VNAF had become a real force in Vietnam. The arrival of the Dirty Thirty also meant that a number of Vietnamese pilots could be released from flying C-47 transports and begin training in fighters, including armed T-28s and the TF-102, a jet fighter.

The United States sent more helicopters to Vietnam as the war expanded and increased Operation FARM GATE personnel to assume a more active role. When a Viet Cong ambush killed 23 South Vietnamese and two Americans in a convoy outside of Ben Cat, the United States provided air power to protect future truck convoys. In 1962, before the air coverage, the Viet Cong ambushed more than 350 convoys. When air coverage was provided, the Viet Cong didn't attack any convoys. That factor led many USAF officers guiding military strategy in Vietnam to believe that air power was key to a victory in South Vietnam.

When a number of transports were destroyed by Viet Cong antiaircraft fire, General Paul Hardin, commander of the Military Advisory Command Vietnam (MACV), requested and received a number of armed helicopters to provide support for the vulnerable transports. The introduction of the UH-1A (Huey) helicopters changed the course of the war and the Huey became a symbol of the war after the United States became fully engaged in 1965 (see Figure 7-2). Even today, the Vietnam War is considered the first helicopter war.

The helicopter received its first real test at the Battle of Ap Bac in early January 1963. For more information about the battle and its significance, see Chapter 4. As for the air war, a hard lesson was learned: Although it was an effective weapon, the helicopter still needed to be refined, and the South Vietnamese required more training before they could put its air mobility capabilities to use.

Figure 7-2:
A Huey delivers ARVN Rangers on an operation in the Mekong Delta.

Photograph courtesy of the Vietnam Archive, Texas Tech University

For the remainder of 1963, the USAF focused on the dual missions of training the VNAF and using its weapons to support U.S. and allied troops fighting the Viet Cong. By the end of 1963, more than 16,000 Americans, including USAF advisors, were in Vietnam. The USAF established itself as a valuable part of American strategy for victory in Vietnam. As the war progressed, its role took on a more significant part in the fight.

Turning a Green Country Brown: Operation RANCH HAND and Agent Orange

One basic problem with U.S. and ARVN troops fighting a war in Vietnam was the territory and environment. The dense jungle of the central highland and mangroves in the Mekong Delta presented the first obstacle, providing perfect cover for the Viet Cong during the war. Another early problem was how the United States could deny the Viet Cong access to their food sources in South Vietnam, especially when the VC controlled so much of the countryside.

The United States and South Vietnam established a counterinsurgency center in 1961 to determine what course of action to take in overcoming these two obstacles and testing the use of herbicides to fight back the vegetation. The recommendations of the center initiated a ten-year program of removing vegetation and effectively denying the Viet Cong vital food supplies and security that the ground cover had provided. This program also started a controversy that continues today, because chemicals used in the project were suspected of causing side effects unknown at the beginning of the operation. For more information on Agent Orange, see Chapter 18.

Spraying your way to victory: Operation RANCH HAND

The destruction of Viet Cong food supplies and exposure of their base areas came under Operation RANCH HAND, which officially began in November 1961. President Kennedy approved the use of three C-123 aircraft equipped with 1,000-gallon chemical tanks (provided through Operation FARM GATE) to apply herbicides on the jungles, forests, and mangroves of South Vietnam. The aircraft arrived in Saigon in January 1962 and began operations January 12. The first mission flown covered major roads north of Saigon, denying the VC the ability to ambush allied convoys from Saigon to Bien Hoa. As the results and effectiveness of the herbicides became apparent, the United States expanded its target list to include VC-controlled areas in the Mekong Delta, denying them valuable food supplies. The target list again was increased to include forest and mangrove areas along the coast that the VC used as cover to launch their attacks and ambushes against allies. Operation RANCH HAND proved an effective tool in the fight against the VC during the early stages of the war.

During the remainder of the Kennedy Administration, the United States experimented with various methods of spraying herbicides over South

Vietnam. By 1965, Agent Orange proved to be the most effective herbicide, and the C-123 was the preferred aircraft for spraying. An estimated 157,000 acres were sprayed over South Vietnam in 1965, reaching a peak of more than 1.5 million acres in 1967 (see Figure 7-3). Agent Orange's (Agent Orange is defined in the "Chemistry 101: What is Agent Orange?" sidebar) effect on U.S. strategy was significant. The herbicide destroyed Viet Cong food sources and cleared jungle and mangrove areas that had been used for cover.

Figure 7-3: A UC-123 maintains a steady altitude of 100 feet above the foliage and a slow speed of 130 knots, assuring complete and even coverage with Agent Orange.

Photograph courtesy of the Vietnam Archive, Texas Tech University

The colors of the rainbow: Orange works

Several types of herbicides were used in Vietnam; Agent Orange is the more commonly known chemical. Various herbicides were used for different types of vegetation. Estimates suggest that more than 19 million gallons of herbicides were disbursed in Vietnam between 1962 and 1971 with 1966 and 1967 receiving the largest amounts of slightly more than 5 million gallons per year. Agent Orange accounted for approximately 60 percent of the herbicides sprayed in Vietnam, or almost 12 million gallons. It was distributed through Vietnam between January 1965 and April 1970 and was used primarily above jungle and broadleaf plants. Other herbicides were used on certain plant crops, such as rice. Before Agent Orange, the United States experimented with Agents Purple, Pink, and Green. The name for the chemical agent came from the colored strip on the container in which the herbicide was stored. While the majority of the herbicides were released over South Vietnam by aerial spraying from Provider aircraft flying, other herbicides were sprayed by hand pump around base camps to clear specific areas of vegetation.

Chemistry 101: What is Agent Orange?

The herbicide known as Agent Orange was developed in the mid-1940s as a weed killer and was used to kill a variety of plant life. Agent Orange contains a mixture of two herbicides: 2,4 dichlorophenoxyacetic acid (2,4-D) and 2,3,5 trichlorophenoxyacetic acid (2,4,5-T). Agent Orange, so named because of the orange bands that were on the 55-gallon drums used to transport the chemicals, was not the first herbicide used in Vietnam. The United States experimented with variations of the dichlorophenoxyacetic and trichlorophenoxyacetic acids and other chemicals, but found that Agent Orange provided the best results. Essentially, Agent Orange contained plant hormone mixtures affecting plant metabolism and resulting in its death. The herbicide often didn't kill trees and other foliage on the first application, but repeated spraying eventually killed the plants. The debate continues today whether Agent Orange had a negative health effect on military personnel who served in areas that were sprayed. Many scientists and advocates have linked Agent Orange to a variety of cancers and birth defects, but others have conducted studies showing that the level of cancers and other health problems in Vietnam veterans is no different than non-Vietnam veterans.

Evaluating Eisenhower's and Kennedy's air war

During the Eisenhower Administration, the USAF focused more on creating and training the VNAF. The United States had its work cut out in South Vietnam, because the VNAF had little to work with after the French left. When Kennedy entered the presidency, he had a different plan in mind for South Vietnam. As Kennedy and his military escalated the war, the USAF took a more active role in the fighting. The USAF continued to train VNAF pilots throughout the 1960s, but in the Kennedy years, USAF pilots began flying into combat and taking significant casualties. As the United States increased its commitment to South Vietnam, it also escalated the air war. When Lyndon Johnson became president, the USAF was ready to step up to the next level, and Johnson didn't wait long to see that happen.

Chapter 8

Air War over Vietnam: 1964–1973

• •

• •

*T*he air war over Vietnam took on several distinct responsibilities, in addition to bombing the NVA/VC troops, and phases from 1964 through 1973. Since that time, the bombing campaign over the Democratic Republic of Vietnam (DRV, also known as North Vietnam) has received the bulk of historical attention, but air operations also involved other significant missions, including those in South Vietnam, that were just as vital to the war effort.

The air war and its different strategies and tactics may seem confusing (although this chapter attempts to clear that up), but it remains one of the most interesting aspects of the Vietnam War.

Speaking the Plane Truth

As the war in Vietnam escalated, so did the number and variety of aircraft the United States flew. Although this section doesn't include all of the aircraft flown over Vietnam, the aircraft listed gives you a good reference point for this chapter and Chapter 9. Use this ready reference as you read the chapters for a better understanding of the different types of aircraft used or if you get confused on what aircraft was doing what.

The U.S. and South Vietnamese Air Force (VNAF) used the types of aircraft described in Table 8-1 to bomb North Vietnam and support the U.S., South Vietnamese, and allied forces fighting the North Vietnamese and Viet Cong

(NVA/VC) in South Vietnam. The U.S. aircraft were involved in a number of mission types, including *reconnaissance sorties* that were responsible for taking photographs of NVA/VC positions and bomb damage. They functioned also as observation flights used to locate and identify NVA/VC positions to call in other air strikes or artillery attacks.

The Vietnam War is often referred to as the *helicopter war.* The helicopter came of age during this time and is recognized as a symbol of the U.S. involvement. The helicopters listed in Table 8-1 are a few of the more recognized ones used by the United States during the war.

It is often forgotten that the aircraft used in the Vietnam War had responsibilities other than bombing and air-to-air combat. A whole series of aircraft were used to move troops and supplies from place to place in Vietnam. Without transportation aircraft, many of the troops in isolated areas would have received neither ammunition nor food and water.

Table 8-1	Early Warplanes and Helicopters Used by the United States, VNAF, and France	
Official Reference	*Also Known as*	*History*
A-6	Intruder	The A-6 began operations in Vietnam in 1965 as an attack plane for the U.S. Navy (USN), although it also was modified for reconnaissance and electronic warfare.
A-7	Corsair II	This jet bomber replaced the A-4 (Skyhawk) that had flown in the early years of the air war. The A-7 could carry up to 15,000 pounds of bombs and was the preferred attack bomber of the U.S. Navy (USN) in the latter part of the war.
A-37	Dragonfly	This plane was originally a trainer aircraft but was converted during the war for the Army of the Republic of Vietnam (VNAF). It was also flown by the USAF. It featured 7.62-mm guns and a faster cruising speed than the A-1 (Skyraider), which it eventually replaced in the latter part of the war.

Official Reference	Also Known as	History
B-52	Stratofortress	This aircraft was the largest used in the Vietnam War and was capable of carrying thousands of pounds of bombs. The B-52 was originally designed to carry nuclear weapons against the Soviet Union but was transformed to carry conventional weapons (bombs) during the Vietnam War. It was said that a B-52 attack would shake the ground miles away and was one of the most feared weapons of the war.
B-57	Canberra	The B-57, originally designed in England, was used primarily as a bomber. It had a large bombing capacity and could stay over its target for a long period of time. The B-57 was also used to destroy DRV anti-aircraft weapons and performed reconnaissance during the war.
F-4	Phantom	The F-4 was one of the most-used planes during the war. It flew in every type of mission for the U.S. Air Force (USAF) and the U.S. Navy (USN). The F-4 was a durable plane that could travel at two times the speed of sound. The RF-4C (Phantom II), an upgraded version of the F-4, served as the primary reconnaissance aircraft over the DRV.
F-5	Freedom Fighter	The F-5 provided the VNAF a low-cost, fast option for their fleet. The F-5 could carry a maximum payload of 5,200 pounds and had two 20-mm guns for air combat.

(continued)

Table 8-1 *(continued)*

Official Reference	Also Known as	History
F-8	Crusader	This jet fighter served as the Navy's primary plane and could travel faster than the speed of sound. The F-8 carried both 20-mm cannons and four air-to-air missiles, an improvement over the F-4 (Phantom), which carried only missiles. The RF-8A, a modified version of the F-8, served as a reconnaissance plane during the war.
F-100	Super Sabre	Introduced into the USAF in 1953, this plane was the first supersonic fighter. During the war, it served as an air-to-air fighter and in reconnaissance and guiding other fighters and bombers to their targets as a forward air controller.
F-104	Starfighter	The F-104 was introduced to Vietnam in 1965 and Thailand in 1966 as an air defense plane. The F-104 proved less than superior in Vietnam and was eventually replaced with the F-4 (Phantom).
F-105	Thunderchief	The F-105 was designed to carry nuclear weapons. In Vietnam, this jet fighter-bomber flew a significant number of missions over the DRV. The aircraft, which flew the majority of missions over North Vietnam, proved to be a valuable asset in the war because of its speed and maneuverability and was the primary aircraft that attacked the North Vietnamese air defense system
F-111	Aardvark	The F-111 was a long-range jet fighter/bomber that was introduced into battle at the end of the war. The 73-foot long plane weighed more than 40 tons but could travel at two and a half times the speed of sound. The EF-111A (Raven), a modified version of the fighter/bomber, was used to disrupt DRV and MiG radar and electronic guidance missile systems. A *MiG* is a Soviet-built aircraft used by the DRV and is described in Chapter 12.

| Helicopters | | |
Official Reference	Also Known as	History
AH-1	Huey Cobra	This modified, thinner version of the UH-1 (Iroquois), described in Chapter 8, was heavily equipped with a 7.62-mm mini-gun, a 40-mm grenade launcher, a 20-mm cannon, and rockets. It was used in a fire suppression and fire support role during the war.
CH-37	Mojave	This helicopter was used by the U.S. Army in search-and-recovery operations during the 1960s. It had a large lift capacity, enabling it to retrieve planes that had been shot down.
CH-47	Chinook	The Chinook replaced the C-37 as a *medium-lift helicopter* (capable of lifting more than 10,000 pounds). It was used to transport soldiers, for medical evacuation, for search-and-recovery, and to move heavy equipment.
CH-54	Tarhe	The CH-54, better known as the Flying Crane or Sky Crane, was used primarily as a *heavy-lift helicopter* (capable of lifting up to 20,000 pounds) and was used to move large equipment such as trucks, jeeps, and artillery. It was also used in rescue and recovery operations to remove destroyed or damaged aircraft shot down by the NVA/VC.
H-3	Sea King	The H-3, which was also called the HH-3 (Jolly Green Giant) by the USAF, was used primarily for search-and-rescue and troop transport during the war.
HH-53	Super Jolly Green Giant	The HH-53 was the successor to the HH-3 (Jolly Green Giant). It served primarily in search-and-rescue operations during the war with a 13,000-pound load capacity (approximately 33 passengers with equipment and a five-man crew).

(continued)

Table 8-1 *(continued)*

Official Reference	Also Known as	History
OH-6	Cayuse	This observation helicopter, also known as the Loach, was used during the war to seek for and identify North Vietnamese Army and Viet Cong (NVA/VC) positions and call in firepower on those positions after they were located.

Reconnaissance/Observation

Official Reference	Also Known as	Its Use
O-1	Bird Dog	The plane was used for observation and Forward Air Controller (FAC) to call in artillery and air strikes against NVA/VC positions.
OV-10	Bronco	The OV-10, a twin-engine propeller-driven plane, was used for reconnaissance and Forward Air Control missions. It could carry up to 3,600 pounds of bombs or rockets in the five weapon stations, which allowed it to be used as an offensive strike aircraft.
SR-71	Blackbird	The SR-71 was used for reconnaissance over Vietnam starting in 1966. It was a long-range plane (2,900 miles) with a maximum altitude of 85,000 feet. The SR-71 was equipped with sophisticated instruments for intelligence gathering.
U-2	Dragon Lady	This plane was used for *high-altitude reconnaissance* (up to 55,000 feet) during the war. It was used extensively against the Soviet Union to photograph missile positions and adapted to the Vietnam War to locate surface-to-air missile sites (a more detailed explanation of these DRV weapons is in Chapter 12) as well as identify other targets for air strikes.

Transportation		
Official Reference	**Also Known as**	**Its Use**
C-124	Globemaster II	Nicknamed "Old Shakey" because of the intensity of vibrations, this plane served as a primary transport for supplies into Vietnam. It could carry tanks, artillery, bulldozers, and trucks, as well as up to 200 fully equipped soldiers.
C-130	Hercules	The C-130 began life in 1954 as a troop carrier. It continued transportation duties during the war, but it was also modified as a gunship and electronic reconnaissance craft.
C-141	Starlifter	This aircraft had jet engines, a first for transports, and was responsible for the majority of large equipment and personnel that arrived in Vietnam. The C-141 had a greater transport capacity and speed than the C-130 because of its more powerful engines.
C-5	Galaxy	This massive transport, the largest in the USAF, could carry almost all of the equipment used by the Armed Forces in Vietnam. The C-5 had a load capacity of more than 100 tons and had the added advantage of being able to refuel in flight.

Taking the War North

The most discussed and debated aspect of the air war in Vietnam was the bombing of the DRV from 1964 through 1973. From the first strike to the north, following the 1964 Gulf of Tonkin incident (flip to Chapter 11), through the final bombing campaigns during Christmas of 1972, the United States believed that its air power would overcome the DRV's ability to resist and would force a negotiated peace settlement. The United States underestimated the will of the North Vietnamese to sustain damage and overestimated the ability of devastating firepower to force an early end to the war party because of self-imposed limitations.

When North Vietnam failed to follow the rules of war (discussed in Chapter 12), the U.S. strategy faltered because it had to follow international law, which restricted its options. The debate continues today as to whether U.S. air power could have changed the outcome of the war if it had not been restricted — the answer is no closer now than it was during the war, however.

Striking north: Operation PIERCE ARROW

When DRV torpedo boats attacked the U.S. destroyer *Maddox* on August 2, 1964 and then allegedly attacked the *Maddox* and *C. Turner Joy* (also a destroyer) on August 4, 1964, President Johnson responded. For more information on this incident, see Chapter 10. He ordered Operation PIERCE ARROW in retaliation for the torpedo boat attack. USN planes struck four of the DRV patrol boat bases and the oil storage facility at Vinh, destroying approximately 25 percent of the facility. The operation was deemed a success because the targets had been attacked even though one pilot, Lieutenant Everett Alvarez, was shot down and captured and another, Lieutenant Richard Sather, was killed. Alvarez, the first USN Prisoner-of-War, spent the next eight years in North Vietnam.

Tit-for-tat: Operation FLAMING DART

The air war started its slow escalation after the Gulf of Tonkin (see Chapter 11). The USAF immediately increased the number of jet fighters in South Vietnam, but then discovered that North Vietnam had moved Soviet-made MiG jet fighters to Hanoi from its training base in southern China. In 1965, more American planes were deployed to South Vietnam to counter the growing NVA/VC threat, which was real and serious (see Chapter 5).

Numerous events may have caused the United States to launch another operation similar to Operation PIERCE ARROW, but it wasn't until the February 1965 Viet Cong attack on Camp Holloway (near Pleiku in the central highlands) that President Johnson ordered a response. That attack on Camp Holloway had left 8 Americans dead and 128 wounded and had damaged or destroyed 16 helicopters and 8 planes.

President Johnson and his advisors believed that a swift and forceful response against North Vietnam would show the North Vietnamese that the United States could not be bullied and would defend itself in South Vietnam. The resulting operation, called Operation FLAMING DART, saw 83 planes — a combination of A-4 (Skyhawks) and F-9 (Crusaders) — bomb the military facilities at Dong Hoi in North Vietnam, dropping 25 tons of bombs in less than 30 minutes.

Welcome to the Hanoi Hilton

Built by the French as a fortress in the late 19th century, Hoa Lo was home for a number of prisoners of war (POWs) from 1964 to 1973. The prison was located in Hanoi and commonly referred to as the *Hanoi Hilton* after being named so by Lieutenant Commander Robert Shumaker, the second American POW.

POWs during the war were divided among several different camps, but after a failed rescue attempt at Son Tay (see the "Raiding Son Tay" sidebar, later in the chapter), the POWs were centralized in a few locations around Hanoi. The Hanoi Hilton became the primary prison camp after the 1972 bombing campaigns.

Conditions in the Hanoi Hilton were far less accommodating than its namesake. Prisoners were isolated from each other, provided with barely enough food to survive, and often tortured to extract confessions of war crimes against the Vietnamese people.

Very little remains of the Hanoi Hilton today, except for a small museum, because the old fortress was leveled to make room for apartments and stores.

The next day, 24 VNAF A-1 (Skyraiders), led by Air Vice Marshall Nguyen Cao Ky and supported by USAF jet fighters, attacked Chap Le and Vinh Linh, north of the 17th parallel. After the attacks, Johnson ordered a halt to Operation FLAMING DART. Rather than cowering in fear, however, the DRV supported a Viet Cong attack on a housing facility for American personnel in Qui Nhon: On February 10, 1964, the four-story building was destroyed, killing 23 Americans and wounding 21.

Outraged, Johnson immediately ordered another round of bombings and, as a result, a combination of USAF and VNAF planes struck Chap Le and Chanh Hoa. Robert Shumaker, an American navy pilot, was captured and taken to Hanoi, where he spent the remainder of the war (and for many in the United States, the escalating conflict in Vietnam was now a war, even if it wasn't a declared one. (See the "Welcome to the Hanoi Hilton" sidebar for more on Shumaker's digs during that time.) Johnson had declared, upon taking office, that he would not lose a country to communism, so the fighting continued to escalate.

The gathering storm: Operation ROLLING THUNDER

Almost immediately following the conclusion of Operation FLAMING DART, the United States resumed its bombing campaign against North Vietnam. On

March 2, 1965, a combination of 45 F-105 (Thunderchief) and B-57 (Canberra) planes completed the first mission of Operation ROLLING THUNDER, attacking the NVA ammunition depot at Xom Bong. (The Navy's version of Operation ROLLING THUNDER was called Operation SEA DRAGON and is examined in Chapter 10.) While the USAF was dropping 120 tons of bombs on Xom Bong, the VNAF struck at the DRV naval base at Quang Khe. Neither mission received serious resistance, but Lieutenant Hayden Lockhart, Jr. was captured. He was the first USAF pilot to become a prisoner of war, a status he held until his release February 12, 1973.

Early in the operation, the USAF was authorized to seek and destroy military targets in selected areas. The military determined the targets, which were grouped into weekly packages, but did not proceed until officials within the Johnson Administration provided political approval.

The *weekly package* would list a number of targets to strike at during the course of a seven- to fourteen-day period during which time these targets would be the primary ones that the United States would attack. In many cases, President Johnson approved the targets and relayed his directives to Secretary of Defense Robert McNamara for its completion. Many in the military worried that they would not be able to conduct the air campaign against North Vietnam if they weren't allowed a free hand in deciding the time and place of bombing missions.

Tuesday Lunch with Lyndon: Restrictions in the air campaign

Johnson once remarked to the media covering the war that he would not let the USAF bomb the smallest outhouse unless he approved. While this might seem an overstatement, there is abundant evidence to suggest that Johnson's tight control on the mission objectives and his restrictions on where the air campaign could bomb thwarted attempts by the USAF and Navy to conduct decisive air operations.

In fact, every Tuesday at 1:00 p.m., senior White House officials met with Johnson for lunch. The Tuesday Lunch Group discussed many of the war's progressions and obstacles, including the Operation ROLLING THUNDER target list and restrictions designed not to destroy North Vietnam but slowly bleed it until there was no alternative but a negotiated peace. Johnson and his advisors believed this strategy was more likely to keep the Soviet Union and Peoples Republic of China (PRC) — two communist superpowers — out of the war. For many involved in the air war over North Vietnam, Johnson and his advisors were micromanaging the war instead of letting those in charge of the military conduct the air campaign.

For this reason (a slow, steady campaign instead of a massive one), during the first phase of the operation, the air campaign was limited to targets south of the 20th parallel. The second phase expanded the mission but prohibited targets within 30 miles of Hanoi, within 10 miles of Haiphong, and near the Chinese border.

The carrot and the stick, part 1

Operation ROLLING THUNDER lasted for more than three years, but was interrupted periodically with pauses and offers of negotiation. This carrot-and-stick approach, however, had a reverse effect on the North Vietnamese. The United States believed that Operation ROLLING THUNDER (which was the stick) would knock some sense into the DRV officials. The United States then offered negotiations (those were the carrot) and halted the air campaign as an incentive to end the war.

DRV officials, however, viewed the carrot-and-stick approach quite differently than the United States had intended. American offers to negotiate were seen as a sign of weakness. North Vietnam was committed to uniting Vietnam and driving out all foreign influence. When the United States first stopped Operation ROLLING THUNDER in May 1965, DRV officials believed America was divided on its war strategy. Agreeing to go to the negotiation table, the DRV used the pause to rebuild damaged areas and strengthen its anti-aircraft weapons around vulnerable targets.

The carrot and the stick, parts 2 through 7

The first bombing pause in Operation ROLLING THUNDER ended six days after it began, with no positive results at the negotiating table. In fact, USAF reconnaissance planes discovered that DRV construction crews had accelerated repairs to bomb-damaged roads and facilities. The second phase of Operation ROLLING THUNDER then continued until Johnson ordered another pause during 1965 Christmas and 1966 New Year and Tet holidays. When this carrot failed to produce desired results, Johnson authorized a larger stick — phase three.

The third phase of the air campaign expanded the target list to include petroleum-oil-lubricant (POL) storage facilities, power plants, and DRV infrastructure that had previously been out of bounds. The first mission of this phase in June 1966 struck at the POL field four miles from Hanoi, destroying the facility. This phase of the air campaign also destroyed the POL storage area near Haiphong and increased the bombings of major roads, railways, and lines of communication. By the end of the third phase, the United States had destroyed two-thirds of North Vietnam's POL facilities and had greatly damaged its transportation system. While the air campaign didn't stop the North Vietnamese flow of personnel and equipment into South Vietnam, it did divert a significant amount of the DRV's limited resources toward fixing the bomb damage.

The United States continued to bomb areas around Hanoi, including factories, rail yards, power plants, and military bases during phases four and five of the air campaign, but it never targeted the city. During the 1968 Tet Offensive (see Chapter 5), the air war over North Vietnam was greatly decreased because of both the weather and the need for all firepower to be centralized in the South. On April 1, 1968, Johnson ordered the suspension of all bombings north of the 20th parallel; all Operation ROLLING THUNDER missions stopped on November 1, 1968, just a few days before Richard Nixon was elected as the next President of the United States.

Does anyone have a spare MiG: Operation BOLO

The North Vietnamese acquired several *MiG fighter/interceptors* from the Soviet Union in 1965 (see Chapter 11 for more information on the MiG). While the MiG-15 and MiG-17 were a potential threat to early bombing raids over North Vietnam, the North Vietnamese Air Force did not become a real threat until 1966 when it acquired newer and more MiG fighters. In September 1966, North Vietnamese used newer MiG-21s with air-to-air missiles, endangering the USAF and Navy bombers. Although U.S. F-4 (Phantom) fighters had superior acceleration and top speed, as well as sidewinder air-to-air missiles that were more reliable than those supplied to the North Vietnamese, the MiG-21 had the advantage in maneuverability. A complete discussion of the DRV response to the air war, as well as DRV aircraft, is available in Chapter 11.

By 1966, the United States had shot down 23 MiG in air-to-air combat with a loss of 9 planes. These favorable odds were not as impressive as the Korean War, however, where the ratio was closer to 9 to 1. As Operation ROLLING THUNDER moved closer to Hanoi and Haiphong in 1967 (see the preceding section), the risk of meeting MiG fighter/interceptors increased. Johnson still refused to allow the USAF to bomb the North Vietnamese air bases around Hanoi and the bases used in PRC (China) for fear of retribution and negative international opinion. Instead, USAF General William Momyer, commander of the Seventh Air Force, and his staff organized Operation BOLO.

Operation BOLO's main purpose was to deceive the North Vietnamese MiG pilots into believing that they were engaging F-105 (Thunderchief) bombers instead of F-4 fighters. The F-105 wasn't as fast or maneuverable as the F-4, so it was seen as a target rather than a threat to the MiG pilots. On January 2, 1967, Colonel Robin Olds led a flight of F-4 fighters that were disguised with paint as F-105 fighters and flew the normal bomber route toward Hanoi. The MiG pilots took the bait and engaged what they thought were slower, less maneuverable bombers only to discover that they had been tricked. In less than fifteen minutes, the F-4 fighters had shot down seven MiGs without any casualties. Operation BOLO was a major victory for the USAF, and it was supplemented four days later when two additional MiG fighters were shot down.

As a result of Operation BOLO, the North Vietnamese Air Force didn't make a significant appearance in the skies over Vietnam until May 1967, when 20 MiGs were shot down in 72 different engagements. Operation ROLLING THUNDER continued to press the restricted areas over Hanoi and Haiphong, scoring major successes on previously untouched bridges, railways, and the Thai Nguyen iron and steel plant near Hanoi.

MiG losses and increased bomb damage didn't deter the North Vietnamese, however, so President Johnson approved the bombing of MiG air bases that had previously been avoided because they were around areas populated with civilians. These targets destroyed a large number of the fighters on the ground, and North Vietnam responded by moving the remainder of its air force to bases within PRC. The MiG continued to be a threat, but was less of one after the tremendous damage inflicted by the United States in 1967.

Taking off the Gloves: Air Power Unleashed

When President Johnson ordered a halt to the bombing campaign over North Vietnam in November 1968, all coordinated efforts to destroy the DRV through air power ceased. President Nixon, who followed Johnson, authorized some reconnaissance missions over North Vietnam throughout his presidency but refrained from a massive bombing campaign until the North Vietnamese struck south in 1972.

There were exceptions to this "calm" over North Vietnam. For example, in May 1970, Nixon ordered reprisal bombings against DRV air defense and supply areas systems after the North Vietnamese fired upon the reconnaissance aircraft. This section, however, discusses the renewed bombing in 1972, which was called Operation LINEBACKER.

The Eastertide Offensive

By early 1972, the United States had withdrawn a majority of its combat troops from Vietnam as a part of *Vietnamization,* the Nixon strategy to turn over the fighting to the South Vietnamese, as discussed in Chapter 6. DRV General Vo Nguyen Giap had determined that it was finally time to launch another offensive into South Vietnam after the military defeat the NVA/VC had sustained during the 1968 Tet Offensive (see Chapter 5). Giap ordered 14 divisions and 26 regiments — approximately 120,000 soldiers — across the border in a three-pronged attack that was supported by 1,200 tanks as well as other heavy vehicles and equipment, in what would be called the Eastertide Offensive (the attack occurred during the Easter holiday in the U.S.). In the course of the invasion, another 80,000 soldiers reinforced NVA positions. It was a classic invasion of a modern army and presented a perfect target for U.S. air power. The Eastertide Offensive demonstrated that the DRV had switched permanently from a guerrilla style of warfare to a more modern, overt strategy. For more information on the Eastertide Offensive, see Chapter 6.

When the NVA crossed the Demilitarized Zone (DMZ) March 30, 1972, and started the invasion, the USAF responded immediately. While the first concern was to support the soldiers on the ground who were being beaten back by the NVA, Nixon also ordered a resumption of bombing against North Vietnam. On April 2, 1972, he authorized missions against military and supply depot targets that were supporting the invasion immediately north of the DMZ; he extended the bombing area to the 18th parallel on April 4. Two days later, the line was moved farther north to the 19th parallel. One week after Nixon authorized the air campaign, 15 B-52 bombers struck the railroad and supply facilities at Vinh. This was the first use of B-52s over North Vietnam since October 1968.

The USAF continued to advance north, finally bombing the military facilities around Hanoi and Haiphong two weeks into the battle. On May 8, 1972, the USN sent six A-7 (Corsairs) and three A-6 (Intruders) on a mission over Haiphong harbor to drop mines and close the harbor to ships. The aircraft, supported by two nuclear-powered destroyers equipped with radar-guided long-range missiles that cleared a path for them, braved surface-to-air missiles (SAMs) and antiaircraft artillery (AAA) fire and dropped their mines in less than two minutes.

Operation LINEBACKER: It really did work

Operation LINEBACKER officially began on May 10, 1972 with three objectives:

- ✔ Continue to destroy the DRV infrastructure and its ability to sustain the invasion.
- ✔ Eliminate the import of supplies coming into the DRV.
- ✔ Stop the flow of DRV supplies and reinforcement from entering South Vietnam.

Unlike Operation ROLLING THUNDER, Operation LINEBACKER didn't have restrictions placed upon it because of President Johnson calling the shots. Instead, Nixon placed the trust of selecting military targets and mission schedules with his USAF and USN commanders. By the end of May, the United States had destroyed most of the major bridges on the border between the DRV and PRC, as well as the bridges between Hanoi and Haiphong and critical points along the railways and roads.

Figure 8-1 shows a bridge that was bombed by USAF F-4 (Phantoms) on May 12, 1972 at Lang Bun on the northwest rail line about 100 kilometers from Hanoi. The rail line is the main transportation link leading from Hanoi northwest to the border of the People's Republic of China. The middle support of this bridge was knocked off center by the bombs, closing it to rail traffic. The result was a significant decrease in the amount of supplies going south. Some estimates suggest that war supplies decreased from more than 160,000 tons per month to 30,000 tons.

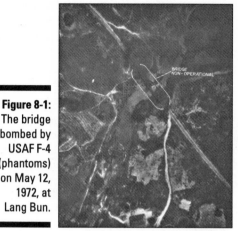

Operation LINEBACKER also introduced some sophisticated technology into the war. The USAF used laser-guided bombs, and the USN employed electro-optically guided bombs to strike at targets that had remained untouched. One example, a bridge linking a major supply line between Hanoi and Haiphong known as the Dragon's Jaw, had escaped American bombs for seven years before a laser-guided bomb destroyed it on May 13, 1972. The USAF and USN also used radar-jamming aircraft to thwart DRV air defenses and used surface-to-air Talos missiles launched from USN ships to ward off the MiG threat to bombers.

Assessing the operation

Operation LINBACKER achieved all of its main objectives:

- As a result of the operation, the DRV wasn't able to sustain the flow of equipment or supplies to support the invasion.

- It could be easily argued that it was air power that halted the invasion and allowed the South Vietnamese forces time to regroup and go on the offensive.

- The operation brought the resumption of negotiations from which the position of the United States and South Vietnam was strengthened after the failed DRV Eastertide Offensive.

- The operation demonstrated that the United States still supported South Vietnam and had maintained enough firepower in Southeast Asia to inflict heavy damage on the DRV.

While Operation ROLLING THUNDER was considered a failure, military historians point to Operation LINEBACKER as a success, because the USAF was allowed to do the job it trained for without restrictions. Critics of the air war in Vietnam argue that the 1972 invasion was not like any previous NVA/VC military operation. Operation LINEBACKER was successful not because of strategy or tactics but rather because the NVA/VC made the fatal mistake of coming out into the open during the Eastertide Offensive.

Negotiations breakdown

When the DRV launched its Eastertide Offensive, Nixon called off peace negotiations and made clear that the United States would not go back to the negotiating table until it could bargain from a position of strength. General Giap's gamble failed as ARVN troops and American firepower stopped all three prongs of the invasion and began pushing the NVA back to the North by June and July. The devastation wrought by Operation LINEBACKER finally brought the DRV back to the negotiating table in August, but unlike earlier in the war, there was no bombing pause. By maintaining the air operations over the DRV, the United States forced the North Vietnamese to drop many of their demands that had stalled earlier talks. Finally, on October 23, 1972, Nixon agreed to stop the air operation after indications that the DRV was ready to resume discussions. Nixon's chief negotiator, Henry Kissinger, declared on October 26 that peace was at hand, but his assertion was premature — the DRV continued to stall in agreeing to a final peaceful resolution. On December 13, the peace negotiation broke down completely again. Nixon issued a final warning to the DRV the next day and after it was rejected, he authorized the most intense bombing campaign of the war, which is discussed in the following section.

Wishing you a merry Christmas: Operation LINEBACKER II

Operation LINEBACKER II, also known as the *Christmas bombings,* was a direct result of several factors:

- ✔ Nixon and Kissinger were frustrated with the DRV's stalling tactics.
- ✔ The DRV had repaired damage sustained during the first Operation LINEBACKER and had re-opened the supply routes between both China and Vietnam and Hanoi and Haiphong.
- ✔ The United States wanted and needed peace in Vietnam.

The DRV offensive failed for several reasons. Air power played a major role in the defeat of the NVA, as did the DRV's inability to sustain the attack because of strained supply lines. However, between Operation LINEBACKER and Operation LINEBACKER II, rail lines had been restored to the point were the DRV was capable of transporting 16,000 tons of supplies per day. There were also indications that the DRV, despite its heavy losses during the Eastertide Offensive, was preparing for another southern attack. Nixon and Kissinger believed that they had just cause in proceeding with a second LINEBACKER Operation.

Operation LINEBACKER II began on December 18, 1972, and lasted 11 days (with a break for Christmas Day). Considered one of the intense periods of bombing over North Vietnam during the war, the operation was the last U.S. bombing operation. The United States dropped approximately 20,000 tons of bombs during the course of the operation with an estimated 1,800 sorties. The workhorse of the bombing campaign over the DRV, the B-52, accounted for more than 15,000 tons and 739 sorties.

The principal areas of attack were around Hanoi and Haiphong, with a concentration on the rail yards, power plants, communication facilities, air defense radar sites, docks and shipping facilities, petroleum stores, ammunition supply depots, air bases, and transportation facilities.

The DRV responded to Operation LINEBACKER II by launching most of its inventory of SAMs against American planes. Few of the approximately 1,000 SAMs remained after the first few days of the operation. Considering the extensive use of SAM and AAA fire during the 11-day period, it is remarkable that the United States lost only 26 aircraft, 15 of which were B-52s.

On December 28, the DRV agreed to re-open negotiations in Paris; the next day, Nixon ordered an end to Operation LINEBACKER II although the United States continued to bomb the DRV south of the 20th parallel until a cease-fire was signed at the Paris Peace Talks. On January 23, 1973, the Paris negotiators signed a nine-point cease-fire agreement effective January 28, 1973 (see Chapter 6).

Providing a Second Chance: Search-and-Rescue

During the course of the war, one of the greatest assets of the USAF and USN during the air campaign was the ability to recover pilots who had been shot down over hostile territory. The search-and-rescue (SAR) mission played a significant role in preserving the morale of the U.S. pilots: Every pilot forced to eject from his aircraft knew that his chances of survival and evading the NVA/VC were greatly enhanced by those in SAR. During the course of the air war from 1964 to 1973, SAR missions rescued more than 2,800 U.S. military personnel and other allied soldiers and civilians. Although 71 SAR personnel were killed and 45 of the rescue aircraft were destroyed during the thousands of sorties, that's a remarkable feat when you consider the harsh elements of Southeast Asia.

Planning for survival: The early mission

The first rescue personnel arrived in South Vietnam in January 1962. The six-member crew was responsible for the creation of a control center and coordination of what would become the search-and-rescue mission. SAR coordination and training of VNAF, however, suffered during the early years for a lack of equipment and aircraft. SAR missions during 1963 and 1964 relied on existing helicopters that weren't designed for search-and-rescue. In Laos, the USAF depended on Air America (see Chapter 14) to rescue downed pilots on missions from Thailand until 1965.

The majority of the early pickups were done with the UH-34 (Sea Horse) and HH-43 (Huskie) helicopter, but after a few failed attempts in which casualties included the rescue teams, the need for specialized equipment became clear. The USAF and the U.S. Marine Corps (USMC) modified these helicopters to suit the needs of search-and-rescue in the hostile climate of Southeast Asia, including a longer cable to hoist pilots stuck in the jungles and better range and loiter time for longer missions. By 1965, the SAR operation added the CH-3 (Sea King) helicopter, which allowed for greater flexibility in rescuing downed pilots. The HH-3 (Jolly Green Giant) and HH-53 (Super Jolly Green Giant) helicopters rounded out the SAR fleet that was responsible for so many lives saved.

Employing search and rescue in a hostile territory

A search-and-rescue (SAR) mission required several elements working together in order for it to be successful. The helicopter was vulnerable to enemy attack and, if it wasn't fast enough, it often provided the NVA/VC with the location of the downed pilot and his crew. Recognizing the need for extra protection, SAR helicopters were supplemented with USAF and USN fighter planes.

How to earn the Medal of Honor

On November 26, 1968, First Lieutenant James P. Fleming, a UH-1F pilot, was returning to his airbase at Duc Co along with four other helicopters when they received an emergency call for help. The five helicopters immediately delayed their return home to go to the aid of a six-man Special Forces long-range reconnaissance patrol. The patrol had been trapped and was about to be overrun. Because the helicopters provided fire support before extracting the patrol, one helicopter was shot down by intense hostile fire. Three of the remaining helicopters were forced to return to their base because of a shortage of fuel, leaving only Fleming. Fleming positioned his helicopter near a riverbank but had to withdraw when the patrol could not reach him because of intense fire. He made a second attempt, despite the amount of weapons fire targeted on him, the patrol leaders' advice to leave, and an empty fuel tank. The helicopter received multiple hits and a smashed windscreen from weapons fire, but Fleming safely rescued all six patrol members. President Nixon awarded the Medal of Honor, the highest decoration in the U.S. military, to Lieutenant Fleming on May 14, 1970.

Raiding Son Tay

The prison camp at Son Tay, northwest of Hanoi, was known to have held up to 50 U.S. pilots. In June 1970, the United States began planning for a SAR mission to raid the camp and rescue the American personnel held in captivity. Before the raid commenced, however, the prisoners were moved to another facility because the water supply at Son Tay had been contaminated. The U.S. planners didn't realize the camp was empty when the mission was carried out November 20, 1970. A flight of A-1E Skyraiders and C-130E aircraft launched a pre-emptive strike around the camp designed to confuse the North Vietnamese while U.S. Rangers landed inside the camp to eliminate the NVA guards and rescue the prisoners. The Rangers killed all of the NVA personnel at Son Tay but discovered that there were no prisoners to rescue. After the 30-minute mission was completed, the SAR force left Son Tay empty-handed. The raid at Son Tay reaffirmed the potential for success of the SAR concept, even though the raid was a failure. After the raid, U.S. POWs were moved into a concentrated area, and no further attempts were made to rescue those held in captivity.

The A-1E (Skyraider) became the aircraft of choice for escorting SAR missions. The Skyraider, a single-engine propeller aircraft, carried an enormous amount of weaponry, including the capability to fire smoke bombs, and could slow its air speed down to work with helicopters in locating and extracting the downed personnel. The Skyraiders would circle the area to protect the helicopters until the personnel were retrieved. A normal mission (not that too many were normal!) consisted of an A-1E dropping smoke on three sides of the rescue area while firing all of its assortment of weapons (bombs, rockets, and 20-mm minigun ammunition) to drive the NVA/VC away from the downed pilots and crew. While not all missions were successful, the SAR mission proved itself invaluable for those pilots and crew who fought in the air over Vietnam.

Medical Aid from the Sky

During the Vietnam War, only 1 percent of those who received a wound in battle died after arriving at a medical facility. This percentage was much less than the 2.5 percent from the Korean War and the 4.5 percent from the Second World War. While many factors, such as better battlefield techniques to care for the wounded and upgrades in medicines, account for the increased survival rate, one of the most important advancements was the medical evacuation system developed during the Korean War and expanded in Vietnam. By decreasing the amount of time between the injury and care in a medical facility (by using aircraft), the chance of survival increased dramatically.

Setting up the system

The first USAF doctor arrived in Vietnam in December 1961. Major George Haworth helped to organize and command the 6220th USAF Dispensary with a staff of five doctors, one dentist, and one veterinarian. The medical facility suffered from a lack of equipment and supplies. The USAF was able to provide one C-123 (Provider) transport from the FARM GATE program (outlined in Chapter 8) to assist in the air evacuations of the most critical patients from Saigon's main air base, Tan Son Nhut, to Japan. Other C-123s were added to the air evacuation, as were C-130s (Hercules), to provide an air bridge between Saigon, Nha Trang, Japan, and the Philippines. After the Gulf of Tonkin incident (see Chapter 11), the air evacuation services increased in Vietnam to include the 1st Medical Service Wing.

Putting the system to work

As the escalation of American personnel in Vietnam continued and the introduction of combat troops meant a rise in the number of casualties, the need for air evacuation rose. The environment of Vietnam was different from the battlefield of Europe or the Korean peninsula. The dense jungles and few roads meant that many wounded soldiers were isolated from traditional methods of retrieval. The United States used helicopters to overcome the obstacle of isolation. The helicopter of choice was the UH-1 (Iroquois), also known as the *Huey*. It was used to get the wounded out of the battlefield and into the safety of the medical facility. The Huey could carry six patients — or more if the situation absolutely demanded it. At the height of medical air evacuations, 116 Huey helicopters were dedicated to this mission. The *Dust-Offs,* as they became known because of the dust stirred by the helicopter blades as helicopters took off and landed (and, by the way, a title that's still used by the military), accounted for a large number of the battlefield casualties that survived the war.

From Here to There: Strategic and Tactical Airlifts

Not all aircraft were involved in engaging the enemy or performing roles such as Dust-Offs and SARs (discussed in the two preceding sections). The USAF also played a major role in the movement of troops both from the United States to South Vietnam and within the country. Strategic and tactical airlifts helped bring supplies to U.S. and allied forces, as well as move troops during operations against the NVA/VC. In strategic and tactical airlifts, the USAF used a number of different fixed-wing aircraft and helicopters. In a country where there were few major roads in rough and unyielding territory, assault from the air was sometimes the only means to engage the enemy.

Searching to destroy: Airlift in a supporting role

During the 1960s, the principal operation performed by ground troops was search-and-destroy, a military tactic described in Chapter 5. Using air power, the United States moved forces into an area of operation to block off escape routes of known NVA/VC forces. Arriving by air meant the United States and its allies avoided road ambushes and costly delays in which the NVA/VC may have escaped or prepared stronger defenses.

The amount of personnel, equipment, and supplies the air transports could deliver in a short period of time was staggering. During Operation BIRMING-HAM, an April 1966 operation near Tay Ninh on the Cambodian border northwest of Saigon, airlift operations provided a daily average of 424 tons of supplies during the first week of the operation. During the course of the operation, more than 10,000 tons of supplies supported the ground troops in their search-and-destroy missions. In many other instances, air power wasn't used in a supporting role but as the primary vehicle to attack the NVA/VC, which used the Vietnamese countryside as protection against attack.

Finding a new way to fight: Airmobility

The first U.S. airmobile unit was formed during the Kennedy Administration. *Airmobility* was the use of aircraft to locate and move troops to engage the NVA/VC. After it was in contact with ground forces, airmobility provided logistical support and coordinated artillery and air power to target the opposition. The concept was attractive because it meant that more military firepower than before could be concentrated in one area and gathered together in a shorter period of time.

In 1962, airmobility was put to the test in Vietnam with the transport of ARVN troops during combat operations. While the ARVN troops didn't perform as well as the United States had wanted, the airmobility concept itself was successful.

The two U.S. divisions in Vietnam that had an airmobility designation were the 1st Cavalry and the 101st Airborne. However, most of the other U.S. units in Vietnam used the concept at some time during the war. An Khe, situated on strategic route 19, was the 1st Cavalry base. Its forces were put into action in November 1965 when the 1st battalion, 7th Cavalry (called the "1/7") engaged the NVA/VC in the Ia Drang valley. The 1/7, whose lineage went back to General Custer, proved that airmobility would work in Vietnam during the operation. Unlike Custer, whose regiment was eliminated by the confederated Sioux at Little Big Horn on June 25, 1876, the 1/7 fought the NVA/VC on their own territory and survived to learn from it.

Using helicopters and transport planes, U.S. and allied forces continued the use of airmobility throughout the war. While early operations had the added advantage of surprise and superior technology, the NVA/VC were able to lessen this advantage as the war progressed. Until the end of the war, the U.S. and ARVN troops used airmobility to counter the advantages gained by the NVA/VC, which had used the rugged and diverse Vietnamese terrain to their advantage.

Spying from the Sky: Reconnaissance Operations

The overwhelming firepower of the USAF and USN couldn't have been utilized as effectively as it was without reconnaissance operations. U.S. aircraft flew thousands of missions over the DRV, gathering intelligence and selecting potential targets (which is how *reconnaissance* is defined) for the bombing campaign. As the air war escalated and the DRV concentrated on its anti-aircraft abilities, the importance of reconnaissance took on more importance.

From air show to showing everything

On October 1961, the South Vietnamese organized an air show in Saigon and invited the United States to display its reconnaissance aircraft, the RF-101 (Voodoo), a twin-engine jet plane that could fly as high as 50,000 feet. The United States had used the RF-101 since the beginning of the year in Laos, assisting the Royal Laotian government in their fight against the Communist insurgency Pathet Lao that threatened to topple the government (see Chapter 14).

The air show was canceled, but the RF-101 was invited to stay to help with rescue efforts resulting from devastating floods in the Mekong Delta and to help the Royal Laotian government. The planes, like those in Figure 8-2, remained in South Vietnam for a month, photographing several instances of Soviet aid toward the Pathet Lao and NVA/VC forces based on the Laos–South Vietnam border. (Within minutes of a reconnaissance plane landing, reconnaissance film exposed on the flight was processed and studied for intelligence information about enemy activities.) When the RF-101 departed South Vietnam, they left their photo unit behind to assist in reconnaissance efforts.

Under Operation FARM GATE (an early Kennedy effort to involve the USAF in South Vietnam that's described in Chapter 7), reconnaissance planes returned to Vietnam in November 1961 with four RB-26s (Invader), a modified version of the old Second World War bomber, and four new RF-101s. When the crisis in Laos was settled in the United Nations, the reconnaissance flights were diverted to South Vietnam. The increase in NVA/VC activity and call for more reconnaissance as U.S. operations became more numerous created a challenge for the USAF and USN planes.

Figure 8-2:
Returning from a reconnaissance mission, an RF-101 lands at the Tan Son Nhut air base.

Photograph courtesy of the Vietnam Archive, Texas Tech University

Reconnaissance over the North

When the United States began its bombing campaign over North Vietnam in 1964, it needed guaranteed military targets. RF-101s led the way in Operation PIERCE ARROW and were the last planes out as they photographed the damage. Reconnaissance missions over North Vietnam had a dual purpose:

  ✔ Identify and photograph potential targets.

  ✔ Provide bomb-damage assessments to determine which targets required additional targeting.

The USAF used *reconnaissance drones* (unmanned aircraft) and the high-flying U-2 to photograph DRV antiaircraft sites. A U-2 plane photographed the first surface-to-air missile (SAM) site in April 1965. Reconnaissance flights over the DRV identified the major supply depots and expanded the potential targets available for Operation ROLLING THUNDER missions by locating additional POL (petroleum-oil-lubricant) sites and military vehicle parks throughout North Vietnam. Without these flights, Operation ROLLING THUNDER and Operation LINEBACKER would not have had as many potential targets.

Reconnaissance missions also provided valuable intelligence on damage assessment. Not all targets were destroyed after the first attempt, and many roads, railways, and bridges were repaired soon after being damaged. Those with strategic value for the DRV were retargeted and attacked until they were destroyed beyond repair. The debate on the success of the bombing campaign against the DRV continues today, but few will disagree that the reconnaissance flights over the North provided valuable information during the course of the war.

Reconnaissance over the South

While reconnaissance missions over South Vietnam didn't have the defined targets they had in the North, the missions were in no way easier. Supporting ARC LIGHT missions, which were often B-52 raids within a predefined area, required detailed photographic imagery of the structures and people in the area before the mission could begin. The United States needed to make sure it wasn't destroying civilian villages, religious temples, or ancient monuments during these raids.

Reconnaissance missions in the south also helped to identify NVA/VC strongholds as well as provide damage assessment photographs for the military intelligence section. Reconnaissance missions provided continuous help during the war in diverse levels of intensity and range. From the siege at Con Thien in 1967, where the planes brought back exact coordinates of NVA/VC artillery sites for the Marines to target and destroy (see Chapter 5), to the nationwide effort to search for the NVA/VC during and after the 1968 Tet Offensive (see Chapter 5), the United States and its allies relied and survived on the intelligence gathered by the spy planes overhead, one of which is shown in Figure 8-3.

Figure 8-3:
An O-1E Bird Dog, flown by a USAF forward air controller (FAC), detected targets for artillery gunners and tactical pilots.

Photograph courtesy of the Vietnam Archive, Texas Tech University

Evaluating the Air War

During the course of American involvement in Vietnam, the role and effectiveness of the air war was a controversial topic of public debate. The discussion has continued in the postwar period with two main lines of argument:

✔ The air war expended a tremendous amount of resources without providing the results to justify the expense.

✔ The air war could have been successful had restrictions not been placed upon it by the political leaders.

Ample evidence supports both contentions. Dependent on your perspective of the Vietnam War, either side seems quite reasonable.

People who argue that the air war was a waste of resources point to the amount of bombs dropped over Vietnam during the war (see the "Quantifying the air war" sidebar). The overwhelming number produced an extraordinary amount of damage, but it didn't lead to a victory nor did it force the DRV to its knees as was intended. The main threads — and some are debatable — of the argument are as follows:

✔ The United States relied on air power to win the war, but the war could be won only on the ground.

✔ In the air campaign over the DRV, the United States failed to realize that bombing a country that had little industry and a large population that was dedicated to victory would not bring them to their knees.

✔ The air campaigns over South Vietnam did more damage than good to the war effort because bombs that were indiscriminately dropped in the countryside recruited more Viet Cong than they killed.

Proponents of the air war disagree with the suggestion that American air power was wasteful. They argued that the strategy and tactics used by the USAF would have been successful had it not been for the interference of politicians in the United States:

✔ Operation ROLLING THUNDER was not effective because President Johnson limited the number of targets based on politics rather than military considerations. Johnson also chose a gradual approach to bombing North Vietnam rather than attacking military targets immediately, which allowed the DRV to stay in the war.

✔ Operations LINEBACKER and LINEBACKER II proved that air power could achieve victory based on the results of each campaign. Operation LINEBACKER resulted in a defeat of the DRV's 1972 invasion attempt, and Operation LINEBACKER II brought about the final peace settlement.

- The United States didn't indiscriminately bomb the DRV and RVN, as some critics suggest. The number of civilian casualties pales in comparison with the Second World War even though three times the amount of bombs fell during the Vietnam War than the Second World War.

- The DRV committed its entire population to victory. The United States, under the laws of war, had every right to bomb military targets next to civilian centers, especially when those targets were placed in such locations because of the civilian population and the propaganda resulting from stray bombs falling on the civilians.

Both sides of this never-ending debate provide compelling evidence to support their contentions. The use of air power in Vietnam continues to evoke debate. It's another example of the controversy that surrounded this most important time in U.S. history.

HISTORIC TRIVIA

Quantifying the air war

During the course of the war, the United States delivered approximately 6,162 million tons of bombs against the DRV and its forces in South Vietnam, Laos, and Cambodia. This amount, almost three times the amount used in the Second World War (2.150 million tons) and 13.5 times the tonnage dropped during the Korean War (0.454 million tons), clearly shows that air power had made dramatic advancements since the last major military campaigns.

The USAF lost 2,257 aircraft (of the approximately 8,500 lost by the United States) at an estimated 3.129 billion dollars with 2,118 killed-in-action and another 3,460 wounded-in-action. The percentage of USAF personnel serving in Southeast Asia who were killed-in-action (2.1 percent) was far less than the percentage for the Army (9.5 percent) or the Marines (22.5 percent). However, the majority of those killed were officers. There were five aces (those who were credited with shooting down at least five DRV planes) during the war, three from the USAF and two from the USN, while 12 USAF pilots earned the Medal of Honor, the nation's highest award.

Chapter 9

Air War over Laos and Cambodia

●●●●●●●●●●●●●●●●●●●●●●●●●●●●●●●●●●●●●●●

In This Chapter

▶ Understanding the early air war over Laos

▶ Supporting the Royal Laotian Army

▶ Bombing the Ho Chi Minh Trail

▶ Air War over Cambodia

●●●

*A*ir operations over Laos and Cambodia in many ways were similar to those conducted over the Democratic Republic of Vietnam (DRV). For more on the air war over North Vietnam, see Chapter 8. These air campaigns were hampered by political restrictions that limited their military effectiveness. Neither campaign achieved the results expected. Laos and Cambodia claimed neutrality during the war even though communist forces supported by the NVA/VC fought against the legitimate governments. The NVA/VC also used Laos and Cambodia to support their war against South Vietnam. The supply line from North Vietnam to South Vietnam, named the Ho Chi Minh Trail, provided continual relief for communist forces fighting against the United States and its allies.

Throughout the war, Laos and Cambodia remained thorns in the side of the United States as it fought to defend South Vietnam. Although air campaigns were successful in temporarily disrupting NVA/VC military operations, they never succeeded in eliminating the threat. Like the early air war in North Vietnam, the campaign against Laos and Cambodia failed to win the day despite the massive number of air missions flown and bombs dropped during an eight-year period.

Neutralizing the Advantage: Air War over Laos

The United States realized that permitting the NVA/VC to take advantage of Laos by moving men, supplies, and equipment from North Vietnam to support the war in the south was intolerable. In addition, the United States would not stand by and allow communist forces in Laos, the Pathet Lao, who were supported by the DRV, to overthrow the Royal Laotian Government.

As a result, the United States designed a series of air operations (see Figure 9-1) to limit the sanctuaries used by the NVA/VC when fighting the war in South Vietnam and to support ground operations against the Pathet Lao. The problem with conducting an air war over Laos, however, was that it bucked international law. As a neutral country in name, if not in practice, the United States was obligated to respect the neutrality of Laos, and yet it could not allow the NVA/VC free movement and a safe haven within that country.

The result was a private war in which the United States did not publicly acknowledge successes or failures in Laos. Although stories occasionally appeared in newspapers, the air campaigns over Laos, which began in 1964, were not considered a significant story until 1969. During the course of the air war, the United States flew almost 500,000 sorties over Laos (one sortie = one plane on one mission) and dropped more than 2 million tons of bombs. Approximately 380 planes and 200 U.S. pilots were lost during the campaigns. The United States never completely denied the NVA/VC sanctuary in Laos during the war nor did it prevent the minimum amount of supplies from reaching the NVA/VC fighting the war in South Vietnam through Laos.

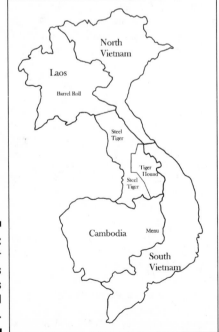

Figure 9-1: Air operations over Laos and Cambodia.

Map courtesy of the Vietnam Archive, Texas Tech University

Starting the campaign: Operation BARREL ROLL

Although President Kennedy may have averted a communist takeover of Laos in 1961 and neutralized Laos through a negotiated United Nations settlement in 1962, Laos never was free of the communist threat. The Pathet Lao controlled the northern provinces in the country and continued to battle the Royal Laotian forces around the strategic Plaines des Jars, bordering the DRV.

The United States paid special attention and gave support to the army of General Vang Pao, whose forces consisted of approximately 5,000 Meo tribesmen trained and equipped by the U.S. Central Intelligence Agency (CIA) and supported by the Civil Air Transport (CAT) and Air America. For more information about the secret war in Laos, see Chapter 13.

In early 1964, the Pathet Lao, supported by the NVA, began an attack in the Plaines des Jars, threatening neutralist forces under General Kong Le and placing the Royal Laotian Government in jeopardy of losing the northern half of its country to the communists. That would have all but assured the overthrow of Prime Minister Souvanna Phouma, and if that happened, stopping the NVA/VC from using the country as a supply-line into South Vietnam would be impossible.

Although President Lyndon Baines Johnson was willing to authorize an air campaign against the NVA/VC forces in Laos, like South Vietnam, he wasn't willing to do it without at least some restrictions based upon legitimate political concerns, such as the possible entry of China into the war or increased Soviet aid to North Vietnam.

Operation BARREL ROLL was the first air campaign against NVA/VC forces in Laos. It began December 14, 1964, with a modest effort — two bombing missions per week with no more than four planes per mission. Using F-105 (Thunderchiefs) originating from the Royal Thai air base at Udorn, Thailand, Johnson wanted to avoid publicity and unwanted questions. The United States, which had to account for its actions and lead from a moral high ground, could not acknowledge the use of an air base in one neutral country to bomb targets in another neutral country in an undeclared war.

Early Operation BARREL ROLL results were disappointing. USAF pilots didn't like restrictions that forced them to go to extraordinary lengths in verifying military targets devoid of any risk of civilian casualties. The restrictions also predefined areas where missions could be flown in northern Laos along the Laotian-DRV border in the Plaines des Jars.

As the war in Vietnam escalated, so did U.S. support for the Royal Laotian Army (RLA) fighting the Pathet Lao. The air war over Laos followed patterns similar to the ground war through 1973. Weather over northern Laos divided the campaign into two seasons:

- **The dry season,** usually October to April, was a time for the Pathet Lao to go on the offensive.

- **The wet season,** usually April to September, enabled government forces and H'mong allies to launch operations into the communist-held territory.

Operation BARREL ROLL missions provided the Laotian forces, which were outnumbered and often possessed inferior equipment, the firepower they needed to strike at the heart of the Pathet Lao. The heaviest fighting occurred during 1967–1969 when H'mong and RLA pushed the Pathet Lao back to near the DRV border only to suffer a serious setback because the Pathet Lao was able to retake most of the area with support from Soviet-made tanks. The two forces jostled back-and-forth in the Plaines des Jars with increased numbers of BARREL ROLL operations offsetting Soviet-made tanks and heavy artillery.

By 1970, the United States was diverting B-52 ARC LIGHT missions in South Vietnam to Laos to prevent a disaster in the Plaines des Jars. (See Chapter 8 for more information on this topic.) On February 17–18, 1970, B-52 bombers dropped more than 1,000 tons of bombs on Pathet Lao forces, and USAF planes flew another 3,000 sorties during the communist offensive before it ended. USAF repeated the performance in 1971 and 1972 as Pathet Lao forces again threatened the Royal Laotian Government. As long as the United States provided air power to support the H'mong and RLA, Laos held off the communist forces.

The United States signed a cease-fire agreement with the Pathet Lao February 21, 1973, a month after a similar agreement was signed with the DRV. The last Operation BARREL ROLL mission concluded two months later. At the same time that DRV forces were rolling into South Vietnam in 1975, Pathet Lao forces also were rolling into RLA territories in Laos. Without the United States supporting the RLA, the Royal Laotian Government also fell. The Pathet Lao occupied the entire country by August 1975, and in December 1975, established the Lao People's Democratic Republic.

Bombing the trail: Operation STEEL TIGER

Supporting the RLA and H'mong wasn't the only mission for U.S. forces in Laos. When Operation MARKET TIME, the blockade that denied the DRV access to a sea route for moving supplies and troops to South Vietnam (see Chapter 10), became fully effective, the DRV increased its efforts to develop a land route for personnel, supplies, and equipment. The Ho Chi Minh Trail, as it commonly was referred to during the war, was a series of roads, trails, and footpaths that traversed Laos and Cambodia from Vinh to several entryways into South Vietnam.

Operation STEEL TIGER began April 3, 1965, less than two months after the beginning of bombing over North Vietnam. STEEL TIGER was designed to complement Operation ROLLING THUNDER, the bombing campaign during the Johnson Administration against North Vietnam (see Chapter 8). It targeted the Ho Chi Minh Trail in Laos (see Figure 9-2) from north of the Demilitarized Zone (DMZ) at the 17th parallel to the southern border with Cambodia. Routes that made up the Ho Chi Minh Trail were established during the Second World War, so the trail was extensive even though the actual roads were primitive. The DRV actively used the trail in the 1960s to counteract the escalation of the war by the United States. The trail was the lifeline for NVA/VC fighting in the south and a significant obstacle to American success during the war.

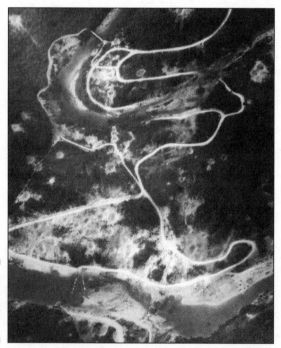

Figure 9-2:
Bombing on
the Ho Chi
Minh Trail.

Photograph courtesy of the Vietnam Archive, Texas Tech University

Operation STEEL TIGER averaged approximately 1,000 sorties per month for the remainder of 1965, with the majority of the flights originating from either Thailand or South Vietnam. The command structure for the operation was complex, and Thai officials demanded that the operations commander be based in Thailand whenever planes took off from one of their bases. Further complicating the structure were other nonmilitary agencies running operations in Laos.

CIA involvement in Laotian operations predated the military's involvement, and it also was very much involved in selecting targets for Operation STEEL TIGER missions. Protecting CIA operatives in the field from exposure or accidental bombing by Operation STEEL TIGER sorties was important and required coordination between various organizations involved in the air campaign.

Organizational lines of command were further muddled when General William Westmoreland, who was commander of the Military Assistance Command, Vietnam (MACV), and who was in charge of U.S. operations in South Vietnam, requested and gained control of the bombing campaign. Although Westmoreland renamed the operation TIGER HOUND for his new area of responsibility, Operation STEEL TIGER remained the name for areas in the interior of Laos and north of the DMZ.

Other political considerations limited available targets in the same way that they had during Operation BARREL ROLL and Operation ROLLING THUNDER missions. Not drawing international attention to the air campaign over Laos was important, because the United States still publicly acknowledged Laotian neutrality. Besides, releasing information about extensive operations may have provided an impetus for Soviet or PRC intervention on a level that the United States could not match. These restrictions produced less than stellar results and caused a great deal of animosity between those flying the missions and the U.S. ambassador to Laos, William Sullivan. Sullivan kept a very tight rein on missions flown over Laos and had the authority of final approval for every mission.

The USAF primarily used a combination of F-4, F-100, and F-105 jets and older WWII-era B-57 and A-26 bombers over Laos with RF-101s and RB-57s for reconnaissance. The C-130 was used during night operations with the B-57 as the USAF bombed the trail at all hours of the day.

Night operations were very important in Operation STEEL TIGER because the NVA/VC used the cover of darkness to conceal movements of trucks on open roads. The USAF used the O-1 Bird Dog and A-1 Skyraider (described in Chapter 7) as forward air controllers (FAC) to search for the truck convoys. When a convoy was located, usually by the careless use of headlights, the FAC called in faster moving fighter/bombers to engage the target. The A-1 also possessed a tremendous amount of weaponry to bomb the convoys, engaging the trucks when possible. Most night operations over the trail, however, ended with no sightings of the NVA/VC and few located more than a couple trucks in a convoy. When the USAF failed to locate convoys or supply depots, planes often dropped their bombs on known trails to create craters. The damage was often only temporary but it was better than doing nothing. Night operations seldom proved beneficial, but the psychological effect was worth the effort. The NVA/VC always had to worry about air attack, day and night, and constantly were on alert for the sound of plane engines overhead. Operation STEEL TIGER continued until December 1968 when it was merged with other operations over Laos. The bombing missions continued until April 1972 under a different name, but the objective did not change.

Igloo White and McNamara's Fence

The United States tried several ways to stop the flow of supplies along the Ho Chi Minh Trail. Technology and creative thinking were not barriers to what the United States planned during the course of the war. One technological device that was used under the code name Igloo White, consisted of small battery-powered acoustic sensors dropped along known routes of the trail. When passing NVA trucks or personnel triggered a sensor, that information was relayed to a computer operator who predicted the route of the truck or personnel and established an interception point for a bombing mission using data stored in a series of computers. Igloo White, on the other hand, was a part of a larger plan cutting surveillance of the trail in two. The McNamara Line, or McNamara's Fence, was a planned barrier of approximately 1,000 meters wide filled with mines and sensor devices and pretargeted for artillery fire. The goal was to completely shut off land routes between North and South Vietnam. Although these and other operations were contemplated and attempted to some degree, the United States never was able to stop the DRV from moving personnel and supplies to the south.

Expanding the air war: Operation TIGER HOUND

In December 1965, General Westmoreland separated the southern half of Operation STEEL TIGER and took over operational control of the air campaign. Westmoreland saw this new air campaign, Operation TIGER HOUND, which was comprised of the area from the 17th parallel to the southern border of Laos and Cambodia, as an extension of the war in South Vietnam. So, he wanted to bypass the restrictions imposed by the U.S. ambassador in Laos.

During the seven years it was employed in Vietnam, Operation TIGER HOUND had two primary objectives:

- Target and destroy NVA vehicles using Laotian roads to move personnel and supplies into South Vietnam.
- Create bottlenecks in the transportation system by destroying strategic bridges and roads necessary for the movement of personnel and supplies.

The rules governing Operation TIGER HOUND strikes were not as strict as for Operations STEEL TIGER or BARREL ROLL. Westmoreland was less sensitive to the political considerations involved in selecting his targets and more interested in the military advantages to be gained by disrupting the NVA/VC supply line, which had become substantial by the end of 1965.

The United States employed a new generation of technology to combat the NVA/VC on the Ho Chi Minh Trail. The reconnaissance version of the F-4, the RF-4C, flew missions with infrared and side-looking radar for maximum intelligence gathering during day and night missions. Pilots also carried Starlight (night vision) technology, which provided them with greater visibility during night missions.

Despite heavy bombing of the trail in 1966–1967, the United States never was able to completely shut it down. The DRV placed approximately 50,000 people along the trail to repair damage caused by the air campaign and support those moving supplies along the transportation network. When a road or bridge was destroyed, the workgroups, frequently young men and women, diverted trucks and convoys around the damaged area when they were repairing it. The movement of supplies seldom stopped, but the passage of materiel south may have taken longer when bombing was at its heaviest. Regardless whether it took three months, six months, or a year, the Ho Chi Minh Trail nevertheless continued feeding NVA/VC forces in South Vietnam and enabling them to match U.S. escalation step-for-step.

Focusing on the trail: Operation COMMANDO HUNT

When President Johnson announced a reduction of Operation ROLLING THUNDER at the end of March 1968 and then halted all bombing north of the 17th parallel a few days before leaving the White House, the effect on the campaign over Laos was significant.

The air campaign over the DRV was designed to bring about a political solution, but the air campaign over Laos was focused on military victory. The end of Operation ROLLING THUNDER meant that the DRV could divert more resources to maintain the Ho Chi Minh Trail and improve the infiltration routes already established earlier in the war.

On the other hand, U.S. sorties over southern Laos increased to 12,800 during November 1968, in part as a response to the strategic value of the trail but also because more aircraft were available for such operations. On November 15, 1968, the new Nixon Administration ordered Operation COMMANDO HUNT. Its dual purpose included disrupting the trail and destroying the NVA moving into South Vietnam to replenish the defeated NVA/VC forces following the 1968 Tet Offensive (see Chapter 5).

Operation COMMANDO HUNT eventually broke down into seven different phases during 3½ years. Each phase had the same basic objective of destroying more of the NVA/VC than could be transported south to replenish their combat losses and preventing the flow of supplies to maintain the existing

NVA/VC forces in South Vietnam. The phases of Operation COMMANDO HUNT usually were tied to the weather patterns over southern Laos. During the wet season, Operation COMMANDO HUNT missions concentrated on disrupting repairs and improvements to the trail, because less convoy traffic traveled the trail. As convoys increased during the dry season, missions refocused on destroying vehicles destined for South Vietnam. As the air campaign against the trail continued during the war, the United States used newer and more sophisticated ways of detecting movement. Seismic and acoustic sensors detected NVA/VC movement without concern for nighttime or poor weather conditions. When sensors indicated heavy movement down the trail, Operation COMMANDO HUNT missions targeted the area in question.

The number of Operation COMMANDO HUNT missions fluctuated based upon other air commitments in Southeast Asia. Those in charge of the air war used Laos, and later Cambodia, as their primary areas of operation not only to test new weapons, strategies, and tactics but also to demonstrate their abilities.

The first two phases of Operation COMMANDO HUNT included a large number of missions, because no other significant air operations were being conducted over Vietnam. Operation BARREL ROLL missions increased in response to the Pathet Lao and DRV dry season offensives, so the number of sorties flown in Operation COMMANDO HUNT (III) decreased.

Phase IV also included fewer sorties because air power was diverted to support the U.S. incursion of Cambodia in May 1970, which you can read about in Chapter 6. Phase V of the operation started out slow because available air power was diverted to LAM SON 719, the ground operation into the main logistics city of Tchepone in Laos that is outlined in Chapter 6. Operation COMMANDO HUNT continued through April 12, 1973, but as the United States departed South Vietnam, fewer aircraft were available for the air operations over Laos, even though DRV activity wasn't diminish.

Pushing the legalities of war: LAM SON 719

After the May 1970 Cambodian incursion, Congress prohibited the use of ground troops outside of South Vietnam. No mention of stifling air power was made in the congressional legislation, and the United States fully participated in air operations during LAM SON 719 without introducing ground troops. For more information on the ground war during these two operations, see Chapter 5. U.S. participation provided a much needed boost in training for the South Vietnamese pilots who, as a result, were able to log more combat flying hours with U.S. guidance. The United States also willingly supported the Army of the Republic of Vietnam (ARVN) in capturing Tchepone and cutting the Ho Chi Minh trail in two.

LAM SON 719 was supposed to buy time for Nixon's Vietnamization program and ensure that the South Vietnam Air Force (VNAF) was prepared to take over air operations after the United States departed Southeast Asia. The United States committed aircraft for moving approximately 13,000 ARVN soldiers and 20,000 tons of supplies to a preinvasion staging area. When ARVN crossed the border into Laos, Vietnamese pilots flew with U.S. pilots in U.S. planes helping to coordinate airstrikes and communicate with the ground troops. When these aircraft were supporting the 17,000 ARVN troops approaching Tchepone, B-52s and C-130s bombed suspected NVA/VC bases.

As we explain in Chapter 6, the ground operation ended in failure, but the air operations faired much better. Air power accounted for the destruction of approximately 20,000 tons of food and ammunition, 150,000 gallons of fuel, 500 trucks, and 100 tanks either damaged or destroyed. The United States flew more than 8,000 sorties and dropped more than 20,000 tons of bombs during LAM SON 719. Although the USAF and USN lost only seven planes, they suffered heavy helicopter losses. At least 100 were destroyed, and 600 were severely damaged. ARVN troops failed to obtain their military objectives, but the operation caused considerable damage to Tchepone and the Ho Chi Minh Trail surrounding the city. The DRV would rebuild, but LAM SON 719 delayed NVA/VC offensive operations for another year.

The Operation COMMANDO HUNT operations ended when the NVA/VC finally struck during the Eastertide Offensive. The coordinated, covert invasion of South Vietnam signaled the end of Operation COMMANDO HUNT, because all air assets remaining in Southeast Asia were diverted to Operation LINE-BACKER (I) in defense against the Eastertide Offensive. As the Eastertide Offensive was turned back, air power continued its focus on bombing raids over the DRV and providing support for the RLA in northern Laos. The Ho Chi Minh Trail became less important after the 1972 Eastertide Offensive, because NVA troops no longer needed to move personnel and supplies through Laos (see Chapter 6). With the United States out of the war in January 1973, the DRV could launch its next attack across the DMZ with little fear of reprisal from U.S. air power.

Over Cambodia

Cambodia was a problem for the U.S. war effort in South Vietnam from the beginning of the war. Cambodia declared neutrality, thereby prohibiting the use of foreign troops on its soil. The declaration of neutrality, however, enabled the NVA/VC to use Cambodia as a safe haven against U.S. and ARVN attack. NVA/VC bases in Cambodia served as sanctuaries and launching points for offensive operations into South Vietnam.

Early in the war, U.S. military leaders recognized the Cambodian problem but political considerations prohibited them from correcting it. President Johnson rejected military plans to destroy the NVA/VC bases in Cambodia and severely limited the ability of U.S. soldiers to engage NVA/VC troops, once they crossed the border.

Prince Norodom Sihanouk, the political leader of Cambodia, continually denied the existence of NVA/VC bases in his country in spite of the overwhelming evidence to support the assertion. After the 1968 Tet Offensive, Sihanouk conceded that a few NVA/VC might be in his country but did little to stop their movements across the Cambodia-South Vietnam border. The United States refrained from pursuing the NVA/VC or targeting their supply lines and bases in Cambodia throughout the Johnson Administration. When Richard Nixon came into office, U.S. strategy changed, and the problem in Cambodia surfaced at the top of the priority list.

Secret bombing campaign: Operation MENU

Shortly after Nixon took office, the NVA/VC launched an offensive from its bases in neutral Cambodia that was designed to overthrow the South Vietnamese government. Although much smaller than the 1968 Tet Offensive, this new offensive raised questions about just how neutral Cambodia really was in the war. General Creighton Abrams, the new commander of MAVC, requested authorization to bomb the NVA/VC bases inside Cambodia to disrupt the offensive.

Nixon authorized the new air campaign. Its missions were named BREAKFAST, LUNCH, SUPPER, DESSERT, and SNACK, all under the operational name MENU. Operation MENU lasted less than 14 months from March 18, 1969, to May 26, 1970, but it resulted in more than 120,000 tons of bombs dropped in a small target area. Operation MENU was a secret bombing campaign designed with three primary objectives:

- Disrupting the NVA/VC 1969 offensive

- Destroying the NVA/VC bases in Cambodia

- Providing time for Vietnamization to work in South Vietnam

Operation MENU made use of B-52 bombers disguised to appear as if they were flying Operation ARC LIGHT missions, which generally supported ground troops (see Chapter 8). The secrecy lasted for more than a year until *The New York Times* ran a story about the bombing mission. In March 1970,

Lieutenant General Lon Nol overthrew the Cambodian government of Prince Sihanouk and asked the United States for help in pushing the NVA/VC out of Cambodia. Nixon responded immediately with the Cambodian incursion, which is described militarily in Chapter 6 and politically in Chapter 14. After the incursion, keeping the bombings a secret no longer was necessary, but the extent to which the United States had bombed the neutral country remained a secret until 1973.

Antiwar activists' outrage (see Chapter 14) against the incursion and what was known of the bombing forced an end to Operation MENU, and so did the early success of the Cambodian incursion. The U.S. Congress prohibited the use of air power over Cambodia with the Cooper-Church Amendment, but that didn't stop the United States from continuing its secret air war over Cambodia.

Continuing the air war: Operation FREEDOM DEAL

After the Cambodian incursion, the U.S. air campaign over Cambodia focused on supporting the forces of Lon Nol and disrupting NVA/VC supply lines through the country under Operation FREEDOM DEAL. It also was successful in blocking the transport of supplies by sea from North Vietnam to the NVA/VC in South Vietnam via the Mekong River.

Air missions took on the additional role of providing air cover for sea and land convoys to Phnom Penh, the capital of Cambodia, and in 1971, the United States used its air power to back an operation to reopen supply roads to the capital.

Communist forces led by a radical faction in Cambodia known as the Khmer Rouge had achieved remarkable success in late 1970, taking over more than 50 percent of the Cambodian territory. U.S., ARVN, and Cambodian personnel had many successes against the Khmer Rouge through 1972, but the communists maintained their hold on most of the country. In early 1973, a massive U.S. air response was the only thing that stopped the Khmer Rouge from marching into Phnom Penh.

With the war in Vietnam over for the United States in January 1973, Congress started applying pressure to end U.S. involvement in Cambodia. Nixon vetoed a bill that would have prohibited funding of U.S. operations in June 1973 and compromised with Republican leaders in the House of Representatives delaying similar legislation and extending U.S. air operations until August 15, 1973. Nixon signed Public Law 93-53 July 1, 1973. After the last mission was completed August 15, the Khmer Rouge launched an offensive in which they captured Phnom Penh by April 1975. Lon Nol's forces surrendered the capital and Cambodia fell to the Khmer Rouge April 17, 1975.

Assessing the air war

During the air campaign over Cambodia, the United States flew more than 16,500 sorties and dropped approximately 383,800 tons of bombs. Despite this massive use of firepower, the United States never achieved its objectives. Cambodia remained a safe haven for the NVA/VC, except for a short period in 1970 when U.S. and ARVN troops occupied border areas. NVA/VC used Cambodia to launch offensive operations into South Vietnam, resupply, and regroup in relative peace. Although the air war often disrupted NVA/VC operations, it didn't destroy their ability to fight from Cambodia. Political considerations played a significant factor, but so did geography and military considerations. The United States attempted to respect Cambodian neutrality despite the air campaigns, even though that neutrality was in name only.

Chapter 10

Navigating the Seas: The Navy's Role

More than 2.6 million sailors served during the Vietnam War — 2,551 were killed in action. Fifteen sailors received the Congressional Medal of Honor, the highest honor in the armed forces, seven posthumously. The United States Navy played a crucial role in the Vietnam War with a three-pronged strategy that included:

✔ Attempting to stop the flow of weapons and equipment from North Vietnam to Viet Cong forces. The North Vietnamese had used water routes for a majority of their supplies until the U.S. Navy adopted a strategy to stop the flow of supplies.

✔ Providing artillery fire support for U.S., South Vietnamese, and Free World forces. Naval gunfire played a significant role in protecting troops under attack as well as weakening North Vietnamese and Viet Cong forces in well-protected fortifications.

✔ Participating in military operations in and around the major waterways of South Vietnam. The Navy used the waterways in Vietnam to its advantage, providing rapid transport of troops and equipment into areas that otherwise were inaccessible.

While the Navy has received less attention in Vietnam than the Air Force, Army, and Marines, it played a crucial role in U.S. strategy. The Navy's success was measured in its ability to stop the flow of supplies by sea, its overwhelming firepower, and, by 1965, its unquestioned domination of the seas.

Arming Themselves for the Sea War

The blue- and brown-water fleets used a number of different ships to combat the North Vietnamese Army (NVA) and Viet Cong (VC). The *Blue Water Navy* used more traditional weapons of war in their fire-support missions, interdiction campaigns, and protection of the fleet. It maneuvered over, and controlled, the oceans and deep seas to the south and east of Vietnam — these waters held shades of blue and thus the name. These ships included aircraft carriers, battleships, cruisers, destroyers, cutters, and elements of the amphibious fleet. U.S. Navy ships of particular note were the first nuclear-powered aircraft carrier, the USS *Enterprise,* and the nuclear-powered guided missile cruisers, USS *Long Beach* and USS *Chicago*, which destroyed a Soviet-built MiG aircraft using a Talos surface-to-air missile over North Vietnam. For more information on the MiG aircraft, see Chapter 11.

Because of the nature of the area of operations for the *Brown Water Navy,* it used a different type of vessel in its battle against the NVA/VC. The Brown Water Navy used patrol gunboats (PBRs), minesweepers, hydrofoils, Swift Boats, and Boston whalers. The Brown Water Navy patrolled the inland waterways and coastal seas in Vietnam, operating in the murky brown waters that covered the country.

The allied naval forces involved during these interdiction operations used a variety of traditional and unusual weapons mounted on their ships and vessels. The Blue Water Navy's firepower consisted of a majority of 3-inch to 8-inch guns, along with the 16-inch guns on the battleship USS *New Jersey*. The size of the gun was defined by the diameter of the bore, or end of the weapon. As technology advanced during the war, allied naval forces added a combination of rockets and guided missiles to their arsenals. The Brown Water Navy used a combination of traditional and unusual weapons in its operations. Water cannons mounted on small vessels poured thousands of gallons of water into earth and log bunkers that had been able to defeat artillery bombardment. Defenders of these bunkers had the choice of staying and drowning or fleeing. Flamethrowers were mounted on Assault Support Patrol Boats (ASPBs) and *Monitors,* a heavily armored craft resembling ships used during the American Civil War, to attack enemy bunkers aside of shallow waterways where other weapons proved ineffective.

Building Up the U. S. Navy in Vietnam: 1954–1964

Contrary to popular belief, the U.S. Navy didn't begin its involvement in Vietnam in the 1960s. The Navy first became involved in Vietnam in 1950 and was involved with training South Vietnamese Armed Forces, thus providing crucial support to the early war effort. Its first operation, one of the largest humanitarian evacuations in U.S. naval history, occurred after the 1954 Geneva Conference and the division of Vietnam at the 17th parallel, as described in Chapter 2.

This is your "Passage to freedom": The 1954 Vietnamese evacuation

One aspect of the 1954 Geneva Agreement was the free movement of Vietnamese on both sides of the 17th parallel for 300 hundred days. The 17th parallel is shown in Figure 9-1. As a result of that movement, almost 750,000 Vietnamese voted against Communism with their feet as they fled North Vietnam. In the beginning, the French believed that only a few thousand would want to leave ancestral lands in the north and refused U.S. assistance. They certainly weren't prepared for the mass exodus.

In August 1954, at the request of the Vietnamese and the French, the U.S. Navy agreed to assist in evacuating Vietnamese refugees to South Vietnam. Operation Passage to Freedom oversaw the movement of 310,000 Vietnamese on U.S. ships from Haiphong to Saigon and Vung Tau (named Cap St. Jacques by the French). The remaining 440,000 Vietnamese departed in what the South Vietnamese called Operation Exodus by air or ground transportation.

The U.S. Navy, under the command of Admiral Lorenzo Sabin, evacuated the Vietnamese personnel, equipment and vehicles used by the French and Vietnamese that the United States did not want to fall into the hands of the Viet Minh. To learn more about the Viet Minh, the precursors to the Viet Cong, see Chapter 2. The movement of people and equipment, and the logistical nightmare of resettling the population in the war-torn South challenged the United States in what would be considered the first major humanitarian effort to aid the Vietnamese people. Passage to Freedom introduced to many in the U.S. military the difficulties of working with the Vietnamese people. The humanitarian nature of the operation outweighed the headaches caused during the 300 days.

Developing the Vietnamese Navy

After Operation Passage to Freedom, American naval advisors worked to help create a South Vietnamese Navy in the late 1950s and early 1960s. Between 1954 and 1959, members of the Navy Section of the Military Assistance and Advisory Group, Vietnam trained South Vietnamese soldiers. For the approximately 80 members of the Navy Section, finding ships was the first task. They did so through a salvage project, reclaiming old French equipment. By 1959, the South Vietnamese Navy had 119 ships and a force of 5,000 personnel, a significant increase if you consider that the South Vietnamese Navy did not exist on its own before 1954.

Brown Water Navy versus Blue Water Navy

The variety of terrain and conditions in Vietnam affected the United States Navy as much as it did the Army, Air Force, and Marine Corps. The Navy established a division of resources to handle the tasks it confronted in Vietnam. The Brown Water Navy, consisting of small and quick ships and boats, used the almost 3,000 nautical miles of near rivers, waterways, and canals, to patrol supply routes and attack the North Vietnamese Army/Viet Cong (NVA/VC) whenever possible. While the focus of the Brown Water Navy was in the Mekong Delta, it extended to all inland waterways. The Blue Water Navy, what is considered the traditional Navy, performed the same missions but, because of the size of its ships, was confined to the South China Sea.

When NVA/VC activities increased after 1959, the U.S. Navy became more active in the South China Sea with several visits by American ships to Saigon. During the crisis in Laos, the Seventh Fleet deployed a task force into the region for use against the Pathet Lao, the communist force threatening the Royal Laotian Army in northern Laos. The crisis was averted, and the fleet returned to normal duties, after a United Nations solution resolved the situation.

During the early 1960s, as the Laotian crisis was resolved in the United Nations, the Kennedy administration continued to emphasize the training of the South Vietnamese armed forces as they struggled against the Viet Cong. When Lyndon Johnson became president, he continued this work so that by May 1964, 235 American naval advisors were in Vietnam while the South Vietnamese Navy increased to 8,162 officers and sailors with a fleet of 44 seaworthy ships and more than 200 other smaller vessels. The South Vietnamese Navy was a formable force by 1964 but it still relied on the United States for training, logistics, and support.

Catalyst to War: De Soto Missions, Oplan 34A, and the Gulf of Tonkin Incident

The U.S. Navy became involved in secret operations against North Vietnam to disrupt the forces near the 17th parallel during the last few weeks of the Kennedy Administration. Kennedy authorized a series of missions to gather intelligence and harass North Vietnamese coastal installations and offshore island facilities. These bases had been used to infiltrate personnel and supplies south of the 17th parallel and were considered a legitimate target for the

United States and South Vietnamese. The U.S. strategy was divided into two strategies, the De Soto Missions and Oplan 34A:

- ✔ President Johnson reaffirmed the De Soto missions in early February 1964 with the use of the destroyer USS *John R. Craig* to gather information about the North Vietnamese radar and air defense installations using electronic intelligence (ELINT). This technology proved useful as the war progressed. The USS *John R. Craig* mission was canceled because of heavy coastal fog and was replaced by the destroyer USS *Maddox* when the weather cleared.

- ✔ The second prong of this strategy, known as Operation Plan 34A (OPLAN 34A), was the use of commando raids. In early November 1963, President Kennedy ordered covert operations targeted against the North Vietnamese coastal sites that contained supplies, radar installations, and artillery positions. The campaign used U.S. naval craft and American pilots transporting small teams of highly trained, elite South Vietnamese commandos (similar to U.S. Special Forces) during the night to cause as much damage as possible.

North Vietnamese sometimes were kidnapped to gather as much information as possible. It was an OPLAN 34A raid on July 30 and 31, 1964, that resulted in the Gulf of Tonkin incident and what many believed was the start of major military involvement for the United States.

The OPLAN 34A mission against the Hon Me and Hon Nieu islands proceeded in the early hours of July 31, 1964, when four Norwegian-built fast patrol boats (PTF) bombarded the islands. The PTFs returned to Da Nang after completing their mission. The USS *Maddox* had monitored the raid during an intelligence gathering De Soto mission. Following a predesigned course in international waters, the crew of the USS *Maddox* spotted five P-4 North Vietnamese torpedo boats approaching their destroyer during the morning of August 2, 1964. Three of the torpedo boats moved closer to the USS *Maddox* in spite of the fact the destroyer fired three warning shots with its 5-inch guns. Shortly after 2:00 p.m., the Maddox opened fire, striking each of the P-4s. Four F-8 fighters, see Chapter 8 for more about the F-8, from the carrier USS *Ticonderoga* supported the USS *Maddox* by sinking one of the torpedo boats and forcing the remaining boats back to their installation.

President Johnson ordered the USS *Maddox* reinforced with the destroyer USS *C. Turner Joy* to continue the De Soto mission, but this time at a farther distance from the North Vietnamese coast. On August 4, 1964, the two destroyers reported being under attack by unidentified vessels. While evidence from investigations after the incident suggest that an attack did not take place, the Johnson administration mobilized and set into motion the legal justification for increased U.S. action against North Vietnam. While the United States never declared war on North Vietnam, Johnson used the Gulf of Tonkin incident to increase the U.S. presence in South Vietnam and show the Vietnamese that an attack on U.S. personnel would not be tolerated.

Gulf of Tonkin Resolution

The Gulf of Tonkin resolution stated that the U.S. Congress approved and supported Johnson, as commander in chief, to take whatever measures were necessary to repel any NVA/VC attack against U.S. forces and prevent further aggression.

The resolution regarded security in Southeast Asia as vital to U.S. national interest and to world peace. The United States invoked the provisions of its Constitution, the Charter of the United Nations, and the Southeast Asia Collective Defense Treaty, enabling President Johnson to take all the necessary steps, which included the use of armed military force, to defend the freedom of the nations that had signed the treaty and asked for the help of the United States.

This resolution gave Johnson the authority to determine when peace and security of the area had been attained according to international conditions created by the United Nations. Only a concurrent resolution of Congress could terminate the president's authority. Essentially, the U.S. Congress gave Johnson a blank check to act in Vietnam.

On August 7, 1964, the U.S. Congress passed the Gulf of Tonkin resolution authorizing the Johnson administration to use whatever force it deemed necessary to defend U.S. assets in Southeast Asia and assist the South Vietnamese in their war against North Vietnam. With no dissenting votes in the House of Representatives and only two negative votes in the Senate, this resolution served as justification for later increases in U.S. military forces in South Vietnam. The Gulf of Tonkin resolution provided a "blank check" for Johnson's escalation of the conflict in Vietnam.

Interdiction by Sea: The Navy's Answer to Bombing the Ho Chi Minh Trail

Before 1965, an estimated 70 percent of the supplies received by the NVA/VC traveled by sea. With approximately 1,200 miles of South Vietnamese coastline to infiltrate with personnel and equipment to supply their forces, the sea routes represented a real danger to the survival of the South Vietnamese government, because the NVA/VC had almost unchallenged access to the coastal towns by which they supplied their forces.

Water, water everywhere: Stopping the North Vietnamese sea supply route with Operation MARKET TIME

To counter the North Vietnamese ability to supply its forces in the south by the sea, the U.S. and South Vietnamese navies joined together on March 11, 1965, in Operation MARKET TIME. The goal of this operation was stopping and destroying the ability of the North Vietnamese to supply its forces in South Vietnam.

On July 31, 1965, the U.S. Navy formed a Coastal Surveillance Force (Task Force 115) that combined ships and planes to cover and guard three defined zones used by the NVA/VC to move supplies from North Vietnam to South Vietnam. The three zones and activities were

- ✔ **Coastal air space reconnaissance:** Aircraft patrolled air space from the 17th parallel in the Gulf of Tonkin to the Gulf of Thailand from a distance of up to 150 miles from the coastline, reporting any suspicious, unidentified ships to Navy elements to investigate.

- ✔ **Blue-water patrols:** Navy destroyers responsible for patrolling closer to the coast, yet still in deep blue water up to 40 miles from the coastline. In May 1965, Coast Guard cutters joined in this responsibility, and in the late 1960s, the Royal Australian Navy supplemented the naval force with guided-missile destroyers.

- ✔ **Brown-water patrols:** The third zone, closest to the coast and in the brown water, was managed by a combined force of the South Vietnamese Junk Force, or Coastal Force, and fast, 50-foot U.S. Swift Boats (see Figure 10-1).

Operation MARKET TIME was extremely effective in stopping the flow of people and material from North Vietnam via the sea. From January 1966 to July 1967, the combined U.S./South Vietnamese force inspected more than 700,000 floating craft and either turned back or destroyed all but one of the large 100-ton transport ships the North Vietnamese used to supply its army in the south. During the next six months, the U.S./South Vietnamese forces encountered no trawlers until February 1968 when the North Vietnamese attempted to resupply its military forces after the failed Tet Offensive (see Chapter 5). All five of the trawlers dispatched by the North Vietnamese were either destroyed or forced to abort the mission. Only one transport ship ever managed to slip through the screen in 1970.

Figure 10-1:
Swift Boats,
among 13
turned over
to the
Vietnamese
Navy in
October
1969, cruise
down the
Saigon-
Vung Tau
shipping
channel on
a training
mission.

Photograph courtesy of the Vietnam Archive, Texas Tech University

The success of Operation MARKET TIME forced North Vietnam to find alternative routes to supply its forces in South Vietnam. While the North Vietnamese used the Ho Chi Minh Trail (see Chapter 10) to supply a large portion of the equipment and personnel needed to fight the war, they searched for alternative sea routes to supply their forces. As Operation MARKET TIME slowly closed the sea routes, the North Vietnamese began placing supplies in ships from neutral countries and sending them to the large Cambodian port of Sihanoukville. These ships came from Poland, Central American countries, and others who were sympathetic to the North Vietnamese and willing to take the risk because of the financial rewards. Because the United States was not allowed to stop and search neutral shipping, the North Vietnamese, therefore, were able to move the much-needed material from North Vietnam to Cambodia. From there, it was transported to the NVA/VC forces in the Mekong Delta.

Patrolling the waterways: Operation GAME WARDEN

While Operation MARKET TIME had achieved a certain amount of success in stemming the flow of weapons and personnel from the North, Navy officials recognized that the Viet Cong still were able to move a significant amount of supplies along the waterways in the Mekong Delta. With the creation of Operation GAME WARDEN and River Patrol Force (Task Force 116) in September 1965, the decision was made to make a serious effort in destroying these lines of supply that flowed in the inland waterways of South Vietnam.

Patrolling the waterways, rivers, and canals was rife with many problems, including:

- ✔ **The large size of the area to be covered.** The NVA/VC had more than 3,000 nautical miles of water passage through which they could move their materials.

- ✔ **The remoteness of water routes.** Many routes were shallow with jungle growing all the way up to the waterline. Conducting night and day patrols of these waterways meant the Navy had to use light and fast, fiberglass-hulled boats known as Patrol Boat — River (PBRs, see Figure 10-2).

The PBRs in Operation GAME WARDEN inspected Vietnamese boats for weapons and illegal supplies, participated in ambushes of suspected VC areas, and provided fire support for allied troops as they maneuvered the maze of waterways in the Mekong Delta.

Figure 10-2:
A PBR-130 glides along the Bassac River to rejoin the other boats of River Section 511 in combat against the Viet Cong.

Photograph courtesy of the Vietnam Archive, Texas Tech University

In addition to boats, two critical elements of Operation GAME WARDEN included:

- ✔ **Air power to locate NVA/VC supply ships and support navy vessels that came under attack.** The U.S. Navy used a squadron of UH-1B Iroquois helicopters called the Seawolves and a squadron of heavily armed OV-10 Broncos airplanes known as the Black Ponies to aid in the interdiction of supplies coming from the Ho Chi Minh Trail and Sihanoukville.

- ✔ **Highly trained U.S. Navy SEAL (sea, air, and land) teams.** The SEAL teams, organized in platoons of 14 men, conducted day and night ambushes, raids, reconnaissance patrols (to gain intelligence on the NVA/VC movements and bases), and salvage operations (to retrieve damaged ships).

Among the best: SEAL teams

The special operations force of the United States Navy, SEAL (sea, air, and land) teams, conducted several missions during the war. The first SEAL teams arrived in South Vietnam in 1962, training South Vietnamese commandos. SEAL teams supported South Vietnamese operations against North Vietnam, including Oplan 34A. After the U.S. commitment of ground forces, SEAL teams were deployed in the Rung Sat Special Zone, searching for and destroying the Viet Cong and providing intelligence and support for the Mobile Riverine Force. As the war progressed, SEAL-team operations spread across the Mekong Delta. These small and effective units provided intelligence, conducted ambushes, supported the barrier campaigns, and organized raids to capture known Viet Cong agents or free allied POWs in the Mekong Delta. The majority of the SEAL-team operations were covert, involving great risk to their members; however, their role in the Vietnam War improved the overall position of the allied forces throughout the Mekong Delta.

To counter the effectiveness of Operation GAME WARDEN, the NVA/VC forces in the Mekong Delta sabotaged major water routes with mines to destroy allied shipping. Although many of the mines they used were from the Second World War or older, they still presented a threat. The United States established Mine Squadron II in May 1966 to deal with the newest challenge. Operation GAME WARDEN lasted until 1970 when the task force was disbanded because its boats and equipment were handed over to the South Vietnamese as a part of Nixon's Vietnamization program, as explained in Chapter 6. The U.S. Navy realized that it had to coordinate with other U.S. forces in South Vietnam to achieve the success it desired. The U.S. Navy turned to the U.S. Army to coordinate activities — the results were better than expected.

The heart of the Brown Water Navy: Mobile Riverine Force

With the battle in the Mekong Delta raging in 1966, the U.S. Army and Navy jointly created the concept of the Mobile Riverine Force (MRF). The Navy element of this force included the River Assault Flotilla 1 (Task Force 117), which was based, in part, on the French experiences with their Dinassauts (see Sidebar "Dinassauts: Division Navales D'Assault") in Indochina during the 1950s. Almost all of the U.S. and South Vietnamese ground units assigned to the Mekong Delta worked with Task Force 117 to increase their mobility.

The MRF relied on control of the waterways in the Mekong Delta to support swift and damaging use of specially trained troops with overwhelming firepower. Adding to its mobility, the MRF not only used bases on the shoreline but also floating Mobile Riverine Bases with access to all of the major and minor rivers in the Mekong Delta.

From February 16 to March 20, 1967, Operation RIVER RAIDER (I) relied on the combined forces of Task Force 117 and the Second Brigade of the Ninth Infantry Division to clear parts of the Rung Sat Special Zone southeast of Saigon. This joint operation was the first between the Army and Navy. On June 1, 1967, it became the proof that was needed to make the concept of the MRF a reality. The MRF conducted a number of operations in the Mekong Delta, keeping the Viet Cong off balance. The MRF remained in existence until it was incorporated into the SEALORDS campaign.

A strategy for victory: SEALORDS

On October 18, 1968, Vice-Admiral Elmo R. Zumwalt, the Commander of Naval Forces, Vietnam (NAVFORCV), created the Southeast Asia Lake Ocean River Delta Strategy (SEALORDS).

The primary strategy of this new organization was

- The complete interdiction of NVA/VC supply routes by sea
- Harassing the NVA/VC in their traditional safe havens
- Pacification of the Mekong Delta (see Figure 10-3)

Figure 10-3: The Mekong Delta was home to the IV CTZ (Fourth Corps) during the Vietnam War and witnessed the majority of naval military operations.

Map courtesy of the Vietnam Archive, Texas Tech University

Dinassauts: Division Navales D'Assault

During the First Indochina War (see Chapter 2) the French organized a force that combined French Army and Navy units working together in the environmentally unfriendly Mekong Delta. The Dinassauts combined the best of the French Navy with the French Army. Army units used naval craft to navigate the waters of the Mekong Delta to respond to units in trouble faster. Because the Mekong Delta had only one permanent highway, the French needed another way to move troops and supplies. They achieved remarkable success with the Dinassauts concept and forced the Viet Minh to reevaluate how they would fight in the Mekong Delta. The United States used the French concept when they created the Mobile Riverine Force.

SEALORDS effectively combined the operations of MARKET TIME, GAME WARDEN, and the Mobile Riverine Force. Admiral Zumwalt (see Figure 10-4) combined all of the naval assets in Vietnam within the IV Corps Tactical Zone (CTZ) — the southern-most region of the country — with the goal of entering all waterways in the Mekong Delta and denying the NVA/VC the ability to use this means of transportation. This strategy was tested earlier in the month when the Coastal Surveillance Force was expanded into the inland rivers in III and IV CTZs. The results were deemed successful when an area that had been dominated by the NVA/VC was retaken while their infrastructure, transportation, and revenue sources were destroyed.

Figure 10-4:
Admiral
Elmo R.
Zumwalt, Jr.
(1920–2000).

*Photograph courtesy of the Vietnam Archive,
Texas Tech University*

One of the most important aspects of the SEALORDS campaign was the use of man-made barriers to interrupt the NVA/VC water routes. Testing the validity of the barrier strategy, SEALORDS designated an operational area, later known as Search Turn, between the Gulf of Thailand at Rach Gia and the Bassac River at Long Xuyen. A combination of South Vietnamese ground troops and naval patrol units, all trained for action in the delta, achieved great success using two canals along the barrier to stop the NVA/VC.

With the success at Search Turn, naval forces expanded the barrier to the Giang Thanh-Vinh Te canal system in Operation FOUL DECK, later renamed to Tran Hung Dao in November 1968. In December 1968, they further expanded the barrier up the Vam Co Dong and Vam Co Tay rivers to the west of Saigon and near the famous Parrot's Beak region on the South Vietnam boarder with Cambodia. Cutting off the Parrot's Beak as an entryway for NVA/VC supplies into the Mekong Delta was one of the primary goals. The operation was known as GIANT SLINGSHOT because the courses of the two rivers resembled a slingshot when viewed from the air.

Spurred by the success of SEALORDS, Admiral Zumwalt ordered a new operation on January 2, 1969, that linked the operational areas of Giant Slingshot and Tran Hung Dao. Continuing the SEALORDS strategy, Operation BARRIER REEF, as it became known, created a continuous line of patrols for 250 miles from the Gulf of Thailand to the mouth of the Saigon River.

The U.S. Navy ended its SEALORDS involvement in April 1971 with the transfer of operations to the South Vietnamese. SEALORDS proved to be a tremendous success in the fight against the NVA/VC, because the barrier system had captured approximately 300 NVA/VC solders and killed another 3,000 while suffering half as many casualties. The Mekong Delta, the area protected by SEALORDS, was the only area not affected during the North Vietnamese's Easter Offensive in 1972.

Zumwalt's Z-Grams

Admiral Elmo R. Zumwalt became Commander of Naval Forces, Vietnam, and Chief of the Naval Advisory Group, U. S. Military Assistance Command, Vietnam, in September 1968. He became Chief of Naval Operations in July 1970, a position he held for four years. He organized SEALORDS and was responsible for much of the Brown Water Navy's success during his Vietnam tenure. While serving as chief of naval operations, his *Z-Grams,* a series of memoranda designed to reform the Navy, brought forth praise and scorn as he attempted to modernize the U.S. Navy.

Ruling the Sea

One advantage the U.S. Navy had during the war was its overwhelming superiority of forces over that of the Democratic Republic of Vietnam (DRV). The North Vietnamese had only a small coastal fleet and nothing to compare with the U.S. Seventh Fleet. As a result, the United States ruled the seas, and the Blue Water Navy was able to coordinate and conduct operations without serious threat of opposition. The U.S. Navy was able to move troops by sea to any point along the South Vietnamese coast and used this advantage to keep the NVA/VC off guard when it moved near the coast.

Using the amphibious force: Naval participation in the ground war

Allied naval forces also played a valuable role in the movement of ground troops during the Vietnam War, moving troops with ease to coastal areas and through inland waterways. The first U.S. Navy action was the March 8, 1965, landing of Marines on the beaches of Da Nang — the event commonly considered the start of the ground war.

The first combat situation involving the amphibious forces in Vietnam was Operation STARLITE. In an effort to destroy the First Viet Cong Regiment in Quang Tri Province, the Third Marine Amphibious Force launched a three-pronged attack. While allied forces formed a barrier around the Viet Cong and pushed them closer to the sea, the Navy landed the Third Marines on the beaches to wait for the Viet Cong and complete the circle. The Navy then directed artillery fire on the Viet Cong area with some significant success. In operations BLUE MARLIN I and II, the Navy again played a role in trying to destroy the main Viet Cong force in I CTZ near the cities of Tam Ky and Hoi An through amphibious landings but failed to achieve significant results.

HISTORIC TRIVIA

Into the Fire: Rung Sat Special Zone

The Rung Sat Special Zone was a swampy area to the southeast of Saigon, strategic for its location near the capital city but also because it bordered the Saigon River leading to the South China Sea. The allied forces conducted several major operations in the zone to find and destroy Viet Cong. While the operations never were successful, they tended to disrupt Viet Cong operations. At one point or another, all Navy plans involved operations in the Rung Sat, including GAME WARDEN, Mobile Riverine Force, SEAL Teams, and SEALORDS.

In the first major and most ambitious amphibious operation in the war's history, Operation DOUBLE EAGLE involved several amphibious landings along the coast in I CTZ. Marines and South Vietnamese troops conducted large sweeps to search for the Viet Cong around Quang Ngai City and Tam Ky. The U.S. Navy also moved allied troops. In Operation DEFIANT STAND, Republic of Korea troops, using American transports, joined an American Marine force to clear the Barrier Island off the coast of Da Nang.

Amphibious operations were used throughout the Vietnam War as a means of quickly moving large numbers of troops anywhere along the Vietnamese coastline. While some military officers questioned the usefulness of the amphibious fleet, maintaining that the strategy for fighting the NVA/VC didn't involve landing on beaches in the manner of the Pacific Theatre of the Second World War. However, the Navy was so effective in this mission that the NVA/VC were forced to abandon the coast as a safe haven. The threat of the U.S. Navy bringing in troops from the sea was real and NVA/VC forces who tempted fate often found themselves surrounded and in peril. The last amphibious operation was in 1975 when the fleet assisted in the evacuations of Phnom Penh (Operation EAGLE PULL) and Saigon (Operation FREQUENT WIND).

Bombing the coast: Operation SEA DRAGON

One of the most significant sea campaigns involving intense bombardment and harassment of the NVA/VC forces operating north of the 17th parallel was Operation SEA DRAGON. From October 25, 1966, to October 31, 1968, the Seventh Fleet raided coastal positions from the Demilitarized Zone (DMZ) at the 17th parallel to the 20th parallel and provided saturation bombing of suspected NVA/VC positions and artillery support for allied troops operating in the I CTZ.

When President Johnson ordered the end of the bombing after the 1968 Tet Offensive, as described in Chapter 5, forces involved in Operation SEA DRAGON were restricted to operating south of the 19th parallel, and the size of the Blue Water Navy was reduced. The campaign ended on October 31, 1968, and naval operations were suspended north of the 17th parallel until the 1972 Eastertide Offensive when elements of the Seventh Fleet bombarded North Vietnamese troops who had exposed themselves to deadly fire. For more information on the Eastertide Offensive, see Chapter 6.

The raids against the coast were designed to keep the North Vietnamese off balance and, at the same time, provide the appearance that the allied forces would and could strike at any place and any time. The favorite targets for these raids were the radar stations, shore guns, maintenance facilities, and supply depots.

The success of the Blue Water Navy was significant in the amount of damage caused to North Vietnam, but it did not stop the flow of personnel and materiel nor did it cause the North Vietnamese to abandon coastal areas for safer havens inland. Instead, the North Vietnamese increased the number of shore gun placements along the raid areas, especially near the Song Giang and Kien Giang rivers. These artillery positions along the coastline caused some damage to the allied forces, yet they didn't deter the raids or presence of the Blue Water Navy.

The bombardment campaigns started in May 1965 when the cruiser USS *Canberra* and an escort of five destroyers lobbed shells on Viet Cong coastal positions. In 1967 alone, the allied naval forces fired more than 500,000 shells against the NVA/VC. Naval bombardment provided such intense fire on the NVA/VC that it accounted for numerous casualties and was responsible more than once for saving allied ground troops engaged with the NVA/VC.

The USS *New Jersey* was the only U.S. battleship involved in the Vietnam War. With its 16-inch guns, it was the powerhouse of the Seventh Fleet and lead the U.S. Navy in providing frequent and effective bombing missions when it served in Vietnamese waters. Working with U.S. forces in the Blue Water Navy, the Australian Royal Navy contributed several destroyers and at least one cruiser between 1967 and 1971.

Assessing the Navy in Vietnam

The U.S. Navy played a crucial role in the Vietnam War in offensive and support roles. Naval forces operated in adverse conditions against an elusive enemy. Patrolling the narrow canals and waterways was a dangerous task because the possibility of ambush or accident was great. Still, the personnel of the U.S. Navy performed admirably, accomplishing their tasks as outlined in the overall strategic plan. The U.S. Navy was successful in interdicting supplies from the North, providing firepower from the sea, and moving troops with relative ease. The Vietnam War, however, was not to be decided on the sea.

Chapter 11

North Vietnamese/Viet Cong Strategies and Tactics

*F*rom 1965 until 1973, U.S. and Army of the Republic of Vietnam (South Vietnam) (ARVN) forces controlled most of South Vietnam's rivers, canals, and coastline. They also enjoyed significant control of the air over Southeast Asia. But despite this naval and air superiority (which you can read about in Chapters 8 and 10), control over the land was another matter altogether. This chapter examines the NVA/VC response to U.S./ARVN strategy and tactics on the ground, sea, and air.

The North Vietnamese Army/Viet Cong (NVA/VC) devised creative methods and strategies and ultimately challenged the U.S./ARVN for control over the ground and people of South Vietnam. Countering the air and sea threats posed by the U.S./ARVN and maintaining their strength, the NVA/VC used the American strategy of gradualism (see Chapter 5) to their advantage, by attempting to control the intensity of the battlefield and engaging U.S./ARVN forces when and where they could inflict acceptable casualties.

The NVA/VC also used various tactics, including terrorism, for maintaining control and influence over the South Vietnamese people and for drafting young South Vietnamese men into the ranks of the VC (see Chapter 12). And, using the geography of Vietnam (see Chapter 1), assistance from their allies (communist China and the Soviet Union), and a bit of ingenuity, the NVA/VC developed a strategy that ultimately enabled them to outlast and survive against a nation and military force more powerful than their own.

Strategizing for Victory . . . Or at Least a Stalemate

When violence erupted in South Vietnam in the mid-1950s, the government under Ngo Dinh Diem (discussed in Chapters 2 through 4) initially faced an internal threat from VC *guerrilla forces.* These VC forces typically engaged in hit and run attacks and terrorism until the VC could gain enough strength to amass and supply larger conventional forces that could challenge and defeat the U.S.-trained and -equipped ARVN forces. Facilitating this transition in VC strategies and tactics, North Vietnam increased its support of the VC by expanding the Ho Chi Minh Trail in 1959.

Although the VC formed larger, more conventional units, the war changed dramatically in 1964 with the Gulf of Tonkin Incidents (see Chapters 5 and 10), when the United States started bombing North Vietnam and in the following year became more heavily involved in the ground war in South Vietnam. At the same time, North Vietnam also decided to commit more materiel and larger numbers of ground troops to the war in the south.

Although the VC received a significant boost from the introduction of larger amounts of military assistance from North Vietnam, as NVA units arrived in the South, problems also emerged. Perhaps the most significant was competition over command and control of military operations in the South among communist political cadres (NVA/VC political personnel) and military commanders. In addition, many NVA soldiers and members of North Vietnamese communist political cadres who went to South Vietnam looked down on and had little respect for their VC counterparts. This turmoil created a competition between the NVA and VC that lasted until the destruction of the VC during the 1968 Tet Offensive, which is discussed in Chapter 5.

After the United States introduced ground units in 1965, the NVA/VC quickly realized that they'd never have enough firepower to truly challenge the United States on the battlefield, and as long as the United States remained committed to sending more soldiers to fight in Vietnam, the NVA/VC never could win an outright military contest. So, instead of trying to match the U.S. superiority in firepower, they chose to use their strongest ally — time — against U.S./ARVN forces. One of the earliest changes in the NVA/VC strategy was exerting greater control over the size and intensity of the battlefield.

The NVA/VC had substantial manpower reserves but couldn't just sacrifice large numbers of men in combat. Rather than holding territory for any length of time, the NVA/VC used mobile bases and chose where and when they'd strike at U.S./ARVN forces. Holding a specific piece of terrain for too long would make NVA/VC units more vulnerable to U.S. firepower, which meant NVA/VC base camps rarely were in the same place for any length of time. The downside was that the comfort levels in NVA camps also declined, because no time or resources were invested on creature comforts. Whereas some U.S. base camps featured basketball courts and other luxuries, NVA/VC soldiers accepted additional hardships when doing so meant less exposure to U.S. bombing and artillery barrages. So, as a major part of their strategy, the NVA/VC opted for mobility. U.S. and ARVN ground forces, on the other hand, chose to establish more static base camps from which to launch their operations.

Although the helicopter still provided U.S./ARVN forces with an advantage in mobility, the NVA/VC base camp design, combined with their strategy, always enabled them to predict the directions from which U.S./ARVN attacks might come. Disadvantages of the mobile NVA/VC camps were much fewer than the advantages gained by being on the move and disrupting the ability of the U.S./ARVN to target and destroy them. The NVA/VC used other things to their advantage in addition to mobility:

- ✔ **Geography:** Use of mountains, hills, rivers, valleys, and other geographical features to mask movement and other activities.

- ✔ **Camouflage:** Used to conceal and deceive, it hides something so that it blends in as if the thing is not there.

- ✔ **Concealment:** Can incorporate camouflage but is also anything that obscures vision or detection. For instance, a thatch wall is visible against a jungle backdrop. At the same time, it conceals the movement of anyone behind it although a person can shoot through it and perhaps kill someone hiding there.

- ✔ **Cover:** Can be camouflaged and provide concealment but more importantly it provides protection, such as a cement wall or a bunker.

These things added tremendously to the difficulties faced by U.S./ARVN forces on the ground, in the air, and on the water.

Fighting with jungles and tunnels as allies

Combating the U.S. advantages of mobility and firepower, the NVA/VC developed various techniques for preventing their forces from being detected and destroyed by U.S./ARVN units.

One basic military technique they used was *camouflage and concealment.* In Vietnam, this meant hiding and using the terrain and jungle to mask movement and activity, especially from U.S. aircraft flying overhead. Most of the Ho Chi Minh Trail, which spanned from North Vietnam through Laos and Cambodia into South Vietnam, meandered through mountainous and dense jungle. Double- and triple-canopy jungles were not uncommon in Vietnam, Laos, and Cambodia. The number of *canopies* refers to the layers of trees and foliage that covers an area. Plant life in a jungle competes for access to sunlight and grows in layers, or canopies, which means that the NVA/VC could cut down shorter, lower brush and trees, making way for their trucks and convoys, but keep taller trees intact, thus completely concealing their movements from detection by air. In some areas, the Ho Chi Minh Trail literally was cut through the jungle like a tunnel. You should read Chapter 7 if you want to see how the South Vietnamese and Americans tried to counter the NVA/VC use of the jungle in this way.

For even more cover and concealment, the NVA/VC used underground tunnels and bunker complexes where they stored, or *cached,* ammunition, weapons, food, fuel, uniforms, and equipment in smaller tunnels and bunkers (see Figure 11-1), saving larger ones for more difficult tasks.

Figure 11-1:
In this example of a NVA/VC tunnel system, U.S. soldiers found food, clothing, medical supplies, documents, radios, and 1,000 weapons with ammunition.

Photograph courtesy of the Vietnam Archive,
Texas Tech University

Tunnel complexes in North and South Vietnam were vast and well designed, providing protection and security when ground, naval, and air forces launched attacks against them. The NVA/VC often built tunnel systems near major rivers and waterways and used the river and canal banks for building and concealing entry and exit points. The NVA/VC also ambushed U.S./ARVN river forces and then used the waterways as avenues of escape to their tunnel complexes. The tunnel systems, often accompanied by bunkers, weren't usually visible by water or air unless the NVA/VC purposefully exposed their positions through an ambush.

Given their extensive use of camouflage and concealment, most of the NVA/VC tunnel systems were located by ground units conducting foot patrols and search and reconnaissance operations through suspected areas of NVA/VC activity. Once uncovered, the only way of rooting out NVA/VC forces from a tunnel complex was sending U.S./ARVN personnel into the tunnel system. Engaging the NVA/VC in the tunnels was difficult for U.S. *tunnel rats,* because they often encountered booby-traps and other hazards designed to injure or kill them.

In many instances, instead of creating new tunnels and bunkers, the NVA/VC merely improved upon the ones used against the French and Japanese. In the war with U.S./ARVN forces, expanding and digging deeper helped the NVA/VC offset the effects of larger bombs, heavier artillery, and naval gunfire employed by U.S./ARVN forces. Because tunnels were invisible to aircraft, bombing missions over suspected tunnel complexes relied mostly on luck and massive numbers of bombs to destroy suspected tunnels and bunkers.

One of the heaviest-bombed and frequently attacked tunnel complexes was around the village of Cu Chi, located to the northwest of Saigon. Despite repeated ground and air attacks against that system, it remained in use throughout the entire war. On several occasions during the war, the tunnels of Cu Chi were thought to be cleared, but the extent of the complex never was fully understood, and NVA/VC never relinquished large sections of virtually miles of tunnels to the U.S./ARVN.

Maintaining pressure and avoiding defeat: The North Vietnamese Army and Viet Cong

The NVA/VC used the U.S. strategy of attrition to their advantage. When larger numbers of U.S. forces appeared on an operation, the NVA/VC tried to choose when and where to fight and then disengaged from combat when overwhelming U.S. firepower pushed their losses too high. The United States nevertheless engaged in several operations that forced the NVA/VC to change their tactics. The success Mobile Riverine Forces and SEALORDS had with using small, fast, highly maneuverable riverboats (see Chapter 10) forced the NVA/VC to reassess how they fought in the Mekong Delta. The NVA/VC countered these highly mobile U.S. forces with hit-and-run tactics. Firefights seldom lasted longer than an hour and were generally over before the full complement of U.S. naval gunfire, artillery, and air power entered the attack.

Responding to the Ground Threat

The NVA/VC responded to U.S./ARVN ground operations in various ways. As described in Chapters 4, 5, and 6, the NVA/VC sometimes engaged in traditional combat operations, fighting against large U.S./ARVN units. But they also used unconventional tactics designed to erode the morale of U.S. units in particular, including the use of hit-and-run tactics, snipers, booby traps, and women as combatants.

The NVA/VC quickly discovered they could keep a large U.S. unit preoccupied by using only a very small detachment of troops. Even better, whenever a small group of NVA/VC wounded several U.S. soldiers while on patrol, they also tied up large numbers of U.S. support personnel. The United States relied heavily on air support for maneuvering its soldiers, and helicopters for medical evacuation (MEDEVAC). As a result, NVA/VC units at times intentionally tried to wound, not kill, U.S. soldiers, forcing the entire unit to stop patrolling so they could bring in MEDEVAC helicopters to pick up and fly the wounded to a nearby evacuation hospital. This type of hit-and-run activity and the fact they often made little contact with NVA/VC units proved demoralizing for U.S. soldiers.

Using booby traps is another effective technique employed by the NVA/VC. *Booby traps* are improvised munitions intended to wound or kill U.S./ARVN soldiers patrolling in an area. U.S. soldiers quickly learned how adept the VC were in that aspect of guerilla war. As with the techniques described in the previous paragraph, the intent was not always to kill. Sometimes wounding a U.S. soldier was better because it to forced the unit to halt its patrol so the wounded could be evacuated by helicopter. The VC set foot traps along likely areas of U.S. patrols. Although horribly damaging to the leg of the victim, the intent of the trap was to wound, not kill.

Responding to the Air Threat

Combating U.S. air power during the war was a difficult task for the DRV. The U.S. had more aircraft and trained pilots than the DRV, enabling it to take control of the skies above the battlefield. However, this superiority didn't stop the DRV from using its available resources to fight against the United States. The DRV response to the American air threat is a story of courage and ingenuity.

Does anyone have a spare MiG?

The DRV used the *Mikoyan-Gurevich (MiG)* jet fighter as its primary aircraft during the war. A Soviet design, the creation of Artyem Mikoyan and Mikhail Gurevich was used to provide air cover against U.S. bombing campaigns over the DRV. Although it didn't succeed in stopping the bombing campaigns, it did challenge American air supremacy over North Vietnam.

The DRV used four versions of the MiG fighter:

- **MiG-17 (Fresco):** Designed to replace the MiG-15 with improvements that enabled it to reach a velocity approaching the *speed of sound* (approximately 775 mph).

- **MiG-19 (Farmer):** A mass-produced fighter considered to be reliable and maneuverable with limited all-weather capabilities.

- **MiG-21 (Fishbed):** A mass-produced small and fast jet fighter able to hold its own with American F-4 and F-105.

The DRV Air Force remained a threat throughout the war but never seriously challenged U.S. air supremacy. The MiG planes seldom had any advantages over faster and more heavily armed U.S. aircraft. Because the DRV recognized that it never could rule the air over North Vietnam, it nevertheless used its air force as a constant threat, forcing the United States to use more aircraft in escorting its bombing missions and to otherwise expend additional resources in its air campaigns.

The antiaircraft war

The North Vietnamese had few options when fighting against the U.S. air forces over the DRV. Early in the air war, the North Vietnamese relied on surplus antiaircraft artillery (AAA and also called "Triple A") left over from World War II, the communist struggle in China, and the Korean War. AAA sites surrounded key military facilities and cities. When U.S. planes flew more frequent missions over the DRV, people were supplied with weapons and encouraged to go out into the streets and add their firepower to that of the AAA in what was described by the DRV leaders as a "wall of lead." They hoped the quantity of bullets in the sky might shoot down U.S. planes.

Rather than striking fear into the Vietnamese people, the air war served as a rallying point for them. By shooting down U.S. planes, Vietnamese people knew they were not helpless, and by capturing U.S. pilots they gained a stronger bargaining position during peace negotiations. As the air war progressed, the DRV found willing allies in the Soviet Union, the PRC, and former Eastern Bloc countries East Germany, Poland, and Czechoslovakia.

The DRV received many AAA weapons from the Soviet Union. AAA relied on a high volume of shots fired (along with some luck) to shoot down U.S. aircraft, so the DRV increased the number of AAA sites dramatically to an estimated 8,000 locations by 1968. As the number of sites increased, the weapons and targeting systems also improved. The DRV used radar guidance to target U.S. aircraft, increasing the likelihood that the AAA would find its targets.

Although AAA sites were effective for low-flying aircraft (see Figure 11-2), U.S. B-52 bombers flew at an altitude beyond their range. Improvements in new targeting systems forced the U.S. to fly at even higher altitudes, thus sacrificing accuracy in its bombing missions.

Figure 11-2:
A DRV antiaircraft artillery unit near Haiphong prepares for U.S. aircraft. The AAA batteries around military facilities in North Vietnam targeted lower flying planes.

Photograph courtesy of the Vietnam Archive, Texas Tech University

Play it again SAM: Taking aim at the U.S. Air Force

Despite their poor kill-ratio, surface-to-air missiles (SAMs) became one of the greatest threats employed by the DRV during the air war over North Vietnam. The U.S. designated SA-2 (Guideline), built as the V-75 in the Soviet Union, was the principal weapon in the DRV arsenal. It was a mobile and relatively easy to operate weapon, carrying a 300-pound warhead at a velocity reaching more than three times the speed of sound. Although estimates indicate fewer than 2 percent of the missiles fired hit their targets, the SA-2 nevertheless was a threat to high-altitude bombers (see Figure 11-3), often forcing the United States to conduct bombing missions at lower altitudes and thereby making the U.S. aircraft vulnerable to AAA fire. The SA-2's electronic guidance system was effective in forcing the United States to alter or abandon bombing missions early in the air campaign and in forcing the United States to develop an electronic combat doctrine to counter the SAM threat.

The DRV set up SAM sites around strategic military areas and vital transportation hubs, a strategy that is discussed in Chapter 8. The SA-2 sites consisted of six launching positions surrounding a radar installation that guided the missiles, which is a procedure adopted from the Soviet Union. The DRV created several more sites than it had missiles to keep the United States off-balance. Because the SA-2 was mobile, the DRV stored missiles in protective bunkers or under jungle canopies unless the sites were set up for operation. The SA-2 equipment was most vulnerable during transportation, during the six hours it took to set up the missile site, and the three hours it took to disassemble the weapon system.

The Soviet SA-7 (Grail) was a hand-held, surface-to-air, heat-seeking missile first introduced in 1966 and used by the NVA/VC in South Vietnam as early as 1969. The SA-7 wasn't very effective against faster-moving aircraft, but it posed a threat to helicopters and propeller-driven aircraft. A constant threat in the air war over South Vietnam, the SA-7 could be carried anywhere and fired at any time. *Countermeasures,* such as flares to mislead the missile, easily deterred the SA-7, but not all aircraft in Vietnam had flares nor could they launch them in time to escape the missile. The SA-7 was most effective when fired at the rear of an aircraft, which enabled it to lock on to the hot exhaust trail behind the aircraft's engine.

Figure 11-3: SAM units, like this one in the 4th military zone in the DRV, targeted higher-flying bombers.

Photograph courtesy of the Vietnam Archive, Texas Tech University

Twisting the Rules of Engagement

When the United States began fighting in Southeast Asia, and especially when it launched air campaigns against the DRV, its principal objective was destroying the North Vietnamese will to continue fighting. According to U.S. military theory, bombing targets in the DRV would force them to the negotiating table and bring peace under American terms. The DRV used this flawed U.S. strategy to its advantage as it countered the air war.

Although the DRV suffered serious damage and many hardships from 1964 to 1972, it maintained itself and the war in the south. By twisting the rules of war, the DRV forced America to conform to international law. In particular, the NVA/VC used the geography of Southeast Asia to capitalize on the unwillingness of the United States to openly violate the laws of war or the internationally recognized neutrality of Laos and Cambodia.

Adopting the media as an ally

The DRV was effective in its use of propaganda during the war. Civilian casualties are bound to occur in any war. Estimates of the number of killed and wounded in the Second World War, for example, ranged in the millions. In Vietnam, the number was much lower, but the impact of civilian devastation proved a more powerful ally for the DRV, for the antiwar movement in the United States, and for the rest of the world.

As the air war intensified over the DRV, reports of devastation and DRV civilian casualties made their way to the United States. Photographs and stories of bombed schools, hospitals, and factories in the DRV became fuel for antiwar fervor. Seldom, if ever, did stories linking bombing damage to DRV tactics of placing AAA or military assets near these structures reach the media or the American public. The DRV maintained international awareness of the bombing damage caused by U.S. air campaigns by keeping the media informed.

Placing the innocent in harm's way

The DRV fought a total war for their survival against the United States and South Vietnam, but the United States never moved beyond a limited war designed to prevent South Vietnam from falling to communism. Total war follows a different set of rules than limited war. The DRV mobilized their entire society and economy to fight the war and all citizens became a part of the national defense. Northern losses to American air power were more readily accepted within the DRV. The people of North Vietnam rallied around the government when the U.S. planes starting bombing. Volunteers and conscripted workers were organized to repair bomb damage and clear debris from towns and roads to enable the people and government to function. Individuals in the DRV were provided with weapons and ordered to go out in the streets during U.S. Air Force and U.S. Navy bombing raids and shoot into the air. Although this form of air defense was relatively ineffective, it improved the morale of the Vietnamese people who had few ways to counter the U.S. bombers.

The DRV also moved strategic military facilities closer to civilian areas, discouraging the United States from targeting the sites. Bombs dropped on these facilities often damaged or destroyed surrounding civilian structures and resulted in the deaths of innocent DRV civilians. The DRV placed AAA and SAM sites near schools, hospitals, or other civilian structures, increasing the likelihood that those structures also would be damaged and further angering and rallying the DRV population against the United States and the war in South Vietnam. Military supply depots were located in heavily populated civilian urban centers. The DRV counted on the United States being reluctant to target these areas because of potential civilian casualties and international reaction. When the United States bypassed these targets for other less politically dangerous ones (see Figure 11-4), the DRV extended the use of such civilian shields around their military targets. The United States eventually attacked these important military sites but with great caution and care. Doing so didn't negate civilian casualties. DRV officials exploited civilian damage by using it in the international arena to condemn the United States and South Vietnam.

Figure 11-4:
A highway bridge, 15 miles northwest of Vinh, is destroyed by a direct hit from a Navy A-6 Intruder's 500-pound bomb.

Photograph courtesy of the Vietnam Archive,
Texas Tech University

Playing on American fears

The DRV also played on the U.S. fears that the PRC and Soviet Union might enter the war, a strategy that was successful until Nixon (see Chapter 6) approached the Chinese in 1972. Based on experiences in the Korean War (see Chapter 3), the United States worried that too much pressure on North Vietnam or attacks along the DRV-PRC border would result in the Chinese entering the war. The United States wasn't prepared to fight an additional 900 million Asians, and the DRV used this U.S. reluctance to its advantage by moving its air force to bases in southern China. Important military factories and facilities also were moved closer to the border for protection against U.S. bombing raids.

The DRV used its total-war footing to its advantage. The entire population of North Vietnam was involved in the struggle against the United States, and all resources were devoted to ousting the United States and overthrowing the South Vietnamese government. In many instances, the U.S. bombing of North Vietnam acted as a rallying point for everyone in North Vietnam to rally against the United States as the common enemy. The United States, however, didn't engage in total war against the DRV and wasn't prepared to accept the staggering losses incurred by the North Vietnamese. As long as the North Vietnamese government kept its people focused on fighting the United States, it maintained a reasonable chance of outlasting the United States. When comparing body counts, the United States didn't lose many engagements during the war. That statistic, however, didn't matter: Success using the DRV's strategy was measured in time and strength of political will. The DRV knew it could outlast the United States the same way it outlasted the French, Japanese, and Chinese before.

Part IV
The "Other Wars"

The 5th Wave   By Rich Tennant

"As part of the pacification program we've brought in medical doctors to teach the villagers basic first aid, disease prevention, and, if any of them are having trouble with their golf swing, we can assist in that area too."

In this part . . .

When looking at the Vietnam War, the most attention is paid to American ground, air, and maritime combat operations in South Vietnam. But Americans were involved in so much more throughout Southeast Asia. In South Vietnam, the "Other War" focused on pacification and winning the hearts and minds of the Vietnamese people. Throughout the rest of Southeast Asia, the "other wars" involved US military and civilian operations in Thailand, Laos, and Cambodia. This part looks at the various activities of the US and RVN as they attempted to pacify and maintain the support of South Vietnamese people. It also looks at American military and civilian activities in the other countries in Southeast Asia and the bearing they had on the war in South Vietnam.

Chapter 12

Winning with the South Vietnamese People

*T*he emphasis of United States policy in Vietnam changed several times over the course of the war. One of the most debated and difficult issues involved what became called, *the other war* or *pacification*. This phrase refers to the efforts of the governments of the United States and Republic of Vietnam (RVN, also known as South Vietnam) to win over and maintain the support of the South Vietnamese civilian population.

Since the creation of South Vietnam in 1954, the civilian population was essential to success on both sides of the war. The South Vietnamese communists or Viet Cong (VC) needed noncommunist South Vietnamese civilians to provide them with support and oppose the RVN government. The VC comprised the group of South Vietnamese people so disgruntled and angry with the South Vietnamese government that they took up arms against that government. The VC applied significant pressure on the South Vietnamese civilian population in order to get the men, materiel, food, and support necessary to fight; in fact, the VC eventually turned to terrorism to get what it wanted. The RVN and United States, on the other hand, needed the South Vietnamese civilian population to resist the VC and not provide any support to the communists. The RVN and United States pressured the Vietnamese people to provide intelligence on VC movements and VC members from their villages. But without adequate security to protect them from VC terrorism, convincing the Vietnamese to turn against the VC became increasingly difficult. The result was a war between the North Vietnamese Army (NVA)/VC and United States/RVN, with the South Vietnamese civilians caught in the middle.

Managing and Relocating the Population

For the decade from 1954 and 1964, most of the fighting that occurred in South Vietnam involved the VC and the Army of the Republic of Vietnam (ARVN). In fact, military forces from the United States and North Vietnam did not become involved in any significant numbers until 1964.

Although the North Vietnamese government (DRV) did provide some financial and material support to the VC, most of the support for the VC came from South Vietnam and the South Vietnamese people. Sometimes, the South Vietnamese people reluctantly and briefly supported the VC. Other times, they provided long-term and enthusiastic support. The trick for the government in South Vietnam was to deny the VC access to the support of the Vietnamese civilian population without alienating or angering these same civilians and, thus, turning them back to the side of the VC. That was no easy feat.

The Vietnamese strategy: Phase 1, Government Reform

In 1954, more than 85 percent of the people of South Vietnam lived in rural communities or villages and engaged in farming. In addition, more than 95 percent of the South Vietnamese were Buddhist. When South Vietnamese President Ngo Dinh Diem took office, he, as a Catholic, had little control over the people or governing infrastructure outside the main cities of South Vietnam. In an attempt to gain political and administrative control, Diem restructured the government and implemented various policies designed to control the rural and urban populations.

Government restructuring under Diem involved removing government officials unknown to him and replacing them with people he could trust. This government reform occurred at all levels, from the national government down to villages. For the most important positions of power, Diem chose family members or close friends. For other positions, Diem chose people based mostly on their apparent loyalty to his government. During the late 1950s and early 1960s, Diem removed many previously elected and appointed South Vietnamese officials and replaced them with fellow Catholics who had fled North Vietnam in 1954 as part of Operation Passage to Freedom, discussed in Chapter 10. The appointment of Catholics from North Vietnam added to many people's mistrust of the Diem government because these new government appointees worshipped the French religion, Catholicism. Further, Diem's appointees spoke a difference dialect of Vietnamese. In Vietnam, this was very important, as a person could be identified by how they spoke Vietnamese and these factors combined to make the impression that Diem's government was filled with French influenced northerners as opposed to Buddhist southerners.

The effects of Diem's government reform and restructuring varied throughout South Vietnam. In some of the mountainous regions, Montagnard tribes people were displaced by groups of Northern Catholic refugees. This alienated many of them and the NVA/VC capitalized on this, getting support from some of the Montagnard groups.

In the cities, Diem's replacement of officials, combined with additional policies in the early 1960s (such as banning the flying of flags other than that of South Vietnam) and popular resentment against his government, led to demonstrations, riots, and fighting in the streets. In the highest-profile incident, this resentment led to the self-immolation (dousing themselves with gasoline and burning themselves to death) of Buddhist priests. As the war progressed and U.S. involvement increased, urban unrest and rioting centered on anti-American attitudes, with calls for the United States to withdraw its forces from South Vietnam (see Figure 12-1).

Figure 12-1:
Buddhist
Monks
demonstrate
in Saigon.

Courtesy of the Vietnam Archive, Texas Tech University

On the rural population, Diem's policies didn't result in immediate violence but did create a climate of mistrust that, with time, ultimately led to violence. Many rural Vietnamese felt that the distant government of Saigon was exerting too much influence over local affairs. This was especially the case when Diem suspended local village elections, violating a long-held tradition in Vietnamese culture that the rule of the national leader ended at the village gates.

But by 1959, Diem concluded that the gates of most villages were not strong enough to withstand communist encroachments. The VC had implemented a policy of terror designed to force the civilian population into supporting the communists by systematically killing political officials, teachers, and other prominent local people who opposed the VC and their demands for support. The Diem government also engaged in heavy-handed activities and arrested and imprisoned anyone suspected of being opposed to his government, under the guise such persons were automatically communists and active supporters of the VC. Under the stress and pressure of this climate of terror and fear, it became almost impossible for the RVN government to effectively administer the rural areas of South Vietnam, which led to President Diem's implementation of various programs that increased his control over the people through rural and village security.

Weeding out the bad and the good: The Agglomeration Centers

Started in 1959, the Agglomeration Centers served as holding areas for two principal groups of Vietnamese people:

- ✔ Those who were trusted and thought to be loyal to the RVN government: Diem's government feared that remote but loyal villages in rural South Vietnam might come under insurmountable pressure and be forced to provide aid and comfort to the VC. In order to protect these loyal citizens, they were relocated to Agglomeration Centers for their security and protection.

- ✔ Those suspected of ties to communists (VC or North Vietnam): This group included people who had relatives in the VC organization or in North Vietnam. Using these vague criteria, local officials banished entire families, forcing them to leave their ancestral homes and lands. Problems that emerged from this are discussed in the section on "Trouble in Agroville paradise."

Serious problems with the Agglomeration Center program quickly emerged. The centers were harsh places to live, and the government provided inadequate economic and social support for the people relocated to them, regardless of whether the people were previously loyal to the government or were suspected of supporting communists. As a result, many loyal Vietnamese became angry and turned against the government. For those suspected of having ties to the VC already, if they had not had ties before, they had reason to create them. For people already opposed to the government, after relocation, they had even more reasons to remain opposed. Making matters more difficult, the criteria used to determine who to relocate also created problems, because just about everyone in South Vietnam had extended family members still living in North Vietnam, including several senior ministers working for President Diem. The program came under fire from within the government and, eventually, other programs took over the issue of population relocation and security. The first of these was the Agroville Program.

Improving on a bad idea: The Agroville Program

Diem announced the Agroville Program in 1959, and he chose one of the most troubled areas of Vietnam at the time, the Mekong Delta region, as the test bed of this new project. Diem officials carefully chose the sites for *Agrovilles,* specially designed villages, strategically placing them along specific highways that would allow larger ARVN forces in the area to quickly move in and provide security whenever necessary. The government drafted villagers in the area to provide the necessary labor to build the Agrovilles. After its completion, the Vietnamese people were forced to leave their ancestral lands and homes and relocate or "regroup" into the new Agroville compounds. The Agrovilles were fenced with entry and exit checkpoints that were manned by armed guards. The villagers in the Agrovilles had to travel to their fields each day, which allowed the RVN government to better regulate and collect taxes from the villagers.

Trouble in Agroville paradise

Problems with the Agrovilles emerged almost immediately. The lack of any compensation or wage payment to the construction laborers created immediate resentment among the Vietnamese people. Although most Agrovilles were constructed during the lulls in rice planting and harvesting, Agroville construction deprived people of their time for leisure or other activities that helped them maintain a better standard of living or even generate modest amounts of additional income. Forcing the laborers to provide their own transportation and food during construction also increased the overall burden on a very poor population.

Making matters more difficult, the RVN government didn't always provide adequate security in the villages or at the Agroville construction sites. The VC still controlled the areas, especially at night, and they harassed the villagers and their families who provided the labor and attacked and sometimes destroyed Agroville construction, further prolonging the burdens of construction on the villagers.

Still other problems emerged of a more delicate nature. In the areas of Agroville construction, some people were forced to relocate their ancestral burial mounds and family tombs to make way for the new buildings and compounds. This was not an easy task, because most Vietnamese people engage in rituals and activities centered on their ancestors, whom they buried in tombs within their rice fields and revered during daily rituals in small shrines in their homes. Adding to the emotional distress many people felt, the government provided no assistance to the people forced to relocate their family tombs. These problems persisted after completion of the Agrovilles, because villagers had to relocate to the Agroville and had to either leave their family tombs or move them closer to the Agrovilles, which upset further the daily pattern of Vietnamese village life and alienated many people.

Although some officials within the RVN government brought these problems to the attention of President Diem, he dismissed them and felt the villagers should be happy that the government was trying to provide them with additional security and benefits. To the average villager, this sounded too similar to the French colonial attitude (see Chapter 2) and increased the resentment many felt toward Diem and the RVN political leadership.

The Agroville program didn't last long. The new compounds came under attack and although the security system worked well during the day, the VC still operated with ease at night. The fences and gates proved futile in keeping out villagers who legitimately lived in the compounds but were also active VC leaders or agents. Worse than all of this, the resentment generated by the RVN policies turned some Agrovilles into active recruiting areas for the VC who found many villagers willing to help them resist what they felt were unfair and unjust demands from an arrogant national government. Although the Agrovilles were well intended and touted as a success by President Diem, the program was abandoned within a year.

Breathing life into a dead program: The Strategic and New Life Hamlets

Diem followed the Agroville program (along with several others designed to provide security to and control over rural Vietnam while denying the VC access to the civilian support base). In 1961, Diem introduced the Strategic Hamlet program, which later became the New Life Hamlet Program in 1964, both of which amounted to Agrovilles on steroids. The differences between Strategic and New Life Hamlets were principally in name, time of implementation, and the amount of money being thrown into the programs with New Life Hamlets receiving more funding.

A bigger, better Hamlet

The Strategic and New Life Hamlet programs differed slightly from the Agroville program but maintained several key elements from their predecessors. Like the Agrovilles, Diem located Strategic and New Life Hamlets along major roads so as to provide rapid security whenever needed. Additional security made it harder for the VC to attack the Strategic and New Life Hamlets and made construction easier. The major differences included increased funding from the U.S. and RVN governments and increased fortification and security of the hamlets. Some Strategic Hamlets were surrounded by walls, barbed wire, and various obstacles, making them more like fortresses than village hamlets and causing some people to wonder whether the Strategic Hamlets were designed to keep the VC out or the villagers in. Other hamlets had just barbed wire and fences like the Agrovilles.

In addition, the United States and ARVN trained and armed the Vietnamese people so they could assist in the defense of their own villages and hamlets. This gave rise to the Regional Forces and Popular Forces (RF/PF), a general term used to define civilian forces who were armed and trained in order to defend their villages, hamlets, and provinces. Because most able-bodied young men were drafted into the ARVN, most of the RF/PF units employed older men as well as women (see Figure 12-2).

Bigger is not always better

Unfortunately, many of the same problems of the Agrovilles persisted into the Strategic and New Life Hamlet programs. Government corruption often meant there were never enough supplies to adequately build a hamlet large enough to accommodate the population forced to build and move into it. Although they had more security, the RVN officials demanded that Strategic and New Life Hamlets fly the flag of South Vietnam. Intended to foster feelings of patriotism, instead the hamlets that flew the RVN flags became targets and they generally came under heavier attack from the NVA/VC units in their area. Many NVA/VC still found it easy to attack the new hamlets, and then fade away into the jungle when necessary.

Figure 12-2:
Girl volunteers of the People's Self-Defense Force of Kien Dien, a hamlet 30 miles north of Saigon.

Photograph courtesy of the Vietnam Archive, Texas Tech University

Other problems emerged, and people resisted the new hamlets for many of the same reasons they resisted the Agrovilles. Sometimes, people watched as government personnel destroyed homes and villages. The people in those communities were then forced to relocate and construct new hamlets from scratch, living in improvised and makeshift huts while they built. Other times, the labor demands for construction took men and women away from their crops during planting and harvesting. Many people did not understand why the RVN government couldn't just provide security and safety to the people while they lived in their homes on ancestral lands. Why did they have to be uprooted and moved to a new location? The government programs lacked any rhyme or reason for many people and, unfortunately, RVN officials did a poor job of explaining the situation to the people, thus failing to win them over. As a result, many Vietnamese people became angry with the government and at best, refused to support these programs. At worst, people became active supporters of the VC.

Backing the hamlets: U.S. support for the early pacification programs and reform

Very early in U.S. involvement, American observers and planners realized the need for reform in South Vietnam. One of the dilemmas facing both Presidents Eisenhower and Kennedy involved getting South Vietnamese President Diem to engage in appropriate political, economic, and social reforms that would help stabilize his country. As discussed in Chapters 3 and 4, Eisenhower and Kennedy found that they could exert very little influence over Diem, despite the massive amounts of aid and assistance the United States provided to South Vietnam. Even with more advisors and money in Vietnam, Kennedy continued to hold limited influence over Diem and his government. Why?

The U.S. policy in Vietnam was in part based on the experiences of the United States and Great Britain in the Philippines and Malaysia after WWII. The lessons derived from each were applied to Vietnam in the hopes that the successes enjoyed in those two countries would be repeated in South Vietnam. From Malaysia, U.S. policy makers and advisors took the model for the Agrovilles and Strategic Hamlets. From the Philippines, they took similar lessons as well as the importance of supporting a strong national leader to hold the country together, but Diem knew of and took advantage of this lesson. Diem understood that U.S. Cold War policy of the containment of communism in Southeast Asia rested on the success of South Vietnam. The more money, material, and advisors the United States sent, the more important South Vietnam became. He also understood that the United States saw him as the indispensable man, the strong national leader who could keep South Vietnam free of communist domination. He aptly understood that he was as important to the United States as was U.S. support to his success.

JFK and the other war

Kennedy and members of his cabinet doubted that the war in Vietnam could be won through purely conventional strategies and tactics. To this end, Kennedy resisted the calls of his Joint Chiefs of Staff (JCS) to introduce and emphasize conventional approaches to the war; instead, he focused on Special Forces and other unconventional programs (the other war).

The importance of the other war received constant reinforcement throughout the early 1960s. As late as 1963, Special National Intelligence Estimates (SNIEs, pronounced "sneeze") from the Central Intelligence Agency (CIA) reported to Kennedy that the war in South Vietnam was an insurgency: an internal civil war between the VC and South Vietnamese government. These reports acknowledged the political activity and rhetorical support coming from North Vietnam and the increase in men and materiel from North Vietnam to South Vietnam, but according to these reports, that activity

remained a small proportion of the overall activity in South Vietnam.
In addition, the VC rebuffed the initial attempts of North Vietnam to reach out and assist them in their fight against the Diem government. In 1964, North Vietnam still played only a minor role in the events in South Vietnam and had little to no control over the VC. By comparison, the United States played an increasing role, especially in providing material and money to South Vietnam, but still had very little control over Diem, ARVN, or any South Vietnamese officials.

It was because of these reports that JFK instituted a counterinsurgency (COIN) policy and strategy in the early 1960s (see Chapter 4). The U.S. Army Special Forces formed the backbone of U.S. COIN strategy.

Freeing the oppressed of SEA: U.S. Special Forces in Laos and Vietnam

The first Special Forces teams were introduced into Southeast Asia in Laos for Operation WHITE STAR, where they helped train Laotians to fight against the communist Pathet Lao, discussed in Chapter 13. The United States introduced additional Special Forces teams into South Vietnam that same year. Their initial missions involved intelligence and reconnaissance missions as part of the Military Assistance Command–Vietnam (MACV) Studies and Observations Group (SOG). They also worked with local civilian groups, and in 1963, they took over work with Civilian Irregular Defense Groups (CIDG) initially organized and run by the CIA.

The CIDG was comprised of groups of mountain tribesmen (Montagnards) in the Central Highlands of South Vietnam, who provided defense and security to their own villages and conducted intelligence and reconnaissance missions along the Ho Chi Minh Trail near Laos and Cambodia. These operations were very successful because the CIDG had intimate familiarity with the local terrain, having lived there all their lives. They had incentives to help U.S. Special Forces teams because they were, in essence, defending their own homes.

The Special Forces teams also engaged in Civic Action; brought in weapons, supplies, and building materials; and provided the villagers with medical and dental care. The CIDG served as an example of what U.S. Special Forces could do in Vietnam — they set up remote outposts (usually on mountaintops), lived near and trained local indigenous forces, won their allegiance by staying with them and providing them with assistance, and conducted reconnaissance operations near the infiltration routes in the border areas. Special Forces base camps were so remote and inaccessible that the only way in was by helicopter or by walking. In addition to working with MACV SOG, CIDG, and other civilian groups, the U.S. Special Forces also trained the South Vietnamese Special Forces, which was the Vietnamese equivalent of the U.S. Army Special Forces.

TECHNICAL STUFF

Specializing in counterinsurgency: U.S. Special Forces in Southeast Asia

The U.S. Army Special Forces evolved out of the Office of Strategic Services (OSS) in World War II, discussed in *World War II For Dummies* by Keith Dickson (Wiley Publishing, Inc.). The OSS trained individuals and small teams of men, parachuted or transported them into remote areas of wartime France, and supported their activities behind enemy lines. The program was such a success that the U.S. military formalized units similar to the OSS teams in 1952 and called them Special Forces. The unit adopted the motto *De Oppresso Liber*, Latin for "free the oppressed."

The primary mission of the Special Forces during the Vietnam era was to enter a hostile country and help train soldiers and civilians deemed on the side of U.S. policy. Special Forces units were organized into 12-person "A-teams," and each team had soldiers specifically trained in various specialized areas, including heavy and light weapons, communications, demolitions, medicine, and other specialties. After members were assigned to a team, they were cross-trained so that if one member was injured or killed, other members of the team can fill in, as necessary.

Kennedy placed significant emphasis on the Special Forces when he became president and increased their authorized strength to 10,000. He later approved their distinctive headgear, the Green Beret (see Chapter 4). He also expanded the Special Warfare Training Center (now called the John F. Kennedy Special Warfare Center) at Fort Bragg, North Carolina, where Special Forces training emphasized counterinsurgency and counter-guerilla operations. As a result, Special Forces became the cornerstone of JFK's foreign policies in opposition to the expansive, communist-supported "wars for national liberation."

A rather small force when compared to the eventual U.S. conventional force buildup, U.S. Special Forces proved highly successful. They operated in the same locations for extended periods of time and got to know the people and terrain. They helped defend villages and bases from attack and provided good intelligence on NVA/VC movements in their areas. U.S. Special Forces activity provided an excellent example of how small U.S. forces could work with and complement local militias and popular forces to provide security and intelligence without placing onerous burdens on government resources or the civilian population. They also complemented certain activities of the U.S. Marine Corps in other parts of South Vietnam.

The Marine Corps' contribution to COIN: Combined action platoons

Like the Special Forces, the U.S. Marine Corps Combined Action Platoon (CAP) program was designed to place Marine units next to villages where they trained the Vietnamese and provided security. The Marines developed the CAP program based on their extensive counter-guerilla and small wars experiences in Latin America during the first half of the twentieth century. CAPs trained Regional Forces and Popular Forces (RF/PFs, discussed in

"A bigger, better Hamlet" section, earlier in this chapter) and provided villages with medical attention, assisted with construction projects, and lent security and stability to villages, helping to protect them against NVA/VC attacks.

Unfortunately, the CAPs weren't popular with General William Westmoreland (see Chapter 5), because they didn't consistently generate high body counts. Marine CAPs didn't engage in battalion-sized operations but stayed near their villages and learned to live, work, and fight with the Vietnamese people. Although they did engage in patrols around their villages, they didn't go looking for large units because they worked in platoon and company size formations. Over time and under pressure from Westmoreland, the Marines moved away from the CAP model and the bulk of their force in South Vietnam participated in more conventional operations and tactics.

Unconventionalizing a Conventional War: Pacification in Vietnam

After the Gulf of Tonkin Incident in 1964, the United States sent large numbers of ground forces into Vietnam to fight against the communist North Vietnamese Army (NVA) and VC. The details of the conventional war in Vietnam are discussed in Chapters 5 and 6.

But it became apparent to many observers that the war in Vietnam couldn't be won alone by conventional tactics and strategies. Many people thought the war in Vietnam was more about winning the allegiance of the people than just defeating NVA/VC forces in combat. President Lyndon Johnson, members of its cabinet, and certain military commanders all agreed that another important part of the American military effort had to be the pacification of the Vietnamese population.

Winning hearts: American Civil affairs

It may seem ironic that the U.S. military in Vietnam engaged in a wartime activity that involved something civil, but they did. *Civil Affairs* (CA) is a rather broad term that refers to various activities that promoted goodwill and an improvement in the standard of living for the Vietnamese people. CA units and American personnel in general engaged in all types of activities:

- ✔ Built roads, bridges, airfields, schools, hospitals, and many other similar buildings, structures, and facilities
- ✔ Dug wells, canals, and irrigation systems

  ✔ Taught various subjects, skills, and trades in Vietnamese schools

  ✔ Engaged in MEDCAP (Medical Civic Action Program), through which they provided medical assistance, prescribed and provided drug treatments, and provided children with immunizations (see Figure 12-3)

Many different types of units and personnel engaged in civil affairs activities. American military engineers built roads and bridges, engaged in irrigation projects, and built various types of buildings throughout South Vietnam. Many American military medical personnel volunteered their free time to assist with MEDCAPs. American soldiers based near villages sometimes volunteered their free time to build schools and hospitals. Many American military and civilian personnel distributed food to refugee camps and needy people throughout South Vietnam.

All of this activity occurred in an attempt to convince the Vietnamese people that the United States was in Vietnam to try to help them, and went a long way toward building goodwill between the American people and the Vietnamese civilian population.

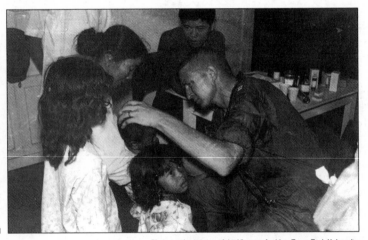

Figure 12-3:
USAF Flight Surgeon Dr Calvin Chapman provides medical services for villagers outside of Saigon.

Photograph courtesy of the Vietnam Archive, Texas Tech University

Winning the minds: Psychological operations in Vietnam

In addition to winning the hearts of the Vietnamese people through civil affairs and other activities, the United States also tried to influence their minds through *psychological operations* or *Psyops*. All of the various service branches engaged in activities designed primarily to convince the NVA/VC to give up and change sides. These operations included:

> ✔ Leaflet and pamphlet distribution
>
> ✔ Radio broadcasts
>
> ✔ Loudspeaker broadcasts, as shown in Figure 12-4
>
> ✔ Military disinformation campaigns

Need a hug? The Chieu Hoi (open arms) program

Although ascertaining the true success of these operations was difficult, one Psyop program generated some impressive, if misleading, statistics.

The most concerted attempt to get NVA/VC soldiers and leaders to change sides occurred under the Chieu Hoi or "Open Arms" program started in 1963 under President Diem and lasting for ten years. The purpose was to convince the NVA/VC that all Vietnamese people were brothers and all should want the war to end. If they did change sides, rallying to the side of the RVN, all would be forgiven, they would be treated well and given medical attention and food, and they could live happy and normal lives in South Vietnam. Eventually the Chieu Hoi program resulted in nearly 160,000 NVA/VC soldiers and political cadre changing sides, far exceeding the initial goals of the project.

Figure 12-4:
A U.S. Navy river patrol boat (PBR) conducts psycho-logical operations using loud-speakers.

The problem with the impressive numbers generated by the program was the difficulty of knowing the true intentions or status of those ralliers to the Chieu Hoi Program. Not all defectors showed up carrying a weapon: The statistics generated with regard to defectors only added to the confusion because, depending on the source quoted, somewhere between 7 percent and 60 percent of defectors did turn in some kind of weapon when they defected. This meant the true status of anywhere between 40 percent and 93 percent of defectors who had no weapons could never be accurately determined. Defecting without a weapon became a problem because the defector could be an NVA or VC soldier trying to get food or medical attention from the U.S. or ARVN facilities, only later to slip away and rejoin their unit fighting against U.S./ARVN forces.

One of the most troubling problems to emerge from the Chieu Hoi program was the difficulty in knowing the true intentions of the defectors. Suspicion emerged in U.S. military units where some defectors became Kit Carson scouts. These defector/scouts worked with Americans and other allies, supposedly providing insight regarding the terrain and enemy activities within their areas of operations. But no matter how much the defectors assured them of their sincerity, most Americans who worked with the Kit Carson scouts felt they could never really trust them.

During the war, people also suspected the NVA/VC had penetrated both government offices and military organizations of South Vietnam. As a testament to that suspicion, after the war ended in 1975, many senior ARVN officers and RVN government officials emerged wearing the uniform and senior officer rank of the NVA/VC. The levels to which the NVA/VC penetrated and compromised South Vietnam surprised many people, including many South Vietnamese who had worked closely with these spies and never questioned their loyalty. Although it is impossible to conclude that the Chieu Hoi program was a complete success, the program shows that the United States and RVN realized it was absolutely necessary to weaken the NVA/VC and used this unconventional approach in an attempt to weaken NVA/VC resources. In this respect, the Chieu Hoi Program was part of the much larger U.S./RVN pacification program that expanded significantly in 1966.

A stronger emphasis: CORDS

After the United States became more heavily involved in ground operations and conventional war fighting in 1965, the other war fell to the background. The Vietnamese people endured many hardships as large military maneuvers tromped through their farms and rice fields and many people had to leave their homes and became refugees, fleeing both no-fire-zones and areas with heavy fighting. Although the United States and RVN tried to alleviate some of the social and economic upheaval caused by the war, in the eyes of many, not enough emphasis was placed on the problem and not enough resources were made available to adequately deal with the growing problems. Although the U.S. military command gave verbal support to pacification projects, General William Westmoreland didn't want to divert the manpower and resources he had focused on the war against the NVA/VC. As a result, many of the refugees and displaced people of South Vietnam had to fend for themselves, and the resentment generated from this lack of support added to the ranks and support provided the VC.

Fortunately, President Lyndon Johnson saw many of the shortcomings of the situation in 1966 and, at a meeting in Honolulu, Hawaii, with Prime Minister Nguyen Cao Ky of South Vietnam, ordered a renewed and increased effort in U.S./RVN pacification efforts. It was thought by Johnson, Ky, and their advisors that the biggest hurdle to successful implementation of pacification was the decentralized nature of the command structure and the competition between the military and civilian agencies working on pacification. To alleviate this problem, Johnson created CORDS (Civil Operations and Revolutionary Development Support — later changed to Rural Development Support), assigned a senior civilian staff member to head the organization, and placed CORDS directly under General Westmoreland, Commander of U.S. Military Assistance Command–Vietnam (COMU.S.MACV). The first director of CORDS, Robert Komer, held the equivalent rank and title of the Deputy Commander of MACV, creating equal status between military and pacification operations.

Winning with Komer and Colby: Pacification on steroids

CORDS personnel expanded almost immediately and at its peak in 1969, involved nearly 6,500 American advisors working with many thousands more South Vietnamese and other nation's counterparts. Komer and his deputy, William Colby, devised the Accelerated Pacification Campaign (APC) and sent out pacification teams to every Hamlet and district in South Vietnam. The primary mission of the CORDS APC teams was to coordinate the pacification and civil affairs programs of the military branches and government agencies. This involved U.S.MACV, Civil Affairs, and other military personnel, along with civilian employees of the U.S. Agency for International Development (U.S.AID) and the State Department, the U.S. Central Intelligence Agency, the South Vietnamese Revolutionary Development Cadre, and other South Vietnamese government and military programs and personnel. CORDS became an immense undertaking and first on the to-do list was establishing rural security.

Winning more hearts and minds? South Vietnam's Revolutionary Development Teams

Created before CORDS, the Revolutionary Development (RD) Teams played an important role in the APC. Started in January 1966, the RD teams, shown in Figure 12-5, included 59 young Vietnamese men and women trained to work in semi-secured hamlets and villages conducting civic action. This included providing medical assistance; building roads, schools, and hospitals; conducting political rallies; tracking down members of the VC; and training volunteers for local security and self defense.

Although important in getting the Vietnamese people involved in the pacification effort, the RD program faced many obstacles. Many RD cadres had to leave their positions due to the ARVN draft. Others deserted because they were moved to areas outside their districts where they didn't want to work. Still others left because of government corruption. In 1967, more than 21,000 RD cadres worked throughout South Vietnam, yet that same year, the RD program lost nearly 8,000 due to various reasons. Regardless of the problems of retention, the RD Teams played a vital role in putting a Vietnamese face on pacification, proving that the RVN government was involved in addressing the many problems of rural South Vietnam. And in addition to the RD teams, ARVN and U.S. advisors provided weapons and training to many RF/PF units and other self-defense forces.

For the unconverted: The Phoenix Program

One of the most controversial programs to emerge from CORDS was the Phoenix Program (called "Phung Hoang" in Vietnamese). Created in December 1967, four years after the assassination of President Ngo Dinh Diem and under the leadership of a new president of South Vietnam Nguyen Van Thieu, the purpose of the Phoenix Program was to neutralize the Viet Cong Infrastructure (VCI). In other words, Phoenix was designed to coordinate the activities of U.S. and RVN military and civilian intelligence organizations to identify and locate — and either arrest, capture, or kill — known Viet Cong leaders. This was not a campaign to engage in conventional battles with VC units; but instead, Phoenix employed small teams called Provincial Reconnaissance Units (PRU) who raided villages or set up ambushes hoping to capture or, if necessary, kill VC leaders. The PRU teams were made up of mostly Vietnamese with one or several American advisors, including U.S. Army advisors and CIA operations personnel.

Almost immediately, the Phoenix program became shrouded in mystery, myth, and controversy. Many PRUs earned reputations as being tough, hard, and dangerous. Without a doubt, the PRUs effectively took the war to the VCI and turned the tables on them. Before Phoenix, the VC had gone into villages and terrorized civilians, killing politicians, teachers, and other innocent civilians. After the Phoenix Program began, however, when VC cadre entered a village, they ran the risk of being captured or killed by a PRU.

Figure 12-5:
Two young members of a Revolutionary Development team, active in refugee resettlement projects, present a Vietnamese national flag to a village elder.

Photograph courtesy of the Vietnam Archive, Texas Tech University

The actual number of known or suspected VCI killed under the auspices of Phoenix is uncertain. Regardless of the actual statistics, Phoenix was ultimately labeled an assassination program, something most Americans found horrible and unacceptable and resulted in an official Congressional investigation. In testimony before the U.S. Congress, former Director of Central Intelligence William Colby acknowledged that the actual number of VCI killed was unknown but could be as high as 20,000. Later statistics put the number closer to 10,500. Of those, roughly 9,000 died during combat with conventional forces. Although the remaining 1,500 killed hardly constituted an assassination campaign, especially when compared to the tens of thousands of assassinations conducted by the VC throughout South Vietnamese villages, Phoenix did suffer some legitimate problems:

- ✔ The inability at times to verify whether a suspect was actually VCI.
- ✔ The alleged use of the PRUs to remove the political competition in certain districts.
- ✔ Public allegations of war crimes and atrocities.

Even the North Vietnamese acknowledged the effectiveness of the program after the war ended. But regardless of the successes and apparent restraint of the program, so much controversy swelled up so quickly that American involvement in Phoenix quickly became limited and ended in 1971. Although the U.S. involvement ended early, when combined with the other programs under CORDS and pacification, Phoenix helped undermine VC activities throughout South Vietnam.

Evaluating victory and defeat in pacification: The Hamlet Evaluation System

Of the many instruments devised by Americans to measure victory and defeat, success and failure, few equal the Hamlet Evaluation System (HES) in their complexity. Designed as a computerized survey, American district advisors had to evaluate each hamlet in their area of responsibility and assign it a letter depending on certain criteria:

- ✔ Ratings of A, B, or C indicated degrees of RVN government control.
- ✔ Ratings of D or E indicated a contested Hamlet leaning to one side or the other.
- ✔ A rating of V indicated a hamlet under VC control.

HES surveys were then sent to a central computer-processing location where an elaborate set of statistics and maps were generated. Over the course of the CORDS program, the HES statistics indicated that the United States and RVN gained increasing control over the rural population of South Vietnam. This was especially the case after the 1968 Tet Offensive, discussed in Chapter 5, which resulted in many killed and captured VC. With the VC out of the way, William Colby, then director of CORDS, tried to capitalize on the opportunity and sent out additional CORDS and security personnel, including PRU teams, and pushed out many of the remaining VC, taking back control over more than 1,000 villages and hamlets. The problem with the HES statistics was that many villages received ratings of A, B, and C, even though no American or ARVN personnel spent much time there, making such ratings questionable.

Although the United States decided to withdraw from Vietnam in 1969 and South Vietnam was defeated in 1975, the successes of certain COIN policies and of pacification before and after 1968 have led some observers to call the fall of South Vietnam a "lost victory." The United States had successfully defended South Vietnam against the combined NVA/VC assault of Tet in 1968 and took advantage of the situation to further consolidate RVN control over South Vietnam thereafter. The question remained, however, whether South Vietnam could survive without continued U.S. military and economic assistance while North Vietnam continued to receive support from both the Soviet Union and China.

Chapter 13

Making Friends and Enemies in Thailand, Laos, and Cambodia

In This Chapter

▶ Building American alliances in Southeast Asia

▶ Finding communism everywhere

▶ Fighting a secret war

▶ Not winning but not losing, either

As strange as it may seem, the war in North and South Vietnam was not fought only in those two countries. When the United States became involved in Southeast Asia, government officials eventually focused a lot of attention and support on South Vietnam, as did the public policies and statements made by the U.S. government during the 1950s and 1960s.

But while North and South Vietnam became the public focus, plenty of action went on behind the scenes in three other Southeast Asian nations, Thailand, Laos, and Cambodia. Although most Americans defined success or failure based on what happened in South Vietnam, the activities and events in Thailand, Laos, and Cambodia proved vital to the overall war effort and are an essential part of the history of the Vietnam War.

Thailand: Supporting the United States

Shortly after World War II, the United States and Thailand established a closer relationship. Although based on many factors and considerations, the powerful anticommunist philosophies of both nations played a prominent role in creating a lasting friendship. In 1950, the two nations signed agreements for nonmilitary cooperation and, shortly thereafter, Thailand sent military forces as part of the United Nations (UN) armed services fighting against communism during the Korean War.

Following the Korean War, with the fall of the French in Vietnam at Dien Bien Phu in 1954, Thailand agreed with the U.S. concerns about communism in Southeast Asia. There existed a historical rivalry between Thailand and Vietnam, because they were two of the most populous and developed nations in Southeast Asia. Thailand and Vietnam especially competed for influence over Cambodia and Laos, because Thailand shared those two nations' western borders, and Vietnam shared their eastern borders, as shown in Figure 13-1. You could say that Cambodia and Laos were a kind of buffer zone between the two more powerful nations of Thailand and Vietnam.

Figure 13-1: Thailand, Laos, Cambodia, and North and South Vietnam.

Map courtesy of the Vietnam Archive, Texas Tech University

When the Viet Minh won over North Vietnam in 1954, Thailand realized that a reunited North and South Vietnam under a communistic and nationalistic government would pose a powerful threat to their position and influence in Southeast Asia. When the United States approached Thailand about membership in a new regional alliance, Thailand readily agreed and became a member of the Southeast Asian Treaty Organization (SEATO), which is discussed in more detail in Chapters 2 and 3.

Thailand and the United States agreed on many issues, and both nations shared concerns about the spread of communism outside of North Vietnam. Both also believed in the *domino theory:* the idea that if one nation fell to communism, neighboring nations were sure to follow, allowing communism to spread throughout the region. A communist movement emerged within Thailand and the government of Thailand believed that its security and sovereignty would be further threatened if communism spread outside of North Vietnam, so it quickly expanded its relationship, including complete military cooperation, with the United States.

Preparing for War: The U.S. military buildup in Thailand

Among the first steps in more U.S./Thailand military cooperation were joint military exercises. The United States sent U.S. Marines and other armed forces to Thailand so that they could train together and gain a better understanding of one another in the event they actually had to fight a common enemy. The two countries didn't have long to wait, because violence broke out in Laos in the late 1950s.

Threatening developments in Laos

The withdrawal of the French in 1954 allowed a group in Laos called the Pathet Lao to expand its support base among the Laotian people. The Pathet Lao first formed in 1950 and allied with the Viet Minh in Vietnam to fight against and remove the French as a colonial power in Indochina (the former name for Vietnam). Philosophically and politically, the Pathet Lao was made up of both communists and nationalists and engaged in a revolutionary movement to counter the French — and then American — presence in Laos. Despite their intentions, U.S. meddling in the political affairs of Laos after 1954 created political instability and provided a rallying point for Pathet Lao activity: Many Laotians saw the United States as just one more colonial power trying to take over their nation.

In the late 1950s, the Pathet Lao received additional supplies and training from North Vietnamese cadres and set up bases along the eastern border of Laos next to North Vietnam. Then, in 1960, fighting erupted between the Royal Lao government and Pathet Lao forces and the fate of Laos became very uncertain. President Eisenhower thought the situation in Laos even more of an immediate concern than the fate of South Vietnam. The importance of the situation was reflected in Eisenhower's briefing to President-elect Kennedy that same year when Eisenhower told Kennedy that the key to victory in Southeast Asia was Laos. After Kennedy took office, the situation in South Vietnam also deteriorated, as fighting continued and riots broke out in Saigon and other cities (discussed in Chapter 4). The overall result of the deteriorating situation in Laos and South Vietnam was an expansion in the relationship between the United States and Thailand.

Expanding the Thai ties: Agreements, bases, operations, and aid

The weaknesses of SEATO became apparent and Thailand sought more substantial assurances from the United States to help defend against communist attack. The two nations signed the *Rusk-Thanat agreement,* and the United States committed to safeguarding Thailand's security against external aggression and invasion, as well as internal insurrection. In exchange, Thailand agreed to establish U.S. air bases in Thailand and allowed U.S. ground forces and CIA personnel in the country. In essence, Thailand became a forward base of operations for both conventional and unconventional operations, and the United States used the bases in Thailand to launch missions into Laos, Cambodia, and North and South Vietnam. All of this was funded completely by the United States, which agreed to provide significant military and economic assistance and aid to Thailand to bolster its military and economy. From 1960 to 1973, the United States invested directly and indirectly more than $2 billion to Thailand. Economic aid from the United States played various roles. The Thai government used the funds to build infrastructure and industry and invested the money to build up the nation. U.S. economic assistance helped Thailand develop one of the strongest economies in Southeast Asia.

Aiding in unconventional warfare, too

One of the most intriguing developments between the United States and Thailand involved the CIA and Thai National Police. Bill Lair, a CIA paramilitary specialist and case officer working in Thailand helped develop and lead the Thai PARU (Paramilitary Aerial Reinforcement Unit). An elite unit of parachutists, the PARU conducted paramilitary operations in both Thailand and Laos. To prepare for operations in Laos, PARU established a jungle warfare training center, where members learned from local Thai villagers how to live off the land and conduct operations in inhospitable and unfamiliar terrain, allowing them to conduct long-range, long-term operations with little resupply.

The PARU were important in several ways, not the least of which was that the group formed an elite, rapid-response unit that increased the internal security of Thailand. More important for the U.S. operations in Laos, members of the PARU conducted operations against the Pathet Lao and North Vietnamese in Laos. The development of the PARU also provided Lair and other CIA personnel with real-world experience, working with the indigenous people of another nation and jointly creating and training paramilitary forces to provide internal security.

This experience was vital to the success of U.S. operations when the United States decided to enter Laos in the early 1960s in order to train and equip Laotians to fight against the Pathet Lao and NVA.

Expanding the Air Force presence in Thailand

The United States Air Force (USAF) made up the majority of U.S. air assets operating out of Thailand and established several air bases from which it launched thousands of sorties from bases like the one at Udorn, Thailand, in Figure 13-2. In addition to USAF personnel and aircraft, these bases also housed U.S. ground forces, personnel from various U.S. governmental civilian agencies, including the CIA, as well as a number of private civilian organizations.

Figure 13-2:
Udorn,
Thailand.

Photograph courtesy of the Judy Porter Collection at the Vietnam Archive,
Texas Tech University

The latter group involved what were thought to be private civilian organizations that conducted and supported missions and operations into Laos, Cambodia, and Vietnam and included Civil Air Transport (CAT), Air America (AAM), Continental Air Services, Incorporated (CASI), Bird and Son, and Arizona Helicopter. Although a tightly held secret for many years even after the war, CAT and AAM were actually owned and operated by the CIA. The other three, CASI, Bird and Son, and Arizona Helicopter were very small in comparison to CAT and AAM but played a vital role in creating the illusion that the activity in Laos was being run by private civilian contractors and not the U.S. government through the CIA.

USAF missions from Thailand

At its peak in 1968, U.S. military forces in Thailand numbered nearly 50,000. Although small when compared to the more than 500,000 in Vietnam, USAF pilots in Laos contributed mightily to the U.S. air presence over the Ho Chi Minh Trail, Laos, and North and South Vietnam. In fact, the majority of official U.S. military operations from Thailand involved USAF bombing missions into Laos and North Vietnam.

USAF pilots stationed in Thailand participated in all of the major bombing campaigns of the war, including Operations ROLLING THUNDER, LINE-BACKER I and II, and many others discussed in Chapters 8 and 9. In addition to the bombing missions, USAF pilots in Thailand flew search-and-rescue (SAR — flying in to find and rescue downed pilots), aerial-resupply, reconnaissance- and intelligence/information–gathering, forward-air-controller (FAC) missions, directing other planes to drop their munitions on specific targets and flying deep into the country to drop off ground reconnaissance teams. Although modest in number, the Thailand-based U.S. operations contributed greatly to the overall war efforts in Laos and Vietnam.

Equipping and training the Royal Thai Military Forces

When the United States and North Vietnam (that is, the Democratic Republic of Vietnam or DRV) signed the Geneva Conventions of 1962 (see the "Relieving the pressure in Laos . . . or at least trying" section, later in this chapter), both sides agreed to stay out of Laos and respect Laotian neutrality. The United States intended to honor that agreement but quickly discovered that the DRV had other plans. The DRV continued to supply the Pathet Lao and failed — with the expansion of the Ho Chi Minh Trail, the trail and road network used to bring men and supplies from North Vietnam to South Vietnam — to cease its activities in the areas along the DRV/Laotian border.

Unlike the DRV, concerns about international relations led the United States to conclude that it should maintain the appearance of honoring the Geneva Conventions but not necessarily hold to the letter of the agreement. President Kennedy and later, President Johnson realized they couldn't actually honor the agreement and watch Laos fall to the Pathet Lao, because the DRV violated the agreements from the beginning. The first step was setting up a support network in neighboring Thailand.

Although the United States decided not to send uniformed military personnel into Laos, it did send a tremendous amount of military equipment to Thailand for use by the Royal Thai Army and other Thai military forces. USAF personnel trained the pilots and U.S. Army and Marine personnel trained the soldiers with the United States paying for everything. In essence, because the United States couldn't send in its own forces, it paid Thailand to send its forces to Laos to fight against the Pathet Lao and NVA. In addition, Thailand did send Royal Thai Army units to fight in South Vietnam to include the Queen's Cobra and Black Panther Regiments.

In addition to U.S. military personnel operating out of Thailand and training Thai forces, the CIA also used Thailand as its base of operations for equipping, supplying, supporting, and helping to lead a Laotian Army of approximately 30,000 soldiers.

Laos: The U.S. Hopes for an Anticommunist Neighbor

Laos was the focus of Presidents Eisenhower and Kennedy, only to be set aside in 1964 by the Johnson administration when the war in Vietnam escalated. But to many U.S. government and military officials, Laos was little different from South Vietnam, and they thought the United States had to prevent the spread of communism into that country in order to remain consistent with the U.S. Cold War policy of containment discussed in Chapter 3. The initial U.S. policy in Laos was proactive as the situation in Laos became increasingly violent and complicated in the late 1950s and early 1960s.

Defining the cultural and political landscape: The many nations of Laos

Many Americans made the mistake of viewing Laos as a nation in the modern sense. In fact, Laos was divided geographically, racially, culturally, and religiously along several lines and contained more than 60 ethnic groups.

- ✔ The lowland Lao people living near the Mekong River are the oldest group of Lao people, and they live rather static lives as farmers and fishermen, engaged mostly in rice cultivation.

- ✔ The highland or hill-tribe Lao migrated more recently from Southern China, Burma, and even Cambodia and live more dynamic lives, engaged in slash-and-burn agriculture.

Slash-and-burn farming literally involves cutting down and burning a forested or jungle area so that the resulting ash provides additional nitrogen and nutrients to the soil, allowing for better farming. But with little else to replenish the nutrients, farmers eventually exhaust the soil and are forced to leave, moving into another area where the slash-and-burn cycle is begun again. Although they moved much more frequently than their lowland cousins, the highland Lao farmed in these cycles and usually remained in the same general areas, rotating to and from areas slashed-and-burned by previous generations of their families.

These significant differences between lowland and highland Lao people added to their mutual fear and mistrust of one another and made the jobs of U.S. personnel working in Laos that much more difficult.

Negotiating the minefield of Laotian politics

One of the stipulations of the Geneva Accords of 1954 (discussed in Chapters 2 and 3) was recognition of Laotian and Cambodian neutrality, but almost immediately, foreign powers intervened, and three distinct groups emerged and competed for control over Laos:

- ✔ The communists: Prince Souphanouvang (one of the Laotian Princes), Pathet Lao, North Vietnam (DRV), Soviet Union, and People's Republic of China (PRC)

- ✔ The non/anticommunists: Prince Souvanna Phouma (another Laotian Prince), General Phoumi Nosavan (the Laotian Army commander), United States, and Thailand

- ✔ The neutralists: Prince Souvanna Phouma, Captain Kong Le (a Laotian Army officer)

Initially led by Prince Souvanna Phouma, control over Laos changed hands several times from 1954 until 1962. Souvanna was noncommunist when it suited him and he received American aid, but increasingly, he leaned toward being a neutralist and wanted to limit or eliminate foreign interference in Laos. Although the United States agreed with the principal of Laotian neutrality, the DRV, Soviet Union, and PRC all continued to provide support, aid, and training to the Pathet Lao.

If the communists refused to honor Laotian neutrality, the United States had no choice but to become involved, as well. Souvanna and Kong Le tried on several occasions to establish coalition governments and even succeeded in convincing Prince Souphanouvang, Souvanna's half-brother and leader of the Pathet Lao, to join them. But because these coalition governments included communist representation, the United States refused to recognize and accept them and continued to provide support to anticommunist and nationalist politicians and General Phoumi, a fervent anticommunist.

U.S. activity between 1958 and 1960 even involved helping Phoumi rig elections so that anticommunist and nationalist leaders won. Angered by the blatant foreign meddling and corrupt elections, the neutralists rebelled. In August 1960, Captain Kong Le staged a coup and put Prince Souvanna back into power. Four months later, in December, General Phoumi and the bulk of the Royal Lao Army (RLA), with ample material and financial assistance from the United States, massed in Savannakhet in southern Laos and staged a counter-coup, attacked Vientiane (the capital of Laos), removed Kong Le and his forces, and temporarily sent Prince Souvanna into exile in Cambodia. Phoumi assumed control over Laos, but Kong Le gathered his neutralist forces and struck an alliance with the Pathet Lao.

This alliance with the communists brought with it material support from the Soviet Union, PRC, and DRV. Kong Le then took his forces, attacked the strategically important Plain of Jars along with the airfield, and drove Phoumi's forces from the area. With the continued support of the communists, Kong Le posed a serious threat to the stability and success of the Phoumi government and heightened concerns in Washington. President Kennedy became increasingly concerned that the United States and the Soviet Union were getting too closely engaged in this war, which could lead to an escalation in hostilities in Laos, or even worse, a direct confrontation between the two super-powers.

Relieving the pressure in Laos . . . or at least trying

President Kennedy engaged in some quiet diplomacy with the Soviet Union and found them a willing audience, because they didn't want a major confrontation with the United States, either. These initial exchanges led to a call for meetings in Geneva in May 1961 and resulted in the Geneva Conventions of 1962. The U.S. position toward Laos changed, and Kennedy turned away from the hard stance of trying to create an anticommunist Laos, instead seeking neutrality. The new Conventions of 1962 called for all parties to respect Laotian neutrality and brought Prince Souvanna back to power.

The problems in Laos did not end, however, as the DRV continued its activities along the border, continued to expand Ho Chi Minh Trail, and did not stop their support of the communist Pathet Lao. In contrast to earlier policies and meddling, the United States responded with temperance and reserve and sought mostly to reinforce and support Laotian neutrality by providing covert and clandestine assistance in order to counterbalance the DRV's blatant disregard for the terms of the Geneva Conventions. The policy that followed became referred to as *the Secret War in Laos.*

Fighting a nonattributable war in Laos

Years after the war, former Director of Central Intelligence (and participant in the Vietnam War) William Colby commented that the United States had to fight a *nonattributable war* in Laos. What he meant was the United States had to engage in war fighting activities but also had to be able to completely deny any involvement, and those denials had to be believable at best and not disprovable at worse. The way by which the United States fought this nonattributable or secret war was through covert civilian operatives, civilian covers, partisan forces, and mercenaries. The war had to be run at a level involving the highest-ranking American officials, including the U.S. Ambassador in Laos, with the CIA controlling operations in the air and on the ground. A uniformed military presence would be a direct violation of the accords, so all U.S. military personnel had to dress in civilian clothes and deny their military associations. For their part, the U.S. military provided only a small percentage of the overall forces operating in Laos, because most U.S. personnel were civilians and the bulk of military forces came from Laos and Thailand.

Fighting from the embassy

Given the importance of being able to deny any involvement, the U.S. ambassadors in Laos became heavily involved in the secret war in Laos. William Sullivan was the most prominent and long-serving U.S. Ambassador in Laos, and he became the most involved, as well, although sometimes to the disappointment of air and ground personnel and military commanders operating in the theater of Southeast Asia. It is purported that MACV Commander General Westmoreland, in particular, didn't get along well with Sullivan, who would routinely counter Westmoreland's order regarding military forces in Laos and would circumvent the military chain-of-command and directly contact the Defense Secretary, without so much as a courtesy call to MACV Headquarters (HQ). Although many of Sullivan's decisions became controversial, few would dispute his intelligence, sincerity, or suitability for the job in maintaining the illusion of no direct U.S. involvement in Laos.

Fighting in Laos: The H'mong and the CIA

When the United States changed its policy toward Laos in 1962, the CIA decided to solicit the support of a charismatic H'mong leader named General Vang Pao.

The H'mong — or Meo, as they are sometimes referred — are members of the large ethnic minority people who live in the mountains and highlands of Laos. General Vang Pao was one of the few senior officers in the Royal Thai Army (RTA) from that segment of the Laotian population. According to various observers, Vang Pao was an extremely effective commander who could balance strong military leadership and discipline with an understanding of H'mong culture and superstition. He was adept at understanding the limits and capabilities of his 30,000-man army and didn't squander his forces just because the country making the requests (the United States) happened to be giving him significant amounts of food, weapons, ammunition, and the money he used to pay his soldiers.

Vang Pao's H'mong army engaged in large numbers of offensive operations against both the communist Pathet Lao and the North Vietnamese, with the advice and support of CIA case officers. The most significant direct combat support provided Vang Pao by the CIA was the U.S. close-air support and aerial resupply from bases in Laos and Thailand. Vang Pao also provided security for the CIA base camps throughout Laos at such places as Luong Prabang, Long Tieng (shown in Figure 13-3), and Sam Nuea. The CIA housed personnel at these bases where the agency set up airfields; cached weapons, ammunition, and supplies; and set up communications networks. Most of the sites were remote and accessible only by air. In addition, the bases housed significant Lao civilian populations, because the H'mong families typically followed and lived with soldiers.

Figure 13-3:
The CIA base at Long Tieng, also called Lima Site 20A (Alternate).

Photograph courtesy of the Vietnam Archive, Texas Tech University

Fighting in Laos: Strategies and tactics

The composition of Vang Pao's forces limited their capabilities. The H'mong Army was too small to directly challenge the larger, well-trained, and well-equipped NVA forces operating on the Ho Chi Minh Trail near the North Vietnamese border. It was these same NVA forces that also provided the Pathet Lao with reinforcements. So the best Vang Pao could usually do was use his forces to harass the NVA and Pathet Lao and disrupt their movements and logistics operations. Vang Pao also used his forces for reconnaissance and intelligence gathering. And the H'mong Army also provided security for the various U.S. bases and facilities throughout Laos.

Very rarely did Vang Pao intentionally engage large NVA forces due to the heavy losses the troops typically suffered in such engagements. Still, by engaging in these other operations, Vang Pao's army effectively defended most of the U.S. bases and tied down between 40,000 and 67,000 NVA soldiers who had to provide security to their logistics operations along the Ho Chi Minh Trail. Absent the necessity to keep these soldiers in Laos, North Vietnam would have likely sent the bulk of these NVA units to South Vietnam where they would have fought and, potentially, killed U.S. and South Vietnamese (ARVN) forces.

The tactical operations conducted by Vang Pao and his H'mong Army focused on northern Laos near the border with North Vietnam, as well as a strategic area called the Plain of Jars (PDJ). The defensive operations took on a more important role in 1967 at a small remote CIA base at Phu Pha Thi, also called Lima Site 85.

Phu Pha Thi: Expanding the conventional role of Laos in the Vietnam War

Control over the Laotian border with North Vietnam by H'mong and U.S. forces provided a great opportunity to expand the U.S. bombing capabilities in Laos. Conducting bombing runs along the Ho Chi Minh Trail in Laos and North Vietnam, as well as targets deeper within North Vietnam, presented constant risks to U.S. pilots. Weather often hindered the accurate dropping of bombs or prevented the bombing of targets altogether. Under the control of the CIA and H'mong, Phu Pha Thi was strategically located 20 miles from the border and only 160 miles from Hanoi.

In 1966, the United States decided to minimize some of the risks to its pilots and increase the pilots' bombing accuracy by placing a Tactical Air Navigation System (TACAN) on Phu Pha Thi. Then, in 1967, the USAF installed a TSQ81, bombing radar guidance system, just in time to contribute to Operation COMMANDO HUNT, discussed in Chapter 9. With the addition of these two facilities at Phu Pha Thi, U.S. pilots could more accurately navigate along the Ho Chi Minh Trail and into North Vietnam, avoid known missile and other antiaircraft sites, and fly more accurately to their targets. In addition, the TSQ81 allowed pilots to be guided to their targets in adverse weather, within almost 50 miles of Hanoi.

President Johnson, the U.S. Military Joint Chiefs of Staff (JCS), and many other advisors in Washington, D.C., thought this was great. Although many people in Laos agreed, some of the CIA ground personnel didn't. Bill Lair and others predicted that the radar and guidance systems would act as magnets to the NVA, who would stop at nothing to destroy the facility along with Lima Site 85. This attack would endanger the CIA and USAF personnel on site, as well as the H'mong contingent providing security. Such a battle would also draw undue attention to the war in Laos at a time when everyone was supposed to be ensuring the secrecy of U.S. activities and operations in the area. No one wanted U.S. violations of Laotian neutrality to be publicized, even if the NVA and other parties involved in the war already knew. This was, after all, supposed to be a nonattributable war.

Unfortunately, almost immediately after discovering the site at Phu Pha Thi, the NVA started building a road network up to the base of the mountain, an indication that it would ultimately send in a large force to destroy the site and facility. In January 1968, two North Vietnamese MiG bi-planes (propeller-driven planes with two sets of wings, one set above the other) flew over the site and fired their guns at the facility. An Air America helicopter chased the two planes, and a crewmember engaged the MiGs with an AK-47 personal assault rifle, shooting one down and forcing the second to crash into a mountain. Two months later to the day, the NVA launched a major offensive on Lima Site 85.

On March 11, the NVA fired artillery onto Phu Pha Thi, and ground forces scaled a steep and mined side of the mountain, avoiding the mines with detectors and surprising the USAF and CIA personnel, as well as the H'mong defenders. Air America pilots flew in and rescued some of the personnel, but at least eleven Americans and many more H'mong never made it out. Although the USAF equipment had been rigged with explosives in the event of just such an attack, no one at the site was able to detonate them, and the USAF spent the next several weeks bombing the site in the hope it would destroy the facilities and equipment left behind. Although the defeat at Phu Pha Thi was devastating to both the U.S. military and H'mong, it didn't become an international incident: North Vietnam didn't make an issue of it, lest its own violations of Lao neutrality come under international scrutiny.

Fighting over the PDJ: Sometimes it depended on the weather

Another strategic area of Laos that many U.S. personnel wanted to control was the PDJ (Plains of Jars). Part of the strategic importance of the PDJ was an airfield at Xieng Khouang, and shortly after the battle at Phu Pha Thi, Vang Pao and his Pathet Lao and NVA counterparts began a game of seasonal tug-of-war to control the area.

The weather played a vexing role in Laos and had varying effects on operations on and around the PDJ. Although it has a fairly wet climate to begin with, Laos receives the bulk of its rainfall during the monsoon season, which typically runs from May to October, when the area receives anywhere between 50 and 200 inches of rain.

Rain affected ground operations in several ways.

✔ Too much low cloud cover hindered U.S. air operations, hampered the movement of the H'mong Army, and could prevent close air support and aerial resupply at critical moments in a battle.

✔ The Pathet Lao and NVA lacked any significant air support capability, and too much rain could slow or completely halt their ground transportation, troop movements, and operations.

✔ During the rainy season, the United States and Royal Laos Air Force (RLAF) couldn't bomb Pathet Lao and NVA forces as easily or frequently.

The result was an ebb and flow in control over key terrain like the PDJ, where the H'mong had greater advantages in air mobility and air support during the dry season (October–May) and the Pathet Lao and NVA enjoyed greater success during the monsoon season (May–October).

A good example of this occurred in September 1969, when Vang Pao and the H'mong Army launched Operation ABOUT FACE, which was designed to recapture the PDJ from the Pathet Lao and NVA. The operations stirred up quite a bit of controversy, because some of the CIA ground personnel were concerned that the H'mong weren't trained or equipped well enough to conduct a massive ground assault against the NVA. Even if Vang Pao succeeded, these observers questioned the likelihood that the H'mong would be able to hold onto the PDJ for any length of time. Regardless of these concerns, Ambassador Sullivan approved support for the operation and in September, Vang Pao and the H'mong captured Xieng Khouang and took over much of the PDJ. They captured a sizable cache of Pathet Lao and NVA supplies, including small and heavy weapons, millions of rounds of ammunition, trucks, tanks, jeeps, more than 150,000 gallons of gasoline, and seven tons of food. But the victory was short lived.

In January 1970, the NVA and Pathet Lao launched a counteroffensive, using tanks, and retook the PDJ. The United States and RLAF flew many airstrikes against the PL/NVA, slowing their advance enough to allow Vang Pao to get some of his forces out of the area. Still, the H'mong suffered serious losses and it wasn't until May 1971 that the H'mong could launch another offensive to take back the PDJ. For the next two years, the H'mong and the PL/NVA engaged went back and forth over the PDJ, each side controlling the area for about six months at a time with neither side gaining a definitive advantage over the other. Still, without a doubt, the U.S. air support magnified considerably the H'mong Army capability, and Air America was one of the most significant organizations providing that support.

U.S. military operations in Laos

In addition to the CIA and Air America, the U.S. military conducted various missions in Laos. Much of this activity involved training, although some U.S. personnel did engage in combat operations.

Training ground forces: Green Berets in Laos

Some of the first U.S. Army Special Forces missions conducted in Southeast Asia occurred in Laos. First introduced in 1959, U.S. Special Forces engaged in Operation HOTFOOT, which involved training the Royal Lao Army to fight against the Pathet Lao. The U.S. forces created the mobile training team model that traveled around Laos and trained the Lao forces, especially those defending the capital of Vientiane, as well as other cities, such as Savannekhet, Luang Prabang, and Pakse.

In an attempt to broaden the ground forces available to fight against the Pathet Lao communists, the United States launched Operation WHITESTAR in 1962. Employing U.S. Special Forces mobile training teams, Operation WHITESTAR focused on the rural highlands of Laos and trained the H'mong soldiers, especially those who joined Vang Pao's Army.

Training and flying: The USAF in Laos

In addition to the U.S. Army Special Forces activity, the USAF also conducted two missions in Laos. First, in 1966 under PROJECT 404, USAF personnel entered Laos and trained Laotian pilots and ground personnel on the proper use and maintenance of the materiel being sent to them. The United States had increased the amount of military aid entering Laos but the provisions of the Geneva Accords made it all but impossible to properly train the Laotian military. PROJECT 404 addressed that deficiency.

In addition to training, some USAF pilots also flew combat missions over Laos. Although this happened under various auspices, the most blatant use of USAF personnel in this context was a Forward Air Controller (FAC) unit called, *the Ravens.* The name Raven was derived from the group's *call sign,* the name they used when communicating on the radio.

Military personnel use code words to identify themselves when talking over the radio, and the FAC unit flying in Laos used the call sign Raven.

The Ravens flew FAC missions throughout Laos, and their principal mission was to direct U.S. airpower over their targets. Flying small, single-engine, slow-moving, and low-flying aircraft, the FAC would sometimes direct pilots to drop bombs or fire guns in relation to terrain feature; other times they would mark the target to be bombed with a smoke rocket. Either way, the Ravens directed U.S. aircraft flying out of Thailand and South Vietnam, providing relief to H'mong ground forces, engaging Pathet Lao and NVA units caught in the open, and disrupting the movement of NVA troops and materiel down the Ho Chi Minh Trail.

Ending the war in Laos and Thailand

When the United States ended the war in Vietnam in 1973, it left Thailand and Laos, as well. The USAF turned over its bases, and the CIA and Air America closed their facilities. Although the loss of revenue had an adverse impact on the Thai economy, the stability of that nation continued into the postwar period because it lacked any serious internal communist threat. Laos was not so lucky.

Dependent on the tremendous amount of military and financial assistance they had received for more than a decade, the RLA, RLAF, and H'mong couldn't hold out long against the well supplied and equipped Pathet Lao and NVA. Vang Pao's Army was overrun in 1975, and he fled Laos to the United States where he has lived since. The Pathet Lao gained control of the Lao government that same year and took over complete control in December, abolishing the monarchy and creating the Lao People's Democratic Republic.

Creating the Largest Airline in Asia: CAT and Air America

Early during U.S. activities in Southeast Asia, the CIA realized the effectiveness of developing an air support capability outside the USAF and military chain of command.

The agency derived this lesson from the experiences of General Claire Chennault and the American Volunteer Group, the Flying Tigers, who flew combat and support missions in the China-Burma-India theater during WWII. Immediately after WWII, Chennault and Whiting Willauer created Civil Air Transport (CAT), Incorporated. As tensions increased in Asia after the fall of China to communism in 1949, the CIA purchased CAT in order to use the cover of the civilian airline to conduct secret intelligence operations throughout Asia. CAT aircraft and pilots supported the French during the French-Indochina War, providing aerial resupply, even during the battle at Dien Bien Phu. CAT civilian air operations stayed the same, and CIA ownership of the airline was one of the best-kept secrets of American activity in Asia during the Cold War.

Air America emerges

As the United States increased its operations in Laos and the rest of Southeast Asia, the CIA recognized the need to expand the air support available in the area, as well. In 1959, the agency created Air America, Incorporated, as a second "air proprietary" operating in Southeast Asia. CAT maintained its base in Japan and continued conducting regular commercial carrier flights, as well as secret missions and operations in support of the U.S. government and military. But although CAT operations continued throughout Southeast Asia, Air America handled most of the flying in Thailand, Laos, and South Vietnam.

Spreading her wings: Air America expands

As the U.S. presence in Laos expanded, so, too, did the need for additional air capabilities. Shortly after the creation of Air America, the CIA sought to expand both the fixed wing and rotary wing capabilities of this new organization. Although helicopters in 1959 were not as powerful as was needed for high-altitude flying, they could engage in more flexible missions and in lowland areas. Eventually, manufacturers addressed the issues of power, and helicopters in the 1960s became powerful enough to operate at some of the highest elevations in Southeast Asia.

In addition to helicopters, the CIA actively sought out aircraft more suited to the terrain and facilities — or lack thereof — in Laos. Most military airplanes need rather long runways in order take off and land safely. Laos had a shortage of airfields, and the mountainous terrain didn't lend itself readily to the construction of long runways. So the CIA bought several types of aircraft, including the Helio Courier and the Pilatus Porter (see Figure 13-4), which are STOL (short take-off/landing) capable. Small and maneuverable, these STOL aircraft could slow to around 50 miles per hour and land on very short, poor quality, dirt runways — some as short as 100 feet with full flaps and the right wind conditions. Although the aircraft couldn't carry heavy cargo, they could accommodate some passengers and materiel, as needed.

Figure 13-4:
The Pilatus Porter was one of the most versatile aircraft in the Air America inventory.

Photograph courtesy of the Vietnam Archive, Texas Tech University

For heavy airdrops and resupply missions, the CIA and Air America also relied on certain tried-and-true military aircraft, including the C-119, C-123, C-130, C-46, Caribou, and several other aircraft with larger cargo carrying capabilities. For these larger aircraft, Air America employed airfreight specialists, also called *kickers,* who loaded and dispensed the cargo over the designated drop sites. These drops included all types of material, including, pigs, chickens, and other livestock; rice and other food; and military supplies that included weapons and what was called *hard rice* (ammunition).

Air America crews transported and delivered literally thousands of tons of food and military equipment and hundreds of thousands of troops and refugees, while providing medical evacuation services, coordinating routine and emergency troop insertions and extractions, and conducting Search and

Rescue missions for downed U.S. and allied pilots throughout Laos. Without a doubt, Air America played an indispensable role in U.S. missions and the overall success in Laos.

The Air America controversy

Like many other aspects of American involvement in Vietnam and Southeast Asia, Air America has become embroiled in controversy and myth. Most of the controversy involved accusations that Air America pilots participated in drug trafficking. Although it is likely that almost all aircraft flying in Laos carried drugs at one time or another, such passengers and cargo were usually H'mong soldiers and civilians who flew with them and carried heroin, mostly for personal use. In fact, the CIA and Air America ultimately took very real steps to prevent any illegal drug activity, including the use of drug-sniffing dogs to inspect cargo. Unfortunately, these rumors have persisted despite the overwhelming evidence that Air America pilots and personnel served in Southeast Asia with dignity and honor.

Caught in the Middle: What About Cambodia?

Like Laos, when the war in South Vietnam escalated, Cambodia found itself caught in the middle between the U.S./RVN/Thailand alliance and the DRV/Soviet Union/PRC communist alliance. In addition, communist groups emerged within Cambodia, further complicating matters. But unlike Laos, Cambodia more effectively maintained its neutrality and didn't suffer internal instability, at least initially.

A princely balancing act

Prince Norodom Sihanouk, a talented politician, emerged to power during the last years of French colonial rule in Cambodia. In 1954, Cambodia gained its independence from the French and, the following year, Sihanouk was elected president. To deal with threats to stability from within Cambodia, Sihanouk invited potential political rivals to join his government and offered them legitimate positions of authority. Some of the communists didn't want to share power and so left for the DRV or went underground. To deal with the threats to Cambodian stability from outside the country, Sihanouk tried to play the United States, DRV, PRC, and other foreign powers off one another but eventually had to choose a side.

The decision for Sihanouk came in 1963 when South Vietnam violated Cambodian territory and neutrality in pursuit of VC soldiers who crossed the border while fleeing the Army of the Republic of Vietnam (ARVN). The United States backed ARVN in the diplomatic exchange that occurred afterward, and so Sihanouk approached China (PRC) for support. In 1963, Sihanouk also concluded that the DRV was most likely to win in the war between North and South Vietnam, so he broke diplomatic relations with South Vietnam and later (in 1965) broke relations with the United States. Sihanouk also allowed the DRV to set up base camps in eastern Cambodia near the border with South Vietnam. These decisions eventually led formerly loyal members of the Sihanouk government to turn against him.

In the meantime, instability in China led Sihanouk to decide in 1966 to approach the United States about renewing ties and diplomatic relations. Because the war in South Vietnam had escalated and expanded rather significantly in the interim, the United States welcomed the opportunity. Sihanouk accepted U.S. military and economic assistance and in exchange, U.S. and ARVN forces could follow and engage NVA/VC forces that crossed into Cambodia, so long as the fighting occurred in uninhabited areas and no Cambodians were injured or killed. Unfortunately for Sihanouk, this agreement led to an escalation of U.S./ARVN air and ground operations in Cambodia.

Communism in Cambodia: The rise and growth of the Khmer Rouge

The communists who decided not to join the Sihanouk government started to recruit and organize members of Cambodia's rural population to form what became the Khmer Rouge. Their leader, Pol Pot, had the initial backing of both China and DRV. Numbering only 4,000 in 1969, the communist leadership received a boost in recruiting in the form of the U.S. Operation MENU, discussed in Chapter 10, when the United States bombed NVA/VC bases in Cambodia, forcing them deeper into Cambodia and disrupting the lives of the Cambodian people. The Cambodian Incursion the next year, discussed in Chapter 6, further destabilized Cambodia and angered many people as ARVN troops took out their anger and resentment on the Cambodian civilian population. By 1975, the Khmer Rouge numbered in excess of 80,000 armed members.

Seizing power in Cambodia: First Lon Nol, then the Khmer

Unhappy with Sihanouk, the United States backed a coup in 1970 while Sihanouk was out of the country. Led by a nationalist and anticommunist,

General Lon Nol, the coup succeeded but couldn't unite the country: The urban populations supported Lon Nol but growing segments of the rural population supported the Khmer Rouge. Lon Nol maintained power principally through significant amounts of American military aid. This changed in 1973 when the U.S. war in Vietnam ended with the Paris Peace Accords and the U.S. Congress cut aid to Southeast Asia, including Cambodia, the following year.

Without U.S. assistance, Lon Nol couldn't maintain power, and the Khmer Rouge seized Phnom Penh, the capital of Cambodia, in April 1975. Mistrustful of its true intentions, Pol Pot renounced his ties to North Vietnam and all other nations and sought to rely solely on China for support.

The killing fields and war with Vietnam

The situation in Cambodia deteriorated rapidly after 1975 when a drought, coupled with a malaria outbreak and unbelievable violence, resulted in the deaths of more than 1 million Cambodians. The killing fields of Cambodia (see Figure 13-5) were littered with the corpses and bones of people murdered or dead from disease or starvation. The situation between Cambodia and Vietnam also escalated in 1977, resulting in a war where the Vietnamese captured Phnom Penh and put into power the Cambodians who fled to North Vietnam after Sihanouk took power in 1955. Vietnam controlled most of Cambodia until 1993 when the UN oversaw elections, and Prince Sihanouk emerged once again and took the throne as King of Cambodia.

Figure 13-5:
The killing
fields.

Photograph courtesy of the Vietnam Archive,
Texas Tech University

What Did It All Mean?

Although South Vietnam, Laos, and Cambodia did ultimately fall to communism, Thailand and the rest of Southeast Asia remained free and democratic. Some postwar observers have argued that although unsuccessful in their primary goal of preventing the spread of communism to South Vietnam, the U.S. involvement in Southeast Asia was absolutely vital in securing the rest of the region. In other words, the fighting in South Vietnam, Laos, and Cambodia allowed for the containment of communism to just those three countries for just long enough. This allowed the other nations in Southeast Asia to develop strong economic, political, and social institutions so that they could withstand any communist threats.

Part V

A War at Home and a Home at War

@RICHTENNANT

STOP THE WAR IN VIETNAM

SUPER ST★RE

A&P

★Picket Signs
★T-Shirts

★ Bumper Stickers
Posters
Buttons

"The antiwar movement seems to be gaining some mainstream acceptance."

In this part . . .

One has to go back to the American Civil War to find the U.S. more divided as a nation over a single event. The Vietnam War brought emotions to a boil as anti-war activists squared off against Vietnam War supporter around the campuses, in the cities, and on the streets across the U.S. In this part, you will learn about the origins of the anti-war movement and the movement to support the forces in Southeast Asia and how each movement developed and intensified as the war progressed. War is never a popular thing though the justifications for it can spur a people to the greatest of sacrifices. For many in the U.S., the Vietnam War was a part of a great struggle against communism that, if left unchecked, could threaten the very things that Americans held near and dear. It was unthinkable that any U.S. citizen would criticize U.S. foreign policy or the American president. The Vietnam War resulted in both as anti-war activist questioned the role of the U.S. in Vietnam and the use of resources taken away from domestic programs. In this part, you will discover the motivations for both sides of the argument as well as how the movements transitioned to the post-war period and helped to shape the generation that followed.

Chapter 14

Protesting the American War Effort

• •

In This Chapter

▶ Beginning the movement

▶ Responding to the escalation of war

▶ Justifying action to mainstream America

▶ Reaching the high-water mark

▶ Ending the war — ending the movement

• •

*N*ot since the American Civil War in the 1860s did the United States experience the degree of domestic turmoil and civil disobedience that it did with the protests against the Vietnam War during the 1960s and early 1970s. Although the antiwar movement formed in response to America's escalation in Vietnam and to what appeared to many to be the senseless loss of life so many thousands of miles away from home, it also challenged the structure of society.

Protesters against the war also questioned the roles of race, sex, and culture and, in some cases, overturned or tried to overturn traditional, long-held values in American society. The methods used to convey the 1960s and early 1970s brand of antiwar sentiment continue even today to stir the kind of controversy that disrupted the lives of so many during that period.

Although the antiwar movement was not the main reason for ending the war in Southeast Asia, it did exert considerable influence on various legislative initiatives aimed at how the United States government conducts foreign policy and war. One of the most significant reasons the movement failed to exert more influence on the war was the movement's splintering and its ineffectiveness during the last years of the war. Still, the seeds planted by the antiwar movement, which modeled itself on the Civil Rights movements in the 1950s and early 1960s, left a powerful legacy in the form of postwar organizations and protestors that were poised to try to change a nation. The rise of feminism and environmentalism are good examples of movements benefiting from the organizational experiences of the antiwar movement. For the United States during the 1960s and early 1970s, the antiwar movement became an integral part of American culture and society. There truly was a war at home and a home at war.

Forming the Origins of the Movement: 1950-1964

During early U.S. involvement in Vietnam, concerns about Southeast Asia were minor. Personnel levels in Vietnam during the presidencies of Dwight D. Eisenhower and John F. Kennedy remained relatively low, and the main focus of the military's attention was on Europe and the Soviet threat. Opposition to American involvement in Vietnam resided within groups, such as the Fellowship for Reconciliation and the War Resisters League, traditionally known for favoring peace and opposing armed aggression and expansion of the United States' commitment abroad.

Following that conflict in Southeast Asia

Opposition to U.S. involvement in Southeast Asia during the 1950s and early 1960s came principally from religious and pacifist organizations that rallied against war and violence.

Two organizations were involved in the early antiwar movement, but neither made a significant impact on the course of U.S. involvement in Vietnam:

- **Fellowship of Reconciliation (FOR).** FOR was founded in England at the start of World War I and came to the United States shortly thereafter. Pacifist A. J. Muste led FOR and protested violence in Vietnam during the 1950s and early 1960s. In October 1964, FOR issued the first public statement endorsing draft resistance as a response to the increasing number of Army advisors sent to Vietnam during the Kennedy Administration. FOR was not a radical organization and did not engage in a public debate against American involvement in Vietnam.

- **War Resisters League (WRL).** WRL was founded as the American branch of FOR in 1932. It also was a pacifist organization that focused on conscientious objection to war (see the sidebar "The conscientious objector" later in this chapter). Under the leadership of David Dellinger, the WRL focused its protests on the expanding U.S. military advisory effort in Vietnam. In May 1964, the WRL sponsored a demonstration in New York City at which 12 men burned their draft cards. In December 1964, the WRL organized the first nationwide demonstration against the Vietnam War, but it failed to attract a large number of protestors or gain national media attention.

Greene's peace

In 1955, Graham Greene wrote *The Quiet American,* which took exception to the policy of the United States in Southeast Asia. Greene's main character was an American who adhered to the Cold War mentality of the time — a firm believer in the Communist monolith, the Domino Theory, religion, and democracy. Greene's primary objective in writing the book was to highlight what he thought was America's mistaken military strategy in Vietnam. The book became prominent as the antiwar movement took shape.

Emerging opponents to Ngo Dinh Diem

Although no serious opponents objected to U.S. involvement during the Eisenhower Administration, a few within the Kennedy Administration and Congress began questioning the role of the United States in Vietnam, especially with the increased oppression of Ngo Dinh Diem, the president of South Vietnam, which is outlined in Chapter 2.

John Kenneth Galbraith, a Harvard economist, warned President Kennedy that Vietnam could escalate into a major war with little likelihood of a definite winner, and Averell Harriman, another Kennedy confidant, counseled against support for Ngo Dinh Diem, arguing that he was not the right man for the job.

The Buddhist Crisis in the summer of 1963, which is described in Chapter 2, caused many of the reporters covering the war to question how the United States could support a South Vietnamese government that was involved in human rights violations. Members of the press, however, seldom questioned the role of the American military's role in Vietnam. Criticism from the media of the increase in American personnel was almost nonexistent. The press corps almost always passed along military assessments of the situation without question to the public, and political critics did not challenge Kennedy's vision and prestige. One main reason why reporters didn't question the military's role in Vietnam was because of the low level of military action involving U.S. soldiers. Casualties were kept to a minimum and the media were less willing to attack the popular presidency of John F. Kennedy and his foreign policy in Vietnam.

The overthrow of Diem and the assassination of Kennedy made President Lyndon B. Johnson's mandate clear — continue Kennedy's policies. Even with the buildup of advisors and commitment in 1964, Congress was reluctant to openly criticize America and the presidency. Only a few outspoken protestors like Senator Ernest Gruening (Alaska) maintained that the loss of American life and waste of resources in Vietnam were not worth the results. He and Senator Wayne L. Morse (Oregon) were the only congressmen to vote against the Gulf of Tonkin Resolution, the overwhelming congressional action (described in Chapter 5) that provided the basis for LBJ to escalate the war.

Some of Johnson's advisors also warned against becoming involved in Vietnam. Undersecretary of State George Ball voiced opposition to the commitment of combat troops in Vietnam, and others, including Vice President Hubert Humphrey and Senators J. William Fulbright (Arkansas) and Michael Mansfield (Montana), cautioned against escalation. Although these men advised against the introduction of combat troops, after Johnson decided to proceed, they supported the 1965 action.

The Focus Becomes Clear: 1965–1966

The few antiwar activists at this point were neither organized nor did they hold the attention of the American public. When Johnson announced the introduction of military combat troops into Vietnam, public opinion supported the move. Most Americans believed that it was the obligation of the United States to assist in the development of South Vietnam and combat the communist insurgency that threatened that country.

And so, as more and more young Americans went to Vietnam and an increasingly more noticeable number of them returned in body bags, the focus of the antiwar movement became clearer and its motivation for protest more understandable. More than 30 new antiwar organizations emerged in 1965 under the tenuous leadership of the National Coordinating Committee to End the War in Vietnam (NCC). The committee's principle function was receiving and distributing information about antiwar activities but it never was able to unite groups across the political spectrum. As the war progressed, the NCC was unable to unite the various antiwar groups that emerged from various parts of American society.

Recognizing religious protestors

Mobilized and led by the Clergy and Laity Concerned About Vietnam (CALCAV) when the Johnson Administration escalated America's military commitment in Vietnam, members of the religious community joined social liberals in taking a stand against the war. The joining of CALCAV with groups such as FOR, NCC, and WRL on the common issue of the Vietnam War strengthened the antiwar movement, enabling it to grow as the war intensified.

Founded in October 1965, CALCAV brought protesting the war to the middle American and, when combined with the organizations involved in the Civil Rights movement, brought several national leaders into its fold. CALCAV was the counter to *radicalism* expressed by people who became frustrated with the failure to end the war through peaceful protest and therefore believed that violence was necessary to show the U.S. government that the Vietnam War must end. In CALCAV's infancy, it focused on moderate alternatives of protest, such as peaceful demonstrations, and concentrated on issues like ending the air war against North Vietnam rather than targeting government facilities that supported the war effort.

In 1967, with Martin Luther King Jr. serving as its chairman, the group was investigated by the U.S. government as a threat to national security. CALCAV responded by releasing a report that accused the United States of war crimes and international law violations. As the war progressed, the group intensified its efforts but at the same time managed to retain its stance as a moderate alternative to the increasingly radical antiwar movement.

Other religious organizations, such as the Catholic Peace Fellowship (CPF) and the National Emergency Committee of Clergy Concerned About Vietnam, focused on using additional strategies to protest the war. These religious groups conducted workshops showing draft-aged men how to apply for deferments and other means of avoiding the draft, including the option of leaving the United States rather than fulfilling the requirements of the draft.

The Friends Committee on National Legislation (FCNL), a Religious Society of Friends (Quaker) organization founded in 1943, called for nonviolent resolution to the war in Vietnam. It advocated pacifism and settling the conflict through the United Nations. The FCNL believed the United States was wasting valuable resources on the military in Vietnam when it could have provided more for human needs in the United States and abroad.

American Friends Service Committee (AFSC), founded in 1917, also a Quaker organization, was committed to social justice, peace, and humanitarian service. After the French left Indochina (see Chapter 2), the AFSC advocated noninterference in Vietnam. The AFSC sent personnel to Vietnam to assist with medical care for the war wounded and provided medical supplies and care for refugee children in Quang Ngai. The AFSC expanded its care in Quang Ngai in 1967 but also sent medical supplies to Viet Cong–held territory. By 1969, the AFSC provided medical supplies to North Vietnam, and its membership became more involved in antiwar demonstrations. The AFSC helped organize the March Against Death rally in Washington, D.C., where demonstrators, walking by the White House, called out the names of U.S. soldiers killed in Vietnam. The AFSC also was involved in exposing the *secret war* in Cambodia and Laos, which is described in Chapter 13.

After the United States departed Vietnam in 1973, the AFSC remained in Vietnam providing relief for the war-torn country with special care for children and agricultural equipment.

Coordinating the colleges

The rise of protests on college campuses was a defining moment in the antiwar movement. In January 1960, a group of University of Michigan students formed Students for a Democratic Society (SDS) to work toward civil rights for African-Americans in the United States. After the Gulf of Tonkin incident, an event that changed the course of the war, which is described in Chapter 11, SDS organized campus demonstrations and teach-ins against the war and circulated "We Won't Go" petitions among draft-aged men enabling them to state that they would not go to Vietnam if drafted into military service.

On April 17, 1965, SDS sponsored a demonstration in Washington, D.C., that was attended by more than 20,000 protesters. As a result, the number of SDS chapters increased to between 300 and 400 with a membership rising to more than 30,000 by the end of 1966. By the mid-1960s, the organization split into two groups, those who wanted to focus only on the Vietnam War and those who held true to the original mission of SDS, the Civil Rights movement. By 1968, SDS organizations on campuses around the nation had become less influential in the antiwar movement. Some SDS members joined more radical elements within the movement, and others continued their protests with other organizations. The last major SDS-sponsored protest, a march on Washington, D.C., occurred in 1969.

SDS members weren't only students who adopted civil rights techniques in their protest of Vietnam. After Johnson announced the commitment of Marines at Danang in March 1965 — for more on the military strategy see Chapter 5 — the faculty at the University of Michigan organized the first teach-in. On March 24, more than 3,000 students and faculty participated in the first teach-in, modeled, after a fashion, on the sit-ins used by the civil rights movement in the 1950s and early 1960s. *Sit-ins* were tools used by supporters of the civil rights movement, in particular African-Americans who converged on public locations — usually a business that had discriminated against them — and peacefully occupied the business by sitting down. These actions were accompanied with educational messages, prayers, and song. *Teach-ins* accomplished similar goals on college campuses. Student leaders and faculty educated participants about:

- The history of Vietnam
- The role of the United States in Southeast Asia
- The war

Thus, participants were more able to critically judge the justification for United States involvement in Vietnam. The success of the first teach-in led to a national teach-in on May 15, 1965.

Profiling an antiwar leader

Tom Hayden, a student at the University of Michigan (pictured in Figure 14-1), was one of the founders of the Students for a Democratic Society. He was the group's first secretary. He also was a leader in the National Mobilization Committee to End the War in Vietnam and an organizer of the 1968 protest at the Democratic National Convention that led to riots in the host city of Chicago. Hayden visited the Democratic Republic of Vietnam twice, once in 1965 and again in 1967, when he accompanied three recently released POWs back to the United States. He is also noteworthy as the one-time husband of another Vietnam War antiwar activist, Jane Fonda. Hayden abandoned his antiwar/antigovernment views in the 1980s when he was elected to the California State Assembly in 1982, serving for ten years, and the California State Senate in 1992 for eight years.

As the American military escalation continued, criticism of the war from leaders of the civil rights movement also increased. These leaders, Martin Luther King Jr. prominent among them, encouraged students to become active in the civil rights and antiwar movements. King argued that the struggle for freedom in the United States was no different than the struggle of the Vietnamese people. The United States needed to focus its attention on resolving its own problems before trying to solve any problems in Vietnam.

The Student Nonviolent Coordinating Committee (SNCC) helped spread King's message, calling for an end to the war and charging the U.S. government with misleading the American people in the reasons for war. SNCC questioned how the United States could resolve the crisis in Vietnam and ensure freedoms associated with democracy when it failed to provide the same for the minority communities in the United States. SNCC supported antiwar activists who refused to adhere to the draft and worked with these individuals to avoid military service.

Going global

The antiwar movement also received support from a number of other countries whose armed forces were fighting in Vietnam. In West Germany, numerous student-led demonstrations in the late 1960s opposed the United States military and the nonmilitary aid provided by West Germany. The organization known as RITA (Resist Inside The Army) operated inside American military bases, organizing demonstrations, sabotaging military property, and assisting those who wanted to desert. Continual protests against the Vietnam War in France, the one-time Indochina ally, were reinforced by President Charles de Gaulle making public statements to the effect that North Vietnam would win the war and warning that the United States should negotiate peace as soon as possible. Australia's antiwar movement paralleled that of the United States in many respects. As Australia became more involved in the war and used *conscription* to fill the ranks, the public questioned why Australians should be drafted to fight in a U.S. war and demanded immediate withdrawal. The effects of this international movement helped solidify and justify the American antiwar effort.

Figure 14-1:
North Vietnamese Premier Phan Van Dong received the antiwar American's delegation.

Photograph courtesy of the Vietnam Archive, Texas Tech University

With the growing commitment of the United States military to Vietnam in 1966, the increase in the number of casualties was inevitable. Until this point, the war had been distant to mainstream Americans going about their daily lives. No one had reason to question the use of American personnel in Vietnam, so the majority of the population accepted that soldiers die in battle.

The Berrigan Brothers

In 1964, Philip Berrigan founded the Emergency Citizens' Group Concerned About Vietnam as an organization combining religious and civic groups to protest the war. Berrigan and his brother, David, were cofounders of the Catholic Peace Fellowship. Although the brothers were opposed to the war from as early as 1964, their antiwar feelings intensified when President Johnson escalated U.S. involvement. On October 27, 1967, the Berrigan brothers and other radical Catholic protesters broke into the Selective Service office in Catonville, Maryland and destroyed draft records. The subsequent trial of the Cantonville 9 pushed many in the mainstream away from the antiwar movement because it was perceived as too radical.

The media in the antiwar movement

There is no question that the media played a significant role in the antiwar movement. As the war progressed, with no end in sight, many of those covering Vietnam began to question the United States role in that country. The media was most significant in bringing the war home to Americans and it used an effective tool, the television, to show to the public the destruction of war. The antiwar movement became national, even international, through the use of the television while many within the media used the Vietnam War and the antiwar movement to gain notoriety.

However, with the growing number of casualties came a growing number of questions from many Americans about what the United States had hoped to achieve in Vietnam and why its resources were being used in that distant land. Although the early antiwar movement was confined to universities and intellectuals, mainstream America became more interested because sons, nephews, cousins, and neighbors were losing their lives. The American people supported their president, but they also needed a reason for their sacrifice.

When the United States started bombing North Vietnam in February 1965, students were joined by average Americans who did not believe the United States was correct in its actions in Vietnam. More people in the mainstream supported President Johnson and the Vietnam War than were opposed to it. But seeds of discontent were planted when no justification for the conflict was forthcoming and the bombing of North Vietnam commenced.

The Opposition Finds Meaning: 1967–1969

Had the Vietnam conflict in 1964 been a brushfire, the war in 1967, by comparison, was a raging inferno. The United States had committed more than 365,000 troops to Vietnam by the beginning of 1967, and the number of casualties had risen to more than 6,600 dead. The events in Southeast Asia were a part of everyday life in the United States and few people had not been impacted directly or indirectly. Public interest and scrutiny paralleled military escalation, and Congress began openly criticizing the Johnson Administration.

Speaking out on the floor

By 1967, Senators Wayne Morse and Ernest Greuning no longer were alone. Members of the Democratic and Republican political parties joined them in the U.S. House of Representatives and Senate. Republican Mark Hatfield won a Senate seat from Oregon in 1966 because of his antiwar platform and other Republicans voiced opposition to the way President Johnson was handling the war.

Several governors joined in opposition to the war, including New York's Nelson Rockefeller and Pennsylvania's William Scranton, both influential members in American politics. More important, Johnson also began losing Democratic support in the Senate from majority leader Mike Mansfield (Montana), J. William Fulbright (Arkansas), George McGovern (South Dakota), and Robert (pictured in Figure 14-2) and Edward Kennedy (New York and Massachusetts). On November 30, 1967, Senator Eugene McCarthy (Minnesota) announced his candidacy for the 1968 Democratic presidential nomination against Johnson on an antiwar platform.

Figure 14-2:
Senator Robert Kennedy and Secretary of State Robert McNamara were on opposite ends of the Vietnam War debate.

Photograph courtesy of the Vietnam Archive, Texas Tech University

The rise of congressional opposition to the Vietnam War was not so much universally against American involvement in the conflict as it was in protest against Johnson and how the military was conducting the war. Many in Congress lamented that an explanation of the U. S. commitment had never been publicly debated, relying instead on the 1964 Gulf of Tonkin Resolution for justification. For a discussion on the Gulf of Tonkin incident and the subsequent resolution, see Chapter 11. A questionable decision by Johnson (based in part on the strength of his conviction that the United States was just in its actions in Southeast Asia) prevented public debate and thereby fueled the antiwar movement by allowing speculation to remain unchecked.

The conservative (military) protest

From the early days of American participation in Vietnam, members of the United States military warned that involvement in the Vietnam War would result in disaster. The warnings were passed on to President John F. Kennedy and later to President Lyndon B. Johnson, but neither took advantage of them. The United States escalated its involvement in Vietnam. From lessons it had learned during the Korean War, the U.S. military warned against a land war in Southeast Asia without clearly defined goals for victory. President Johnson straddled the middle course between total war and working toward his "Great Society." Not wanting to upset either the political left or right, he ended up alienating both. In the late 1960s, military leaders, including General William Westmoreland and Admiral Ulysses S. Grant Sharp, argued against the way the war was being fought. Joined by influential Senators Barry Goldwater (Arizona) and Strom Thurmond (South Carolina), these conservative protestors maintained that the United States should either fight the war to win or get out of Vietnam. These leaders believed that political constraints were holding back the military and making winning the war much more difficult for the United States. Senator Robert Dole (Kansas) actually introduced an amendment to repeal the Gulf of Tonkin resolution. Although pressure from the right existed, it hardly compared to the political burden from the left.

When members of Congress turned against President Johnson, he showed no sympathy. Public debate to justify American involvement in the Vietnam War was not an option for Johnson. As noted Johnson historian Robert Dalleck argues:

- ✔ Johnson formulated policy and created legislation in private. Public debate did not fit into his style.

- ✔ Johnson's personality lent itself to unilateral action rather than open debate, and it dominated those around him. He did not encourage discussion contrary to his own view.

- ✔ Johnson had a great sense of loyalty to those who fought and believed that opposing a conflict in which Americans were risking their lives was treason.

- ✔ A public debate would recognize and legitimize the antiwar movement.

Most important, Johnson believed that most Americans supported the war effort, which eliminated the need to have a debate.

Many scholars have argued that a public debate in early 1965 or 1966 would have satisfied the vast majority of Americans who opposed radicalism but were frustrated with the seemingly endless and bloody war in Vietnam. The failure to conduct such a debate allowed many to believe that the president had something to hide in America's involvement.

The conscientious objector

The Vietnam War saw the rise of conscientious objection as a means of protesting participation in the conflict. A *conscientious objector* is someone who refuses to serve in the Armed Forces for religious or moral reasons. One of the more famous conscientious objectors was boxer Muhammed Ali who gained the status citing religious beliefs. The Department of Defense approved conscientious objector status in 1962 and yet conscientious objection was practiced in all major wars. After 1962, however, individuals had to prove to their local draft board that their conscientious objection was legitimate. As the Vietnam War escalated, the number of conscientious objectors increased. In 1971, approximately 4,400 military personnel applied for the status. Becoming a conscientious objector did not excuse one from service or participation in the Vietnam War. In fact, many conscientious objectors went to Vietnam as medics and served their country honorably in nonviolent ways. Conscientious objection remains a viable option today for those who want to serve their country in an alternative fashion.

Questioning credibility and the Light at the End of the Tunnel

Throughout 1966 and early 1967, the antiwar movement became an increasingly legitimate concern within the political establishment. More influential politicians voiced support for the protestors. Gaining momentum, the antiwar movement became more visible and vocal. The military's reporting of the war and the response of the media enhanced the antiwar movement's claims that serious difficulties were happening in Vietnam.

The body count was one aspect of the *war of attrition* — a strategy devised to kill more North Vietnam Army and Viet Cong (NVA/VC) soldiers in South Vietnam than the DRV could replace in a timely manner. This strategy, used in Vietnam in 1966 and 1967, is described in Chapter 5. Because few indicators showed whether the United States was winning the war, using the number of NVA/VC killed in action justified American tactics and helped gauge whether the United States was coming out on top.

However, the use of the body count is highly inaccurate and open to criticism. The problem: Officers were encouraged to provide these statistical results for the war managers in Washington. The numbers never were accurate because some officers inflated their body counts to advance their careers or they simply guessed because guerrilla warfare in the jungles and rice paddies of Vietnam made counting bodies difficult. In 1967, members of the media began questioning whether numbers the military was providing were accurate, because the NVA/VC continually matched the U.S. escalation, fielding an army when their casualty numbers suggested they'd otherwise be unable to do so.

The credibility gap emerging between what the military said and what it did added fuel for the fire in the antiwar movement. The credibility gap wasn't limited to the military. President Johnson and politicians justifying the war often were discovered providing only part of the truth when discussing U.S. strategy and tactics in Vietnam. Questions put forth by war critics went unanswered, and debate on the course of the war often was structured by the Johnson Administration to provide only a minimal amount of information.

Mobilizing in spring to end war in Vietnam

In 1967, a new coalition emerged in the antiwar movement. The Spring Mobilization to End the War in Vietnam consisted of academics, students, radicals, and old liberals. Included in the leadership were long-time members of the antiwar movement A. J. Muste and Martin Luther King Jr., Dr. Benjamin Spock, and Stokely Carmichael. The primary goal of the organization was to coordinate national antiwar demonstrations.

The first target date was April 15, 1967, with one demonstration on the East Coast and another on the West Coast. More than 130,000 people joined the march in New York City, including approximately 150 men burning their draft cards. Almost 70,000 protested in San Francisco. The event was the largest single organized protest of the war up to that point and created an impression that the antiwar movement had the support of the average American.

Rock'n'roll rebels

A new generation of rock music became an effective tool for the antiwar movement during the 1960s, just about the time U.S. Army Sgt. Barry Sadler's *Ballad of the Green Berets* became the anthem for patriotism and the military in Vietnam. Although mainstream rock music during the earlier period of the conflict was nonpolitical, as the war progressed, several musicians began using their music as a platform against the war. Performers such as the Animals, Crosby, Stills, and Nash, and Bob Dylan used their music to protest the war. Jimi Hendricks, an Army veteran, the Rolling Stones, and the Beatles were heard in the fields of Vietnam and in the streets of the United States. For the two such distinct places, music had much meaning, helping define the time and place for all who listened to it. Songs such as Louis Armstrong's "What a Wonderful World," Country Joe McDonald's "I-Feel-Like-I'm-Fixin'-to-Die Rag," and the Animals' "We Gotta Get Out of This Place" remain powerful reminders of Vietnam for Vietnam veterans. For many, as the antiwar movement entered the mainstream, it became more acceptable for musicians to express their political views through music. Whether rock music followed or led the antiwar movement still is debatable. It is true that some musicians swayed with the times, and in the late 1960s, antiwar feelings were strong. It also is true that rock music served as a unifying and focusing force for members of the antiwar movement who committed to the objectives in spirit if not body.

In October 1967, a demonstration against the war brought more than 100,000 people to Washington, D.C. Half of the protesters marched on the Pentagon only to be met and stopped by armed U.S. Army personnel. Flowers and songs were met with guns in a highly publicized event that gave the odd feeling that the United States government was under siege and overtly authoritarian in its response. Many people outside the antiwar movement believed that the presence of armed military personnel at antiwar demonstrations was a strong indication that American society was unraveling.

Talking about Tet: 1968

The antiwar movement gained strength and popularity in the United States in 1967. At the end of January 1968, however, with the beginning of the Tet Offensive, the antiwar movement found a new purpose. Many within the United States felt betrayed by the military and government, which they believed had lied about the progress of the war effort. The NVA/VC were able to launch a major nationwide offensive — their largest of the war to date — even though military and political leaders had assured the American public that the war was almost over. For more information about the 1968 Tet Offensive, see Chapter 5.

General William Westmoreland, commander of the United States Armed Forces, became a symbol for the antiwar movement and was renamed "General Waste-mor-land" as the loss of life increased. Leaders in the antiwar movement cited the effectiveness of the Tet Offensive to rally support for their cause, and other influential community leaders within the United States reacted to the new set of circumstances. For example, Walter Cronkite, the anchorman of *CBS Evening News,* questioned America's ability to win the war in Vietnam, fearing that the conflict would end in stalemate.

In the 1968 New Hampshire presidential primary, Senator Eugene McCarthy did so well against Johnson that Senator Robert Kennedy announced that he also would run against Johnson in the Democratic Party primaries. Johnson realized his fear that the antiwar movement would gain legitimacy if it reached mainstream America and was thereby brought into public debate. This post-Tet environment assured that the movement and public debate about U.S. Vietnam policies would be present and growing in strength as long as the United States remained involved in the war.

The Tet Offensive confirmed the existence of a credibility gap that served as a signal to the more radical elements of the antiwar movement that it was their time to act. From March through May 1968, the SDS chapter at Columbia University increased the level of its protests by taking control of several campus buildings. The New York City Police Department reacted against the radicals resulting in violent confrontations, shutting down the entire campus. Campus protests intensified not only at Columbia but also at campuses throughout the country.

On college campuses in the United States, it seemed that the war would not end as promised. Demands for more personnel in Vietnam increased. Westmoreland called for a significant increase in the number of troops to take advantage of the military disaster of the Vietnamese offensive. The end of special deferments for graduate school and teaching meant the campus was no longer a safe haven from the war. Students who continued their educations past undergraduate studies to avoid the war no longer were protected from the draft. Many on college campuses joined in the antiwar movement as a result of the end of the deferment.

It's an election year . . . the whole world is watching

On a March 31, 1968 in a nationally televised broadcast, Johnson stunned the American people and the world when he announced that he would not seek reelection in the November election. For supporters of McCarthy and Kennedy, the hope of gaining the presidency became a real possibility and antiwar leaders recognized that the war would be at the center of the presidential debate.

The antiwar movement and the American people suffered a great loss in June when Robert Kennedy was assassinated. McCarthy carried the antiwar banner into the Democratic National Convention but didn't have Kennedy's charisma or support from the Democratic Party's old guard that Hubert Humphrey possessed. The antiwar movement used the 1968 Democratic National Convention in Chicago to bring the public debate to the front pages.

Inside the convention, delegates debated a full range of issues, but the war took center stage. The delegates adopted a platform plank that supported Johnson's handling of the war in the early morning hours, thus avoiding press coverage when the streets outside the Chicago Amphitheatre were in turmoil. Antiwar activists took to those streets in protest of the war only to be met by Chicago police, Illinois State troopers, and the National Guard. Mayor Richard Daley ordered the removal of demonstrators who failed to obtain a permit to protest beyond an agreed upon area near the convention. Daley's order set off violent clashes. Many watching the coverage thought that the fabric of America was coming unraveled.

The televised demonstrations and police clashes led many into believing that the Democratic Party could not lead the United States out of the crisis at home and in Vietnam. Protestors, on the other hand, knowing the advantages of media coverage in getting their antiwar message out, chanted: "The Whole World is Watching" as they marched down the streets.

Reacting to Nixon

When Richard Nixon entered the White House in January 1969, the antiwar movement waited to find out what policies he would introduce for the war. Protesters, however, did not wait long. The first organized antiwar demonstration during Nixon's administration occurred in March when the Women's Strike for Peace (WSP) organized a large-scale antiwar event. The WSP had been active since the early 1960s and represented many mainstream American women who were concerned with the loss of life in war.

Nixon's announcement of *Vietnamization* — turning the war over to the South Vietnamese as described in Chapter 6 — in June and the beginning of American troop withdrawal with the first 25,000 returning to the United States in August should have deflated antiwar pressures. Many within the movement, however, believed that Nixon was moving too slowly, arguing the thousands of casualties during the first six months of his administration proved that Nixon wasn't serious about ending American commitments in Southeast Asia.

As a result, the antiwar movement responded by organizing a national day of protest. The Vietnam Moratorium Committee and the New Mobilization Committee to End the War in Vietnam organized an October 15 Moratorium Day Demonstration, encouraging people to take off from work and school and participate in organized protests against the war. Although determining the exact number of participants is impossible, estimated numbers reached the 1 million mark. New York City Mayor John Lindsay declared the day one of mourning with flags flown at half-staff, and several trade unions supported the demonstrations, recommending that their members participate. The antiwar movement gained unstoppable momentum after the traumatic events of 1968. 1968 was a defining year in the Vietnam War with the Tet Offensive, but it also changed the United States. In 1968, two well-respected leaders in the United States — both antiwar activists — were assassinated. The deaths of Senator Robert Kennedy and Martin Luther King Jr. scarred the United States, and so did the fall of Johnson. 1969 brought with it a series of revelations that strengthened and focused the cause of peace.

Kent State, Jackson State, and the End of the Movement

The antiwar movement was at a crossroads with the introduction of Vietnamization and the winding down of the war. The protest, it seemed, was successful after Nixon promised his "Peace with Honor" solution and began withdrawing the troops.

The Trial of the Chicago Eight . . . Seven

After the controversial post convention, eight antiwar leaders were charged with conspiracy and crossing state lines with the intent to commit riot in August 1969. The trial of the Chicago Seven — the eighth member, Black Panther Party Chairman Bobby Seale (see the section "Bobby Seale and the Black Panthers," later in this chapter), was so disruptive that his trial was separated from the others — became a showcase for the antiwar movement. Defendants Tom Hayden (Students for a Democratic Society), Jerry Rubin (*YIPPIE* — Youth International Party), and Abbie Hoffman (YIPPIE) treated the trial with disdain and used it to their advantage. The judge, Julius Hoffman, issued 175 counts of contempt to the seven defendants and their lawyers with sentences of two to four years. Seale also was charged with contempt and sentenced to four years imprisonment. The jury found the group innocent of the conspiracy charge; however, all but two, Lee Weiner and John Froines, were found guilty of intent to riot. Although the guilty verdict brought sentences of five years imprisonment and $5,000 fines, none of the eight served any of their sentences. In 1972, the Seventh Circuit U.S. Court of Appeals overturned the sentences while most of the contempt charges were dismissed.

Vietnamization required a strong South Vietnam to work and this, in turn, meant the United States had to turn to the offensive, buying time for their ally to train. The antiwar movement misunderstood Vietnamization as it focused only on bringing back American soldiers alive. Antiwar leaders argued that Nixon had betrayed his promise of ending the war. When stories emerged regarding American atrocities, combined with the violations of Cambodia's neutrality and an attempt to conceal how the United States became involved in the war, the antiwar movement made one last push to end the war.

Revealing the hard truth: The Pentagon Papers and My Lai

The March 1968 event in the village of Son My, termed the My Lai Massacre, which is described in Chapter 5, and the Peers Commission that investigated the incident provided more evidence for those protesting the war that Vietnam was a black mark on the United States. When the media revealed in 1969 that American soldiers shot women, children, and elderly people in the village without any direct provocation — the villagers, whose village had been named "Pinkville" maintained strong connections to the Viet Cong — the backlash was immediate. The military's attempt to cover up the event didn't help and neither did the government arguing that the incident was an aberration at a time when its credibility already was in question.

My Lai was unique. Even U.S. soldiers were disgusted with the actions of a few undisciplined soldiers. However, My Lai became the rallying point for antiwar protestors who thereafter labeled everyone in uniform as "baby killers." The My Lai incident became public shortly after the November 1969 Moratorium Day demonstration and was followed only days later by news of Nixon's secret bombings inside the Cambodian borders, which is examined in Chapter 9.

In 1967, Secretary of Defense Robert McNamara ordered a study about the history of U.S. involvement in Vietnam. Using classified and internal documents from government sources, *The Pentagon Papers* detailed American strategy and tactics of the war from 1945 through 1967. A RAND Corporation researcher named Daniel Ellsberg had access to the documents used to produce the study and decided to release the classified study to Neil Sheehan, a reporter for *The New York Times* and a Vietnam War correspondent. Ellsberg was frustrated with the U.S. government's handling of the war and believed, the release of the documents would help to reveal the sinister and reckless actions of the U.S. government.

The legacy of the antiwar movement

In the same way that the antiwar movement benefited from the organization and expertise of the civil rights struggle, other organizations learned from the antiwar protests. All of these movements had reshaped the American landscape by the end of the twentieth century. Many activists within the antiwar groups began questioning traditional roles of gender, race, and class. Gender inequality was a significant problem in the antiwar movement. Other movements rose out of the antiwar movement as it slowed down during Vietnamization or splintered into radical factions.

In 1969, the Women's Liberation Front organized at Stanford University in antiwar fashion exposing the inconsistencies in the university's policies toward women. Another group, the Chicago Women's Liberation Union (CWLU), organized in the 1960s and participated in civil rights and antiwar demonstrations. CWLU leaders applied the lessons they learned from the Vietnam War and the antiwar movement to the struggle for gender equality. The rise of the women's movement in the late 1960s and into the 1970s is seen as a positive legacy of the antiwar movement. Women who would lead the movement into the 1970s received their foundations with the civil rights and antiwar movements in their youth. Women's liberation would not have experienced the growth or success that it did without the precedents set by the antiwar movement.

Other causes that benefited from the antiwar movement were environmental and consumer protectionism. Groups representing these causes organized along the same lines as the antiwar protestors and, although their causes didn't receive the same amount of attention as the Vietnam War, they benefited from using the same strategies and tactics. Thus, the enduring characteristic of the protest movements wasn't that antiwar activities ended the war, but rather that recognizing individuals united in a common cause can provide pressure for change.

Despite government attempts to block publication of the study — the decision ultimately reached the Supreme Court — three versions of the papers were released to the public. *The Pentagon Papers* confirmed that the U.S. strategy in Southeast Asia was flawed and provided some evidence to support the notion that American foreign policy had reacted to the events in Vietnam instead of guiding them. Although motivated by legitimate security concerns and the desire to protect classified information contained in the leaked documents, the fact that the United States government tried so hard to keep the study out of the public's hands provided the perception that it had something to hide from the American people. Following the news of My Lai and the secret bombings of Cambodia, accepting this perspective was not that difficult.

The May Riots

Nixon ordered U.S. troops into Cambodia in May 1970 to destroy NVA/VC troops and supply bases that had used that neutral country as a safe haven during the war. The backlash to invasion, or incursion as the Nixon Administration called it, was intense. If the United States was withdrawing from Vietnam, how could it expand the war into Cambodia? On the heels of My Lai, the bombings, and *The Pentagon Papers,* this action caused many within the movement to believe that Nixon had no interest whatsoever in leaving Vietnam. Demonstrations against the Cambodian incursion blossomed on college campuses throughout the United States with less restraint than usual.

Protesters believed that Nixon had violated their trust by expanding the war into neutral Cambodia when he pledged to disengage American military personnel from Southeast Asia. The antiwar movement was not impressed by Nixon's statement that the incursion was necessary to buy time for the South Vietnamese to train their forces. The antiwar movement didn't bother becoming concerned with Cambodia's role in providing a safe place for the Viet Cong inside its borders and ignored this method of occupation and invasion into South Vietnam. The antiwar movement was concerned with ending the war in Vietnam; military strategy and tactics were not a consideration within this overarching goal.

From Syracuse University in the Northeast to the University of California at Berkeley on the West Coast, nationwide protests on college campuses halted end-of-the-semester activities: Barricades went up and mass gatherings occurred. Most of the demonstrations were allowed to run their course as local and state police watched demonstrators to ensure that they did not cause serious damage.

But unfortunately, the protests at Kent State and Jackson State universities became deadly. Demonstrations against the Cambodian incursion began May 1 at Kent State University with some minor property damage to the university. However, the Reserve Officers' Training Corps (ROTC) building was destroyed the next day and the National Guard was introduced to contain the demonstrations. Tear gas was used to disperse the May 3 student protests, but during the May 4 protests, National Guardsmen fired into a crowd of approximately 2,000, leaving four dead. Two of the casualties were protesters, but the other two were innocent bystanders. The university and scores of other colleges and universities across the country closed that day, fearful that more violence might occur. President Nixon ordered an investigation by the President's Commission on Campus Unrest, which concluded in September that the National Guard's action was inexcusable and yet criticized the protesters for helping to create the situation in which the tragedy occurred.

On May 14, two African-American students at Jackson State University were killed in their dormitory after local and state police fired into it in response, they claimed, to a sniper who had fired at them. The President's Commission on Campus Unrest found no evidence to support the policemen's claim. Compared to the outcry from the Kent State University deaths, the tragedy at Jackson State University, a black college, received less attention. Many within the African-American community believed that this incident was a result of the color of the victims' skin and that it helped to fuel the fires of the Black Power movement, as described later in this chapter.

The violence of the May 1970 campus demonstrations had not reached the level that it had the previous year. Reports of violence occurred on only 1 in every 25 campuses, but the significance of the nationwide campus-led protests and the six deaths at the hands of law enforcement officers and the National Guard were significant to the movement. An event at the University of California, San Diego, culminated the events of May. Reminiscent of earlier Buddhist self-immolation in protest against Ngo Dinh Diem, George Winne Jr. walked to the public center of that campus with a sign reading, "In the name of God, end the war," and using gasoline and a match, set himself on fire. This act helped define the May 1970 riots and the tragic nature of the Vietnam War.

The response by Congress to the Cambodian incursion pleased the antiwar movement. Senators John Sherman Cooper and Frank Church attached an amendment to the military appropriations bill, which funds the U.S. Armed Forces, prohibiting the use of troops and advisors in Cambodia and the use of the Air Force over Cambodia. The House of Representatives passed similar legislation; however, it did not include the air space over Cambodia in its final passage. Nixon's response to the two amendments was strong, because he was worried that their impact would lessen the American bargaining position during peace negotiations. However, he was unable to gather enough Congressional support to overturn the amendments by veto. During the same Senate debate on the Cooper-Church amendment, Senator Bob Dole (Kansas) introduced an amendment repealing the Gulf of Tonkin Resolution. That resolution was the original justification for United States intervention in Vietnam.

Speaking Out about Their Experiences: Vietnam Veterans Against the War

The antiwar movement argued that the Vietnam War was immoral and unjust. Because most who were involved in the movement had never been to Southeast Asia or experienced the war in Vietnam, their credibility with mainstream America always was in question. As military personnel returned from their tours of duty, some veterans joined the antiwar movement, thus adding a level of integrity to the movement and its call to end the conflict.

Founded in April 1967 with six veterans marching in an antiwar demonstration in New York City, Vietnam Veterans Against the War (VVAW) used the first-hand experiences from the war of its members to protest United States involvement in Vietnam by organizing a series of unique demonstrations in an effort to get their point across. We describe these demonstrations in the sections that follow.

Operation RAW

In September 1970, VVAW organized Operation RAW (Rapid American Withdrawal), a journey from Morristown, New Jersey, to Valley Forge, Pennsylvania. Between 100 and 150 individuals, dressed in camouflage and carrying plastic M-16 rifles, conducted theatrical military sweeps of the area between the two historic towns, capturing and torturing prisoners and shooting innocent civilians in mock skirmishes along the route. Although individuals, not all of whom were Vietnam veterans, met opposition in the form of oral insults and an occasional thrown vegetable along the route, more than 1,000 supporters greeted them at Valley Forge. Providing the average citizen with an understanding of the horrors of war was the purpose of Operation RAW.

Winter Soldier Investigations

When the My Lai incident was revealed, discussed in the "Revealing the hard truth: The Pentagon Papers and My Lai" section earlier in this chapter, military and political leaders maintained that it was an aberration. Many within the antiwar movement, however, dismissed this claim and members of the Vietnam Veterans Against the War came forward providing evidence of other incidents (although on a smaller scale) that were similar to My Lai.

From January 31 through February 2, 1971, the VVAW helped organize the Winter Soldier Investigations in Detroit, Michigan. The purposes of the investigation were

✔ Exposing the truth about Vietnam from the perspective of the antiwar movement

✔ Ensuring that the My Lai incident was not forgotten

✔ Pushing Congress toward some type of action

On April 5, 1971, Senator Mark Hatfield (Oregon) recognized the investigations and called upon President Nixon to take the charges leveled by the VVAW seriously. He also urged Nixon to understand that the Winter Soldier Investigations and the conviction of Lt. William Calley, who led the soldiers in the massacre, raised moral questions of whether U.S. actions in Southeast Asia were justifiable. Hatfield maintained that he didn't agree entirely with all of the testimony provided in Detroit but argued that honorably discharged veterans had a right to be heard and their allegations taken seriously.

Hatfield called for further investigations to discover whether violations of the Geneva Convention and other international agreements had been committed. He called for Congress to:

✔ Include the testimony presented by more than 100 honorably discharged veterans in Detroit in the *Congressional Record.*

✔ Give the testimony to the Department of Defense and the Department of State so that it could be fully investigated.

✔ Set up Congressional committees to conduct hearings on the policies governing the use of military force in Indochina and their relation to international agreements the United States had ratified.

✔ Form a special commission that would investigate in full these matters and that would provide a forum to assess the moral consequences of U.S. involvement in Southeast Asia.

Hatfield's motion was not opposed. The Winter Soldier Investigations had achieved their main objective, which was investigating military misconduct in Vietnam and legitimizing the existence of a problem with the United States Armed Forces.

Operation Dewey Canyon III

In February 1971, on Abraham Lincoln's birthday (February 12), a small group of veterans threw their medals and service ribbons on the White House lawns in protest of the war. These men didn't want to be praised for their actions in Vietnam. The symbolic success of this action caused the VVAW to organize a larger demonstration with the same purpose in April 1971. The protest was further punctuated by the presence of mothers of soldiers who were killed in Vietnam.

This event, Operation Dewey Canyon III, was named after two military operations in Vietnam, the first to stop the flow of supplies from Laos and the second in support of the South Vietnamese Army's Lam Son 719 operation into Laos, which is described in Chapter 6. VVAW members staged mock search-and-destroy operations similar to Operation RAW in Washington, D.C., and tried to turn themselves in at the Pentagon for war crimes. On April 23, they staged a rally on the steps of the United States Capitol, where approximately 700 veterans (the exact number who had actually served in Vietnam was disputed) denounced the war and threw their medals away.

Splintering from the Rest: Radicalism

The main goal of the antiwar movement was the war's end. When Vietnamization (see a detailed discussion of this strategy in Chapter 6) started showing the desired effect and American combat troops were withdrawing from Vietnam in June 1969, reasons for keeping the movement together were few. Although the majority of America simply wanted to return to normalcy, radical elements splintered from the main antiwar organization arguing that the cause would not end until the war ended. The final act of the antiwar movement included not only the radical elements but also the Congress and president. The Vietnam War had changed a generation and the antiwar movement played a role in that change.

From the frustration within the antiwar movement with the continued persecution of the Vietnam War, several radical elements emerged that believed that only violence would change America. The principle forms of violence included

- Bombing
- Bank robberies (to fund the movement)
- Breaking into government facilities (to destroy documents)
- Using intimidation (to further the antiwar cause)

Weathermen-ing the storm

The Weathermen, an outgrowth of the breakup of SDS (see the "Coordinating the colleges" section earlier in this chapter), were the most prominent of the radicals who believed that any means justified the end. Violence was an acceptable form of protest when it was the only way the United States would end the Vietnam War.

In October 1969, as the trial of the Chicago 7 transfixed the antiwar community, the Weathermen promised an assault on Chicago. During these *Days of Rage*, the Weathermen threatened to unleash 20,000 protesters into the city. Between

500 and 700 radical militants gathered in Lincoln Park to march on the hotel where Judge Julius Hoffman, who presided over the Chicago 7 trial, lived. Along the way, the group deviated from its original goal toward the destruction of property. On October 11, three days later, approximately 150 Weathermen fought with police in Haymarket Square, resulting in more than 100 being arrested.

The majority of the antiwar movement, including the emerging radical Black Panthers, condemned the violent actions of the Weathermen. The events of October were overshadowed with the first Moratorium to End the War in Vietnam on October 15.

On August 24, 1970, a bomb detonated in the Army Mathematics Research Center on the campus of the University of Wisconsin, Madison. Although police received warning of the attack, they didn't have enough time to alert anyone in the building. The bombing killed one and injured three others and was one in a series targeting research centers that supported military research, but it was the first by the Weather Underground, or Weathermen. Within two weeks after the bombing, the Federal Bureau of Investigation (FBI) identified and caught three of the four bombers (Karleton and Dwight Armstrong, and David Fine). Leo Burt was identified as the fourth bomber, but was never located.

Bobby Seale and the Black Panthers

Remembering that the early antiwar movement found its roots in the Civil Rights movement of the late 1950s and early 1960s is important, because, although the two movements had intertwining goals, some believed that the antiwar movement actually had steered the focus away from unfinished Civil Rights goals for Civil Rights.

One group, the Black Panther Party for Self-Defense, led by Bobby Seale and Huey P. Newton, argued for a radicalization and combination of both movements. Seale and Newton put forward a ten-point platform for the Black Panthers:

  ✔ **Freedom** — the power to determine the destiny of the black and oppressed communities.

  ✔ **Full employment** — giving every person employment or guaranteed income.

  ✔ **End to robbery of black communities** — the overdue debt of 40 acres and two mules as promised to ex-slaves during the Reconstruction period following the emancipation of slavery.

  ✔ **Decent housing fit for the shelter of human beings** — the land should be made into cooperatives so that the people can build.

✔ **Education for the people** — that teaches the true history of blacks and their role in present day society.

✔ **Free health care** — health facilities that will develop preventive medical programs.

✔ **End to police brutality and murder of black people and other people of color and oppressed people.**

✔ **End to all wars of aggression** — the various conflicts that exist stem directly from the United States ruling circle.

✔ **Freedom for all political prisoners** — trials by juries that represent our peers.

✔ **Land, bread, housing, education, clothing, justice, peace, and community control of modern industry.**

The platform did not promote violence, but Seale and Newton advocated the use of force to achieve their goals, including active resistance against those that stood in the way of racial equality.

Preventing It from Happening Again: Congress and the End of War

Starting in March 1969, Nixon and Secretary of State Henry Kissinger (the main negotiator for the United States at the Paris Peace Talks) attempted to negotiate an end of the war with the North Vietnamese. Although the first years of the negotiations proved frustrating for the United States, it enabled Nixon to proceed with Vietnamization and appease some of the moderates within the antiwar movement. He could point to the attempt to achieve peace while at the same time expanding the war to provide South Vietnam with an opportunity for victory. Although this strategy seemed effective for gaining support with those not actively involved in the antiwar movement, it only alienated those involved in protesting the war. Nixon, however, was satisfied with the support from the *Silent Majority,* a section of the U.S. population that Nixon believed supported his policies in Vietnam (see Chapter 6).

In 1972, Nixon sought reelection against Senator George McGovern (South Dakota) whose platform included an antiwar element. McGovern argued for immediate withdrawal from Vietnam while Nixon countered that the United States would leave Vietnam, but on its own timetable. Nixon achieved an overwhelming result receiving 61.7 percent of the popular vote and 521 of the 538 total of electoral votes.

The reelection of Nixon was a disappointment for those within the antiwar movement. Even though American troops were coming home in greater numbers (approximately 159,000 remained in Vietnam by the end of 1971), the antiwar leadership didn't trust that Nixon would end the war. When the United States responded to the 1972 Eastertide Offensive, a North Vietnamese offensive described in Chapter 6, those who remained a part of the antiwar movement tried to organize massive protests but failed to attract the numbers reached during 1970.

True to his word, Nixon continued negotiating with the North Vietnamese — with only a brief interlude during 1972 — and achieved a tentative peace agreement in October 1972. When the North Vietnamese appeared to be stalling about reaching a final agreement, Nixon ordered a short period of intense bombing against the North Vietnamese cities of Hanoi (the capital) and Haiphong to bring the North Vietnamese back to the negotiating table. The Christmas bombings, as they were be labeled, are examined in Chapter 8. By that time, the antiwar movement had splintered so badly that it was not able to organize a successful resistance to the bombing campaign.

The Paris Peace Agreements, signed January 27, 1973, effectively ended American military involvement in the Vietnam War. The end of the war also brought a return of POWs and allowed the majority of the American public to ignore the Vietnam War and the years of U.S. involvement. The majority of Americans didn't want to think about the Vietnam War, but rather to put it behind them.

For people who participated in the antiwar movement, their main objective had been successful. American involvement in the war was over. The antiwar movement was credited with a few additional victories before the final collapse of South Vietnam. Soon after the United States ended its military involvement in Vietnam, Congress passed the Case-Church Amendment to the bill funding the State Department on June 19, 1973. The amendment stated that, "on or after August 15, 1973, no funds herein or heretofore appropriated may be obligated or expended to finance directly or indirectly combat activities by United States military forces in, or over, or from off the shores of North Vietnam, South Vietnam, Laos, or Cambodia." This amendment made it almost impossible for the United States to respond to North Vietnamese violations of the Peace Agreements and sealed the fate of the Republic of Vietnam, which had relied upon American firepower for survival. The amendment passed by votes of 278–124 in the House of Representatives and 64–26 in the Senate. The wide margins by which the measure passed meant that it was immune from a presidential veto.

Empowering Congress with the War Powers Act

Many within the antiwar movement never forgot the overwhelming victory Nixon achieved in the 1972 election and resented his second term as president.

When the Watergate scandal was exposed, people within the movement were energized for a short period, rallying behind the call to impeach President Nixon.

Nixon resigned the presidency on August 9, 1974, receiving a full pardon from his successor Gerald Ford and leaving Ford to deal with the final defeat of the South Vietnamese government. For those who participated in the antiwar movement, the Nixon resignation was an added bonus to their original cause.

Shortly after the Cambodian incursion, Senator Jacob K. Javits introduced legislation limiting the power of the president to use military force without congressional approval. The senator's War Powers Resolution was debated in Congress for nearly three years. With the decline of American armed forces in Vietnam and the Watergate scandal and investigation in full force, Congress passed the legislation that became know as the War Powers Act. The following points were the basis for the legislation:

- ✔ The president was required to provide a written report to the Speaker of the House and President of the Senate within 48 hours of introducing American military personnel on foreign soil. This report had to justify why the action was necessary and how long the troops would be required to stay.

- ✔ The president was to end all military involvement on foreign soil before the 60th day unless Congress declared War and specifically authorized the use of force.

- ✔ The president needed congressional approval to extend the use of armed forces for an additional 30 days if Congress did not declare war.

- ✔ Congress had the right to order the president to remove troops before the 60-day deadline if it thought the action unnecessary.

Watergate

After the release of the Pentagon Papers in 1971 (see the section "Revealing the hard truth: The Pentagon Papers and My Lai" earlier in this chapter), the Nixon Administration organized a group of individuals, known as "The plumbers," to acquire information about leading Democratic and antiwar protestors. The information then was to be used as leverage against Nixon's "enemies" to keep them in place. In June 1972, the plumbers broke into the Democratic National Committee headquarters, which was based in the Watergate office and apartment complex on the banks of the Potomac River. The illegal acts, justified by Nixon as necessary for national security, became a symbol of his presidency and eventually led to a hearing in the committee on the judiciary and Nixon's resignation and to stronger Congressional measures to curb the power of the presidency.

The War Powers Act restricted the ability of the president to conduct an aggressive foreign policy and required the presidency to include Congress in future military operations. Nixon vetoed the legislation, but his political strength had been weakened so much by the Watergate scandal that Congress easily overrode the veto on November 7, 1973. The War Powers Act remains one of the strongest pieces of Congressional legislation to rise from the Vietnam War.

The American people were tired of the Vietnam War, and Congress, sensing the mood of the nation, cut the military and financial assistance it was providing to South Vietnam in 1974. Further cuts occurred in the 1975 budget. When North Vietnam launched its 1974–1975 offensive, it achieved surprising success. The question whether the United States would come to the aid of its ally after the violation of the Paris Peace Accords was answered when increasing evidence of war wariness made it impossible for President Ford to provide promised assistance and Congress rejected his overtures. The North Vietnamese offensive gained momentum and reached Saigon in April 1975. On April 30, 1975, Saigon fell and the South Vietnamese surrendered to North Vietnam. The war was over, but the cost had been high. Millions of South Vietnamese woke the next day to an uncertain future and without a country.

Assessing the antiwar movement

In assessing how effective the antiwar movement was in ending the Vietnam War, perspective plays a significant role. Each side of the debate has ample evidence to support their contentions and continue the debate about the question.

Antiwar advocates argue that the movement was the primary reason the United States ended its involvement in Vietnam. Without any doubt, the antiwar movement caused the public debate that Johnson had refused to recognize. Protestors questioned many traditional issues and practices and were successful in the passage of legislation to place checks on the president's ability to wage war. Concluding that the antiwar movement made many within the United States more aware of the situation in Vietnam and made them question the role of the United States in that country, also is reasonable.

However, those who made the military and political decisions that started, maintained, and ended the war have argued that the antiwar movement was nothing more than a nuisance. If they are to be believed, then the antiwar movement had little effect on the decision to deescalate.

Chapter 15

"The Sound of Silence": Supporting the American War Effort

The Vietnam War was seen as a great divider between segments of American society. Not since the American Civil War had the people so harshly debated the state of the union and the future of the country. Lost amid American antiwar demonstrations and public recognition of protest leaders were Americans who supported the call to arms and believed that the war in Vietnam was necessary and just. The number of people who supported the war was a majority through 1968, but they did not organize, demonstrate en masse, or seek media attention. When they did march, however, it usually was in connection with patriotic events. The American flag was their symbol, and showing the proper respect for the flag as a sign of support for soldiers who fought in the war was enough for them.

During the time that this "Silent Majority," as Richard Nixon called it, remained a force throughout the 1960s and 1970s, it never had as much of an impact as the antiwar movement. The strength, size, and conviction of the U.S. government supporters require recognition in the war at home.

Building a Nation with White and Blue Collars: 1954–1963

After the conclusion of the 1954 Geneva Conference, Operation PASSAGE TO FREEDOM began, evacuating North Vietnamese refugees to the South (as described in Chapter 11). The addition of almost 1 million refugees to the south — plus the emergence of a new government fighting for survival against a communist insurgency — created a difficult situation for South Vietnam. In 1954, it was apparent that the South Vietnamese needed economic assistance if it were to survive. After the French left during the 1954–1955 period, the United States came to the aid of South Vietnam to maintain the government and provide relief to the people. Figure 15-1 shows the kind of help given.

Figure 15-1: Dr. T. A. Dooley, PHC A. B. Cory, Dr. J. M. Anderson, and Dr. E. G. Gleason work on the water pump of purification unit for a refugee camp at Haiphong.

Photograph courtesy of the Vietnam Archive, Texas Tech University

Introducing academia in Vietnam: The Michigan State University experiment

In an effort to stabilize his country, South Vietnamese President Ngo Dinh Diem accepted assistance from the United States. The United States started a number of projects — building schools, hospitals, houses, and roads — during the 1950s to improve the lives of the South Vietnamese people. U.S. technicians worked in Vietnam to improve food crops and medical care as well as provided advice on how to form and run a government. These U.S. actions were designed to strengthen South Vietnam in order for it to survive and compete with North Vietnam in Southeast Asia.

HISTORIC TRIVIA

Dooley's Passage

Americans found out about the destructive nature of the Viet Minh from a firsthand account of Operation PASSAGE TO FREEDOM by Dr. Thomas Dooley, who served aboard the USS *Montague.* Dooley was one of the few Americans who spent a considerable amount of time in the northern camps assisting the refugees. His book *Deliver Us From Evil* told of the miserable conditions of North Vietnam and the mistreatment by the Viet Minh of Vietnamese, most of whom were Catholic and wanted to start a new life south of the 17th parallel. Dooley treated Vietnamese refugees from the North who had been tortured by the Viet Minh for wanting to escape south or because of their religious beliefs. He rejected the communist notions that denied freedom of religion, speech, and action that he observed while in Haiphong. This book, two more that followed, and Dooley's public appearances after returning to Southeast Asia to set up medical facilities in Laos shared a common theme: how the evils of Communism pointed to the necessity of doing something, no matter how small, to help people in that region.

Dooley's work compelled many others to help and, as a result, supported movement by the United States to become more involved in Vietnam during the 1950s. Several organizations answered Dooley's call, supporting efforts by the United States to build a nation in South Vietnam and to continue supporting the objective of providing a better life for people there who were fighting Communism.

TECHNICAL STUFF

The U.S. effort, called *nation building,* provided South Vietnamese President Diem with extensive financial and technical assistance for military, social, and administrative reforms. Diem, in turn, relied on the advice of Wesley Fishel, a political scientist, as well as other experts, all of whom were associated with the Michigan State University technical assistance program. Fishel and Diem, who shared many commonalities, including strong anticommunist views, formed a friendship that lasted until the Vietnamese leader's death in November 1963. From May 1955 to June 1962, Michigan State University provided advice and planning in several areas that were of importance to South Vietnam's survival, including reforms in its police force, economy, social structure (ethnic relations), and its Constitution. The task of reforming South Vietnam was a daunting challenge, but the Michigan State University group proved worthy of the task. Unfortunately, it would take more than the Michigan State University experts to build South Vietnam.

The failure of nation building, however, was not the result of poor advice. Instead, difficulties fighting the Communists in South Vietnam, combined with the authoritarian personality of Diem, worked against the nation-building process. Another problem was that a majority of the U.S. officials associated with the Michigan State University group knew very little about Vietnam, its history, or its people, which led to misunderstandings and a poor working relationship. Diem's regime failed to gain and hold the confidence of the people and, at the same time, alienated American officials who believed they knew what was best for Diem and South Vietnam.

Buddying up: American Friends of Vietnam

If Michigan State University was the equivalent of a group of blue-collar workers getting their hands dirty in Vietnam trying to build a nation, then American Friends of Vietnam (AFV) was its white-collar counterpart. Formed in December 1955, AFV, also known as the Vietnam Lobby, promoted President Diem in the United States and worked to raise money and lobby Congress and other influential statesmen for the South Vietnamese cause.

AFV publicized a simple mission: Save South Vietnam from Communism. Among its ranks were many influential Americans including many prominent Catholics, the Archbishop of New York Cardinal Francis Spellman, Supreme Court Justice William O. Douglas, Senators John F. Kennedy and Mike Mansfield, and chief of the U.S. Military Assistance Advisory Group–Indochina, General John O'Daniels. AFV effectively publicized the crisis in South Vietnam and solidified Diem's role as the leader of this embattled country despite critics who argued that AFV misled the American people about Diem's practices. In 1963, after the assassination of Diem, the group split regarding the direction that the United States needed to take in Vietnam.

Bear Any Burden, Pay any Price: 1961–1963

When John F. Kennedy entered the White House in 1961, the United States commitment in Vietnam was still only minimal. The United States had been actively involved in nation building for six years without much success. The Viet Cong, on the other hand, had been able to maintain its strength and increase pressure of the South Vietnamese government.

South Vietnam was not on the minds of the American people in the early 1960s, but President Kennedy made sure that the public understood the necessity of preserving democracy around the world. Kennedy appealed for the continuing support from the American people for South Vietnam: "Let every nation know that we shall pay any price, bear any burden, meet any hardship, support any friend, oppose any foe to assure the survival and the success of liberty." And the American people responded to Kennedy's appeal.

Public support for Kennedy's Vietnam policy was not as much a reaffirmation that the United States was doing the right thing in Southeast Asia as it was a general response to Kennedy's anticommunist strategy. After the Cuban Missile Crisis, when the Soviet Union tried to put nuclear missiles in Cuba and brought the United States to the brink of war with the Soviet Union, the threat of Communism became more of a reality. Before the crisis, the majority of Americans trusted that the commitment of the United States to Southeast Asia was the right thing. After Cuba, the American public accepted any strategy that projected a strong American foreign policy.

Kennedy also was keenly aware that the United States needed other countries to fight in the war against Communism. Having more allies would help further justify United States action and make it easier for the American public to accept the greater commitment in Vietnam. Strong pressure on Free World countries in Asia and the Pacific that were opposed to Communism yielded commitments from Australia and Korea to provide advisors as early as 1962. Other countries followed as the war escalated. These alliances contributed much toward assuring public support for the war in its early stages. For more about U.S. allies, see Chapter 5.

The American public responded to Kennedy's appeal to share in the burden of preserving liberty. He signed an executive order in March 1961 creating the Peace Corps with R. Sargent Shriver as its leader. Congressional approval of Peace Corps legislation in September 1961 mandated that it provide assistance to countries in need, promote American understanding and ideals, and discover more about other people in the world. Organizations such as the Peace Corps created a certain activism within American youth and resulted in stronger acceptance of Kennedy's overall foreign policy initiatives.

The War Has New Meaning: Johnson's Vietnam: 1964–1966

When Lyndon B. Johnson assumed the presidency, he was faced with a growing conflict in Vietnam and forced to respond to events in that country at the same time he was trying to lead the United States out of its own personal tragedy — the assassination of President Kennedy. Johnson advanced his political career by working behind the scenes to pass important legislation and promote his political agenda. He was a respected member in every political institution with which he was involved. When he became President, Johnson continued to work behind the scenes but also had to reveal his plans publicly. It was important for him politically and personally to gain the approval of the American people for his policy. Johnson was not as successful in his public pronouncements as he was when he working within the political system to achieve his goals. This shortfall would hamper his Vietnam policy throughout his presidency.

The overwhelming passage of the Gulf of Tonkin Resolution in August 1964 and the American public's reaction to America's early use of force (Gallup Polls gave Johnson a favorable rating in a range of 60 percent to 70 percent) provided him with the justification for continuing efforts in Vietnam.

Noting that the majority of Americans supported the war effort during his presidency was important for Johnson, because it wasn't until the 1968 Tet Offensive (examined in detail in Chapter 5), during the last few months of his term, that supporters of the war temporarily were in the minority. The antiwar majority is examined in Chapter 14. At that point, war supporters were overshadowed by more vocal opposition from antiwar activists, who, as a result, garnered better coverage from the media and more attention from scholars examining the war.

A war involving "Many Flags"

Early in the war, the Johnson Administration placed an emphasis on gathering allies for the American cause. Allied support helped the American people justify the increasing commitment of U.S. troops in Vietnam and assured them that America wasn't fighting the Vietnam War alone but rather that the international community supported its efforts.

"Many Flags," as the Johnson Administration named the program, had mixed results. The United States pointed to 37 different nations that supported the war against North Vietnam; however, many antiwar activists were critical of the list, arguing that it was not a legitimate representation of support for the war. Although five allied nations (Australia, New Zealand, the Republic of Korea, Thailand, and the Philippines) provided assistance to South Vietnam, their contributions to the war effort were not enough to silence antiwar protestors from arguing that the United States was alone in fighting the war. In the case of South Korea and Thailand, the antiwar activities argued that because the United States was paying for the troops, the Koreans were nothing more than mercenaries.

Pairing religion and war

Many religious organizations also provided assistance as the United States helped secure Vietnam from Communism. Although many of these organizations preferred a nonviolent solution, they saw the evils of Communism as a greater threat than the hostilities.

The Mennonite Central Committee (MCC), an organization founded in 1920 and dedicated to helping people in need around the world, entered Vietnam in 1954 and remained throughout the war, providing relief for people who had suffered from the devastation of the French-Vietnamese conflict (see Chapter 2) and people who had been resettled after Operation PASSAGE TO FREEDOM, as described in Chapter 11.

Members of the MCC went to South Vietnam to help the people build school and medical facilities and other infrastructures designed to improve their day-to-day lives. In 1966, the MCC, Church World Services, and Lutheran World Relief coordinated their efforts by forming Vietnam Christian Services; however, the MCC left the VCS in 1972 after being criticized for expanding its humanitarian aid to North Vietnam in 1968 (see Figure 15-2).

As the war escalated, Christian organizations struggled when trying to reconcile their support for the United States with their pacifist beliefs. Although elements in each organization opposed the war, general support existed for the United States fighting to improve lives of the South Vietnamese people.

Nongovernmental support for the war effort

The United States received support from a number of organizations from within and outside of the country. It was an important part of the U.S. war effort to show that it was not alone in aiding the South Vietnamese (see Figure 15-2). The following organizations not only provided assistance but also helped justify the American commitment to Southeast Asia:

- **The International Rescue Committee (IRC):** Established in 1933, the IRC was an all-volunteer group that was one of the organizing agencies coordinating aid for Vietnam and support for the fight against Communism. Its focus was on providing relief, protection, and resettlement services for people affected by the war.

- **The Cooperative for American Remittances to Everywhere, Inc. (CARE):** CARE first entered South Vietnam in 1954, responding to the dire needs of people resettling from the North. *CARE packages,* a sampling of items needed for day-to-day health and well-being, greeted refugees as they departed American naval transports in Saigon during Operation PASSAGE TO FREEDOM, as described in Chapter 11. CARE continued providing relief for war victims and supporting American actions to improve the lives of the South Vietnamese.

- **The United Nations International Children's Emergency Fund (UNICEF):** Founded in 1946, UNICEF was designed to provide support for the one set of people within the population that was not able to take care of itself — the children. UNICEF began working in South Vietnam in 1954, providing the basic necessities required for a young person to survive. UNICEF continued its involvement in Vietnam and with those opposed to the violence associated with war by helping to reinforce the basic tenet of U.S. involvement in Vietnam, which was providing a better life for its people.

HISTORIC TRIVIA

Romancing the war: John Wayne and Hollywood

In 1968, John Wayne produced, directed, and starred in *The Green Berets,* a movie that tried to depict the harsh realities of the war in Vietnam. The plot of the film, decidedly pro-American, was designed to stir patriotic feelings of the people who viewed it. The film ends the day after a climactic battle with the Viet Cong, showing the survivors moving on to fight another battle to save Vietnam. Sgt. Barry Sadler's *Ballad of the* *Green Berets,* a musical tribute to the Special Forces, plays in the background as the film comes to a close. Sadler's 1966 hit became the song used by war supporters as a counter to the blossoming antiwar music of the late 1960s. Songs and songwriters of the antiwar movement soon washed out Sadler's lone voice. His ballad, however, still stirs the hearts of those who supported the war.

Figure 15-2: Dr. Joanne T. Smith of the Vietnam Christian Service examines a patient at the Salvation Army's clinic at the Chanh Hung Rehabilitation Center.

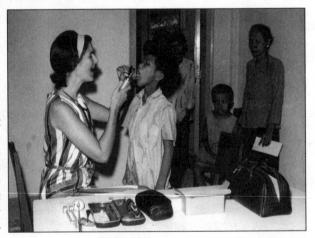

Photograph courtesy of the Vietnam Archive, Texas Tech University

Writing to win: The loyal press

Early in the war those who reported the war supported the United States commitment to Vietnam by following the line that military and government provided to them without question. Military and government reports showed U.S. progress toward the defeat of the NVA/VC while neglecting the growing strength of the NVA/VC in South Vietnam. Many journalists covering Vietnam were experienced war correspondents from World War II and the Korean War, who knew government procedures and respected its position.

When Harrison Salisbury of *The New York Times* reported on civilian damage in North Vietnam caused by Operation ROLLING THUNDER (as examined in Chapter 9), few in the press picked up the story — most because they didn't want to appear critical of the American military. Even the My Lai Massacre story (see Chapters 5 and 15) was held for several months before being released so that facts about the event could be confirmed. This professional constraint would not be evident as the war progressed into the 1970s.

Contrary to popular belief, the media didn't run amuck denouncing the American soldier and war effort throughout the entire war. As the war escalated, and no definable strategy for victory emerged, some of the reporters in Vietnam became doubtful of official U.S. military reports and increased their investigative reporting.

The War Comes to Middle America: 1967–1968

In 1965, most Americans supported the war — or at least they were showing ambivalence toward protestors. In supporting the war, this majority focused more on their day-to-day lives — they weren't holding rallies or carrying signs in support of the war the way their antiwar counterparts were doing. But when the antiwar movement expanded its original call from ending the war to also rethinking social values, many within the United States responded to what they considered un-American activities. This response came from all walks of life, including Congress and the average American. When antiwar protesters traveled to North Vietnam to support the DRV against the United States, it caused many who had supported the war from behind the scenes to come forward and make their voice heard. The response came in many forms except for the one that garnered the most public attention, the mass protest. Still, supporters of the war organized parades and speeches at public venues to rally the United States behind the flag, the president, and soldiers fighting in Vietnam.

Aiding the president: Congressional and political support

Even when some in Congress were voicing opposition to his handling of the war, President Johnson continued receiving support from Republicans and Democrats who backed him and the military.

Former President Dwight Eisenhower supported the escalation of the war in Vietnam, even though his administration had tried to limit U.S. involvement. Eisenhower believed that the people protesting the war were coming close to committing treason, and, because Eisenhower continued receiving the admiration and respect of many in the United States, his voice was acknowledged. Eisenhower strongly supported Richard M. Nixon in his 1968 presidential bid because of Nixon's more active military policies for pursuing the war. Ironically, however, those Eisenhower despised — the antiwar protestors — praised him for not becoming involved in the war.

When Ronald Reagan ran for Governor of California in 1966 on a platform that included support for the war and a promise to take care of the problem of the student protestors at the University of California at Berkeley, the people of California responded by overwhelmingly electing him to that state's highest office. Reagan was not alone in rallying the American people against the antiwar movement and arguing that the war was justified.

Welcoming home the families

Not every Vietnam veteran experienced the same welcome upon arriving back in the United States. Many veterans recount being greeted by antiwar protestors blaming them for American involvement in the war or discovering that returning to a normal life would take longer than expected. No hero's welcome and no parades greeted returning Vietnam veterans; the nation was divided and few people felt like celebrating.

Most families, however, provided a war reception for their brothers, sisters, and the boys and girls next door. They defended American action in Vietnam and the American soldier and they made up the group to which Nixon made his appeal in November 1969, just when the antiwar movement was reaching its apex. The majority of America — Nixon's Silent Majority — believed that the efforts of the United States in Vietnam were justified and supported the military.

Hard hats confront long hair

The rise of the antiwar movement and its image of the longhaired, drug-induced student protestor sparked a reaction from blue collar America. On May 8, 1970, a group of New York construction workers demonstrated against antiwar protestors. The demonstration ended in a violent skirmish.

Countering the May 1970 protests and the earlier confrontation between construction workers and antiwar protestors, the Building and Construction Trades Council of Greater New York organized a rally and demonstration in support of President Nixon and the American servicemen in Vietnam. Led by Peter Brennan, these self-declared *hard hats* marched down the streets of

New York City representing not only the labor unions but also Americans who believed in patriotism, American democracy, and the flag. This more peaceful demonstration was designed to represent the majority of America and provide an avenue for people belonging to the Silent Majority to raise their voices in support of the U.S. war in Vietnam.

Riding the right's support: Nixon finds an ally

From Richard Nixon's perspective, the 1972 election reaffirmed his Vietnam War strategy over the previous four years. Nixon won reelection to the presidency over Democratic challenger George McGovern who had campaigned on an antiwar platform. McGovern advocated pardoning draft dodgers and ending all military involvement in Southeast Asia at the same time that Nixon was launching two of the most destructive air campaigns (described in Chapter 9) against North Vietnam in 1972, during the height of the campaign season.

Nixon relied on the conservative right and the Silent Majority for support during the election and for seeing him through the "peace with honor." He won the reelection with one of the largest majorities in United States presidential campaign history. Silent or not, for the course of the war, the political right in the United States and the majority of Americans supported the military in Vietnam and remained a mainstay for the president.

Nixon's greatest domestic strategy in the war at home against antiwar protestors was the war's end. When he announced Vietnamization in 1969, he deflated the antiwar movement. However, he was quick to reignite the passion of the movement with secret bombings of and the incursion into Cambodia.

Nevertheless, Nixon recognized that the American withdrawal from Vietnam would lessen, and eventually end, the protests. When Nixon's National Security Advisor Henry Kissinger was negotiating an end to the war, Nixon gained supporters who were tired of the war, tired of the antiwar movement, and ready to return to normalcy. The American public supported the air campaigns in North Vietnam and military reaction to the North Vietnamese 1972 Eastertide Offensive, as described in Chapter 6. Nixon ensured continuing support by not reintroducing troops. As the war was ending, Nixon's opponents began refocusing their energies away from Vietnam and toward him. You can read more about the president who ended the war in Vietnam but found himself out of office the next year, forced to resign and accept a pardon from President Gerald Ford, in Chapter 6.

HISTORIC TRIVIA

Will the Silent Majority please speak up?

On November 3, 1969, Nixon addressed the nation to discuss his plan for ending the war in Vietnam. He appealed for the "Silent Majority" not to abandon the United States to the antiwar movement. He planned to end the war by winning the peace — or achieving "peace with honor" for the United States. Nixon needed the Silent Majority behind him to succeed:

"I want to end the war to save the lives of those brave young men in Vietnam. But I want to end it in a way which will increase the chance that their younger brothers and their sons will not have to fight in some future Vietnam someplace in the world. And I want to end the war for another reason. I want to end it so that the energy and dedication of you, our young people, now too often directed into bitter hatred against those responsible for the war, can be turned to the great challenges of peace, a better life for all Americans, a better life for all people on this earth. I have chosen a plan for peace. I believe it will succeed. If it does succeed, what the critics say now won't matter. If it does not succeed, anything I say then won't matter.

"I know it may not be fashionable to speak of patriotism or national destiny these days. But I feel it is appropriate to do so on this occasion. Two hundred years ago this Nation was weak and poor. But even then, America was the hope of millions in the world. Today we have become the strongest and richest nation in the world. And the wheel of destiny has turned so that any hope the world has for the survival of peace and freedom will be determined by whether the American people have the moral stamina and the courage to meet the challenge of free world leadership. Let historians not record that when America was the most powerful nation in the world we passed on the other side of the road and allowed the last hopes for peace and freedom of millions of people to be suffocated by the forces of totalitarianism.

"And so tonight to you, the great Silent Majority of my fellow Americans, I ask for your support. I pledged in my campaign for the presidency to end the war in a way that we could win the peace. I have initiated a plan of action, which will enable me to keep that pledge. The more support I can have from the American people, the sooner that pledge can be redeemed; for the more divided we are at home, the less likely the enemy is to negotiate at Paris. Let us be united for peace. Let us also be united against defeat. Because let us understand: North Vietnam cannot defeat or humiliate the United States. Only Americans can do that."

Part VI
The Part of Tens

The 5th Wave   By Rich Tennant

"...and let that be a lesson to you!"

In this part . . .

The Part of Tens has become a trademark of all *For Dummies* books and each chapter in this part contains information on ten important issues or subjects that are good to know about and are interesting and entertaining as well. In addition to discussing controversial postwar issues and various myths about the Vietnam War, we also discuss other important resources you can use so you can learn more about the Vietnam War on your own. The material in this part is designed to make you think about the Vietnam War in different ways as it provides different, controversial, and sometimes contradictory views on the war itself and the postwar world in which we live.

Chapter 16

Ten Myths of the Vietnam War

In This Chapter

▶ Debunking myths about race

▶ Correcting misperceptions about American veterans

▶ Putting the antiwar movement and the media in their place

*T*he Vietnam War was one of the most controversial events in modern U.S. history. Not since the Civil War has any one event divided the nation. The emotions rising out of the Vietnam War retained their intensity during the postwar period. Along with those emotions certain myths about the war developed and were perpetuated in years that followed. We think the following ten myths from the Vietnam War (in no particular order) have caused the greatest controversy and greatest harm to an objective understanding of this important time in U.S. history.

More Minorities Served and Suffered Greater Casualties than Caucasians

This statement often is used in support of an argument that the Vietnam War was a backdrop for social and cultural culling that targeted ethnic minorities for service in the Vietnam War with little concern for the consequences. But the contention that African American soldiers bore the brunt of the dangerous combat missions and incurred a higher casualty rate than Caucasian soldiers simply is not true.

This myth is continually repeated in Vietnam War debates despite clear and readily available evidence to the contrary. The National Archives and Records Administration lists the official Killed-in-Action (KIA) from the Vietnam War at 58,193 — a number that most scholars of the war agree on. African American soldiers suffered 7,264 KIA or 12.5 percent of the total KIA. Caucasian soldiers suffered 50,120 KIA or 86.1 percent of the KIA. These figures are close to the percentage of each group as a part of the overall U.S. population. According to the 1970 census, 88 percent of the American population was Caucasian and between 10 percent and 11 percent was

African American. When compared to the representation of casualties in the Vietnam War, the numbers are too close to support the argument that African Americans were exposed to greater risks than Caucasian soldiers. Although it is true that the politicians who guided the war from Washington, D.C., were Caucasian, they were more interested in fighting communism in Southeast Asia than in targeting a specific race in America to fight the war.

More People Drafted than Volunteered

Many people arguing that the Vietnam War was unpopular throughout the United States try to prove their point by stating American men and women didn't volunteer but instead had to be drafted to fill the ranks of the U.S. Armed Forces in Southeast Asia. Unfortunately, people making this argument are relying on another myth about the Vietnam War.

Depending upon your source, between 2.7 million and 3.4 million U.S. personnel served in Southeast Asia during the war. Selective Service (the U.S. government department in charge of making sure the armed forces have enough personnel) records indicate that approximately 650,000 draftees served in Vietnam. This figure represents approximately 19 percent to 25 percent of the total number of servicemen who went to Vietnam. Of those who were drafted, 17,672 (30.4 percent) were KIA. The majority who served in Vietnam volunteered for military service. Every woman who served in Vietnam volunteered for the assignment.

Although motives for volunteering varied, and some were motivated to volunteer because they knew they were going to be drafted and they at least wanted to select the type of job and unit to which they would be assigned, arguing that more men and women were drafted to Vietnam than volunteered is incorrect.

War Reporting Changed U.S. Policy

One of the more controversial subjects during the war and in the postwar period has been the role the media played and the effect it had on the Vietnam War. Contrary to what many people think, recent research and writing about the Vietnam War proves the media didn't have as powerful an impact on the decisions being made by U.S. war leaders as many people think.

Early in the Vietnam War, the media and the Johnson Administration agreed that the media would be provided with access to the political and military decision-making process so long as they respected the rules of reporting a war — not showing violence and death on television but rather reporting what actually was happening in the war. Until 1968, the media adhered to the agreement, but as the Johnson Administration moved away from fully disclosing facts, the media began investigating the war for themselves. During the Nixon Administration, the media became more of an opponent to the government and the military. Still. it can be argued that the media reporting neither changed decisions coming out of Washington, D.C., nor caused the United States to end its involvement in Southeast Asia.

At the same time, the effects of the media should not be dismissed as irrelevant. The Vietnam War was the first war to be broadcast on television. Although dramatic and powerful, television imagery of the war didn't directly affect political or military decisions. Instead, television graphically and visually portrayed the war to the American people and showed them what war does to another society and people. Most Americans had never experienced war and, with the exception of Pearl Harbor, no major battles had been fought on U.S. soil since the nineteenth century. The American generations of the 1960s and 1970s learned about the horrors and realities of war through the televised Vietnam experience, discovering on a daily basis that war is nothing like a Hollywood movie.

The way the media covered the war in Southeast Asia evolved over time. Before 1968, media coverage tended to be more positive. Some observers argue that this changed with the 1968 Tet Offensive. When it became apparent that President Johnson no longer believed in the U.S. policy in Vietnam (discussed in Chapter 5 above), the media more openly challenged U.S. policy. Rather than changing public opinion, it appears that the shift in media coverage from positive to negative reporting reflected the tone of American public opinion. Rather than acitng as an active agent of influence, by reflecting public opinion, the media acted as a magnifier and focus for the growing skepticism regarding the Vietnam War. In this way, negative media coverage following Tet 1968 made it much more difficult for the Nixon Administration to escalate the war and provided powerful impetus for them to seek a peaceful resolution on terms acceptable to the U.S. and their allies.

Vietnam Veterans Suffer Higher Rates of Alcoholism, Drug Use, and Divorce

At the end of the war, many popular portrayals showed Vietnam veterans as unstable and unproductive members of U.S. society. Reports based on questionable data suggested that Vietnam veterans were alcoholics, drug addicts, homeless, unemployed, and couldn't maintain stable marriages or relationships. The fact is, however, that most Vietnam veterans are like most Americans and the overwhelming majority of them are neither alcoholics nor drug abusers, most of them have homes and successful careers, and many have remained married to their spouses.

So how did this myth become so entrenched in American popular culture? The answer is primarily the media. Whether through news coverage, television drama, or big-screen Hollywood movies, most depictions of Vietnam veterans since the war have focused on negative stereotypes.

Successful and productive Vietnam veterans also failed to debunk the myth, because they were turning inward during the 1970s and early 1980s, refusing to speak of the war and their postwar successes because of their perception that Americans didn't care about hearing their side of the story. In addition, admitting that you were a Vietnam veteran could subject you to ridicule or discrimination because of the negative stereotypes. Many people did not want to admit they were Vietnam veterans because people would think they were unstable.

The sad fact is that since the war's end, some Vietnam veterans have faced great difficulties as a result from their wartime service. Some Vietnam veterans are alcoholics, drug abusers, unemployed, homeless, and multiple divorcees. But is this group of troubled veterans larger as a percentage within the Vietnam veteran community than the same group of people within American society in general? No. Further dispelling this myth more recently are increasing numbers of people who openly identify themselves as being Vietnam veterans. The vast majority of these men and women are successful and contributing members of their communities. No statistics are available that show Vietnam veterans suffered from higher rates of alcoholism, drug abuse, or divorce than average Americans.

Antiwar Protests Forced U.S. to End War

One of the more enduring myths of the Vietnam War is that the antiwar movement forced an end to the war. Some who believe in this myth, usually the men and women who protested the war, argue that the movement forced the U.S. government to change its policies and end the war. Although some decisions made by the U.S. government were influenced by public opinion, most significant military and political decisions were primarily based on wartime Vietnam and Cold War realities.

The Johnson Administration didn't limit the bombing of North Vietnam because of antiwar activism. It limited the bombing because of available targets and fears that the Soviet Union and the Peoples Republic of China might enter the war. Johnson's decision not to seek the nomination of the Democratic Party in 1968 wasn't caused by the burgeoning antiwar movement. The reason he didn't run for reelection was that he became frustrated with the war wreaking havoc on his Great Society legislation and domestic policy agenda and because he didn't see an end to the war after the 1968 Tet Offensive. As described in Chapters 6 and 14, the Nixon Administration rarely paid attention to the activities of the antiwar movement, and thus it didn't play a role in determining military or political strategy, tactics, or policy toward Southeast Asia.

The U.S. Lost in Vietnam because of "Rules of Engagement"

Considerable irony surrounds this particular myth regarding the Vietnam War. *Rules of Engagement,* or the rules that governed American behavior in Vietnam, existed in Vietnam for several reasons:

- Some rules were in place to prevent the accidental killing of innocent Vietnamese civilians in rural areas where U.S. forces patrolled but had difficulty identifying Viet Cong soldiers.

- Other rules were meant to prevent the spread of the war or the introduction of other nations' forces into the fray. This rule was especially true regarding the selection of bombing targets in North Vietnam and the fear of China and the Soviet Union entering the war.

- The intent of still other rules was limiting the killing of civilians or limiting damage to certain civilian structures during bombing raids of North Vietnam such as hospitals, schools, or dike systems.

So, from 1964 until 1973, the rules of engagement prevented

- American forces from bombing every possible target in North Vietnam
- The overt use of American military force in Cambodia and Laos
- A ground invasion of North Vietnam

However, by asking yourself whether rules of engagement contributed to a failure of U.S. policy in Southeast Asia, you discover that arguing that they did is contradictory to the historical facts of the war.

What is so odd about this myth and criticism of American policy in Vietnam is that it contradicts the accomplishments of American and South Vietnamese forces during most of the war. The goal of U.S. policy in Southeast Asia from 1954 until 1973 always was the preservation of a noncommunist South Vietnam, as discussed in Chapters 3, 4, 5, and 6. This policy remained in place during the U.S. conventional military presence from 1965 until 1973. During that eight-year period, the United States, South Vietnam, and allies succeeded in protecting South Vietnam from communism despite the rules of engagement. In 1972, the United States had all but completely withdrawn from Vietnam when North Vietnam launched its Eastertide Offensive, covered in Chapter 6, attempting to conquer South Vietnam and destroy the small remnants of American ground forces still in the country. The armed forces of South Vietnam, with some American assistance, successfully repulsed the North Vietnamese offensives and defeated them. Within a year, the United States signed the Paris Peace Accords and officially withdrew the remainder of U.S. forces from Vietnam.

How could the U.S. rules of engagement have contributed to the fall of South Vietnam when the United States succeeded in its policy objectives up to the point when they officially and completely withdrew U.S. forces? The answer is that the rules of engagement did not contribute to the fall of South Vietnam because they no longer mattered and no longer were enforced when South Vietnam was defeated in 1975. But the myth about rules of engagement ties in to another prominent myths of the war.

U.S. Forces Won Every Battle but Still Lost the War

This statement is a myth on several levels. First, some people believe that U.S. forces literally won every battle during the war. As you discover in various chapters in this book, the U.S. forces winning every battle simply is not the case. Although arguing that U.S. forces won a majority of the battles is easy, they also lost some. The events at LZ Albany, during the battle for Ia Drang Valley in 1965, discussed in Chapter 5, are a good case in point, but other examples also point to U.S. losses.

The validity of this position also depends on how you define "win." The United States defined winning in Vietnam in terms of the numbers of North Vietnamese Army and Viet Cong (NVA/VC) killed in comparison to U.S. losses. When U.S. forces inflicted more casualties, they won. However, the NVA/VC defined winning in terms of their ability to engage U.S. forces at places and times of their choosing, thus inflicting casualties on U.S. units and then withdrawing so they could continue the fight for as long as possible until the U.S. forces withdrew completely from South Vietnam. In this context, both sides *won* many of the battles. From the U.S. perspective, U.S. forces won nearly every battle because, in most instances, they killed more NVA/VC. Yet the NVA/VC also won from their perspective, because they usually chose the place and time of combat, inflicted casualties on U.S. units, and survived until U.S. forces left South Vietnam.

North Vietnam Controlled the Viet Cong

This Vietnam War myth grew out of a larger and more powerful myth that developed early in the Cold War: Communism is *monolithic,* meaning that communism was an ideology and philosophy centrally directed and controlled by the communist leadership of the Soviet Union. It wasn't. This idea stemmed from the declaration by the Soviet Union in the early 1920s that it would foster and support the spread of communist revolution throughout the world.

After WWII, when communism replaced fascism and totalitarianism as the great evil in the world, wherever a communist movement or revolution emerged, the United States and its allies saw the hand of the Soviet Union. That is what occurred when communist insurgency broke out in South Vietnam during the 1950s and many people saw the communist North Vietnamese being manipulated by the Soviets.

There are problems with this myth: It overlooks basic human and diplomatic relationships. Although the Viet Cong in South Vietnam may have received symbolic support from North Vietnam, they received little to no material or financial support from North Vietnam until the mid-1960s. In addition, according to former South Vietnamese Premier General Nguyen Khanh and other South Vietnamese leaders, most of the early Viet Cong leaders were born in and lived in South Vietnam, emerging from the educated classes of that country. So, they were not North Vietnamese infiltrators.

But perhaps the most important factor in dispelling this myth is the ample proof that the North Vietnamese and Viet Cong didn't always agree on strategies and tactics or what postwar Vietnam would be like. Many conflicts between communist leaders on both sides emerged to the extent that leads some observers to argue that one purpose of North Vietnam's decision to launch the 1968 Tet Offensive, discussed in Chapter 5, was to get rid of the southern elements of the Viet Cong — an actual, if unintended, consequence of that failed uprising.

Tet 1968 Was a Surprise, but the U.S. Won

Like some of the other myths discussed in this chapter, this one is a myth on several levels. First, as is discussed in Chapter 5, the Tet Offensive of 1968 was not a surprise. Nearly every Tet holiday during the war witnessed attacks that ended the holiday cease-fires. But no one anticipated the widespread attacks on cities throughout South Vietnam; furthermore, the lengthy siege at Khe Sanh surprised many people. So, saying that Tet 1968 had some surprising elements is possible, but few had anything to do with what happened in South Vietnam.

More important and surprising events occurred in the United States that challenged the assertion that the United States won the 1968 Tet Offensive.

Similar to the myth of American battle victories, the outcome of the Tet Offensive depends on who is defining victory or defeat. It is true that United States and South Vietnamese forces killed or captured nearly all of the Viet Cong who attacked throughout South Vietnam and suffered comparatively fewer casualties in return.

In addition, U.S. forces held onto Khe Sanh, discussed in Chapter 5. So, in a narrow and military sense, you can say that the United States and South Vietnam won the Tet Offensive tactically. But few major battles during the Vietnam War occurred without political considerations or consequences. In that respect, the Tet Offensive ranks as one of the most decisive engagements during the Vietnam War and resulted in the loss of popular support for the war. The tactical victory in Vietnam became a staggering strategic defeat back in the United States. Divorcing war from politics is not possible, because they are extensions of one another. Losing politically and strategically during Tet 1968 completely overshadowed and negated the tactical victory against the Viet Cong and North Vietnamese. Tet 1968 was no surprise, but it was a defeat in the minds of the American people and therefore a defeat in Vietnam.

Most Americans Engaged in Atrocities

This myth is perhaps one of the most troubling and disturbing to come out of the Vietnam War. The roots of this myth are evident in the My Lai Massacre Without a doubt, this event was a horrible but isolated incident in which an American platoon under poor leadership killed women, children, and elderly people. Unfortunately, for some people, this incident translates into an assumption that all U.S. military forces in Vietnam must have been doing the same thing. Antiwar protesters latched on to the massacre at My Lai, calling veterans "baby killers" and chanting, "Hey, hey, LBJ, how many kids did you kill today." These same people failed to realize that U.S. soldiers from another American unit stopped the massacre and prevented the senseless killing of even more Vietnamese civilians in My Lai.

Nothing indicates that atrocities at the hands of Americans occurred in Vietnam with any frequency. In fact, indications point to the opposite being true. Although anecdotal and official evidence exists that isolated acts of cruelty and brutality occurred, most of these crimes resulted in *courts-martial,* or military trials, of individuals involved, their removal from Vietnam, and imprisonment. Most American men and women serving in Southeast Asia did so with great dignity, professionalism, and respect for the Vietnamese people.

Chapter 17

Ten Resources for Studying the Vietnam War

A wealth of information about the Vietnam War is available from many sources. You can find materials from government agencies, university archives, libraries, veteran associations, and personal Web sites of the men and women who were there. The following list of the "Top Ten" resources on the war is just the tip of the iceberg and is intended to provide you with a sample of the more important materials that are available, and representative examples of the many other types of materials you can access to discover more about this controversial part of twentieth-century history. Plenty of stuff is out there, and this guide will alert you to the hazards of using certain types of materials.

You need to critically examine all materials that you encounter regarding the Vietnam War. Although many of the documents in the Vietnam Archive come from the veterans and participants themselves and from government sources and oral history interviews conducted with the actual participants, you must never just accept these materials as completely accurate. Government record-keeping isn't perfect, and people's memories are fallible. Keep that in mind when you review materials from the Vietnam Archive and every other source.

The Vietnam Project at Texas Tech University

The Vietnam Project at Texas Tech University (www.vietnam.ttu.edu) is divided into four parts:

✔ **The Vietnam Center.** Since its establishment in 1989, the Vietnam Center has sought to involve a broad spectrum of academics and veterans representing all aspects of the American Vietnam experience. In recent years, the Vietnam Center has facilitated the development of cooperative programs between various Texas Tech University departments and Vietnamese academics.

In pursuit of its mission to encourage continued study concerning all aspects of the American Vietnam experience, the Vietnam Center developed an active conference and symposium program.

✔ **The Vietnam Archive.** The Vietnam Archive exists to

- Collect documents and memorabilia related to the Vietnam War and the collective experience of those affected by the war and its aftermath.

- Preserve archival material in a state-of-the-art facility located on the campus of Texas Tech University.

- Encourage dissemination of information from the archive to all who are interested in learning more about this critical time in United States and world history.

- Promote the study and understanding of the Vietnam War, the nation of Vietnam, and the history of Southeast Asia.

✔ **The Virtual Vietnam Archive.** The Virtual Vietnam Archive was initiated in December 2000 with the objective of *digitizing* (creating scanned copies for the Internet) all noncopyright material in the Vietnam Archive. The Virtual Vietnam Archive enables everyone interested in studying the war to conduct research directly from universities, schools, libraries, and homes. Of equal importance, it enables Vietnam veterans — those who actually served — to access records that may be of importance to them.

✔ **Oral History Project.** The Oral History Project is committed to preserving the history of the wars in Southeast Asia from the perspective of all participants, regardless of country of service. The oral history staff has interviewed men and women from the United States, Vietnam, Australia, and New Zealand. Staff members also attend Vietnam veteran association reunions documenting oral histories and explaining about The Vietnam Project at Texas Tech University.

The Vietnam Veterans Memorial Fund

In 1979, the U.S. Congress authorized the formation of a nonprofit organization to build a national memorial to all Americans who served in the Vietnam War. The Vietnam Veterans Memorial Fund (VVMF) (www.vvmf.org), led by Jan Scruggs, worked toward and achieved this goal in 1982 with the unveiling of The Wall. Two statues honoring the servicemen and women who served in the war were added in 1984 and 1993. After completing its main objective, the VVMF remains active in maintaining and securing the three-acre memorial site. In the 1990s, the VVMF expanded its original mission by providing educational outreach so that younger generations (those who were born after the war ended in 1975) can gain a better understanding of the significance of the war on the United States during the 1960s and 1970s.

The VVMF is active in creating high school curriculum about the war and offers, free-of-charge, *Echoes From The Wall: History, Learning and Leadership Through the Lens of The Vietnam War Era,* a publication that helps high school teachers create lesson plans and Vietnam War units. (You can contact them via regular mail at 1023 15th Street, NW, Second Floor, Washington, DC 20005; 202-393-0090.) In 1996, the VVMF also organized *The Wall That Heals,* which includes an educational exhibition and a half-scale replica of The Wall. The VVMF partnered with Winstar Communication, Inc., to develop a computerized legacy of the war that enables people who knew someone listed on the wall to offer electronic remembrances. The VVMF also organizes events at the memorial and provides free name rubbings.

Many organizations like the VVMF attempt to remain above politics and political issues. But doing so isn't always possible or realistic. When reviewing materials that come from nonprofit, governmental, and other organizations, you need to keep in mind that political and personal agendas and issues sometimes may affect the materials you find or interpretations with which you're presented. This is true for most sources regarding any subject, but the more controversial the subject, the more likely you'll encounter this problem. So, for Vietnam, beware!

Foreign Relations of the United States Series

The official published documentary record for the Department of State is located in the *Foreign Relations of the United States* (FRUS) series. FRUS volumes for the Vietnam War provide a representative sample of the significant documents that helped shape U.S. foreign policy in Southeast Asia during the Eisenhower, Kennedy, Johnson, and Nixon administrations.

Many of these volumes are available online at `www.state.gov/www/about_state/history/frus.html`. FRUS volumes include documents from the presidential libraries, the Department of State, the Department of Defense, the Central Intelligence Agency, and other U.S. government agencies. Many FRUS volumes about the Vietnam War are available free-of-charge on the above Web site. In addition, paper volumes still can be purchased through the U.S. Government Printing Office; phone, 202-512-1800.

Vietnam War Bibliography

Although several resources list books, articles, and documents about the Vietnam War, three stand out for usability and completeness. Based at the Clemson University, historian Edwin Moise and his staff of graduate and undergraduate students have compiled a significant list of material on the Vietnam War.

- ✔ The Web site (`hubcap.clemson.edu/~eemoise/bibliography.html`) is organized by subject headings. If you're interested in learning more about a specific aspect of the war, this Web site is an excellent starting point.

- ✔ Another bibliographical resource is the electronic database for America: History and Life, located at many university and some public libraries . Using keywords such as "Vietnam War," you can access articles and book reviews from many of the more prominent journals and it provides an excellent list of dissertations and other published works.

- ✔ Texas Tech University lists thousands of books and dissertations located in The Vietnam Archive in its library catalog. If you cannot find a book on the subject about which you're interested in your local library, there is an excellent chance that you'll be able to find the relevant information at the Texas Tech University Library Web site (`www.lib.ttu.edu`).

America's Longest War by George Herring

First published in 1979, George Herring's *America's Longest War* is an excellent next step for readers interested in learning more about how the United States became involved in the war and how U.S. diplomacy shaped, and was shaped by, the events in Southeast Asia. The book now is in its fourth edition and has been expanded and organized to account for new scholarship and more-recently declassified documents.

As you continue your studies of the Vietnam War, we provide this caution: As many different perspectives of the Vietnam War exist as books that are written about it. You shouldn't believe everything you read — except this book, of course — and rest assured that whenever you read a book that has something about the war with which you disagree, the next book you pick up will probably counter the first.

The National Archives and Presidential Libraries

The National Archives and Records Administration (NARA) is the official archive for all U.S. government and military records. NARA is one place where you can find many *primary source materials* (documents and materials generated at the time by the principal players and offices).

Most Vietnam War–related materials are part of Record Group 472 within the National Archives system. NARA also has various branch archives throughout the United States and visitors are welcome to visit these local offices. The nationwide facilities and centers are listed at www.nara.gov; phone, 866-325-7208.

In addition, the National Archives administers the presidential library system, which is an extremely important resource for learning about the Vietnam War. Each U.S. president chooses the site for his or her official library and each library usually houses all of the official records and documents from that president's administration. Here are the presidential libraries with relevant information about the Vietnam War:

✔ **The Harry S. Truman Library:** The Truman Library provides materials related to American policies and support for the French against the Viet Minh for the period from 1946 to 1951. For more on Truman's policies in Southeast Asia, please read Chapter 2.

  Web site: www.trumanlibrary.org

  Address: 500 West U.S. Highway 24, Independence, MO 64050-1798

  Phone: 816-833-1400

  Fax: 816-833-4368

  E-mail: truman.library@nara.gov

✔ **The Dwight D. Eisenhower Library:** Eisenhower provided support for the French during their war from 1951 until 1954. After that, the United States became heavily involved with the internal politics of South Vietnam and provided increasing amounts of materiel and economic aid to South Vietnam. For more on Ike's policies in Southeast Asia, please read Chapter 3.

  Web Site: www.eisenhower.utexas.edu

  Address: 200 SE Fourth Street, Abilene, KS 67410-2900

  Phone: 785-263-4751

  Fax: 785-263-4218

  E-mail: eisenhower.library@nara.gov

✔ **The John F. Kennedy Library:** JFK significantly increased the U.S. commitment in Vietnam and Southeast Asia by sending more men, materiel, and economic aid to the region. For more on JFK's policies in Southeast Asia, please read Chapter 4.

Web site: www.jfklibrary.org

Address: Columbia Point, Boston, MA 02125-3398

Phone: 617-929-4500

Fax: 617-929-4538

E-mail: kennedy.library@nara.gov

✔ **The Lyndon Baines Johnson Library:** LBJ committed the first conventional U.S. military forces to South Vietnam and oversaw the Americanization of the war in Vietnam. For more on LBJ's policies in Southeast Asia, please read Chapter 5.

Web Site: www.lbjlib.utexas.edu

Address: 2313 Red River Street, Austin, TX 78705-5702

Phone: 512-916-5137

Fax: 512-916-5171

E-mail: johnson.library@nara.gov

✔ **Richard Nixon Presidential Materials:** Because he resigned from office, the Nixon presidential materials are split between the National Archives at College Park, Maryland, and his Library and Birthplace Museum in Yorba Linda, California. The official presidential materials are located at the National Archives in College Park, Maryland, and his personal papers are located in Yorba Linda, California. For more on Nixon's policies in Southeast Asia, please read Chapter 6.

Web site: www.nara.gov/nixon/

Address: National Archives, 8601 Adelphi Road, College Park, MD 20740-6001

Phone: 301-713-6950

Fax: 301-713-6916

E-mail: nixon@nara.gov

Web site: www.nixonfoundation.org/index.shtml

Address: The Richard Nixon Library, 8001 Yorba Linda Blvd., Yorba Linda, CA 92886

Phone: 714-993-5075

Fax: 714-528-0544

✔ **The Gerald Ford Library:** Gerald Ford served as president for only a brief time, during which South Vietnam fell to communism.

Web site: www.ford.utexas.edu

Address: 1000 Beal Avenue, Ann Arbor, MI 48109-2114

Phone: 734-741-2218

Fax: 734-741-2341

E-mail: ford.library@nara.gov

Military Archives and Research Facilities

In addition to the National Archives, branches of the military have developed specific institutions dedicated to collecting and preserving historical materials. Here is a list of specific military branches with brief descriptions of the materials you can expect to find:

✔ **U.S. Army:** The U.S. Army has two offices that collect and preserve historical materials. The U.S. Army Center of Military History houses official unit histories and many other institutional materials, including oral history interviews. The U.S. Army Military History Institute usually collects personal materials that include letters, diaries, memoirs, photographs, and much more. It also conducts oral history interviews. To learn more about the U.S. Army in Vietnam, read Chapters 5 and 6.

- **U.S. Army Center of Military History**

  Web site: www.army.mil/cmh-pg/

  Address: 103 Third Avenue, Fort McNair, DC 20319-5058

  Phone: 202-685-2704

- **U.S. Army Military History Institute**

  Web site: Carlisle-www.army.mil/wsamhi/

  Address: 22 Ashburn Drive, Carlisle, PA 17013-5008

  Phone: 717-245-3096

✔ **U.S. Marine Corps:** The U.S. Marine Corps (USMC) also has two principal organizations dedicated to collecting and preserving historical materials. The Marine Corps History and Museums Division focuses on official USMC materials and the Research Archives at the Marine Corps University focuses more on personal collections. Both institutions have oral histories and other materials. U.S. Marine operations are discussed in Chapters 5, 6, and 12.

- **The Marine Corps History and Museums Division**

  Web site: hqinet001.hqmc.usmc.mil/HD/Home_Page.htm

  Address: 1254 Charles Morris St. SE, Washington Navy Yard, DC 20374-5040

  Phone: 202-433-3447

- **The Marine Corps University Research Archives**

  Web site: www.mcu.usmc.mil/MCRCweb/archive.htm

  Phone: 703-784-4685 or 703-784-4538

  E-mail: archives@tecom.usmc.mil

✔ **U.S. Navy:** The Naval Historical Center is the principal repository for the U.S. Navy, located at the Washington Navy Yard in the District of Columbia. The U.S. Naval Historical Center collects official documentation, including unit histories, deck logs, ship records, oral history interviews, and personal collections. The U.S. Navy in Vietnam is discussed in Chapter 10.

  Web site: www.history.navy.mil/

  Address: 805 Kidder Breese Street SE, Washington Navy Yard, DC 20374-5060

  Phone: 202-433-3170

✔ **U.S. Air Force:** The U.S. Air Force Historical Research Agency is the principal repository for U.S. Air Force historical materials. It houses unit histories, personal collections, oral histories, and many other materials. U.S. Air Force operations are discussed in Chapters 7, 8, and 9.

  Web site: www.au.af.mil

  Address: 600 Chennault Circle, Maxwell AFB, AL 36112-6424

  Phone: 334-953-5834

✔ **U.S. Coast Guard:** Although few people realize it, the U.S. Coast Guard played a significant role in the Vietnam War. The primary repository for historical materials for the Coast Guard is the U.S. Coast Guard's Historian's Office, which manages a museum and document collections for the Coast Guard.

  Web site: www.uscg.mil/hq/g-cp/history/collect.html

  Address: U.S. Coast Guard, 2100 Second Street, SW, Washington, DC 20593-0001

  Phone: 202-267-1394

  Fax: 202-267-4309

Vietnam Order of Battle by Shelby Stanton

Vietnam Order of Battle by Shelby Stanton is the definitive source on the order of battle for American and allied Army forces that served in Vietnam. This large volume contains detailed information about nearly every Army unit that served in Vietnam. Beginning at the division level and working down to company and sometimes platoon levels, it includes detailed information for combat infantry units and combat support and service support units. Readers will find detailed information about and photographs of uniforms, equipment, weapons, vehicles, aircraft, and many other subjects.

Vietnamese Archives, Libraries, and Museums

In addition to American sources, information about the Vietnam War is available at various facilities in Vietnam. The most important include the:

- ✔ National Archives in Hanoi and Ho Chi Minh City
- ✔ Vietnam History Museum in Hanoi
- ✔ National Library of Vietnam in Hanoi

In addition, the People's Army Military Archive and Library is located in Hanoi, and several museums are dedicated exclusively to the Vietnam War. Although we can provide contact information for some of these facilities, the museums and some of the libraries usually are the only facilities readily open to the public.

The Vietnamese National Archive and military archives are difficult to contact, and you must gain prior approval before you can gain access to these facilities. And, even though access to the facility may be granted, access to specific physical records isn't guaranteed. Making research a bit more difficult for most Americans is the fact that the materials are, of course, located in Vietnam and are written in Vietnamese. We provide this information with the hope that in the future, Vietnam will make its materials more easily available and perhaps even post some materials on the Internet. Until that happens, information from these sources will be helpful only to those people willing to travel, be patient, and learn to read Vietnamese.

- ✔ **Vietnam History Museum**

   Address: Pham Ngu Lao Street, Hanoi, Vietnam

   Phone: 84-4-825-2853

✔ **National Library of Vietnam**

Address: 31 Trang Thi Street, Hanoi, Vietnam

Phone: 84-4-825-2643

Fax: 84-4-825-3357

E-mail: hdan@nlv01.gov.vn

The Internet

Some of the more interesting types of Web sites include the ones produced by individual veterans. These sites usually contain personal stories about service in Southeast Asia. They may also contain images from photographs and slides and even audio and video from the war. Some Vietnam veterans' Web sites also contain documents from their days in the service, including letters, military orders, official records, unit after-action reports, and more.

In addition to individual Web sites, many veteran associations also have dedicated Web sites to the men and women who served in their units during the war. These association sites act as online meeting places for veterans and as community posting sites for materials related to their collective service in Southeast Asia.

Just remember to be careful and critical of what you find on the Web and always question Web pages as sources of fact. Some sites provide actual historical documents and materials, enabling you to draw your own conclusions. These probably are the more trustworthy among the sites that you encounter.

Chapter 18

Ten Postwar Concerns and Issues to Think About

● ●

In This Chapter

▶ Honoring the Vietnam veteran

▶ Forming veteran's organizations and other postwar concerns

▶ Normalizing U.S.–Vietnam relations

▶ Looking at postwar effects on people

● ●

During the years following the Vietnam War, a new set of issues and concerns was introduced for those who served in the war and for a nation that was undergoing a period of healing from one of the most divisive periods in its history. For many Vietnam veterans, the 1970s and 1980s reinforced the negative perceptions that emerged at the end of the war. Many veterans thought they were living in a nation that was ungrateful to them for their service and that blamed them for the fall of South Vietnam to communism. Many veterans also thought the United States turned its back on soldiers who fought and died in defense of U.S. ideals in Vietnam.

Vietnam veterans face many additional issues, including the need to safeguard their history and return the honor lost to them during the war. Many veterans are frustrated, coping with issues such as Agent Orange and Post-Traumatic Stress Disorder (PTSD). The Veterans Administration and government bureaucracy only added to their sense that the United States didn't appreciate them or their service. More recently, as Vietnam veterans have regained their identity, they've become viewed in a more positive light in American society.

The Wall: The Vietnam War Memorial, Grieving, and the Return of Honor

In November 1982, the Vietnam War Memorial Wall was dedicated on the National Mall in Washington, D.C. Known as "The Wall," it was the culmination of several years of work led by Jan Scruggs and the Vietnam Veteran Memorial Fund (VVMF). See Chapter 17 for more information on the VVMF.

The Wall consists of 140 black granite marble panels that stretch almost 500 feet from end to end. The two ends of the wall are shorter and the two middle panels are ten feet high. The names of every American killed during the Vietnam War are engraved on the black granite, representing their personal and individual sacrifices. The wall itself is physically cut into the surrounding landscape with certain panels misaligned, resembling a jagged gash, symbolizing the war as a collective wound. In addition to the black granite representing the color of mourning, its highly polished surface reflects images of visitors, drawing attention to their roles and sacrifices during the war. The design of the names also is symbolic, because it tells the day-by-day tragedy of death during the war. The names of the first soldiers killed begin at the middle-right panel of the memorial and continue to the right so that the last soldier killed is on the middle-left panel. The design represents a completed circle, from first to last person killed, which further represents the ending of the war and the beginning of coping with the tragedy of the collective sacrifice.

The creation of The Wall represents the beginning of national and collective grieving after the war. Created as a sacred space, veterans, families, friends, Americans, and others can gather there to share their stories and begin grieving for those relatives, friends, and colleagues killed in the war. The Wall also provided an opportunity for Americans to begin discussing and debating the war and its legacies in a constructive and respectful manner.

Vietnam veterans organized and created the memorial and assumed responsibility for its preservation and protection. Vietnam veterans continue to maintain a 24-hour-a-day, 7-day-a-week presence at The Wall, not only guarding over their memorial but also providing information and educational resources for visitors and assistance for veterans, families, and friends who are searching for the specific names of Americans killed during the war.

In 1996, the VVMF realized that there were many people who could not come to Washington, D.C., so it created a one-half scale replica of the wall. The traveling wall, known as *The Wall That Heals,* has been to over 100 cities in the United States and, in 1999, was displayed in Ireland.

The Rise of Vietnam Veteran Associations

After the war ended, many Vietnam veterans had a difficult time finding comfort and camaraderie in the places that were familiar to veterans of previous wars. Many Vietnam veterans found the halls of the American Legion and the Veterans of Foreign Wars (VFW) posts closed to them. Not until the late 1980s did Vietnam veterans begin organizing unit associations enabling them to reunite with their former brothers-in-arms, celebrate their collective service and sacrifices, and grieve for those in their units who were killed in Southeast Asia.

Unlike the VFW and American Legion, which organized along geographic regions, Vietnam veteran associations organized more by the military units in which the veterans served, providing a greater continuity and cohesion in preserving the groups' history — a significant side effect of the rise of Vietnam veteran associations. Vietnam veteran associations developed unique identities in the postwar period, offering their own places of comfort and camaraderie that had been denied them within traditional veterans' organizations. Vietnam veterans also used many resources, such as unit records at the National Archives (for more information on the National Archives, see Chapter 17), to find former members of their units. The Internet also plays a significant role in this process, because Vietnam veterans have established numerous Web sites and discussion groups, seeking and finding those with whom they have shared experiences.

The Role of the Veterans Administration

The Department of Veterans Administration (VA) was formed in the 1930s, bringing together several government agencies that previously had provided assistance programs for U.S. veterans. The VA was formed as a result of a crisis within the First World War veterans' community. Many complained that the federal government had ignored their needs and failed to provide promised assistance that was due them after serving their country.

The VA has continued to assist veterans since the 1930s, and veterans continue to complain about the bureaucracy of the VA when they file for compensation and support. After the Vietnam War, veterans were frustrated with the VA's system, requiring the completion of numerous and lengthy forms to receive benefits they believe they were due. The situation became even more complicated when the decision was made to compensate veterans for exposure to Agent Orange and for suffering from Post-Traumatic Stress Disorder (PTSD). Veterans had to provide their own documentation proving they qualified for such benefits. You can read more about Agent Orange and PTSD in sections about those topics later in this chapter.

The VA provides a series of special programs for helping veterans in the United States. The VA offers

- ✔ Assistance for homeless veterans, helping them regain some balance in their lives
- ✔ Employment assistance to ease the transition from the military

> ✔ Educational benefits for college
>
> ✔ Specialized studies to determine health risks based upon experiences and exposures while employed in the U.S. Armed Forces

VA hospitals, a prominent part of the VA support system, are located throughout the United States and provide medical attention and support to veterans in need. For more information about the Department of Veterans Affairs, its programs, and history, please visit their Web site at www.va.gov.

Post-Traumatic Stress Disorder

According to the National Center for Post-Traumatic Stress Disorder (PTSD), PTSD is a psychiatric disorder that occurs following an experience with or witnessing of life-threatening and traumatic events such as combat. Vietnam veterans who suffer from PTSD usually are diagnosed with other related psychological disorders, including depression, substance abuse, and memory loss.

PTSD isn't a new phenomenon caused by the Vietnam War. Many veterans from all wars have suffered PTSD, but to them it was known by different names, such as shell shock, combat fatigue, combat exhaustion, and combat stress. Approximately 30 percent of military personnel who served in Vietnam suffered, at one time or another, from PTSD. Only about 7.8 percent of the general population of the United States suffers from PTSD.

PTSD manifests itself in many ways. You can neither predict the disorder nor anticipate the degree to which it will affect someone. Veterans who experience mild forms of PTSD immediately after experiencing trauma can suffer from intense episodes of PTSD during inactive periods of their life (such as retirement or medical illness), during veterans' reunions, or on anniversaries of major events in the war, which often rekindle memories of the traumatic event. Not only does PTSD affect the individual who suffered through the trauma, it also affects the people closest to the veteran. Family members, friends, and co-workers often cannot understand the nature of PTSD or why it causes the veteran to act a certain way. Higher rates of marital and family problems are not uncommon in families in which a veteran suffers from PTSD. Because PTSD is difficult to diagnose, many veterans suffer from the disorder without understanding their condition. They therefore often fail to seek proper assistance. Other veterans believe they can handle PTSD symptoms, which sometimes cause more significant episodes as the disorder progresses.

Although no single form of treatment or cure works for everyone who suffers from PTSD, the National Center for PTSD maintains that the best treatment for the disorder is a combination of creative psychotherapy and drug therapy. Individual and group therapies have been beneficial for Vietnam veterans suffering from PTSD. For more information about PTSD and centers that offer assistance to veterans suffering from this disorder, contact the National Center for PTSD (www.ncptsd.org) or the Department of Veterans Affairs.

The Wannabe Veteran: People Who Fake a Vietnam War Experience

When Vietnam veterans returned home from the war in the 1960s and early 1970s, few identified themselves as veterans. The stereotype of the Vietnam veteran described in Chapter 16 reinforces this inward-looking approach through the 1970s and early 1980s.

In the mid-1980s, the perception and profile of the Vietnam veteran changed. As the Vietnam veteran came of age and became part of the managing class and leadership within the United States, being a Vietnam veteran no longer was bad. Vietnam veterans attained high positions in the U.S. government as members of the Senate and House of Representatives and as leaders in business, industry, and academia. Vietnam veterans identify themselves with the Vietnam War, taking pride — publicly — in their experiences and service to their country. With the rise in status of Vietnam veterans came a population of individuals who didn't serve in Vietnam but claimed they did to gain attention, receive undeserved awards and honors, and request benefits they did not earn: The *wannabes*.

Vietnam veterans take it upon themselves to root out wannabe Vietnam veterans, exposing them as fakes. For Vietnam veterans who served their country and spent so many years feeling that their status as veterans was negative, the wannabe is the greatest insult imaginable. When you search for the silver lining to this dark cloud, you find that the status of the Vietnam veteran has been returned to them at such a positive level that individuals want to emulate rather than ignore them.

And Vietnam veterans are not alone in dealing with this phenomenon. Historical evidence points to the emergence of wannabes after all of America's wars dating back to the Revolutionary War.

U.S. Prisoners of War and Missing in Action (POW/MIA)

One of the more controversial and long-standing issues facing the United States and Vietnam during the postwar era concerns U.S. personnel who still are listed as missing from the Vietnam War. The controversy actually started during the war with both sides using the issue of American POWs to gain political leverage during the Paris Peace Talks.

As part of a signed agreement between the United States and North Vietnam (DRV), the DRV promised to return all U.S. personnel being held as prisoners. Based on the official list of U.S. POWs maintained by the U.S. Department of Defense, the DRV kept its promise, releasing all of the U.S. prisoners in March 1973. However, as part of a lasting mythology surrounding the Vietnam War, many people believe to this day that the United States abandoned military personnel still alive and captive in Vietnam. Although no significant proof of this abandonment exists, it may be possible that the Viet Cong in South Vietnam held some U.S. personnel who didn't survive or make it to prisons in North Vietnam.

What probably has fueled this controversy most was the politicization of the personnel still listed as Missing in Action (MIA). Again, as part of the bargaining and negotiating for peace in Paris during the war, the United States decided to list many more men as missing than was actually the case. Although U.S. pilots may have witnessed aircraft being shot down, when they weren't able to state with absolute certainty that the pilot and crew had died, then the pilot and crew of the downed aircraft were placed on the MIA list, even when the aircraft crashed into the jungle or ocean and regardless if the crash resulted in an explosion.

At the end of the war, the list of U.S. personnel considered MIA contained more than 2,500 names. The Vietnamese government hasn't always cooperated with U.S. efforts to account for and find the remains of these missing U.S. personnel, because the United States reneged on war reparation provisions of the Paris Peace Accords. But the initial reluctance of the Vietnamese to help the United States account for American MIAs leads some people to conclude that Vietnam still is holding U.S. prisoners and covering up what happened to many of the missing. The Vietnamese deny allegations that they have held any additional American prisoners and have been cooperating with American personnel trying to account for American MIAs.

In fact, the United States established the most comprehensive program in the history of warfare to account for military personnel listed as missing from the Vietnam War. This effort began in 1973 with the creation of the Joint Casualty Resolution Center. It continues today involving the Defense POW/Missing Personnel Office (DPMO), Joint Task Force Full Accounting (JTFFA) in Southeast Asia, and the U.S. Army Central Identification Laboratory in Hawaii. More than 600 missing cases have been resolved, and, based on a massive amount of data collected to date, nothing has been found to substantiate claims that the United States either abandoned personnel in Southeast Asia or that U.S. prisoners still exist there. These agencies and offices still are investigating the remaining 1,900 MIA cases from the war. The issue continues to be a stumbling block to fully normalizing relations between the two nations.

Relations between the United States and Vietnam

Another significant postwar issue has been the restoration of relations between the United States and the Socialist Republic of Vietnam. Although Vietnam indicated early on that it wanted to establish a normal relationship with the United States after the war, President Jimmy Carter found that mounting any support in the United States for pursuing such a course in 1976 was impossible. Americans remained bitter toward the war and supported a trade embargo against Vietnam. For a while, the issue of normalizing relations with Vietnam constituted a political "third rail" that few politicians would touch.

Of the many issues standing in the way, the fact the Vietnam was ruled by a communist government probably was most important, followed closely by the POW/MIA issue. But because Nixon began normalizing relations with Communist China in the early 1970s, the fact that South Vietnam fell, coupled with the POW/MIA controversy, probably had far more lasting negative effects. Adding even more stress to the relationship between the two nations, Vietnam invaded and occupied Cambodia in 1979.

Positive steps were taken, however, in 1987 by President Ronald Reagan. He established a special emissary dedicated to resolving MIA issues with Vietnam. Although little progress toward actually resolving MIA cases was made until the creation of JTFFA in 1992 (see previous section), this move by Reagan in 1987 was an important first step. The fall of the Soviet Union in 1989, the opening of Eastern Europe to democracy and free markets, and the collapse of its own economy gave Vietnam little choice but to address the issues that concerned Americans most. Vietnam withdrew from Cambodia and promised more cooperation in resolving cases of U.S. personnel listed as missing.

In 1991, President George H. W. Bush announced an agreement that ultimately lifted the embargo, began accounting for MIAs, and established a U.S. consulate in Vietnam in 1992. Since then, the United States softened its position toward Vietnam, and in 1994, President William Clinton officially ended the embargo. The following year, the United States officially recognized Vietnam, sending its first official U.S. Ambassador to Vietnam when the two nations exchanged diplomats in 1996. For that position, President Clinton chose Douglas "Pete" Peterson, a former U.S. Air Force pilot who was shot down over North Vietnam in 1966, captured, and served six years as a POW.

Although the relationship between the United States and Vietnam improved dramatically during the 1990s, several issues remain hotly contested between the two nations. Of particular interest for Americans are the POW/MIA issue and the treatment of ethnic minorities in Vietnam. Of concern to the Vietnamese are war reparations and the long-term effects of Agent Orange.

The Effects of Agent Orange

The use of herbicides in Vietnam has a lasting impact on war participants from both countries. Operation RANCH HAND and the use of *defoliants,* or herbicides, in Vietnam are discussed in greater detail in Chapter 8. In Vietnam, birth defects, sterility, cancer, and other health issues are attributed to the use of Agent Orange, which contained the contaminant dioxin. Similarly, little is different for many Americans claiming to suffer from the same and other illnesses because of exposure to Agent Orange during the war. However, one such difference is evident in the fact that many Vietnamese still are exposed to the chemical on a regular basis, but Americans, on the other hand, are not.

Postwar concerns about Agent Orange involve determining whether illnesses and diseases actually are caused by exposure to Agent Orange and dioxin, and, if so, determining appropriate levels of compensation for people who became ill after being exposed. One problem, however, is that no agreement can be reached on whether Agent Orange and dioxin truly are the cause of the diseases and illnesses. Two camps have emerged, espousing that:

✔ Diseases are caused by dioxin. This group relies principally on scientific studies conducted in the United States and Vietnam that provide statistical correlations between the incidence of certain diseases and illnesses for certain American veterans and Vietnamese populations.

✔ No evidence currently exists supporting dioxins as the cause of the illnesses. This side of the argument cites scientific studies that show that no significantly higher incidence of most diseases is evident in people exposed to dioxin and no scientific research proves whether or how dioxin causes such illnesses or diseases.

The result of the disagreement has been the creation of some strange alliances, because some American and allied Vietnam veterans and the Vietnamese people share common concerns and interests in determining that dioxin is responsible for myriad diseases and illnesses.

A class action lawsuit brought against the herbicide manufacturers in 1979 on behalf of U.S. and allied veterans resulted in an out-of-court settlement that has compensated some veterans for their illnesses. Because this issue involves more than the participants in the war and because some of the diseases are alleged to have a detrimental effect on children being born in the United States and Vietnam, Agent Orange and dioxin probably will remain one of the longer-lasting concerns and controversies in the postwar era.

Vietnam Syndrome

Americans supposedly have suffered a syndrome since the end of the Vietnam War. President Richard Nixon coined the term *Vietnam Syndrome,* which describes several side effects or consequences of the Vietnam War, including that Americans:

- ✔ **Never again want to repeat the mistakes made in Vietnam.** They never want to enter into foreign policies that may lead to another war like the Vietnam War. The "no-more-Vietnams" attitude and expression are applicable today, and most foreign policies that send U.S. forces overseas are compared with the Vietnam War.

- ✔ **Are much less trustful of their government officials and institutions as a result of the Vietnam War.** American skepticism toward and mistrust of the government increased substantially during and after the Vietnam War. Many people who lived through the war can attest firsthand that their faith in U.S. officials and government institutions declined in direct response to lies and deceptions made during the war. As a result, the American people and media are more apt to thoroughly question American military deployments, especially when the goals and purposes of military deployments are not well understood by the people.

- ✔ **Are much more reluctant to commit U.S. forces overseas, more averse to risk, and less willing to suffer significant casualties in certain types of conflict.**

- ✔ **Appear to be less willing to accept significant casualties in contemporary war scenarios and limited conflicts.** However, it's fairly safe to say that Americans would bear any burden and accept the necessary casualties to win, if they ever are faced with an enemy bent on the total destruction of the United States. As for U.S. policies in places like Somalia, where no real direct threat to the security of the United States exists, American tolerance for casualties has, indeed, been low.

After the Gulf War, President George H. W. Bush declared, "We have finally kicked the Vietnam Syndrome." But not everyone agrees. Many Americans remain skeptical of their government. Vietnam still is raised as a litmus test for American foreign policies, even for the war on terrorism in Afghanistan. Only future deployments of American military personnel and the unfortunate loss of lives will reveal whether Americans really have kicked the Vietnam Syndrome.

Negative Depictions of U.S. Veterans of the Vietnam War

As a postwar issue, the negative depiction of U.S. Vietnam War veterans ties into some of the myths about the Vietnam War that were discussed in Chapter 16. From the perspective of U.S. veterans, Hollywood films usually are the worst at depicting the Vietnam War and portraying the experiences of Vietnam veterans. Hollywood started making movies about Vietnam during the war, but the more controversial and negative portrayals of the war and U.S. veterans occurred after the war ended.

One such early movie was *Taxi Driver* (1976), which focused on a disgruntled Vietnam veteran obsessed with pornography and prostitution. In 1978, *The Deer Hunter* depicted some of the social and psychological effects of the Vietnam War on members of a small American town. *Coming Home* focused on an antiwar theme and starred Jane Fonda, the actress who is most despised within the Vietnam veteran community. Other early films included *Apocalypse Now* (1979), based on the Joseph Conrad novel *Heart of Darkness,* which depicted the war as being fought by a bunch of crazed and blood-thirsty Americans, and *Hair* (1979), a hit Broadway musical turned movie that is an antiwar hippie cult classic.

Films of the 1980s and 1990s have not done much to resurrect either the Vietnam War or the veterans who fought there. The two popular action series, *Rambo* and *Missing-in-Action*, although teaming with fight scenes and explosions, did more to fuel the POW/MIA conspiracies in the United States, as discussed earlier in this chapter, than anything else. Movies like *Platoon* (1986), which although written and directed by a Vietnam veteran, only mud-died American perceptions by depicting U.S. combat soldiers as drug abusers or alcoholics and showing them committing war crimes. In 1987, *Full Metal Jacket* emphasized the dehumanizing effects of military training on young American men going off to fight in Vietnam. Other movies like *Air America* (1990) depicted American civilian pilots in Laos as being involved in the heroin trade.

The fact is the vast majority of U.S. personnel serving in Vietnam never committed any war crimes, they maintained their humanity, and American pilots who flew in Laos had nothing to do with the drug trade. However, because these movies tended to inflate unsubstantiated or isolated incidents, many Americans believe they are representations of the norm of activities of American men and women who served in Southeast Asia during the Vietnam War.

Many U.S. veterans of the Vietnam War believe more recent films such as *We Were Soldiers* (2002) more accurately portray them and their war.

Index

• D •

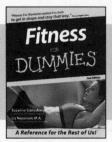

FOR DUMMIES®

A world of resources to help you grow

TRAVEL

0-7645-5453-0

0-7645-5438-7

0-7645-5444-1

Also available:

America's National Parks For Dummies
(0-7645-6204-5)

Caribbean For Dummies
(0-7645-5445-X)

Cruise Vacations For Dummies 2003
(0-7645-5459-X)

Europe For Dummies
(0-7645-5456-5)

Ireland For Dummies
(0-7645-6199-5)

France For Dummies
(0-7645-6292-4)

Las Vegas For Dummies
(0-7645-5448-4)

London For Dummies
(0-7645-5416-6)

Mexico's Beach Resorts For Dummies
(0-7645-6262-2)

Paris For Dummies
(0-7645-5494-8)

RV Vacations For Dummies
(0-7645-5443-3)

EDUCATION & TEST PREPARATION

0-7645-5194-9

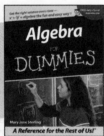

0-7645-5325-9

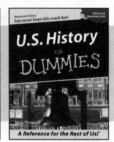

0-7645-5249-X

Also available:

The ACT For Dummies
(0-7645-5210-4)

Chemistry For Dummies
(0-7645-5430-1)

English Grammar For Dummies
(0-7645-5322-4)

French For Dummies
(0-7645-5193-0)

GMAT For Dummies
(0-7645-5251-1)

Inglés Para Dummies
(0-7645-5427-1)

Italian For Dummies
(0-7645-5196-5)

Research Papers For Dummies
(0-7645-5426-3)

SAT I For Dummies
(0-7645-5472-7)

U.S. History For Dummies
(0-7645-5249-X)

World History For Dummies
(0-7645-5242-2)

HEALTH, SELF-HELP & SPIRITUALITY

0-7645-5154-X

0-7645-5302-X

0-7645-5418-2

Also available:

The Bible For Dummies
(0-7645-5296-1)

Controlling Cholesterol For Dummies
(0-7645-5440-9)

Dating For Dummies
(0-7645-5072-1)

Dieting For Dummies
(0-7645-5126-4)

High Blood Pressure For Dummies
(0-7645-5424-7)

Judaism For Dummies
(0-7645-5299-6)

Menopause For Dummies
(0-7645-5458-1)

Nutrition For Dummies
(0-7645-5180-9)

Potty Training For Dummies
(0-7645-5417-4)

Pregnancy For Dummies
(0-7645-5074-8)

Rekindling Romance For Dummies
(0-7645-5303-8)

Religion For Dummies
(0-7645-5264-3)

Available wherever books are sold. Go to www.dummies.com or call 1-877-762-2974 to order direct

FOR DUMMIES

Helping you expand your horizons and realize your potential